COLIN WILSON:

THE MAN AND HIS MIND

Howard F. Dossor left the pastoral ministry of Congregationalism to enter the field of education in which he has been both a teacher and a senior administrator for the past twenty-five years. He has recently taken early retirement from La Trobe University in Melbourne, Australia where he lives, in order to work as an educational consultant and to write. He has had a long-standing interest in the writings of Colin Wilson and has visited Wilson on several occasions at his home in Cornwall, England to discuss his ideas with him. Howard F. Dossor houses at his home what is probably the most comprehensive collection of Wilson's work ever assembled and gives regular lectures on Colin Wilson and his work.

Colin Wilson

COLIN WILSON

THE MAN AND HIS MIND

Howard F. Dossor

ELEMENT BOOKS

© Howard F. Dossor 1990

First published in Great Britain in 1990 by
Element Books Limited
Longmead, Shaftesbury, Dorset

Front Cover photograph by Daniel Farson
Photograph of Howard Dosser (back cover):
Mike Leonard, Lenscape
Cover design by Max Fairbrother
Frontispiece photograph © 1989 by Stathis Orphanos
Designed by Roger Lightfoot

Phototypeset by Input Typesetting Ltd, London
Printed and bound in Great Britain by
Dotesios Printers Ltd, Trowbridge, Wiltshire

British Library Cataloguing in Publication Data
Dossor, Howard F.
    Colin Wilson : the man and his mind.
    1. Fiction in English. Wilson, Colin, 1931–
    I. Title
    823.914

ISBN 1–85230–176–7

FOR
ELIZABETH, HOWARD AND CHARIS

Contents

Acknowledgements

I would like to acknowledge the kindness of the following publishers from whose publications quotations have been used in this book:

Aldus: *Alchemy – The Ancient Art*; Almqvist & Wiksell: *An Odyssey to Freedom*; Aquarian Press: *Lord of the Underworld*; Arrow Books: *Sex and the Intelligent Teenager*; Ashgrove Press: *The Bicameral Critic*; John Baker: *Brandy of the Damned*; Bantam Press: *Jack-the-Ripper*; Arthur Barker: *Beyond the Outsider*; *Origins of the Sexual Impulse*; *Man Without a Shadow*; *Encyclopedia of Murder*; *Encyclopedia of Modern Murder*; *Eagle and Earwig*; *Necessary Doubt*; *The Glass Cage*; *Rasputin and the Fall of the Romanovs*; *The Mind Parasites*; *The Philosopher's Stone*; Blond & Briggs: *The Schumacher Lectures*, Vol. 2; Bodley Head: *Contraries*; Book Club Associates: *The 'Fifties*; Borgo Press: *Anti-Sartre*; Bossiney Books: *My Cornwall*; Brans Head: *Science Fiction as Existentialism*; Briggs & Associates: *The Laurel and Hardy Theory of Consciousness*; Chicago Review Press: *The Violet Apple and the Witch*; Collier Publishing Co: *Collier's Encyclopedia*; da Capo: *Against the American Grain*; David & Charles: *Aries 1*; Faber & Faber: *Success Stories*; Leslie Frewin: *A Casebook of Murder*; Victor Gollancz: *The Outsider*; *Religion and the Rebel*; *The Craft of the Novel*; *The Strength to Dream*; *New Pathways in Psychology*; *The Age of Defeat*; *Ritual in the Dark*; *Adrift in Soho*; *The World of Violence*; John Goodchild: *The Angry Decade*; Grafton: *Spiderworld*; Granada: *A Criminal History of Mankind*; *The Misfits*; *The Janus Murder Case*; Harrap: *Afterlife*; *the Essential Colin Wilson*; Hart Davis: *Order of Assassins*; *The God of the Labyrinth*; Hart-Davis MacGibbon: *The Space Vampires*; Hodder & Stoughton: *The Occult*; *Mysteries*; Hutchinson: *Introduction to the New Existentialism*; *Poetry and Mysticism*; International Universities Press: *The Psychoanalytical Forum*, Vol. 3; Michael Joseph: *Henry; Out of Step*; *Soho in the 'Fifties*; Latimer New Directions: *Strange Powers*; Lost Pleiade Press: *The Unexplained*; McGraw-Hill: *Challenges to Humanistic Psychology*; McKay: *Time to Murder and Create*; Frederick Muller: *The World of Colin Wilson*; New English Library: *Poltergeist*; *The Killer*; *The Personality Surgeon*; Nijhof: *The Sexual Revolution in Modern English Literature*; Oxford University Press: *Order and Surprise*; Pauper's Press: *Autobiographical Reflections*; Philosophical Library: *Existentialism and Thomism*; Progress Press: *Twentieth Century English Literature*; Reader's Digest: *Tales of the Uncanny*; Regnery: *Modern Gloom and Christian Hope*; Rider: *Access to Inner Worlds*; Routledge & Kegan Paul: *The Essential T. C. Lethbridge*; Salem House: *The Contemporary Literary Scene*; Southern Illinois University Press: *The Literary Rebel*; Neville Spearman: *The Necronomicon*; Tallis Press: *Juvenile Homosexual Experience*; Tarcher: *The Outsider*; Twayne: *Colin Wilson*; University of Georgia Press: *The Sounder Few*; Vision, Barnes & Noble: *The Novels of Colin Wilson*; The Sexual Dimension in Literature; Warner Books: *The Philosopher's Stone*; Weidenfeld & Nicolson: *The Face of the World*; *The Black Room*; *The Anatomy of Horror*; *In Anger*; Cecil & Amelia Woolf: *Voyage to a Beginning*.

Foreword

When the author of the present book, Howard Dossor, came to see me in Cornwall – a gentle, earnest man – I was fascinated to learn that he had been a clergyman before becoming a university administrator, and even more so when he told me that it was after a serious illness that he decided to devote himself to writing about my work. I found this flattering but rather worrying; I was inclined to wonder if he was seeing me as a kind of 'religious existentialist', basing his view largely on my first two books, *The Outsider* and *Religion and the Rebel*. And even when it became clear to me that I was doing him an injustice, and that – incredibly – he is familiar with all my books, I still felt a certain anxiety. I have long accepted that the chief difficulty with my work is that it covers too wide a field – from existentialism to criminology and the paranormal – so that even sympathetic readers often fail to see the wood for the trees.

About twenty years ago, a television director working for BBC2 was persuaded by a friend that there was an interesting documentary programme to be made about me; he had already made successful programmes on such figures as Schoenberg and Beckett, and was eager to accept the challenge. He spent several days with me, while I tried to sketch out my basic ideas, concentrating on my 'new existentialism' and trying to show its application in various fields, from the history of the novel to the study of the paranormal. I noticed an increasingly desperate look in his eyes, and was not surprised when, at the end of three days, he confessed that he couldn't see his way to making the programme; he felt I was trying to say 'too much', and he could think of no way of 'packaging' it for television viewers. I bore him no grudge; I would have had the same problem if *I* had been asked to direct it.

Now oddly enough, the central theme of all my work is a fairly simple one. Most of us find life pretty hard work, yet any serious crisis gives us a glimpse of what Chesterton called 'absurd good news', the recognition that it would be *so easy* to live in a state of continuous delight. Sartre remarked that he had never felt so free as when he was in the French Resistance, and was likely to be arrested and shot at any moment. We experience these 'flashes of freedom' again and again, and every time they leave us dazzled and yet deeply frustrated – frustrated because the answer seems so *near*, yet we seem unable to hold on to them. Still, the basic solution seems relatively clear: that the invisible net that entangles us is sheer triviality, our tendency to get 'stuck' in the minor problems of everyday life – particularly those involving personal relations. (Sartre went straight to the point when he said, 'Hell is other people.')

In the nineteenth century, the writers we call the Romantics were obsessed by the same problem. They experienced ecstatic glimpses of freedom when it seemed obvious that life is infinitely marvellous and exciting. But these 'moments of vision' meant that they found everyday life, with its repetitive triviality, miserably discouraging. Hence the high rate of suicide and early death among these romantic 'Outsiders'. My first book *The Outsider* could have been entitled *Moments of Vision*, for this is what it was essentially about.

Of course, all children experience these 'moments of vision', as Wordsworth pointed out, then the 'shades of the prison house begin to close', and most of us come to accept that life is pretty dreary and disappointing after all. Even so, few of us go as far as Schopenauer or Samuel Beckett, and conclude that it is all a kind of confidence trick. In a sense, this is a pity, for it is only when we come close to total pessimism that we are goaded into asking the important questions. Perhaps this is why the English are so disinclined to reflect on these matters. Because we have not been invaded since William the Conqueror, we have developed the 'small island' mentality – tea at the vicarage and cricket on the village green. None of our great writers have raised the question of why we are alive and what we are supposed to do now we are here.

It was because I experienced fairly frequent 'moments of vision' throughout my childhood and teens that I always maintained a fairly high level of optimism. There was also the fact that I was obsessed by the 'vision of science'; by the age of eleven, I was reading books on physics, chemistry and astronomy with the same enthusiasm as the Sherlock Holmes stories or *King Solomon's Mines*. So when, in my mid-teens, I began to read works by modern writers, I found most of them infuriatingly boring. The more I learned of modern culture – and a non-stop habit of reading meant that I learned a great deal – the more I became convinced that something had gone badly wrong since the nineteenth century. The 'romantic vision' had ended in the despair of the 1890s; and this, in turn, had led us into the swamp of pessimism that most contemporary writers seem to take for granted. I could hardly wait to start writing my own books to explain how and why I hated it so much.

I once said that this problem lay across the road of modern culture like a fallen tree, and that no real progress could be achieved until it had been bulldozed aside. And since no one else seemed to be doing anything about it. I decided that I had better try and make a start on my own. My first attempt, *The Outsider*, achieved an instant success that was far greater than anything I had expected. This was soon counterbalanced by the indifference or hostility with which its successors were received. I soon became aware that, in making myself understood, I was faced with two problems. The first was that I had been born in the wrong country; England has no tradition of interest in ideas, and British critics were simply not interested in what I was trying to say. But the second was that it would have been hard enough in any country, because what I was trying to say covered too wide a field. For me, it made sense to deal with the problem in books like *Religion and the Rebel*, *The Age of Defeat*, *The Strength to Dream*, *Origins of the Sexual Impulse*, and even *An Encyclopedia of Murder* and a book on music; but it was clear that the critics merely felt I was meandering aimlessly from subject to subject.

Fortunately, that initial success meant that I had a fairly wide international audience, even if my books never sold enough copies to make me rich, or even reasonably affluent. So I continued to write, and was glad enough to build up a small audience of readers who seemed to understand what I was doing. But as time went by, I got used to the idea that I would remain a literary 'outsider', and that if there was ever a general understanding of my work, it would probably be after my death.

When the typescript of the present book arrived, I must admit that it took me several weeks before getting around to reading it. This may sound odd, but it springs from a curious reluctance to read about myself. It was not always so; when *The Outsider* first came out, I naturally read everything that appeared about me. But I soon began to notice what I called 'the distortion effect' – that even with the friendliest of critics or interviewers, the article seldom bore much relationship to the book, or to what I had actually said. It was rather like looking into a mirror and finding that your face is quite unrecognisable, with one ear bigger than the other and your nose distorted like a turnip. Under these circumstances, even the vainest person would get out of the habit of looking into mirrors.

The first thing I noticed about Howard Dossor's book was the alarmingly ambitious breadth of its coverage: philosophy, psychology, criminology, occultism, critical theory, even sexology. With such an array of subjects, it would not have been surprising if the treatment of some had been less thorough than of others. But what impressed me when I began to read was a sense of his own obsessive seriousness. Within a dozen pages it was obvious that his interest in me is due, to some extent, to his interest in the people I write about: Nietzsche, Gurdjieff, Kierkegaard, Sartre, William James, Bernard Shaw, Paul Tillich, Hermann Hesse . . . I regard my own work as a kind of existential jigsaw puzzle, in which apparently disparate parts lock together to make a whole. And in that sense, Howard Dossor is as much a jigsaw addict as I am. But because he has brought together the parts of my own jigsaw puzzle between two covers, he has made it far easier to see the pattern. Moreover, as he quoted things that I had forgotten I had ever written, I found that *I* was also grasping the total pattern more thoroughly. After I finished reading it, I found myself picking it up and dipping into it at random, for the sheer pleasure of coming upon things that I had half-forgotten. It became clear that, unlike the television director, Howard Dossor has had no difficulty in seeing the wood for the trees. He understands what I am trying to do as well as I do myself – in some respects, perhaps even better.

The Outsider came out shortly before my twenty-fifth birthday; in a few days time I shall be in my sixtieth year. Most of the intervening period has been spent working in a kind of vacuum. This is why Howard Dossor's book gives me such an enormous sense of satisfaction, and why I see it as a kind of watershed in my life.

Colin Wilson

Introduction

IT is now seven years since any substantial study of the work of Colin Wilson has been published. 1983 saw the appearance of Gunnar K. Bergstrom's doctoral thesis, *An Odyssey to Freedom*, but this deals only with four themes in Wilson's novels. In the preceding year, Nicolas Tredell had published *The Novels of Colin Wilson*, another treatment of the fiction only. In fact, for the most recent analysis, we have to go back to 1979, to the publication of the useful but slight – 63 pages – treatment by Clifford P. Bendau and published by Borgo Press. 1988 saw the publication of the Festschrift edited by Colin Stanley but this volume is intended to be celebratory rather than critical. Surprisingly, the basic text on Wilson remains *Colin Wilson* by John A. Weigel, a volume that was published as long ago as 1975.

This is an extraordinary state of affairs, particularly when we recall that Wilson's was one of the most successful literary debuts in the English-speaking world of the twentieth century. It is all the more inexplicable when it is realised that this writer has subsequently produced in excess of eighty books. It is becoming increasingly clear that the time is ripe for a full assessment of this Outsider.

In fact, there seems to be a need for three distinct books. The first of these might be a biographical study, for Wilson's life demonstrates a great deal of insight into – and comment upon – the literary enterprise in England in the mid-to-late twentieth century and it is, like the life story of any developed writer, intrinsically interesting. But the biography may have to wait until after his death. The difficulties associated with writing the life of any living subject are well attested to by accomplished biographers and anyone who attempts the task will need the resilience of a Robert the Bruce. Yet we may take consolation in the fact that eventually such a work will come. It is impossible to believe that a life such as Wilson's will be ignored by the literary and cultural historians of the twenty-first century. Even in our own age, the social historians of the Fifties felt an obligation to give him at least passing notice.

The second Wilson volume that seems to be required is an evaluation of the professional critical response that has been made to his work. From being at the very centre of critical applause in 1956, Wilson has been relegated to a position where his work is actively reviled or curiously ignored. On publication of each new volume, we are reminded by Sunday newspaper reviewers that he is not to be taken seriously; indeed that he is to be resisted as insignificant. Few writers in our age could have attracted so many negative reviews as Wilson. The enigma is well-represented by the Melbourne *Age*, which devoted a half page of its literary review to a passionate rejection of his *A Criminal History of Mankind*. Often, one wonders why the reviewers bother to note him at all. But then one realises that he has a vast readership. Though subjected to such critical scorn, he is yet read as much as any other contemporary writer. There is an obvious paradox here and the analyst who helps us resolve it will be rendering a useful service. But indications are that this volume will have to await the emergence of a new generation of critics who can be spared the ignominy of having to recant their own critical judgements.

The third book, of course, is the book that Wilson himself wants to see written. It is an intelligent, critical evaluation of his philosophy. Admittedly, there are those who would blanch even at the application of this noun to his work and who would suggest that his ideas are more like an undisciplined outpouring based on his ill-digested reading. But such a reaction simply will no longer hold. If there are those who wish to argue that his work is insubstantial, then it is time they produced their evidence rather than contributed further to the demeaning attack on the writer himself. On the other hand, if there are those who consider that Wilson is a major philosopher, then it is time for them to say so and present the evidence in support of *their* contention. There can be no doubt that a writer who has given so much of his life to an intense examination of the human condition deserves a more intelligent response than that currently given to his work. This is not to plead Wilson's case: it is to insist that the most appropriate response to a lack of intelligence is a more developed intelligence.

The present book is none of these desirable volumes. It is, rather, a preliminary amalgam of the three. It is a stop-gap that is intended to further the debate in the hope that at least one of the three required works – and preferably the third – will be forthcoming. It is an unabashed attempt to express a personal appreciation of a philosopher and artist who has had a profound influence upon the life of the writer and upon the culture of our age. Above all else it is a statement of a personal indebtedness to a literary and philosophical giant of his own age, who has helped make the 'crooked places straight and the rough places plain'.

This book seeks to set out the views of Wilson on the range of interests that have occupied him over his lifetime. Of course it would be better if the reader went directly to Wilson's own writing but that is a formidable task, given that there are now something like eighty volumes. This might be regarded as a useful précis of that opus and is a deliberate attempt to show that Wilson's work is centred upon a single theme that is addressed again and again, in no matter what form – fiction, literary essays, philosophy, drama, social comment – his writing happens to take. This, it might be argued, is a useful objective, for it is becoming increasingly clear that many readers do not have an overview of his work. There are those who concentrate on the science fiction; those who concentrate on the criminal case-histories; those who are attracted to his studies of popular figures in the worlds of psychology and alternative lifestyles. There is evidence that many have not taken the trouble to relate these different works to each other or to the central theme that links them. And the fact is that each of them is best understood as an expression of that theme.

Following the division of writers, by Isaiah Berlin, into hedgehogs and foxes, Wilson has insisted that he is a hedgehog. The fox knows many things and speaks with authority on a range of human interests. The hedgehog knows one thing and repeats it at every opportunity for he is so certain of its veracity and usefulness that he believes all men should comprehend it. Wilson has spread himself over a wide range of literary forms but he has never deviated from his central single concern. It permeates everything he has written.

Wilson's philosophy has to do with the nature of human

consciousness. Perhaps no-one has gazed on this facet of our identity with more intensity than he has done.

Over a period of approximately fifty years he has reflected on the mind of man, convinced that it holds the key to all the mysteries that confront us. He has turned to history's philosophers and artists in a determined effort to assess their contribution to our understanding of our own mental processes. In the final analysis, however, despite the intensity of his enquiry and despite the arguments others have provided for him, it is Wilson's own insights that are expressed in his work. It is true that he is an interpreter and a synthesiser but he is also an intellectual pioneer.

It is worth noting, in passing, that a careful reading of Wilson provides an intelligent introduction to the rich panorama of man's philosophical endeavour over the ages. It would be difficult to identify a writer who has made more extensive use of the literature produced by that endeavour. Wilson's philosophy is firmly based in the best tradition of human thought.

Perhaps the best way to approach this present work is to imagine oneself in a theatre. The curtain is up and the play has begun. All the ingredients of the theatre are at work. We might liken Wilson's publications to the stage. Wilson himself is, of course, the playwright. The chapter on psychology is the set; well-lighted here and dim there; sparse here, beautifully decorated there; full of colour here, drab there. The chapters on sexology and criminology are the most prominent characters; one seductively attractive but mysterious – fascinating but enigmatic; the other a dark, repulsive figure upon whom we can scarcely look; a misshapen hunchback who fills us with dread. Fiction is the sub-plot; the intricate counterpoint to the main ideas being played out before us. In our hands, we hold the programme notes – the critical theory – which provide us with the historical and artistic background against which the play has been produced. We know that tomorrow we shall read the critical response in the morning papers, telling us how we should assess what we have seen. To complete the image, we might regard the aphorisms at the end of the book as the memorable one-liners that will linger in the mind long after the evening has passed.

But all of these are but the elements of the play. We shall not take a character home with us; nor the setting. What will remain with us is the plot – the philosophy. For days afterwards we shall roll it in our mouths like a lozenge, tasting it and extracting every last trace of its flavour. And where will all of this happen? It will happen in what Peter Brook has called *the empty space*; in that area where the auditorium meets the proscenium arch – the place where the miracle of drama occurs. But we shall give it another name. We shall call it *consciousness*.

The analogy has one decided weakness. In this work, the elements are capable of mingling. What has been written in consideration of Wilson's occultism might well have been written in relation to his psychology. His criminology and his sexology are intertwined. His fiction is a critical theory in itself. But we need not despair that we are therefore condemned to a poor night's theatre. All we need do is set our concentration on the central theme and all the other elements will fall into place.

Wilson has been accused of having no interest in society. He is widely understood as concentrating on the individual to the exclusion of the group. But this is to misunderstand his concern for the individual and to harbour a false antithesis between the self and society. This can be demonstrated.

Wilson's theme – his philosophy – is prophetic but if this statement is to make any sense it is necessary that we understand what prophecy is. Today, the word is understood as meaning the capacity to foretell the future but it is used here with none of this sense. The Old Testament prophets were not men who predicted tomorrow. In fact, they were not particularly interested in tomorrow apart from in its being a consequence of the present. Their attention was focused on the present condition of their world. Amos looked about him and saw a community from which the quality he called 'righteousness' was missing. For him, righteousness was the product of a correct relationship with God and it was missing from the society precisely because men had averted their gaze from God. The consequence was social injustice in which 'the needy want for a pair of shoes'. Amos, Hosea and the other prophets of the eighth century BC were concentrated on *this* world and on the spiritual condition of their people. Amos warned his people that if they did not return to a 'righteous' way of life, injustice would continue. Amos was a social reformer whose vision of a just society was based on a religious faith: it was this that gave him his identity as a prophet.

Wilson sees a society that is characterised by social collapse. Since the end of the nineteenth century there has been a steady espousal of pessimism with a concomitant increase in the incidence of social disorders such as crime. There has been a marked breakdown in communal adherence to traditional standards and no adequate new standards have been identified. Modern man is iconoclastic. Wilson sees crime, particularly sexual crime, as a manifestation of this collapse in values. He argues that when human beings are in rebellion, they are rebelling against a breakdown in the value system that had previously sustained them.

There is some point in this collapse of values. The beliefs that held earlier civilisations together are no longer adequate to the sophistication of modern man. Thus, for example, Wilson is not unduly perturbed by the collapse of Christianity. For almost two thousand years, that faith played a central role in pointing man beyond himself and it was indispensable during that period. Today, however, it cannot satisfy man because its myths are inadequate. With the scientific revolution, man came to comprehend that his destiny was in his own hands. The tragedy is that so many have refused to follow through the consequences of that insight. Rather than accept the challenge, they have settled for the pseudo-comfort of indolence. And the inevitable result of that negative decision has been the emergence of an overwhelming sense of boredom.

Just as the fundamental social problem of the eighth century BC was identified by Amos as being 'unrighteousness', so Wilson has identified the present central problem as being boredom. Humanity is in a malaise that is the direct result of a lack of purpose. And if Amos found a remedy for unrighteousness in a religious faith, Wilson finds his remedy in a sense of purpose. Wilson is a prophet of purpose.

A society cannot be renewed of itself. Just as it is composed of individuals, so it is the individual who must be renewed. Wilson has concentrated on the single human being in his struggle to discover a level of authenticity for himself. When he first glanced about himself in the late Forties and early Fifties, he identified a modern archetype and gave it a name that has passed into the language – the Outsider. The Outsider was the direct indication that something was profoundly wrong with our society. Then, when he looked closely at himself, Wilson realised that there was an element of the Outsider within himself. What is to be observed in the literature that he has produced since is a personal account of his struggle with – and his victory over – that Outsider. The old prophet, Amos, would have been comfortable with Wilson's struggle and its outcome, for he understood that the beginning of social renewal lies in the renewal of a single individual. The new existentialist depicted by Wilson is a paradigm for a renewed humanity.

Wilson speaks of the need for a new religion. But it is not an institutionalised form of worship that he is advocating. We get closer to his meaning if we use the word 'spiritual' rather than 'religious'. He argues against materialism; against the crass greed which leads men to think of their destiny in terms of the things they can accumulate. Man's future lies within his own mind and if there is to be a human advance we must look inward.

This is no argument for unhealthy introspection. We must look, not simply below the surface of our mind but into its depth. Nor should we focus exclusively on the content of the mind; we must examine its very function. The mind is an instrument of intention. It is essentially designed to project the human species forward into a future which it has itself fashioned. The essence of Wilson's philosophy is the notion that we are our own creator as well as designer of our own destiny.

For Wilson, religion is a function of that part of ourselves about which we know least – the will. Religion is the relationship between a human being and life itself. It is an openness to life; an exploration of all the experiences that constitute our living. The inclusive nature of religion is fundamental. Wilson quotes Whitehead:

Nothing can be omitted, experience drunk and experience sober, experience sleeping and experience waking, experience self-conscious and experience self forgetful, experience intellectual and experience physical, experience religious and experience sceptical, experience anxious and experience carefree, experience anticipatory and experience retrospective, experience happy and experience grieving, experience dominated by emotion and experience under self-restraint, experience in the light and experience in the dark, experience normal and experience abnormal.[1]

This embrace of the whole of life is crucial to Wilson. Man must learn to move out of the corners of his own mind and into the centre. There *are* more things in heaven and earth than are dreamed of in man's philosophy and it is only as our awareness of these things develops that we shall begin to comprehend what we are.

Like all great philosophers and artists, Wilson takes us into the world of our values. Human beings cannot survive without a sense of values and it is Wilson's contention that the higher the values, the greater the man. And great values are immediately available to everyone. Simply by an act of commitment to the highest values, man is capable of taking a giant step forward. And the reverse is true. An examination of our contemporary culture reveals a social chaos that is the inevitable product of an inadequate set of values.

Today, for countless human beings, Dostoevsky's Underground Man still expresses something of their essential condition:

> We're so unused to living. We often feel something like loathing for real life. And we're all agreed; it's better in books. So what is it we scratch about for? What do we cry for? What do we beg for within ourselves? And it would be worse for us if our stupid whims were indulged. Loosen our chains and I assure you we would all immediately beg to be put back under discipline. I see you're angry with me. 'You're only talking about yourself and your underground misery. Don't dare to speak for all of us'. Excuse me, gentlemen. I've only carried to a logical conclusion in my life what you didn't dare take more than half way. And you call your cowardice common sense. You confused yourself with a self-deception. So perhaps I turn out to be more alive than you. Look harder! After all, we don't even know where real life is lived nowadays, or what it is. We don't know whose side to be on, what to love, what to hate, what to respect or to despise. We even find it difficult to be real human beings with flesh and blood of our own. We're ashamed of it. We're always striving to be some unprecedented kind of generalized human being. We're born dead. We've long since ceased to be sons of living fathers. We've become more and more contented with our condition. We've acquired a taste for it. Soon we shall invent a way of being born from an idea.[2]

This is the definitive statement of the Romantic existentialist. It is a cry of pain – but it is also a rejection of inauthenticity.

Dostoevsky may have written the last sentence in irony but it may not be too much to contend that with his exploration of a New Existentialism, Wilson has identified the idea that will lead to the rebirth of humanity. Wilson has taken the anguish of the underground man and transformed it. The energy into which it is changed is experienced by Niall in the Delta in Wilson's *Spider World*:

There was a silence, but this time he felt a flicker of hope; it was as if the empress plant was reflecting on his question. Then he experienced a faint tingling sensation in the skin of his forehead. It reminded him of something; for a moment he was unable to remember what. Then, as the tingling increased, he remembered. It was the sensation of felt pads pressing against his forehead in the white tower. Suddenly, he was aware of his body lying on the ground, with his head pillowed against the foot of the stump. Then there was a sensation as if he was floating clear of his body, while the tingling increased until it became an intense glow of pleasure. This time he was aware of what was happening. The plant was making an immense effort to raise the level of the life-vibration, until it could be absorbed directly by the human organism. But it was almost impossible; the plant itself was not on a high enough level to transform the crude life-force of the earth into the intense vibrations required to stimulate the human brain. There was something heroically self-destructive in its efforts to raise him to a high level of perception.

Then something happened; as the plant's energy flagged, another force seemed to take over. With absurd ease, it filled Niall's brain with a flood of white light, in the midst of which there was a sound not unlike the vibrations of a gong. Then, once again, it was as if the sun had risen from below some horizon of his inner being, and he was flooded with a sensation of overwhelming power, surging up from his own depths. This immense power was attempting to force itself through the narrow doorway of his body, as some roaring torrent might try to force its way out of a narrow canyon. Mixed with the exultation there was a recognition that if this continued, his body would be destroyed. But this appeared unimportant; his body seemed a mere encumbrance.

Then, because he knew the power had its origin inside himself, Niall took control of the force.[3]

This is the destiny Wilson posits for humanity: an experience of a power that lies at our disposal so that we can renew ourselves at will. It is an image as important as that of the Fall in the book of Genesis. When it is grasped, man will take his next step forward.

Perhaps it is permissible to close on a personal note. Late in 1983, I was diagnosed as having a thoracic tumour. It is impossible to describe the emotions that swept through me. Essentially, there was a resignation. I simply placed myself in the hands of the medical team that surrounded me. I knew the seriousness of the situation and contemplated my own death – but with a measure of detachment. I certainly did not wish to die but there was little in life that excited me. Eventually, the upper lobe of my right lung was removed and I was declared free of cancer. I returned home within a matter of ten days and there reflected more deeply on my life. It seemed that I should select my experiences more intelligently; that I should direct my energies to satisfying my own vision rather than responding to the whim of others. I wanted to take more responsibility for myself.

I had been familiar with Colin's works for almost thirty years – since the publication of *The Outsider*. I had thought that I understood what he was arguing. It seemed to me that the most important thing I could do with my life was to focus my attention on his ideas. I had collected a number of his essays and papers from various journals and I wrote my first letter to him, asking if I might try to have them published. In characteristic modesty, he wrote to say that I was welcome to try but that it was unlikely that any publisher would be interested in such pieces. Within a few weeks, Robin Campbell of Ashgrove Press had agreed to put them into print under the title *The Bicameral Critic*. I wrote a short introduction in which I argued Colin's value as a writer and philosopher. Shortly after submitting the manuscript, I decided to go to meet this man who had so stimulated my mind. I wrote again and asked if I might visit him. In September 1984, I travelled to Tetherdown, his home in Cornwall.

When I arrived, Colin was out on his daily walk. His wife, Joy, showed me into the lounge and left me for a few minutes to work in the kitchen. I had arrived right on dinner time – a discourtesy I have managed to repeat on subsequent visits. As I sat in the chair, waiting, I heard Colin's voice as he entered the house. Within a few minutes, he came into the lounge and crossed the floor. 'Hello, Howard,' he said, in a manner that suggested we had been intimate friends for the whole of our lives. It was not so much a welcome as an extension of the writer–reader relationship I had enjoyed for so long. I recall being aware of his physical size – he is a big man. It surprised me, for his photographs had left me with an image of a much slighter physique.

For four days, I listened while Colin expounded his ideas. He answered my questions with patience and as I listened I began to realise that I had not begun to comprehend the essence of his thinking, nor imagined the breadth of its application. I saw much of his philosophy in the man himself. There was an extraordinary correspondence between the man and his ideas. Here was a human being who had not only wrestled with the fundamental questions but who had moved profoundly towards their resolution. But this was not a man who had 'arrived'. It was a man still involved in the pilgrimage represented in the title he gave to his autobiography – a *voyage to a beginning*.

Since that first visit, I have maintained contact with Colin on a regular basis. I have also spoken with a number of his friends and have continued to accumulate his writings. I have spent four years rethinking my way through his publications and am still surprised, when I return to a particular volume, to find a sentence that I am certain I have never read before. If I believe that his books contain the highest wisdom, it is because I have listened as carefully as I can to his arguments. I can do no better than commend those arguments. They are reflected in this book and if it helps others comprehend them, it will have served its purpose.

1

The Man

IN his introduction to Sidney Campion's, *The World of Colin Wilson*, Wilson argued that autobiography and biography have little place in the life of an existential writer. While Campion had written a volume which spelled out much of the detail of his life and given only secondary consideration to the ideas he had expounded, Wilson would have preferred that the ideas had been given prominence. Yet we must remain grateful to Campion, for his work makes available two extremely important documents – the book itself and a sixty-page *Autobiographical Note* which Wilson wrote as a briefing guide for Campion. To date, the *Autobiographical Note* remains unpublished. In addition to this there is the Paupers' Press edition of *Autobiographical Reflections*, the autobiographical portrait in the Gale Research Company's *Contemporary Authors*, an essay published in *Encounter*, namely *An Autobiographical Fragment: 'On Margate Sands . . .'*, which was an extract from the more fully developed Autobiographical Introduction to *Religion and the Rebel*. Finally, we have the autobiographical *Voyage to a Beginning* and a great deal of personal reflection spread throughout Wilson's other books. Thus there is extant a large body of material on the life of Colin Henry Wilson.

Wilson was conceived three months before the marriage of his parents, which took place at Christmas in 1930. He was born in Leicester at 3.30 a.m. on 26 June 1931. His father, Arthur, was employed in one of Leicester's many shoe factories and his character reflected his working-class background. He was seldom at home, preferring the company that offered itself in the local pub and leaving his young wife to care for the children – Colin was followed by two brothers, Barry and Rodney and a sister, Susan. Four noisy children were almost too much for him and a great deal of his time was spent in warding them off. It seems that Colin was a particular burden to his father, forever demanding attention and frequently getting into mischief. Gradually, Arthur's discomfort in the home began to affect his relationship with his wife. In a letter to Campion, Wilson writes:

I think Mum got disillusioned with marriage pretty early. It must have been pretty difficult for her with (four) children always fighting and yelling and a home to run on about three pounds a week. She was often in tears, and used to tell me about her worries from an early age. She didn't have many women friends – I can count only three or four in the past twenty years – and used to spend all her free time reading magazines about romance or murder, or books borrowed from the library.

When I say that Mum got disillusioned with marriage, I don't mean that Dad beat her, or got drunk every night, or anything like that. They used to row sometimes, but they were both having a hard time of it. Dad used to take me and Barry out for a walk every Saturday evening and buy us sweets. On Saturday night he and Mum went to the Spinney Hill Club and they used to bring us back a bar of chocolate and an orange for Sunday morning. We were . . . very fond of Dad until I was about seven, when he began to develop stomach ulcers and became so unpredictable and irritable that we kept out of his way for days at a time.[1]

Arthur's own father had been killed in the First World War and some of the impatience Colin observed in him may have sprung from the fact that he had been required to assume the role of 'man of the house' and take care of four brothers and a sister. Certainly, this role made him into a dominant personality who needed to have things go as he wished. Wilson's mother acknowledges that she was attracted to him because he seemed more mature than most other men of her acquaintance. But this maturity did not run to embracing four children and it seems that Arthur brooded over the fact that he had been 'forced' into marriage. Wilson records that it was only after the publication of

The Outsider that Arthur began to call him 'son' and display a sense of pride in him.

Wilson's relationship with his mother was much more satisfactory. Annetta Wilson (*née* Jones) – but universally Hattie – was a romantic who escaped from the humdrum of her housework, whenever she could, into the fantasies of *True Romance*. She spent a great deal of time in conversation with her children, particularly Colin, who seems to have been favoured, not only by his mother but by his grandparents, aunts and uncles as well. In an expression of his intellectual honesty, the reflections on her marriage that she shared with him were conveyed by Colin to his schoolteacher. Wilson comments as follows on the relationship he shared with his mother:

> It was never what you'd call a Proustian relationship. I was very fond of her, of course, and would listen endlessly to her stories about her childhood. (It was always the same formula when she was ironing: 'Tell us about when you were a little girl, Mam'.) But I hated being caressed, or any hint of sentimentality. I could never work up the least sympathy or understanding for the relationship that Lawrence describes in *Sons and Lovers* or Proust in *Swann*. It was a relation based largely on curiosity and explanation; she never tried to hide anything from me, and explained the 'facts of life' when I was about six. She also talked with complete frankness about grown-up affairs – her opinion of various friends and acquaintances.[2]

The nature of the relationship between his parents might suggest that Wilson's childhood was an unhappy one. In fact, it was not so. Essentially, he did not live in the events that took place in his home. Although he did not learn to read until he was seven, he regarded that ability as a form of magic and from then on he lived in the universe of literature. He spent hours in his bed reading boys' weeklies, *True Romance* and *True Detective*, a practice that infuriated his father. With Barry, he discovered the world of the cinema and he has acknowledged that the silver screen had a profound impact upon him. There, on a Saturday afternoon, he shared the company of Joe E. Brown, Laurel and Hardy and countless others. It was not long before his reading and the cinema drove him to writing and he was soon producing long stories which he read to his brother in the bedroom at night. One of his earliest inventions was a character named Stark, who buried himself in country roads, only to rise suddenly to terrify unwary motorists. Imagination was Wilson's pathway to the fullness of life.

In 1942, Wilson became interested in science. His mother had given him a chemistry set. His grandfather, who was an air-raid warden, managed to supply him with magnesium and gunpowder. A lucrative business developed as Wilson made 'bombs' and sold them to his school friends. He mixed iodine crystals with ammonia which he poured on to floors at school. When the liquid dried, it produced a series of small explosions when somebody walked on it. Wilson saw himself as belonging to the distinguished halls of science and he turned his attention to a voracious reading of any science book or magazine he could lay his hands on. In fact, his first 'book' was a summary of all the scientific knowledge in the world. He wrote a twenty-page letter to Sir Arthur Eddington, seeking an explanation of what the universe was all about. It was never delivered because Eddington had died a year before it was written.

At about the same time, his interest in science fiction blossomed. He worked assiduously at building up a collection of magazines and soon had over forty assorted copies of monthlies such as *Astounding Stories* and *Thrilling Wonder Stories* – an accomplishment made all the more ingenious by dint of the scarcity of copies during the war years.

At the Gateway school, he was always slightly above average but he did not distinguish himself. He constantly scribbled in his notebook rather than pay attention to his lessons. In the spring of 1946, he contributed the following brief passage to the form notes in the school magazine. 'This year, IVx indulged in the doubtful pleasure of potato picking. It took the form's united efforts to cheer up Hathaway at the prospect of missing French. We did, however, learn some very novel English from the farm hands.' These are probably the oldest of his published words still extant. But it was in a clay-modelling class at school that he saw, for the first time, the fundamental problem that has occupied him as a philosopher and writer ever since.

In childhood, I had often had the sudden feeling that the world is basically delightful and wonderful – that the sense of magic that we experience at Christmas or on a clear Summer morning

is somehow realler and truer than the 'ordinary' world we see
on a wet Monday morning. Now, suddenly, I began to suspect
that this was just a comforting delusion. This reached a frightening intensity one day in the clay-modelling class at school,
when we were discussing the question of the size of the universe. We agreed that the visible universe of stars has to come
to an end somewhere. But how long does space go on for? If
you were in a space ship as fast as light, and you reached the
end of the galaxies, would you simply go on forever and ever
into total emptiness? As we talked about this, I suddenly experienced a sensation of cold fear in the pit of my stomach. It was
obviously impossible that the universe could go on forever and
ever; it was equally impossible that it could suddenly stop.
Reason, which had always seemed so reliable, now seemed to
contradict itself. I felt emotionally drained and totally alone. It
was no good turning to my parents or grandparents, as I had
when I was a child; no good appealing to teachers or vicars.
No-one knew the answer . . . I felt that I was carrying around
an intolerable burden of knowledge, a burden that seemed far
too heavy for someone of my age. It seemed clear to me that
all these people walking through the streets, going about their
business, were impelled by delusions. Parents, schoolteachers,
city councillors, Members of Parliament, saints, philosophers
– even scientists – were motivated by 'feelings' that would not
bear examination.[3]

The young Wilson tried to relieve this 'intolerable burden' by
writing an essay on the relativity theory of Albert Einstein. When
he had finished it, he was overwhelmed with a sense of futility,
believing that he had plummeted so deeply into unbelief that he
would be obliterated by God. He tells how he crept into the bed
he shared with his brother in an endeavour to find some solace
but there were evenings when his young brother's body was so
cold that he seemed to be dead. Wilson felt that he had destroyed
every chance of being able to reconcile himself to life. He was
surprised when he woke up the next morning and concluded that
God either did not care or did not exist.

Wilson left school when he was sixteen. He had hoped to
undertake a degree course in science but he lacked one of five
credits he needed for admission to a university. He decided to
work in a factory but found the work – weighing bales of wool

– completely stultifying. After two months he left and took a position as a laboratory assistant in his old school while he pre-pared to take the examination he needed. Again he found the work boring and spent most of his leisure time in writing. He filled ten large notebooks of a journal over the space of a year, then destroyed them. He submitted several stories and plays for publication but they were all returned. One of the plays he wrote at this time was a long three-act sequel to Shaw's *Man and Super-man* which he called *Father and Son*.

Shaw was one of the greatest influences on the teenage Wilson. One Saturday night he had heard *Man and Superman* on the radio. He told Sidney Campion later:

> When I heard *Man and Superman* on the radio, I became immedi-ately fascinated, for here was a man with a message that struck a responsive chord. His outlook seemed to be my outlook. He was writing what I was thinking. I borrowed some of his plays, which I read without fully understanding them. Yet I had a sufficient background of knowledge to find them interesting, and to give me a desire to re-read them. I began to see that they were amusing as well as intellectually stimulating. This was a fresh experience and new vistas were opening up to me. Whenever I picked up a Shaw book, I had the feeling of entering upon a voyage of discovery.[4]

The overwhelming sense of futility persisted. It became so oppressive that, during the summer of 1947, he decided to commit suicide. In the school laboratory, he unstopped a phial of cyanide and was about to drink it when he suddenly experienced a flash of insight. He could see himself raising the phial to his lips and could feel an agonising pain in the pit of his stomach. It was as if he were two people, one of whom was a self-pitying adolescent who wanted to kill himself, the other the real Wilson. He recounts that he did not really care about the first of these people, nor about anything he might do, but he knew that if he swallowed the poison, the real Wilson would be killed. He was flooded with a sense of relief and replaced the phial on its shelf. In his own way he had experienced the same sensation felt by Graham Greene when he played Russian Roulette with his brother's revolver. For Wilson, the event marked the beginning of a control over the futility that had plagued him for so long.

Relationships between Wilson and his co-workers in the laboratory began to deteriorate and when his examination result proved to be unsatisfactory, his supervisor suggested that he should find other work. At home, he was again under attack from his father who felt that he should have gone to work instead of having gone to a secondary school. His younger brother was already working and contributing something to the family income. One evening, a fierce argument developed between Colin and Barry and the brothers came to blows. Wilson felt that the last connection with his family had been broken.

From the school laboratory, Wilson went into the public service. He was given a job in the Leicester office of the Collector of Taxes. His supervisor was J. W. Sidford, to whom Wilson was later to dedicate the English edition of *Voyage to a Beginning*. Sidford was encouraging to Wilson and took his literary aspirations seriously. He gave him a copy of Howard Spring's *Fame Is the Spur* to read in an attempt to convince him that 'life' was a more important area of study than 'philosophy'. Sidford also encouraged him to undertake an examination to qualify as an established civil servant. Upon passing the examination, he was transferred to the tax office at Rugby.

But Wilson took his restive mind with him when he went to Rugby and that city soon closed in upon him. It was here that he had his first unpleasant relationship with a landlady. He was ordered out of her house and found lodgings in a local hostel. He relished his new-found independence. With money he had received as a grant to help him relocate in Rugby, he bought a bicycle and took the first real holiday of his life. As he cycled through the Lake District, he felt as free as he had ever done but it was a freedom that was to end upon his return to Leicester. There, waiting for him, was his summons to enlist in the Air Force.

Whenever in his early teenage years Wilson did something to upset his father, the latter had fulminated with, 'Wait 'til they get you in the army – that'll knock some sense into you.' The words rang in Wilson's ear as he arrived at Bridgenorth in Shropshire for his 'square-bashing'. But for the first few weeks, he was able to accept the discipline and the jocular male bantering with ease. Gradually, however, the absurdity of the regimen became apparent. He wrote to his grandmother:

We've been on the rifle range training all afternoon. That means they march us for miles and miles to a remote field and then tell us we're surrounded by the enemy. Personally, I never do anything. The corporal told me to lie on my stomach and snipe at the enemy as they came over the crest of a hill. I asked where the enemy was; he said I had to imagine them. I said; 'Can't you imagine I'm shooting them instead of making me lie on my stomach?' He called me a 'bloody horrible gremlin', which is one of the nicest things I've ever been called. I wish I knew what he meant. The corporal says I hold a rifle as if it's a cross between a baby and a billiard cue. I said I'd never seen a cross between a baby and a billiard cue, but I bet it took a lot of practice to hold a rifle as if it were one.[5]

Wilson has shared a keen sense of humour with his mother all his life. She still chuckles at his account, in *Voyage to a Beginning*, of being dressed in girl's clothes as a child. Doubtless she would have been equally amused by the ruse he used to get himself discharged from the Air Force.

One evening, Wilson, who had been placed on a charge for untidiness, reported to the guard room. One of the guards began a conversation which seemed innocent enough but soon he was suggesting that Wilson should tie him up and beat him. Wilson was very upset at the suggestion but passed it off as a joke. Some time later, the incident came back to his mind when he was on another charge for letting his hair grow too long. When he was asked if he was not ashamed of himself, he could contain himself no longer and burst out in a diatribe against the services, complaining that they were like boy scout organisations. Expecting to be detained in the guard room, he was surprised when the officer asked if he might not prefer a transfer. Wilson suggested that he might be made a medical orderly but when he was told that he would have to have a better excuse than a simple desire to be rid of his present station, he knew he had to find a convincing argument. He recalled the earlier experience in the guard room and 'confessed' to being homosexual. Eventually, this 'confession', which he sustained through psychiatric examination, led, not to his transfer to the Medical Corps, but to his discharge.

He returned home to his parents. On 3 May 1950, he wrote in his diary:

I have lived at home for three weeks now. I have done little work besides digging the front garden and helping the vicar to dig his garden. Apart from that, I have thought, read the Bible and the Gita, *Thus Spake Zarathustra*, and Rabelais. I have learnt a little of the art of not getting bored, which is tapping the universal energy at its source. I have practiced the primary steps of ballet in my bedroom, and various other exercises, to prevent myself from fossilizing. I am waiting for the Air Ministry to send me my long awaited cash and discharge papers. Now I am tired of both, and am leaving home tomorrow. My aim – to avoid the boredom of offices and other forms of routine, and the state of mind they engender (a state downright dangerous to life). My intention – to support myself as best I can; if possible to get a job on the stage. My hopes – the gods. It is such a queer arrangement of a world, and there's so little you can do to get to know its workings. We seek in the depths of our being for some reality. We discover that the depths of our being have no intention of showing us Reality. Its message is 'Go back to your world of motion and play your part'.[6]

Wilson is not, nor ever has been, homosexual. He confesses that it is a condition which puzzles him. His own sexual energy, in its purely heterosexual form, presents him with more than enough to reflect upon. He had his first sexual experience at the age of eighteen with Sylvia, a girl he met while he was working at a fairground. It was the typical resolution of curiosity and satisfaction of a pervasive sensuality that marks most first sexual encounters, rather than an act of commitment associated with love. For Wilson, it was a thing in itself – except that it made real and present what had previously existed only in his imagination. For Sylvia, it was the beginning of a dream of marriage. Their meetings persisted over a short period until Wilson decided that he had to move on. He made plans to visit a penfriend in Strasbourg.

En route to Strasbourg, Wilson stayed in Paris for a few weeks in the Duncan Akademia, founded by Raymond Duncan, the brother of Isadora Duncan, as a centre for Actionalism – Duncan's theory that reality can be grasped only through action rather than reflective thought. What had at first seemed an affinity between their ideas soon proved, however, to be mutually exclusive intellectual positions and Wilson pushed on to meet up with his penfriend. Again, however, there was little to which he could relate. His friend had embraced Communism while Wilson, if he was inclined towards any established system of belief, was more attracted to Catholicism than to anything else. Within six weeks of leaving England, he was back in Leicester.

Much to his father's delight, he soon found work – this time in a local steelworks. The job proved to be a turning point in his life for while in it he began to date the company nurse, a woman named Betty, who was ten years his senior. Before long, Betty became pregnant and Wilson submitted to the insistence of his parents that he should marry her. The day after the wedding, Wilson left for London to try and find accommodation and work, planning to have Betty join him as soon as he was established. He found work in Holborn, repairing the roof of St Etheldreda's church. He took a single room in Kentish Town as a base for the search for a flat. Two months later, Betty joined him in a room in East Finchley. For several months, they were happy, with Wilson enjoying a sense of security and responsibility. While he did not relish his work – he was now in a plastics factory – there was real satisfaction for him at night when he worked on a novel entitled *Ritual in the Dark*. However, their relative comfort was soon disturbed when they were forced to find another room. Their son, Roderick Gerard – the second name being that of one of the central characters in *Ritual in the Dark* – was born and their new landlady insisted that they vacate the flat for a visitor from Australia. Betty and the baby returned to Leicester while Wilson took a room in Golders Green.

Then, for a period, their luck changed. Betty returned to London and took a job as a nurse to an elderly gentleman. They lived in his house and Wilson had the first real opportunity since his marriage to spend time writing. But it did not last and as they again moved from dwelling to dwelling, their marriage began to collapse. Eighteen months after it had begun, it was over.

In the ensuing months, Wilson worked as hard as he could on his novel. During this period, he met a young woman named Laura del Rivo, author of *The Furnished Room*. Laura played an important part in Wilson's life but so did a rapidly expanding circle of friends which included Bill Hopkins – the most brilliant man Laura had ever come across – Stuart Holroyd and Alfred Reynolds. Together, these three men were to have a profound influence upon Wilson which was to launch him into literary fame.

Reynolds was an expatriate Hungarian who had moved to

England in the early Thirties. He served with the British army during the Second World War and was given the job of retraining young Nazi prisoners of war. Reynolds' method, in classes with the prisoners, was simply to let them talk about their political beliefs and then question and challenge them gently on matters of detail. In fact, they deNazified themselves as they came to see the essential absurdity of the Nazi creed. Many of these prisoners were so grateful to Reynolds that after the war they returned home and set up chapters of an organisation which was called The Bridge. Groups met in Holland, France and Scandinavia on a regular basis. The fundamental principle which held these people together was a variety of anarchism – a belief that men do not need to be kept in place by authority but will respond to a positive expectation.

In the early Fifties, The Bridge was beginning to decline on the mainland but Reynolds was trying to build it up in England. He invited Wilson to join and for a time they were both involved in a recruiting drive. This involved Wilson speaking at Hyde Park and other venues. It was not long, however, before both realised that their ideas were almost diametrically opposed. Both subscribed to Nietzschean ideas but while Reynolds appreciated that philosopher's denunciation of the Christian ethic, Wilson was attracted to his loathing for mediocrity posing as Christian tolerance. While Reynolds preached Anarchism, Wilson preached a form of Outsiderism. It was not long before Wilson was banned from meetings of The Bridge, yet he and Reynolds both agreed to maintain their friendship – they had too much respect for each other's intellect to do otherwise.

In an account of The Bridge, written six years after for *Encounter*, Wilson tells of a subsequent meeting with Reynolds.

We met again recently for lunch. It was obvious within the first five minutes that the same total failure to communicate still exists. The personal element has become too strong; we react uncontrollably, like chemical compounds. The difference of temperaments makes any real discussion of ideas impossible. This is a pity, since I feel that, in many ways, he was right. I have changed in the six years since I first met him, although not entirely in the way he predicted. I no longer regard the Church as the necessary antithesis of modern materialism, and political freedom seems no longer so irrelevant to the question of man's absolute freedom. But the basic differences remain. I would not like to try the experiment of attending another Bridge meeting. Alfred, no doubt, feels the same.

I was amused by a story he told me about one of his 'disciples'. When *The Outsider* was published, a young man who had been particularly opposed to me approached Alfred carrying a newspaper. 'You misled me about Colin. A journalist here says he's a genius. Why didn't you tell us?' Alfred assured him gravely that the journalist was probably exaggerating. Eighteen months later, when my *Religion and the Rebel* was published, the same young man bought one of the posh weeklies to the Bridge meeting. 'You were right about Colin. This man here says he's not a genius. I apologize for doubting your word'. It is to Alfred's credit that he pointed out that a critic in a posh weekly may be as fallible as a penny-a-liner in a low-brow daily. I hope the lesson has taught the disciple to think for himself.[7]

The particular event that led to Wilson's banishment from meetings of The Bridge was a reading on the role of the intellect in literature. Wilson, with the aid of Stuart Holroyd, carefully prepared a script. Holroyd read from Donne and Marvell, while Wilson read from Blake, Eliot and Rilke. The passages selected were in fact an attack on Reynolds' humanism: more significantly, they probably provided both Wilson and Holroyd with the germs of their first books.

Bill Hopkins spent much of his time attempting to launch a journal which was to be called *The Saturday Critic.* Wilson warmed to him although, to begin with, he found the Welshman's writing full of a vague romanticism. Eventually, he came to see that there was a vast difference in their style. Hopkins wrote in the tradition of the French writers Musset and Hugo, while Wilson had followed English writers like Eliot, Hume, Shaw and Yeats. The two exchanged manuscripts – Hopkins was writing *The Divine and the Decay*. *Ritual in the Dark* was returned to Wilson with a note from Hopkins which read, 'Welcome to our ranks! You are a man of genius.'

The heady days on the fringe of The Bridge are recalled by Holroyd:

If anything made us cohere as a group, Bill, Colin and I, it was a shared conception of man as a creature with spiritual hunger, a dynamic evolutionary drive. We held that mystical experiences, visionary states of consciousness, moments of ecstacy, of joy, of world- and life-affirmation, were not only relevant to life but should be the chief object of man's endeavour. 'Religious Existentialists' we called ourselves. 'Spiritual Fascists', we were called by our critics. The time was not very hospitable to unsectarian religious thinking. Official philosophy in the universities was dominated by the logical positivists, whose horror of metaphysical statements was hysterically spinsterish, and the prevailing intellectual orthodoxy was that of the New Left, whose preoccupations were political and social. To both groups, 'spiritual' was a dirty word which was partly why we tended to use it as a rallying call. Or, rather, Bill and Colin did.[8]

Wilson began to see more of Holroyd than of Reynolds and together they discussed a great deal of poetry. Holroyd wanted to establish a poetry journal and a great deal of time was spent in preparing essays for the first issue. It was when Wilson saw one of Holroyd's essays that he made the decision to put away the manuscript of *Ritual in the Dark* for the time being and turn to a book on the Outsider in literature.

At this time, Wilson had completed his first play, *The Metal Flower Blossom*, which recorded the Bohemian life of a group of young adults in Soho. In fact, it was based on life at Chepstow Villas in Notting Hill Gate, where Wilson lived with a young journalist named Tom Greenwell (subsequently chief leader writer for the *Yorkshire Post*), Stuart Holroyd, John Braine and a number of young women. Wilson did work in Soho but he was careful to avoid its fatal attraction; an invitation to spend countless lazy days in the bars and clubrooms talking away the great books that needed to be written and the great paintings that needed to be painted. *The Metal Flower Blossom* was never published but it was not lost, becoming the basis for Wilson's second novel, *Adrift in Soho*.

The theatre has held an ongoing fascination for Wilson. In 1956, shortly after the successful staging of John Osborne's *Look Back in Anger*, at the Royal Court Theatre, one of the theatre's directors, George Devine, asked Wilson to write a play for the Court. Wilson set to writing *The Death of God* but when he submitted it to Devine, it was rejected, partly on the advice of a poet named Ronald Duncan, who thought it contained more philosophy than drama. A bitter argument developed and again Wilson suffered a great deal of bad publicity as a result. The play is now located, in manuscript form, in the Ransom Humanities Center in the University of Texas at Austin. The university bought it from someone who apparently stole it from Wilson's room.

The whole affair ended with Wilson meeting Duncan who revealed that he had lost a job as a literary critic because he had refused a newspaper's request to write a 'suitably scathing' review of *Religion and the Rebel*. Wilson and Duncan began a friendship which lasted until Duncan's death from cancer in 1982. Wilson was given the manuscript of a book on which Duncan had been working at the time of his death, *Marx Refuted*, completed it and saw it through to publication by Ashgrove Press.

On 18 November 1956, Wilson was a participant in a symposium at the Royal Court, chaired by Kenneth Tynan. The other members of the panel were Ben Levy, Wolf Mankowitz, John Whiting and Arthur Miller. Wilson used the occasion to criticise contemporary theatre, explaining that, whereas there was a tendency to highlight the microscopic detail in a character's life, the best playwrights, such as Shaw, were interested in providing a telescopic view of more universal human questions. He was attacked in a derisive manner by Mankowitz and some members of the audience, although some others in the audience called out that he should be permitted to express his views. Wilson remembers that as they all left the theatre, Marilyn Monroe, who was with Miller, pressed her shoulder against his and left him wondering if it was an expression of support or of something more intimate.

Other plays written by Wilson include *Viennese Interlude*, which was a first draft of his only published play, *Strindberg, 71 Mattmannerstrasse*, which was his first treatment of Arthur Lingard (*The Killer*) and which was lost on a bus, and *Mysteries*, a three-act dramatic form of *The Janus Murder Case* which was produced in Cardiff in 1979.

Inexorably, Wilson was moving towards the phenomenal popular acclaim that was to greet his literary début. But first there was to be another sojourn in France. Disappointed with the failure to get his play on the stage, he travelled to Paris where he soon found work selling subscriptions to *The Paris Review*. Shortly afterwards, he was joined by Bill Hopkins. They lived together and drank and talked into the night. Wilson recalls that they were engaged in an endless 'will-to-power' struggle which was essentially a manifestation of their different temperaments. They subsisted on the sale of a few subscriptions. Wilson wrote to his mother:

> I want to stop trying half-measures and compromises. My one aim in life is to become the foremost writer in Europe. From what I can see of the literary life over here, there's no-one to stop me. I've contacted a couple of English magazines and one of them has offered me some work that will keep me alive at all events. Anything can happen if I have enough courage and determination. I'll let you know if any real luck turns up. Paris is a difficult place to get a foothold in.[9]

But there was no change in his luck. After a week or so, Hopkins returned to London and Wilson followed him a few days later. Back in London, in order to avoid having to work while he tried to write, he bought a sleeping bag and began to spend his nights on Hampstead Heath. 'That's right, Col,' said Hopkins, 'build up the legend.'

From the Heath, Wilson cycled down Haverstock Hill through Belsize Park and into the British Library. There he spent day after day writing his manuscript on the Outsider in literature. Angus Wilson, who worked in the Library, noticed him writing and offered to read the manuscript. Impressed with it, he forwarded it to Victor Gollancz, who immediately offered to publish it as simply *The Outsider*.

The critical praise heaped on Wilson and his first book was unparalleled in twentieth-century English literature. Edith Sitwell, Phillip Toynbee and Cyril Connolly all attributed major importance to the work and genius to Wilson. It has been suggested that many copies were purchased as 'coffee-table books' but for every hundred purchased as a symbol of intellectual astuteness, five were bought by individuals who instantly breathed a sigh of relief that the endless struggle raging within the depth of their psyche had at last been acknowledged. Their private torment was now public: they read its first sentence with a shock of recognition – 'At first sight, the Outsider is a social problem.'

Stuart Holroyd paints an interesting portrait of the newly successful Wilson:

> Colin was a queer mixture of the ascetic and the *bon viveur*. He
> spent lavishly on expensive wines, malt whiskies and long-
> playing records, but cared little what he wore or ate or what
> his surroundings were like. As his guest, one had to be prepared
> to drink wine like a Saxon war-lord and at the same time
> listen to a lecture on philosophy or literature or to a complete
> performance of some obscure operatic masterpiece that he had
> recently unearthed. It was a basic tenet of his philosophy that
> man must strive to be a god and will never attain to the status
> until he learns to focus his mind like a laser for long periods of
> time; and it seemed to be a basic function of his hospitality to
> provide the conditions for practice in such concentration.[10]

It would be easy to lampoon Wilson's behaviour in the few
months following the publication of *The Outsider*. It is true that
he did himself little good with his self-promotion in the media.
Yet the media was a stern taskmaster, particularly for a man of
Wilson's age and background. Nor was the apparent egotism as
blatant as the press made it appear: his self-image was always
healthier than most and now, on the dizzy heights of success, he
was not about to pretend that he was a temporary phenomenon
on the literary scene or that what he had written was of no more
value than the latest Raymond Chandler novel. Again, he was
not helped by his friends. Daniel Farson, who had met him
just a few days before the book was published, interviewed him
informally at the Devon home of Daniel's father, Negley Farson
and published the interview in the first edition of a new magazine
entitled *Books and Art* under the title 'Colin Wilson Explains MY
GENIUS'. Wilson was deeply hurt by the interview and it is to
his credit that he wrote to Farson expressing his disappointment
but insisting that their friendship had not been impaired by it.
The two men remain close companions today. It is also important
to realise that while the press depicted the newly published young
author as an egotistical buffoon, he continued to write, for it was
less than a year after the publication of *The Outsider* that *Religion
and the Rebel* appeared.

It was the infamous horse-whipping episode that finally drove
Wilson from London. Three years before the launching of the

book, he had met a girl named Joy Stewart, who was eventually to become his second wife, in Lewis' Department Store in Leicester and had begun to spend time with her. She moved to London and one evening, was invited to a meal at Wilson's room. As they ate, the door flew opened and Joy's parents entered the room, her father brandishing a horse-whip. 'Aha! Wilson, the game is up!' declared John Stewart, in what Wilson saw as a melodramatic farce. When Stewart lifted the whip however, Wilson pushed him aside and he fell to the floor. The whole outburst had been caused by Joy's younger sister, who had found one of Wilson's journals in which he had written some notes for *Ritual in the Dark*. The young girl thought the writer must be a sexual pervert and told her parents.

The next day, the newspapers were full of the story. It was syndicated throughout the world and was published in the *Sydney Morning Herald*, which also published the following editorial under the heading 'Hip Hip Hurrah for Aha!'

> The first words the father used were, 'Aha, Wilson, the game is up'. The key word here is not 'game' or 'up', as some may suppose, but 'Aha' which is an exclamation of long and honourable lineage. Although it achieved its full effect in times past only when accompanied by the twirling of a moustache with one hand, leaving the other free to wield a rapier, (horse) whip, walking stick or cane, it could, with the proper intonation, strike terror into the heart without any of these violent accessories. Those, however, were the days when young men had not acquired that quaint but disarming riposte, 'Sez you', which has paralyzed many a modern papa, even in his own parlour . . . [There is a] most urgent need to restore some element of drama to the rather flabby relations between indulgent fathers and the modern suitor. We could all start with the London 'Aha!' that has echoed around the world and gradually work up to 'Presumptuous villain! Dost thou provoke my wrath?' It certainly would be a change from 'O.K. Have it your own way'.[11]

In the face of such a press, Wilson took Joy to Devon. When it became apparent that this was not far enough away, they went on to Ireland but returned to England shortly thereafter. He was offered accommodation in a cottage in Cornwall and accepted it gratefully. Eventually, he was to buy a home nearby and remain there for the next thirty years. In 1973 he recalled these events with a remarkable objectivity:

> My mistrust of the overnight fame proved justified. As the success rolled on like some giant snowball, and *The Outsider* went through impression after impression, people naturally began to ask if I was all that brilliant and original and if I deserved so much publicity and praise. England's 'intellectual establishment' felt that they had been stampeded, and people who had never joined in the praise took the opportunity to say they'd never considered the book much good anyway. By Christmas it seemed that every critic in England was ready to admit that the whole thing had been an absurd mistake. I was utterly and totally 'discredited' as if I'd been a confidence swindler who had been publicly exposed. There was still plenty of publicity but now it was uniformly hostile. Victor Gollancz, who had sold 40,000 copies of the book, as well as selling it to America and a dozen foreign publishers, saw his investment dwindling. He advised me to take a job and spend five years writing my next book. When I showed no sign of accepting this advice, he suggested I move to a cottage in the country and try to keep out of the newspapers. Early in 1957, sick of the atmosphere of hostility in London, I decided to try out his suggestion. I rented a room in a huge old house near Totnes, belonging to Hugh Heckstall Smith, a retired headmaster; but it was lonely without Joy. I returned to London and more publicity. A poet living in the same house in Notting Hill Gate, asked me if I'd be interested in renting his cottage near Mevagissey. One weekend, in early March, we travelled down by train and spent the evening at a Guest House owned by D. S. Savage, a literary critic in Mevagissey. The next morning a taxi drove us out through Portmellon, up an incredibly steep hill that we had cycled down three years earlier (on a holiday) and on to the farm at the top of the hill. Down a long, muddy track, we found the cottage.[12]

Oddly enough, the press played a significant part in Wilson's resolve to continue with his work – but not the British press. Shortly after the publication of *Religion and the Rebel*, he travelled to Oslo to lecture. As he stepped off the plane, he was met by a number of journalists who wished to interview him. He was astonished at the barrage of questions they directed at him; not because of their volume or their complexity but because none of them was concerned with his personal life – with his 'genius', his alleged sexual activities or his income. They were concerned with his interpretation of Sartre's philosophy; with the manner in which his existentialism differed from that of Camus. In contrast to the mean-minded harassment of the English press, he found his new interrogators willing to ascribe considerable intellectual merit to his work. The effect was to alter his defensive stance and re-awaken that sharp inner certainty that had surged through him as he worked on *The Outsider* before its publication. He reasoned that if the sheer nastiness of English journalism was not universal, there had to be an audience to whom he could address himself with some confidence of being understood.

Back in Cornwall, Wilson went on to complete *Ritual in the Dark*, then wrote the *Encyclopedia of Murder* (with Patricia Pitman), *The Age of Defeat* and *Adrift in Soho*. In London, Gollancz continued to be concerned. He wrote to Negley Farson on 1 July 1959:

> I'm desperately worried about Colin. Ever since the first big success, I've been trying – with a really tremendous expenditure of time and energy – to save him from a disastrous future: but he has defeated me. I am fond of him, and still believe in him: but the trouble is that he has got into such a financial mess that he just can't wait until he has something to say, but must go dashing off and writing the first thing that comes into his head. He has already either published or written almost as many books as you have in your whole life: and you know, better than most, how important the long, crystallising, simmering process is.[13]

When Wilson finally submitted *Ritual in the Dark*, Gollancz read it immediately. Once again, on 17 July 1959, he confided in Negley Farson:

> I read it last weekend – an enormously long thing of, I think, at least 150,000 words. It is a horribly nasty book – indeed, I should go so far as to call it a foul book – and [say] that I would not dream of publishing it in any ordinary case. It also has an absurd ending, which I think I could persuade him to

change: and quite revolting passages, which I am sure, he would be willing to cut out, or at any rate modify. But for all this, it has a great deal of merit – a strong narrative gift, the power to evoke excitement (of an exceedingly unpleasant kind) and a kind of desperate, if adolescent, sincerity. Moreover, the basic idea – that even a multiple sexual murderer is seeking to enhance life – is a horribly perverted form of truth. Any unprejudiced reader of the book could have no possible doubt of Colin's possibilities.[14]

Wilson's relationship with Gollancz was generally unstable. He acknowledges the publishing skills which helped to ensure the financial success of most of his early books but in a review of Ruth Dudley Edwards' biography, *Victor Gollancz*, he concludes:

Aldous Huxley wrote a novel called *The Genius and the Goddess* about a great scientist who was also a supreme egotist and the moral problem of judging such a curious monster. This book raises it all over again with frightening persistence. There can be no doubt that VG was, in many of his actions, almost a saint: there can also be no doubt that he was a bully, an egomaniac and a self-deceiver.[15]

Wilson considers Negley Farson one of the most remarkable men he ever met. The two spent a considerable amount of time together discussing philosophical issues and the role of the writer. Farson was an alcoholic and his son, Dan, tells a story against Wilson in which the latter, hearing Negley say that he would like a drink, indicated that he had a bottle of brandy in his car. As he left the room to fetch it, Negley's wife, Eve, muttered, 'You may be a genius Colin; but you're a damn fool!' It was a sharp barb, using as it did, the heading of Daniel's published interview which had caused Wilson so much anguish.

Another giant of the literary world with whom Wilson had more than a nodding relationship, was Henry Williamson, the author of *Tarka the Otter*, the *Flax of Dreams* tetralogy and the fourteen volumes of *A Chronicle of Ancient Sunlight*, and a man for whom Negley Farson had little time. Wilson describes his meeting with Williamson:

I met Henry Williamson under amusing circumstances in 1957.

I was staying with the writer, Negley Farson, who lived a couple of miles away from Henry, on the coast of North Devon. I'd heard all about Henry from Negley's son, Dan, and from Kenneth Allsop, whose novel, *Adventure Led Their Star*, had been deeply influenced by Williamson's early writing. I had read *Tarka the Otter* in my teens and been enormously impressed: I was not critical enough to feel it was overwritten, and saw it only as a magnificently objective portrait of the wild moorland country and its inhabitants. So I was surprised to hear that Henry was not much liked in the Georgeham area of North Devon, and that most of his friends were sooner or later alienated from his neurotic egoism. Negley and his wife Eve had quarrelled with Henry long ago; so if Dan wanted to see 'the hermit at Ox's Cross', he had to keep his intentions secret. One afternoon, Dan and I and my girlfriend Joy set out ostensibly for a stroll along the beach – in fact to visit Henry. Like everyone else, I was struck by his good looks and his military bearing. Joy, predictably, thought he was stunningly attractive. Henry's wife, a pretty girl who had been a teacher of gymnastics, gave us tea, and Henry produced his latest manuscript and read us a dozen pages or so. I expected it to be about animals – or possibly about the First World War (he had just written *The Golden Virgin*). In fact, it was a defence of his attitude to fascism, specifically to Sir Oswald Mosley's Union Movement. I had met Mosley and found him brilliant and enormously likeable; so this was a matter on which we immediately established a bond of sympathy. Henry read on for what seemed like hours, with the consequence that it was dark when we left. Dan asked me what I thought of him, and I said I'd found him impressive but perhaps rather too talkative.[16]

Over the years, Wilson himself has frequently been accused of being a fascist. He wrote a long three-part essay entitled 'The Fuehrer in Perspective' for *Books and Bookmen*, the first part being published in the issue of September 1974. A careful reading shows that his interest in Hitler was related more to his psychology than to his politics and that Wilson saw him as an example of a personality type he was writing about as the 'Right Man'. That Wilson has persistently adopted a non-political stance is demonstrated by the fact that the political philosophy of Nazism does not get a mention in the index to *A Criminal History of Mankind*.

Almost all the published biographical material on Wilson ceases at or near this point in his life. It is as if, from the time he moved to Cornwall, his life disappeared into his work. In one sense this is true but there remains a personality beneath the writing that is intensely interesting and the time may have arrived for a second volume of his autobiography to be written. One result of this lack of personal detail is the common notion that he has remained steadfastly in Gorran Haven but in fact there have been numerous forays beyond that idyllic setting which reveal a great deal more of the man.

Shortly after the publication of *The Outsider*, he visited Germany as a lecturer under the auspices of the British Council. He has lectured since in Scandinavia, Belgium, Spanish Majorca, Japan, Australia, several times in the United States and extensively in his native United Kingdom. In 1966 he was a Writer in Residence at Hollins College in Virginia. The position had been created for him earlier in the year when he was lecturing in the United States. He tells of the arrangements being made thus:

Our host told me that [Calder] Willingham [author of *End as a Man*] had turned down a job as Writer in Residence at a girls' college. I mentioned this to Willingham, and within ten minutes, I had the job. He simply picked up the 'phone, got on to the college, and said: 'I've got an English writer here – Colin Wilson'. . . . He put his hand over the 'phone and asked me, 'Did you write *Hemlock and After*?' – then, back into the 'phone, 'Yeah, he did. He wants to be a Writer in Residence there. Shall I put him on to you?' I was handed the telephone. The professor on the other end asked: 'Are you married?' I said I was. 'Good. Do you expect to publish anything next year?' I said I had about four books in the works. 'Fine. Can you start in September? We pay $12,000 for the year and travelling expenses for you and your family, and you get a house on campus.' It was as simple as that.[17]

The attempt to sift out unmarried men from the girls' college was wasted on Wilson. He recounts:

I found, to my surprise, that a crowd of girls is no more interesting than a crowd of boys. In fact, it is possible to form a sort of flirtatious relationship with your class on this understanding – rather as you might flirt with the twelve-year-old daughter of a friend. My students used to take a certain pleasure in putting me off my lecturing stride by crossing and uncrossing their legs at crucial points, until they discovered that I tried to stare brazenly up their skirts. They then waited until I took drinks from a mug of water before crossing their knees; so I bought a mug with a glass bottom. (Actually, it was impossible to see anything but a blur through the water, but they didn't know that). . . . The mini-skirt made me focus a realization which, I suppose, is obvious enough, but which had never struck me before. Teenage girls are naturally sentimental creatures; sex is not a physical act but a corollary of romance. They don't understand the male urge to satisfy the *will* by the act of penetration. They want to be petted and caressed, and perhaps rather adored as an incarnation of the *Ewig-weibliche*.[18]

In 1974, Wilson was back in the United States, this time for six weeks at Rutgers University in New Jersey. It was here that he produced *The Craft of the Novel*, in which he expressed profound insight into the nature of fiction and its potential impact upon both writer and reader. It was also here that he met up again with a local journalist, Daniel Grotta-Kurska, who had interviewed him in England some months earlier, for *Oui*, a Hugh Hefner magazine 'for the man of the world'. The interview was important in that, in response to the question, 'What has been your main achievement?', Wilson responded:

Before me, Western philosophy tended to be fatalistic. This pessimism has been particularly obvious over the last century and a half. I think that probably, historians writing a cultural history in the future will say that I represent a kind of watershed. Quite suddenly, with me, the tide of pessimism turned.[19]

Such thinking represents a bold – some would say arrogant – self-image yet it seems reasonable to argue that Wilson's prediction may yet be validated. It is certainly difficult to identify a more persistent exponent of an optimistic insistence that man is moving towards the realisation of his own potential.

Through Grotta-Kurska, Wilson met Arthur Rosenblum, founder of the Aquarian Research Foundation. Wilson found Rosenblum to be an interesting 'mystic' who believed in the unseen world and wanted to investigate it scientifically. He acted as a liaison between people who had reported having unusual experiences and people who were unable to accept the existence of 'unnatural' phenomena. Wilson was so impressed with Rosenblum that he wrote an introduction to his book, *Unpopular Science*. This gesture was a clear indication that Wilson has remained open to new forms of thinking. It also demonstrates his willingness to encourage the unknown writer. To date, he has written introductions to no less than sixty-five volumes by other authors.

For Wilson himself, one of the most important trips he has made was his visit to Finland, at the invitation of a correspondent named Matti Veijola, in the summer of 1981. He had been working extremely hard, meeting publishers' deadlines for *Rasputin: A Novel* for the Reader's Digest anthology, *Tales of the Uncanny* as well as *Poltergeist!* for the New English Library. This pressure of work probably accounts for the poor editing work done on the latter volume – by far the most poorly proof-read of all his publications. Normally, Wilson is meticulous in his handling of galleys and had the text of *A Criminal History of Mankind* substantially reset after the copy editor had varied Wilson's style and inserted the footnotes into the text. He records that in the months leading up to the Finland visit, his emotions had placed him under enormous strain and he had relied heavily on his power of reasoning. Thus he was pleased when he arrived at Helsinki on his way to Vittakivi, an Esalen-like Institute founded by American Quakers after the Second World War. It was at the airport, waiting to be driven to his destination, that he met Brad Absetz.

To begin with, Wilson found Absetz friendly and apparently very relaxed. It was not until later, when he learned of the personal experiences that Absetz and his wife had had to endure, that he realised how much effort had been required to produce the calmness that the man seemed to exude.

Some years earlier, Absetz and his wife decided to adopt a child but the boy they were given soon began to make extraordinary demands upon their time and energy. Eventually he was diagnosed as having cancer and this finally led to his death. Absetz's wife passed into a period of extreme grief and she spent prolonged periods of time in a comatose state, ridden with guilt and self-recrimination, despite her husband's efforts at reassurance. For several years she was in and out of hospital and Absetz felt that his last ounce of energy was fast disappearing. Then, unexpectedly, he found a new source of energy within himself and with practice found that this energy could be facilitated by an 'inner gesture of permissiveness'.

Wilson was instantly and intensely interested in Absetz's story and pursued it to the point where he was so convinced that his subject had achieved a fundamental insight into the realisation of human potential, that he decided to write a book on what Absetz had taught him. Later in 1983, *Access to Inner Worlds*, a slim 143-page book, was published in London by Rider. Many regard it as Wilson's most important book of the past ten years. Certainly it made it clear that there were positive connections between his writings on the occult, and those on human psychology and the new existentialism. For those who have no knowledge of the work of Wilson, it is probably the best starting point. Its final paragraph reads:

> [Absetz] does not regard his present situation as some kind of ultimate. All stages are transitional. Absetz seems to me to have made an important discovery about how we can enter into a new relationship with the unknown areas of the mind. Yet his own experience had not been so much one of 'access to inner worlds' as of an active collaboration with that 'other self' in *this* world. He remarks that new possibilities 'will open up as I become stronger and clearer in my ability to will the inner gesture of change-over from my usual mind-directed level of conscious behaviour to the movement-impulse level'. He recognizes that the present stage is as rudimentary as a baby's first efforts to walk or use its hands for grasping. 'Whether the strengthening of my will will lead only to more sustained and continuous periods of living from that level, or whether it will also lead to new levels of experience, I do not know'. Neither is it important that he does not know. All that matters is to know that in our generation, in the last part of the twentieth century, a new direction of evolution has suddenly opened up in front of us.[20]

Away from home, on the lecture circuit, Wilson is a formidable individual. Few who hear him speak can fail to be impressed by the fine structure of his addresses, the personal style of delivery, or the force of his argument. He draws extensive quotations from his memory, never using a note, and has a flair for teasing out of each word or sentence the last ounce of meaning and relevance to his argument. He has the presence of an actor on a stage; yet he is never pretentious or manipulative. Few speakers can match his capacity to enthrall an audience for two or three hours.

This personal presence that Wilson has is to be understood as a consequence of his world view. The man who accepts himself as a vitally growing organism, will possess the capacity to project dynamically to an audience. The root problem of the stammerer lies within himself – in his devalued self-image. The effective use of language, whether of the body or oral, is a mark of a personality that is well integrated.

Since the time he was able to write, Wilson has maintained a journal. He still has many of the black school exercise books he filled as a child – two of them are in the Ransom Humanities Center collection in Texas. Doubtless, many have been lost and we know that he has destroyed some. Once, while out on a visit and finding himself without anything to write on, he asked for some paper and was given a bound volume containing about five hundred blank quarto sheets. The volume had the word *Rehfisch* embossed on its spine. Wilson kept it and has maintained his diary in matching volumes, each with the same inscription and numbered consecutively. In 1986, he completed the seventeenth such volume. When his definitive biography comes to be written, these will be of inestimable value to the biographer. In addition to the written journals, he keeps an audio record on cassette tape.

Some flavour of the journals – and a reflection of his constant intellectual activity – is indicated in the entry he wrote for the day on which he left England for his lecture tour of Japan and Australia – Thursday, 23 October 1986, a day which began in the Ariel Hotel in London. The following text is unedited.

Up at 8 and watched TV news, then breakfast (buffet again) at 9 – hard-fried eggs, hard bacon and baked beans . . .

The 'great secret' is involved with putting the will into gear. It is usually passive, like S.K.'s (Søren Kierkegaard's) school-boy, listening blankly to the teacher; then he focuses on the beetle in the inkwell and gets into gear.

I woke up on the train yesterday, and refused to sit staring blankly. I concentrated (not too hard) and went into gear. That is, instead of behaving as if you were in a meaningless or boring world, you generate alertness and look at it as if trying to grasp all the meaning behind this '2% awareness'. (I coined the phrase 'the 2% world' 2 days ago, reflecting on Brunner's observation about 'cutting out' 98% of our sensory input.) Our central problem is simply to stop being passive, like babies who rely on their parents . . . The mind is supposed to be the controller. The problem is one of gears. We don't know how to use our gears. When we lost Sally in Cheltenham, I went down to a lower gear and my troubles vanished.

Japan Airlines No. 422. Left Heathrow 2.45 (after 2 hours at airport). First class lounge. They wanted to give us two separate seats but we managed to get this changed.

Large meal on plane and good wine.

In Japan for a period of only sixteen days, Wilson delivered a total of three lectures; one in Tokyo, one in Hiroshima and the key one, in honour of the Buddhist monk, Kukai, at Koyasan on the north-eastern coast of the Inland Sea. There were numerous interviews and television and radio appearances. His books are widely read in Japan and a great many of his works, including early ones, are still available readily in Japanese translations. A new paperback edition of *The Outsider* was published in Japanese as late as February 1988. Earlier, Japanese editions of that book were published as college texts, with explanatory notes included.

From Japan, Wilson proceeded on his first visit to Australia. He flew to Melbourne while his wife went to Queensland to visit a brother who lives there. In Melbourne, Wilson lectured three times in ten days, twice at La Trobe University where his key lecture was entitled *The Untethered Mind*. Again, his lectures were supplemented by radio and television appearances and the daily press expressed considerable interest in him. There can be no doubt that his work has a very wide readership, not only in English-speaking countries, but throughout the world.

While in Melbourne, Wilson stayed on the La Trobe University campus. An entry from his diary, written there, gives another indication of his endless analysis of the human condition:

One thing disturbs me about this campus. Although so idyllically attractive, like something out of H. G. Wells' utopian novels, it has a lot of litter – beer bottles, soft-drink cans, newspapers, plastic bags, cardboard plates – often thrown away within feet of a litter bin. The students obviously have no feeling of responsibility about tidiness – a contrast to Japan, where street litter is minimal. This is, in a sense, the beginning of criminality – a feeling of 'just me and nobody else'.

Apart from his frequent excursions away from Cornwall, Wilson remains in touch with the world through a prodigious correspondence. Daily, bags of mail arrive at his home – and almost as many leave it. It is the exception rather than the rule for him to leave a letter unanswered and most responses are completed in a very short period of time. His correspondence reveals much more than a sociable man trying to keep in touch with other people. It expresses his ongoing attempt to make greater sense of the world. One example must suffice. In a recent letter he wrote:

I find that what really cheers me up is that, as I approach sixty, I seem to be really seeing things in proper perspective at last and getting some of my most important ideas. The most important of the last year have been the notions of 'upsidedownness' and 'completing'. (Both are explained in my new book, *Beyond the Occult*.) But I have also developed what I think to be one of my most important insights. This is a kind of extension of Husserl's Intentionality, but seems to me to go much more to the point, as Husserl continued to think of Intentionality as 'the mental in-existence of the object'. It has suddenly struck me very clearly that our problem is that when we *do* something physically, we fail to do it mentally as well. And when you do something physically but not mentally, you haven't really done it at all. When Paris is in bed with Helen for the first time, he is making love to her mentally as well as physically.

It's a strange thought, isn't it? Imagine a boxer about to climb into the ring, and you say to him: 'Look, it's no use just hitting your opponent on the chin. That won't even shake him. You've got to hit him on his *mental* chin with your *mental* fist before he'll fall down.' . . . Most of us spend most of our time doing things merely physically, and failing to do them mentally as well. In fact, worse still, *undoing* them mentally while we do them physically, not sure whether we want to do them or not![21]

And it is not only mail that arrives at Tetherdown. Over the years, a host of visitors have called there – to express their appreciation of his work or to seek his assistance in addressing a literary, personal or philosophical problem. Wilson does not keep a guest book but if he had maintained a record of his visitors over the years, it would have read like a *Who's Who* of prominent personalities. When he was asked by *Punch* magazine, what he would like to receive for Christmas, he was tempted to request a single summer at home, free from visitors: in fact, he chose a number of long-playing records. Given the generosity with which he gives his time to visitors, it is all the more difficult to comprehend his extraordinary productivity.

Tetherdown is a writer's home. It is a conglomeration of books and more books; records and more records. It is an environment that generates ideas. It presents a forbidding challenge to the regimented librarian, with no apparent order to the collection and with books under every cushion, upon every window ledge and even on a shelf in the toilet! A rear bungalow, especially constructed to hold more books, has become, over the years, almost a solid block of human intellectual achievement; a bound repository of wall-to-wall wisdom. Wilson says that although he is ESP *thick*, he does seem to have some capacity for dowsing. Anyone who has observed the facility with which he can retrieve, instantly, any particular book he wants at a given moment, will find this an easy claim to accept!

At home, Wilson is very much a family man. Although it must be admitted that family life revolves around his disciplined writing, he ensures that he has time to spend with his family each day. During their school years, he drove his children to school each morning, spending the driving time discussing philosophical concepts with them and encouraging them to develop their own intellect. In the evening, after his day's work and his walk along the local Dodman cliff with his dogs, he has his meal with his wife and friends. His mother lives with him, although a large part of her heart is always in Leicester, and his three youngest children, born to Joy, are never far from his concern. The youngest, Rowan, has just gone up to Oxford while the older two, Sally and Damon (named after the prominent Blakean scholar, John Foster Damon), call in whenever their studies permit. Roderick, his first son, by Betty, visits frequently with his wife. There are constant 'phone calls to Betty, to whom he gave the rights for *Poetry and Mysticism*. His literary life rubs off on his family. Joy has produced an evocative photographic record of the St

Austell Bay area as it was at the turn of the century. Damon assisted in the compilation of *The Encyclopedia of Unsolved Mysteries*.

The influence of his wife, Joy, should not go unnoticed. She has an intense interest in his work, even though she must suffer somewhat in its production. She listens sensitively and responds perceptively to his intellectual ruminations, challenging those assertions which offend her own standards of philosophical integrity. Not to be overwhelmed in the presence of the man she knows as a partner, as guardian of his health she strenuously denies him the slice of apple pie he tries to cajole from her; defends herself when he gives vent to the frustration that must be the mark of every writer. Her role in public gatherings, at cocktail parties, book launchings and lectures is clearly defined: 'Have you met . . . ?' she asks, moving in on the three elderly matrons who threaten to end Wilson's creativity by displaying a total misunderstanding of everything he has ever written. But, above everything else, in his home and in his life, she guarantees what Father Brocard Sewell, quoting Eric Gill, has called 'the cell of good living'.

It is to be acknowledged that Wilson, like most men, is a complex of explosive temperament but few men can match the endeavour he puts into self-control. When he feels enraged, he calms himself with the simple mental exercises he has developed. When he finds himself dreading the constant demands upon his time, he challenges himself to give more of himself. When he travels, he allays his annoyance by utilising the time in reflective thought. When he reads bitter critical attacks on his work, he reminds himself of Shaw's injunction always to remain good tempered. In his writing, he is a model of self-discipline – how else could he have produced such a huge body of work. When his mind and his typewriter are locked in an uncompromising stand-off, he simply types on, knowing that suddenly there will be a 'click' in the brain, after which the keyboard will receive the flow of words with a creative willingness.

Wilson is regarded by his friends as the most generous of men. And his generosity is not limited to the presentation of a copy of his latest book or an evening meal to visitors. He gives liberally of his time, of his ideas and of his intuitive understanding of human needs. Nor does he simply respond to needs: he anticipates them with an accuracy that springs from a heightened sensitivity.

His life is in total accord with his philosophy; the one giving stimulus to the other.

Random evaluations of Wilson by those who know him provide important insights into his personality. Writing of the early days of their relationship, Daniel Farson writes:

> My interview with Colin was reported in various newspapers, with such headlines as: 'Colin (I'm a genius) Wilson'. This was to be the pattern of his publicity. I did not help. Though he was, and is, the most constant of people, I found it difficult to remain constant about him. I had met few people who were so spontaneous or shared their own enthusiasms so generously. We became inseparable companions. But there were times when I felt I was guiding a visitor from Mars.
>
> 'Look', I exclaimed, pointing across the street, 'there's Princess Margaret'.
>
> 'Really,' said Colin, 'is that a person or a public house?'
>
> And when Kenneth Allsop drove us to stay with my parents in North Devon, he mentioned myxomatosis.
>
> 'What's myxomatosis?' asked Colin.
>
> In one way this naivety was delightful. He explained he was so busy reading books that he had no time for newspapers, which accounted for his ignorance of everyday life, and his remarkable knowledge of literature. When he wrote, he typed straight on to the page without corrections so that the manuscript might have come from a typing agency. I envied him this gift. When he gave a quotation, he did so, incredibly, from memory, an achievement which rebounded when the inevitable mistakes were discovered and he was accused of carelessness.[22]

Nicolas Tredell presents the following overview of Wilson's life:

> His life has taken him through a series of situations which exemplify major features of culture and society in twentieth century Britain. The culturally deprived working-class background; the voyage through the 'lower-depths' of post-War Britain; the spectacular leap to success through the power of mass communications, a power as dangerous and unstable as nuclear energy; rejection, derision and neglect, reinforcing cultural isolation; and a slow working back to an established position. Throughout all this, because of all this, Wilson has had

to create his own cultural context, using the material to hand. To do this is to make one's own mapping of reality, and ultimately, if one is driven by metaphysical needs as Wilson is, of the universe. Wilson may seem eccentric: in this, he is central. He has carried out, in an explicit and sustained way, an activity which anyone who reflects on his life in depth, and has a hunger for seriousness, must carry out today, in our age of cultural pluralism and debasement. He has made his own world, for lack of another.[23]

In the brief text he wrote to accompany his photograph of Wilson, Cecil Beaton observed:

He proved to be militantly intellectual. Random remarks about our mutual acquaintances were always in terms of whether they had read the philosophers who interested him. *A propos* of a neighbour of mine (I had only known her as a delightfully domesticated old lady) he enthused, 'Oh, you should hear her talk about Swedenborg!' But it was clear from the outset that here was a person who wasted little time in the usual impedimenta of gossip. He preferred to discuss the topics he wrote about, and he described a sadistic novel he had completed, sadism being a subject on which he was extremely well-informed. The new 'insider' was somewhat deprecating about his success. Oh yes, the newspapers had given considerable space to him; but what really mattered was that certain people he respected had taken him seriously. He may, as has been reported, consider himself a genius, but there is no visible arrogance in him, nor any mock modesty either. He seems to be a very natural phenomenon.[24]

Father Brocard Sewell, as early as 1968, observed:

It ought to be realized by now, when the noise of early sensationalism and controversies has died down, that Colin Wilson is a serious writer whose main concern is with ideas. But if this is beginning to be understood, the public has not yet accepted Mr. Wilson's claim that he and Mr. Bill Hopkins are the only two geniuses alive today. But in all probability there is still plenty of time for this assertion to be made good. I certainly know of no-one more likely than Mr. Wilson to end his days as a revered and patriarchal centenarian to whom the term 'genius' is almost fated to be applied. . . . If genius lies in the prosecution of great designs through unremitting hard work and refusal to admit defeat, then Colin Wilson has the basic qualities of genius. Perhaps, also, the genius is the man who never accepts boredom or unfulfilment.[25]

In the publisher's blurb, written for the Llewellyn Publications' edition of Ted Holiday's *The Goblin Universe* in 1986, for which Wilson wrote an extended Introduction, he is described as 'one of the most well-respected and important Renaissance thinkers of the twentieth century'. In accord with this evaluation, there are those who believe that he is, in the precise meaning of the term, a 'universal genius' and that as such, he belongs in the intellectual tradition and human *avant garde* in which such figures as Michelangelo and Emanuel Swedenborg have their place. It is too early to pass a final judgement upon Wilson: he may have as many as another thirty years of creative writing ahead of him. What is already clear is that he has produced an enormously important body of work that deserves the attention of the widest possible audience.

2

The Philosophy

THE essence of the philosophy of Colin Wilson has its roots in the intellectual tradition which flourished throughout the Western world from 1770 until 1850 and which was known as Romanticism. Any real appreciation of his ideas must begin with an examination of that movement.

Romanticism derives its name, not from any notion of romantic love but from the vernacular language, Romany, that was in widespread use in Southern Europe following the collapse of the Roman Empire. It was, accordingly, a movement in which simplicity played an important role. In large part, it was a reaction against the neo-Classical movement, with its elevated language and structured subject matter. Romanticism concentrated on the commonplace and expressed its interest in factual detail in a direct and simple language. Folk tales, folk music and popular stories, which had been ignored by Classicism as lacking in sophistication, were given a new prominence. In fact, Romanticism regarded the prevailing classical culture as artificial.

While a considerable body of well-known historic literary figures, including France's Diderot and England's Horace Walpole, and even Samuel Johnson, may be regarded as having meandered uncertainly between a 'classical' and a 'romantic' celebration of life, it was not until Jean-Jacques Rousseau published his widely acclaimed *Confessions* that the essence of the new philosophy was given full expression. Following its publication, Rousseau earned himself the title, the 'Father of Romanticism'. The contemporary historian of philosophy, Jacques Barzun, has written of him:

Rousseau, the first to break openly with the doctrines of the Enlightenment, sets forth in his works and in his life, almost all the ingredients of the new movement: he repudiates the ideal of elegant upper-class leisure and preaches modern bourgeois family life as we know it today; he defines the principles of democratic society and representative government; he makes religious feeling once again a legitimate emotion; he reforms prose style, anticipates the theory of music drama and revolutionizes the aims and methods of education; he delves into the recesses of the self through his *Confessions* and makes of Nature, not indeed a primitive state of ignorance to which we should turn back, but an ideal norm ahead of us towards which all our explorations of heart and mind should tend.[1]

But Wilson has argued that Romanticism had its origins in the revolutionary thought of the great English physicist, Isaac Newton. Through his vast 'System of the Heavens', *Principia Mathematica*, Newton had relocated man within the universe, giving him the possibility of acquiring unlimited knowledge. This was in stark contrast to an understanding of man which saw him as subservient to God and capable of knowing only what God chose to disclose. Suddenly, with Newton, Adam and Eve were set free from the divine injunction that they should not eat of the tree of knowledge.

Newton was the true father of the French revolution, not Rousseau. The storming of the Bastille was a symbolic act; it was the official coronation of Newtonian man as Lord of the Universe. The Marquis de Sade wrote a curious pamphlet called *Frenchmen, one more effort if you want to be Republican*, in which he told his countrymen that they should follow their execution of the king with the execution of God. And he took, in one stride, the step that has taken other European thinkers a century and a half of nervous edging forward: the idea that values are relative, and that therefore all men should adopt Rabelais's motto: 'Do what you will'. In a sense, de Sade's pamphlet might be regarded as the true assault on the Bastille. It was the first great gesture of Romanticism: the formulation of the question: 'Why is man not a God?'

This was a question that would never have occurred to the men of earlier centuries. They took their limitations and their sufferings for granted. New Romantic man asked questions. He was outraged that he should be a prisoner of the body, a captive of the earth. The great symbol of Romantic man is Byron's Manfred, standing on a mountain top and shaking his fist at God.[2]

The Romantic Revolution – like all revolutions – had the effect of cutting people off from their past. There could be no return to the earlier values; only a forward thrust, aimed at a restructuring of the fabric of life. Romanticism produced men of passion who were determined to play a part in the redesigning of the social and cultural order. These were men who were determined to be innovative and who were not afraid to look questioningly at the unknown. They welcomed diversity and sought to define their world in accord with a broader vision.

But most of all, the Romantics looked within themselves and at humanity as a whole. They elevated history as a valuable source of information on human nature. They studied men in order to find Man. They examined nations without imperialistic motives, in order to enrich their common European culture. And they embraced religious faith and intellectual enquiry with a renewed passion. They were urgently busy with the task of filling out their lives.

> At its best, the Romantic spirit cherishes both experience and tradition, both emotion and reason, both religion and science, both folk art and its sophisticated off-shoots, both form and substance, both the real and the ideal, both the individual and the group, both order and freedom, both man and nature. Its aim, precisely, is synthesis.[3]

Jacques Barzun points out that in many respects, Napoleon Bonaparte epitomises the Romantic man:

> He was the man who, starting from nothing, had become statesman and conqueror – the self-made man in an era of 'careers open to talent'; but more than this he was the prototype of the man of genius, because regardless of his aims, he had the three supreme qualities – the imagination to conceive of great plans, the ability to grasp correctly a multitude of details (what we loosely call 'realism'), and the tireless energy that

kept adapting reality to his imagined plans with the greatest speed and accuracy possible.[4]

Romanticism expressed itself politically in the French Revolution but it found its most complete expression through the creation of a new literature which was characterised by a high degree of realism. The novel as a literary form, was a product of the Romantic movement, which also gave poetry and drama a renewed popularity and influence. It was the Romantic writers who introduced the notion of 'local colour' – a literary device which utilises detail to enable a reader to enter more completely into the imagined world of the writer. The new literature was an attempt at reflecting the human condition in order that it might be studied with greater objectivity and moulded 'closer to the heart's desire.'

It is a popular misconception that Romanticism was uninterested in science. In fact, it was characterised by a 'biological revolution' which saw major advances in the study of zoology, ethnology, anthropology and psychology. The evolutionary theory of Charles Darwin was, in one sense, a crystallisation of the Romantic conviction that becoming was no less important than being. The Romantics studied man both within and without. Whatever refused to surrender its secrets to their artistic examination was subjected to their scientific enquiry.

Wilson is drawn naturally into this Romantic tradition – and it is again Barzun who helps us understand why.

> Some critics have concluded that the Romantic outlook is doomed to failure because it tries to reconcile the irreconcilable. The fact is that twentieth century culture is still eager to achieve this reconciliation. Like Romanticism, it starts from man and accepts the contradictions within him. Man is both great and helpless, destined for glory and for wretchedness, endowed with reason and driven by an irrational life-force. He cannot give up or withdraw from his earthly effort for, as Pascal in the seventeenth century and our modern Existentialists have pointed out, he is 'embarked', engaged in the struggle before he knows there is one. Hence the Romantic valuing of the qualities that may see him through; energy, daring, capacity for experience, courage, intellect and imagination.[5]

But if the nineteenth century began in a blaze of human assertiveness, it was to end in a world-weary, defeated pessimism. Goethe's Faust, even aided by the superhuman powers of Mephistopheles, believes that human freedom remains limited and that man can finally 'know' nothing. Instead of using the power he has to press onward towards the godhead, Faust satisfies himself with the physical comfort of Gretchen's bed! Faust represents the ultimate inadequacy of Romanticism. In the late 1890s, the poet Ernest Dowson lamented:

> The fire is out, and spent the warmth thereof
> This is the end of every song man sings.

Wilson argues that Romanticism failed because men came to believe that the pathway to the godhead was strewn with too many obstacles. Many Romantics were sick men for whom life seemed a denial of all they wished to believe. Aspiration and experience were contradictory. Constant talk of 'ecstasy' and 'rapture' drained the words of meaning: a lack of purpose with its attendant sense of boredom began to pervade the human mind. Perhaps, suggests Wilson, Romanticism failed because the notion of man as god was thrust upon man too early – before he was capable of responding in an appropriate manner. Having enjoyed the comfort and stability of the eighteenth century, man was suddenly challenged to attain maturity overnight.

In the work of Hermann Hesse, Wilson detects a recapitulation of the history of nineteenth-century Romanticism. In early novels, such as *Peter Camenzind*, *Demian* and *Siddartha*, the central character is a kind of pilgrim seeking out an ideal with energetic enthusiasm. A later work, *Steppenwolf*, centres around a middle-aged man whose life oscillates between moments of grand vision and others when suicide appears to be the only option available. Finally, in his last important novel, *Magister Ludi*, he creates his own religion – a humanistic ritual that fails to satisfy his deepest needs.

Almost imperceptibly, Romanticism underwent a change and became the movement that is today known as Existentialism. This name was first used by the Danish Christian philosopher, Søren Kierkegaard, himself a Romantic. Kierkegaard was a man deeply embittered by his relationship with his father. He seems to have had a certain arrogance which tended to isolate him from other people. He became engaged to a seventeen-year-old girl named Regina Olsen but then broke the engagement, apparently enjoying the sense of power that this gave him. He wrote a large volume entitled *Diary of a Seducer*, in which the main character possesses a girl and then discards her. But he also wrote of more substantial things:

> One sticks one's finger into the soil to tell by the smell what land one's in. I stick my finger into existence – it smells of nothing. Where am I? Who am I? How did I come to be here? What is this thing called the world? What does the word mean? Who is it that has lured me into the thing, and now leaves me there? How did I come into the world? Why was I not consulted, why was I not made acquainted with its manners and customs, but was thrust into the ranks as though I'd been bought from a kidnapper, a dealer in souls? How did I obtain an interest in it? And is it not a voluntary concern? And if I am compelled to take part in it, where is the director? I would like to see him.[6]

Kierkegaard argued that religion was central to the fullness of life. He bitterly attacked Hegel who had only reluctantly admitted religion to his philosophical system, and accused him of a lack of passion. For Kierkegaard, passion was always religious passion – a craving for a sense of purpose – and it could not be engendered by the intellect alone. What makes a man a Christian, according to Kierkegaard, is not the fact of baptism or the acceptance of certain doctrines but the *intensity* with which he experiences the truth of the Gospel.

Although a minor philosopher in his own right, Kierkegaard introduced a number of concepts which were to be taken up by a number of twentieth-century philosophers such as Heidegger, Sartre and Camus. It was primarily through these thinkers that Existentialism was to come into full bloom.

Martin Heidegger and Jean-Paul Sartre were both students of Edmund Husserl, the founder of the phenomenological school and the exponent of exciting new ideas on the nature of human consciousness, to whom we shall return later. Heidegger and Sartre both contributed significantly to the spread of Existentialism although there was considerable intellectual distance between them. Heidegger was convinced of a need for Western man to return to a pre-Socratic intellectual climate in which reason had

not yet assumed a total control over philosophy. Like Kierkegaard, Heidegger saw severe limits attaching to reason's capacity
to uncover truth but, unlike the melancholy Dane, he did not
believe that a religious faith could provide answers to the perennial
questions. He placed considerable trust in the poet's capacity to
provide important insights. His careful examinations of guilt,
anxiety, our consciousness of time and our apprehension of death
were important contributions to the development of Existentialism.

Jean-Paul Sartre was relentless in his own examination of
experience. Simone de Beauvoir reported that

> torpor, somnolence, escapism, intellectual dodges and truces,
> prudence and respect were all unknown to him. He was
> interested in everything and never took anything for granted.
> Confronted with an object, he would look it straight in the
> face instead of trying to explain it away with a myth, a word,
> an impression or a preconceived idea: he wouldn't let it go
> until he had grasped all its ins and outs and all its multiple
> significations.[7]

Sartre, like his teacher Husserl, also engaged in an attempt to
define consciousness. He seemed to have been more interested in
our consciousness of other people than in self-consciousness and
the question of human relationships caused him great intellectual
anguish. Among his best-known dictums are the notions that
'Hell is other people' and that 'Man is a useless passion'. Sartre
wrote extensively on what he called 'bad faith' – a form of self-
deception that he found to be one of the central characteristics of
contemporary man.

Sartre was preoccupied with the question of human contingency. But, as Wilson argues, contingency is a concomitant of
passivity which is best defined as an absence of will. Lifeless
objects are perfectly contingent. Man can only feel himself contingent when he allows himself to become an object. Wilson assesses
Sartre's concern thus:

> Sartre calls . . . contingency (or meaninglessness), nausea. And
> it becomes, in a sense, the cornerstone of his philosophy.
> Human beings are so wrapped up in themselves that they treat
> reality as if it was there for their convenience . . . They take

things for granted with a kind of silly conceit. They are not
interested in the real complexity of things; only in what happens
to suit their self-absorbed little purposes. If they are suddenly
forced to admit that things exist in their own right, they experience a kind of distress, like a child confronted with a page of
mathematical equations. This is nausea – revulsion.[8]

Sartre's friend, Albert Camus, accepted Heidegger's belief that
man can only experience the fullness of his existence when he
confronts death directly. Camus' novel *L'Etranger* translated into
English as *The Outsider*, introduces Meursault, a man characterised
by an overwhelming indifference to life, even when he is confronted with the death of his own mother. It is only when he
himself murders a man that he begins to experience the faint
stirring of a sense of life within. For Camus, the central image
for Existential man is that of Sisyphus, who had offended the
gods and was punished endlessly by having to roll a boulder to
the top of a mountain only to watch it roll down again. Camus
declared that we must imagine Sisyphus contented at his perpetu-
ally meaningless task.

Existentialism, as understood by Wilson, is a philosophy that
concerns itself centrally with freedom. Yet, by the middle of the
twentieth century, it had lost its way. This was the case because
none of the great existential thinkers – not Hamann, Kierkegaard,
Jaspers, Heidegger, Sartre or Camus – could see that there are
values that lie beyond man – that is, beyond his everyday consciousness. Sartre insisted that man is free, but he was unable to
decide what man should do with his freedom. It was not enough
simply to say that man could do what he liked with his freedom
for, as Wilson points out, freedom for anything is really freedom
for nothing. In the thought of Sartre, man is free but the world
is empty and meaningless.

Sartre's Existentialism was fundamentally negative. Even his
concept of freedom ends in pessimism for it is a freedom in which
the meaning of the world has to be accepted without justification
and without excuse. Man, according to Sartre, is 'condemned
to be free'. Existentialism, like nineteenth-century Romanticism
before it, ended in despair. Wilson comments:

The basic impulse behind Existentialism is optimistic, very
much like the impulse behind all science. Existentialism *is*

Romanticism and Romanticism is the feeling that man is not the mere creature that he has always taken himself for. Romanticism began as a tremendous surge of optimism about the stature of man. Its aim – like that of science – was to raise man above the muddled feelings and impulses of his everyday humanity, and to make him a god-like observer of human existence.

Now, if we turn to Sartre and Heidegger, we can instantly see why their Existentialism is so unsatisfactory. The great trumpet call of optimism no longer sounds. There is no clear way forward. Heidegger concluded that, with the exception of a few great poets, man achieves 'authenticity' only in the face of death. Sartre's analysis of the human situation leads him to feel that there is no 'life-purpose' for all men, no absolute values. The only good is the relative one of human welfare; so the only possible way forward lies in commitment to socialist politics. All roads are blocked but this one. Philosophy is now a closed subject, for there is no point in thinking further; we shall only keep returning to the recognition that all roads are blocked but this one.[9]

But Wilson was unwilling to accept this negative understanding of Existentialism. He insisted that, properly understood, Existentialism, like Romanticism, is not a body of beliefs or an intellectual creed but an intellectual and emotional perspective from which an interpretation of life is attempted. It is a commitment to the view that life is to be understood in deeply personal terms or it is not to be understood at all. Existentialism is an attitude that insists on the relevance of meaning and which persistently seeks to uncover that meaning. Thus, Existentialism may be religious or atheistic but whichever of these it is, it will place man in a posture of questioning the nature of his experience. Wilson writes:

The ideally great Existentialist . . . would have the ability to use his will power in analysis, and yet at a moment's notice to become completely negative, transparent and receptive. There would, that is to say, be complete *self-control*. And here we see that the concept of Existentialism involves inevitably the idea of self-discipline and self-transformation – the *religious* idea. For the existentialist, then, thought can never be 'abstract'; it is always involved in a concrete situation. He never treats the universe as if he were sitting apart from it all, in a celestial armchair, 'logicising' about it. When the field of his own immediate being is no longer in question, he ceases to think and again becomes the artist-poet. For the existentialist, the only form of abstract thought which is not unutterable nonsense is mathematics and this is because mathematics is the dumbbell exercise of the existentialist, his mental gymnasium. But essentially, existentialism is not a building of an intellectual system. It is the building of an insight, a building of many insights into a total vision, an attempt to extend the consciousness, to extend the sphere of the living being into the unliving. It is made of moments of insight of the kind that come to the poet.[10]

In 1956, Sartrean Existentialism was one of the most vital forces in French culture, Sartre himself was a major cult figure and existential ideas were in evidence in books, popular magazines, films, theatre, poetry and even in some forms of popular music. This then, was the intellectual climate into which Wilson introduced his concept of the Outsider.

Wilson's first book, indeed his entire life's work, must be seen against the background of his own unique interpretation of Existentialism. He insists, quite correctly, that Existentialism is a passionate protest against the prevalence of mere logic. It is a demand that intuition and vision should be admitted to the canon of learning. Existentialism's basic concept is that of the stature of man. Existentialist philosophers would commence an analysis of man's stature by pointing out that while there are times when man feels supremely happy and confident, there are other times when he feels substantially less than human. A study of the cause of this extreme variation in man's self-image is the central task of philosophy.

Wilson assembled a vast range of Outsiders, included Barbusse, Hemingway, Van Gogh, T. E. Lawrence, Nijinsky, Schiller, Shelley, Coleridge, Rimbaud, Rilke and Proust. As he treated them individually and thought his way through their lives and writings, there emerged a dramatic picture of a substantial community which testifies to the fact that life possesses a depth which is seldom fathomed. It is precisely this depth that the Outsider seeks. But Wilson's book is not merely a description of the public figure who feels alienated from his culture. It is an historical review of the emergence of a human type over the past two or three centuries. It is the identification of a new response by a group of individuals to the changing circumstances in which man continually finds himself. It is, in the most profound manner, a defiant statement of affirmation in the face of those forces which threaten to annihilate man.

The Outsider is not an oddity. He is a composite of a host of individuals, living, breathing, agonising their way through contemporary culture with its dehumanising processes, its insensitive organisation and its rationalised mayhem. Nor is the modern Outsider confined to Western culture. He is present in Japan and throughout South East Asia. He is visible in the Middle East. He cuts across cultures and religious dogmas for he is searching for something more permanent than anything that can be contained in nationalism or in any historic religion.

The Outsider's sensitivities are highly sharpened. In fact he may see himself as a Sensitive surrounded by Insensitives. This is not because he is arrogant or self-deceived but because he sees deeply into the heart of things. Indeed, he sees too deeply, too much, for his own peace of mind. He is under some inner compulsion to acknowledge the genuine significance of people and events. He feels himself to be outside all established conventions, all social orders and even all interpersonal relationships – even those in which he is himself engaged. The Outsider's prevailing sense of unreality makes it virtually impossible for him to love. In the light of this description, it would be easy to conclude that the Outsider is no more than a psychologically disturbed human being. But this is not so. In a profound sense, he is *too* sane. He cannot acquiesce in the mindless mores of his culture or the childish mythologies by which so many of his contemporaries live. Retreat into the grey world of mental illness is not an option to him for he is essentially incapable of self-deceit.

Perhaps the most important fact about *The Outsider* is that it is quintessentially, a personal journey through his own psyche and identity, made by Wilson in the twelve months of 1955. It is simply one of the most integrated attempts of our time to look with honesty and courage at the state of a mind which refuses to feel at home in a dehumanised world. *The Outsider* is Wilson's personal confrontation with meaninglessness. It is his wrestling with Jacob's angel. It is, as he himself acknowledged to T. S. Eliot, his own wasteland. The Outsider is Wilson himself, pressed in a cruciform against Barbusse's hotel wall with his eye to the events – birth, copulation and death – unfolding within the next room.

Those who have not read the whole of the Outsider cycle are on dangerous grounds if they purport to understand Wilson. If they have read *The Outsider* and *Religion and the Rebel*, they will be inclined to see him as continuing the pessimism set in motion by the Romantics and carried forward by Sartre. If they have read only *Beyond the Outsider*, they will doubt whether Wilson has seen the depth of despair he claims to have mastered. No, the seven volumes (*Introduction to the New Existentialism* is included) of the Outsider cycle is a single work and it is one of the most seminal works of our century. Even then, it must be acknowledged that it does not stand alone. It is the cornerstone of a profound literary production, now represented in over eighty volumes, that is stunning in its consistency and its vitality.

What then, does the Outsider cycle say? What is the philosophy of Colin Wilson?

In writing *The Outsider*, Wilson was doing more than cataloguing the lives of Romantics and Existentialists. He was attempting to resolve some of the questions that burned in his own mind in relation to his own existence. He was also looking for a way forward for Western philosophy.

> The Outsider, then, is a man who is haunted by a sense of the futility of life. Most of the modern Outsiders I dealt with felt that there was no way out of this impasse. But to some degree, a closer examination showed that this attitude is due to the peculiar conditions of our civilisation. Spiritual standards have almost ceased to exist, and Freud and Karl Marx have done a thorough job of convincing us that all men are much the same: subject to the same kind of psychological and economic pressures. If the modern Outsider finds the world an unrelieved prospect of futility, it is because his training and conditioning have made it difficult for him to see any meaning in the notion of *increased intensity of mind*.[11]

For Wilson, Existentialism is essentially a confrontation with one's self. It takes as its central question, 'What shall a man do with his life?' Thus whatever questions it might have to ask about the nature of the universe are secondary. The salvation of the individual, rather than a comprehensive intellectual system, is the end objective of Existentialism. Fundamentally, this salvation must be worked out by each man for himself. In his attempt to express his real self, the individual must learn to stand alone. One man's self-expression must be achieved over against the self-expression of all other men. As Wilson points out, the greatest achievements in human history, whether in music, painting, poetry or even philosophy, have been accomplished by men who have learned to be supremely alone.

Mankind's first business is self-knowledge. But this does not come easily, as Wilson notes:

> The man who watches a woman undressing has the red eyes of an ape; yet the man who sees two young lovers really alone for the first time, who brings out all the pathos, the tenderness and uncertainty when he tells about it, is no brute. He is very much human. And the ape and the man exist in one body.[12]

Nor is this simply a matter of human psychology. There is a universal reference here – a hint of what Paul Tillich has called *the ground of being* and a consciousness that our highest aspirations are incapable of realisation without the maximum exertion of will and energy.

Modern man is a divided man. He is outside himself looking upon himself with a nostalgia for unity. He is outside his own society, for he has no centre within himself and can identify no centre within others to which he might address any communication. He is divided from his past and from his future. He is divided from his dreams. Ultimately, he is divided from his own life for he experiences life, not so much as living but as drifting.

Wilson's analysis of this existential drift led him to one of the most original insights of contemporary psychology. Reflecting on the fact that we can get into our car, turn the ignition key and then suddenly find ourselves at our destination without having any recollection of having made the journey, Wilson saw that much of our living is done for us by what he called *the Robot*. In the case of our driving the car or typing a letter, the Robot is a useful ally but a problem arises when the Robot takes over and robs us of the quality of life in domains where quality is the very thing being sought. In fact, we have become overly dependent upon the Robot and have handed over more and more of our living to it. Wilson has caught his own Robot listening to the music he wanted to hear and even making love to his wife! In such circumstances, we might well ask, with T. S. Eliot, 'Where is the life we have lost in the living?'

> The structure of the Robot restricts our capacity to feel. We keep learning things and packing them into the realm of the Robot until we are like some archaeological site, it gives us pleasure but the moment the Robot takes over, the pleasure vanishes.
> It should be noted, however, that this pleasure is recoverable. We may become acquainted with the symphonies of Beethoven through the radio and finally become so familiar with them that they cease to be a source of pleasure. Years later, we buy a good record player and the latest versions of the symphonies and find that our pleasure in them is just as intense as when we first discovered them.[13]

Soon after identifying the Robot, Wilson had a second insight which was closely related. In a small village in Huntingdonshire, called St Neot, he himself slipped across a threshold of indifference. This threshold, which he called the *St Neot Margin* is a line on one side of which is an active participation in life while on the other there is a passive withdrawal from life. In the St Neot Margin, there is a willing acceptance of pain and suffering. It is a resignation to a lower level of existence. It is a reflection of the fact that we know more about what we do not want than about what we do want.

> The St Neot margin is a problem of human purpose – or rather, lack of purpose. Man's strongest impulses are negative: revulsion from death or pain, the need for security. . . . One would expect that a creature with such strong negative impulses would have equally strong positive ones, that the power of his revulsion from death would indicate a profound sense of purpose, an equally powerful appreciation of life. Yet the lives of these creatures are wasted in trivialities. They are like spoilt children who kick and scream when they are told it is time to go to school, and yet who are bored and listless at home. It is not surprising that many nineteenth century materialists refused to recognize an evolutionary urge in man. Everything he has created has been for negative reasons -- fear of discomfort and

of death. He thinks in terms of 'freedom from' this and that, but never of 'freedom for' some ultimate purpose.[14]

It is in this context that Wilson believes we have called ourselves Man too early.

Together, or singly, the Robot and the St Neot Margin are capable of producing an overwhelming sense of boredom in the human soul by robbing it of a sense of immediate participation in events and experiences and Wilson has insisted that his sense of boredom is critical to the condition of contemporary man. Not only is it a problem in itself, but, as two lines from W. H. Auden indicate, it produces a negative feedback which perpetuates the condition:

> Put the car away. When life fails,
> What's the good of going to Wales?

This is the problem. We are confronted by a life-failure which is self-perpetuating. We are like children on a holiday for whom the sense of fun has been exhausted after the first few days or, in another of Wilson's powerful images, we are like grandfather clocks being driven by watch springs.

But if Wilson is adept at describing the essential existential problem, he is equally at home in moving in the direction of its resolution. He comprehends that the beginning of man's salvation lies in the fact that he is aware of his self-division. He has an intuitive understanding that:

> the visible world is a deliberate deceit hiding an internal reality which is so glorious that all men would be drunk with ecstasy if they could see into it. . . . [that] . . . most of us are blinded by our feelings and have no sense whatever of inward reality. . . . [that] . . . our reactions to things and people – a gloomy day, our dislike of someone we have to work with – keep us aware only of the surface of the world.[15]

Man wants unity. He wants balance. He wants, in short, to cease being an Outsider. He wants to refine his self-perception and to understand the human soul and its working. He wants to escape triviality and learn how to express himself fully.

The Outsider is man *in extremis*. Having delineated him with such artistry, Wilson realised the enormous importance of his portrait. He warns:

> If you are living a very ordinary dull life at low pressure, you can safely regard the Outsider as a crank who does not deserve serious consideration. But if you are interested in man in extreme states, or in man abnormally preoccupied by questions about the nature of life, then whatever answers the Outsider may propound should be worth your respectful attention.[16]

What answers are propounded by the Outsider? The last two chapters of *The Outsider* are called 'The Outsider as Visionary' and 'Breaking the Circuit'. The first chapter of *Religion and the Rebel* is entitled 'The Anatomy of Imagination'. These chapter headings give a direct and clear indication of what Wilson regards as the resolution of the Outsider's dilemma. They reflect the beginning of his preoccupation with what he called *breakthroughs to pure consciousness* or what Abraham Maslow was later to call *peak experiences*. The chapter headings are the pathway which lead us beyond the Outsider and into the heart of Wilson's philosophy.

Wilson insists that if we are to extend consciousness, we need to know something about how consciousness works. In *Religion and the Rebel*, he deals extensively with Whitehead and the notion of *prehension* which argues that consciousness has a grasping function – that it reaches out with octopus-like tentacles and attempts to clutch at and devour large pieces of reality. He writes:

> If life is to advance a stage higher, beyond the ape, beyond man the toiler, or even man the artist, it will be through a further development of the power of prehension.[17]

But it is not enough simply to clutch wildly at reality. There must be a purpose, an intention to our assimilation of experience. At the centre of our construction of an extended consciousness there must be an architect to develop the designs and ensure that the plans are being followed satisfactorily. Thus Wilson applies Husserl's theory of *intentionality* as a mechanism for prehension.

Wilson provides a set of examples to indicate how intentionality works:

(a) If I stare at clouds, I can see various shapes or faces. If I look elsewhere for a moment, the faces will have vanished – not because the clouds have changed, but because I only 'saw' the faces by carefully *adjusting* my attention so as to notice certain things and exclude others.

(b) When my small daughter falls down, I can see her actually making up her mind whether she will cry or not – whether she will allow herself to feel hurt or upset, or whether to get on with the game.

(c) Sometimes, one can get drunk on two glasses of beer, and sometimes one can drink whisky for a whole evening and still feel sober. Drunkenness is only partly physical; to a far greater degree, it depends on intentionality.

(d) When I feel sick, I can usually prevent myself from being sick by a certain attitude of mind – a deliberate summoning of my healthy energies. This, of course, applies generally to our physical condition. Headaches are usually a matter of intentionality.

(e) I may go to bed feeling completely exhausted, unable to fix my attention on anything. If someone aroused me because the house next door had caught fire, the sleepiness would vanish.

(f) I meet a man I have often seen at a distance – perhaps on stage or television – and I am startled that his face is unlike my mental picture of it. I realise that when I saw it at a distance, I only saw certain of its characteristics and my imagination added the others – mostly by a process of association of ideas, recalling faces that he reminded me of. Yet watching him on television, I could have sworn that I was merely 'seeing' him, and not adding anything at all.[18]

Intentionality may be triggered by the emotions, or by the body. It can operate on many levels and may be almost conscious. Thus, an experience that would normally be unpleasant, such as being talked into seeing a film or a play that does not hold real interest, can be made pleasant by the deliberate decision that it will be so. Intentionality is frequently the real cause of an action that is perceived as being mechanical. When a stone is dropped from a hand, it is easy to think of the falling as being 'natural' – but it has been caused.

The significance of intentionality can be indicated simply, thus:

> When we look at something, we *throw* our attention at it, like
> a stone. If we stare at it passively without this effort, we fail
> to notice it – like reading the page of a book when our minds
> are elsewhere and being unable to remember what we have
> read. We grasp meaning as the hand grasps an object. The
> important corollary is that if we wish to see more meaning we
> have to tighten our grip, heighten our intentionality.[19]

Consciousness is the instrument with which man seeks to illumi-
nate the world. It follows that if man operates his consciousness
at a reduced level of intentionality he will see less of the world
than is available to him. In a profound sense, the world he sees
will be a devaluation of the real, full world. It would be as if he
tried to examine the riches of an art gallery lit by nothing more
than a candle. Sartre had rejected the pivotal Husserlian contention
that a man has a 'real me' above and beyond consciousness; a
'transcendental ego'. When Sartre looked within himself, he saw
nothing but a void. The effect of Sartre's rejection of this notion
was that he was left without a self to 'fire' attention at the universe. He was dependent upon impressions 'floating' upon him.
Sartre's character Roquentin, in *Nausea* and Camus' heroes, suffering from an acute sense of absurdity, are incapable of pulling back
the bowstring, so that the intentional 'arrow' drops at their feet
rather than flying to impale the object of their desire.

Wilson highlights the critical importance of what he calls the
'Husserlian Revolution':

> Husserl points out that if philosophy finds itself in a cul de sac,
> this is simply because it has so far been a half-measure – like
> science. Science may appear to hurl man out of his world of
> provincialism and prejudice; but Husserl has shown that man's
> prejudices go a great deal deeper than his intellect or his
> emotions. Consciousness itself is 'prejudiced' – that is to say,
> intentional. I am born into a situation that includes my family
> background and my social background, and I shall grow up
> with certain intellectual and emotional prejudices that are the
> result of these. Science may help me to shed most of them.
> But I am also born with habits of perception that have been
> slowly achieved over millions of years, and which science leaves
> untouched. Admittedly, some of these perceptions broaden as
> I get older: I may develop a sense for music or poetry or

religion. But these things will only make clear to me what it is that torments Faust: that mere knowledge – of science, philosophy, etc. – has no radical effect upon my essential being as a glowing fragment of life, striving to be more alive. If knowledge is really to fire my *whole* being and cause it to expand, it must not be capable merely of exploding my child-hood prejudices and releasing me into a broader world of universal knowledge; it must also enable me to understand my inner being: what happens, for example, to my consciousness when I am moved by great music. If this can be done, then the immense release that science promises can become a real possibility. In being able to stand aside from my habits of perception, I shall have discovered the secret of poetry and mysticism.[20]

Wilson has also drawn attention to another characteristic of consciousness: that is, by nature *relational*.

Consciousness has a web-like structure. Things have meaning, significance, in so far as they are related to other things. If I am reading, and my attention wanders, I stop 'taking it in'. This is not simply because I have ceased to fire my attention at the page, but because I have ceased to actively grasp the meaning of earlier pages, and to keep adding the meaning of each new sentence to what I have already grasped. In the case of a difficult book, or a problem in mathematics, this tendency to 'lose the thread' is very obvious. If you do not make the effort to 'connect up' the latest stage of the argument with all that has gone before, the latest stage will become meaningless. If I am sitting in a train, looking at the world that goes past, I am not aware of having to 'connect up' the things I now see with my past experience. But this is because I do it unconsciously. The fact remains that 'seeing' things, understanding them, responding to them, is a matter of making connections with dormant areas of my mind. In order to understand anything, we have to make the mental act of 'connecting up' with other things. (And there is also an important corollary to this: the more things I can 'connect it up' with, the more meaningful it becomes.)[21]

Wilson further draws out the significance of relationality:

Philosophy has been saddled with a narrow and passive idea of the word 'meaning'. The meaning of a sentence or a mathematical formula is quite precisely definable because both are abstractions to which we have assigned the meaning in the first place. But the 'meaning' of all other things, a book, a passage of music, a patch of green grass, can never be pinned down like this. Every object in the universe is like a fragment of bone upon which an archaeologist could construct a whole prehistoric animal; perhaps a whole epoch.

Hesse's *Steppenwolf* describes how the taste of a glass of wine makes him aware of Mozart and the stars. He means that the web has suddenly become bigger and Mozart and the stars have become realities.[22]

When we look at a cube, we can see only three of its six sides. Our mind 'supplies' the other three sides and we accept that we are looking at a cube. In the same way, when we listen to music by Mozart, we hear the various sounds of musical instruments being played simultaneously. If we want to hear the symphony, we must use our mind to connect the sounds to the melody, the harmony and all the other elements that together constitute music. Our mind does this for us – but only if we permit it. If we are in a state of boredom, we will hear each note as a grating sound. If we admit the relationality of consciousness and connect the sounds, not only to each other, but to what we know about Mozart and about ourselves and about man . . . the music becomes richer and richer. We begin to move beyond boredom.

Young lovers provide an example of the relationality of consciousness. When they kiss for the first time, the male sees in the female much more than the girl he holds in his arms. He sees her as Paris saw Helen, or Dante saw Beatrice. She is the essence of the eternal feminine. She is the physical embodiment of the biological will to motherhood and the emotional security of the family. Thus, in such a situation, the male himself feels a transformation. He experiences himself as an embodiment of the eternal masculine – Casanova, Caesar, Faust. Nor is this a simply juvenile fantasy. It is as real as anything that the young couple have ever experienced before. Their relationship has facilitated the relationality of consciousness and they vibrate, like a spider's web extended between the branches of a tree, under the influence of a myriad sensations that convince them that life is beautiful.

It is the triple concept of prehension operating through intentionality and relationality that distinguishes Wilson's existentialism from that of Jean-Paul Sartre. Sartre's theory held that reality extends beyond our power to grasp it so that our lives appear to be contingent and without meaning. Wilson saw that Sartre's 'nausea' was in fact the cause rather than the product of his philosophy. With these new insights at his disposal, Wilson was able to lay the foundation of his New Existentialism.

With characteristic modesty, Wilson recognizes Friedrich Nietzsche as the father of the New Existentialism. Nietzsche was a philosopher in whom the passion for truth was a discipline; a discipline which turned him into a visionary. A follower of the religious figure, Zarathustra, he had much respect for Christ but rejected Christianity, like Shaw, as being founded by an immature Paul of Tarsus. In the intellectual tradition of the mystic philosopher and theologian, Jacob Boehme, Nietzsche was a self-disciplined ascetic who gave himself to the strengthening of his vitality by concentrating on satisfying positive needs. He refused to crush his own personality by subjecting it to indignities.

Nietzsche saw man as being a tightrope between a beast and a Superman. The Superman was the outcome of man's endeavour to transcend himself. Nietzsche preached the idea of 'eternal recurrence' as the foundation for an essentially optimistic philosophy. He encountered considerable opposition to his Master–Slave theory, according to which some men were masters who were capable of immense will-power while others were slaves whose short-sightedness led them to seek nothing more than material comforts. Nietzsche pleaded with men to become their own master and strive for perfection.

Notwithstanding the important contribution made by Nietzsche, Wilson's New Existentialism stands alone as a uniquely twentieth-century philosophy of optimism. It begins by seeing man as a dual being continually engaged in an internal battle and it clearly identifies the two selves in this dual being. The first lives in the present and is cautious in his approach to life. He is limited in his grasp of reality. His essential characteristic is cowardice and his highest value is personal security. He takes few risks and spends most of his time in a defensive posture. The other self is aware of altogether broader horizons. From time to time he catches glimpses of a joy, a beauty, a sense of power, that are all completely beyond the imagination of the coward. This self is fully aware of the misery and pain that abound but is determined that these negative factors will not be given the central place in his interpretation of the human condition. He understands that freedom is an absolute power and that it can be used to defeat the sense of contingency and all the other miseries that present themselves to man. He believes that misfortune is just another name for human stupidity and self-pity. He has even come to suspect that death is a form of suicide. In essence, he is the eternal optimist. He believes that human reason, powered by the will to freedom, is capable of surmounting any problem life might present to him.

The New Existentialism, then, reduces the problem to its simplest possible form. Life consists of an ongoing struggle between our vision of an inner freedom and power and a sense of restriction and boredom. It asserts that the resolution of this problem lies in the facilitation of life's evolutionary potentialities. It insists that man's attainment of ultimate freedom will finally disclose the truth about contingency – that it is an illusion.

> The New Existentialism concentrates the full battery of phenomenological analysis upon the everyday sense of contingency, upon the problem of 'life-devaluation'. This analysis helps to reveal how the spirit of freedom is trapped and destroyed; it uncovers the complexities and safety devices in which freedom dissipates itself. It suggests mental disciplines through which this waste can be averted.[23]

The New Existentialism is not based on a delusion. Wilson is not given to some absurd notion of an unlimited self. He knows all too well that man is of this earth. What he rebels against is the notion that man must be restricted by his *intellect*. He cannot accept a definition of man that is couched *purely* in terms of what is already known of him.

> The problem, as Sir Julian Huxley has stated, is to redefine man in terms of possibility and limitation. It might be said that human history has been working towards such a synthesis. Ancient literature – the Greeks, the Old Testament – felt that life is fundamentally tragic, since man is a creature. The early Romantics went to the opposite extreme, and decided that man is born for absolute freedom – that man is really a 'god in exile'. They acted on this belief after the manner of a man who feels that he should be able to fly like a bird by flapping his hands, and tests the theory by leaping off the roof. The impact

of reality startled them so much that most of them died of despair. But man is neither a creature nor a god; he is somewhere between the two, and his evolution depends on recognising the precise nature of his limitations. He can occasionally experience the state of mind in which Van Gogh painted *The Starry Night* or in which Nijinsky wrote *I am God*; but nature refuses to allow man to live in this state for too long. It would destroy his usefulness as the evolutionary spearhead. As Aldous Huxley pointed out in *Doors of Perception*, a certain limitation is necessary if the work of civilization is to continue.[24]

The New Existentialism, in its essence, is an examination of the ways in which human consciousness, with its intentionality and relationality, might be extended to enrich human life. This is a matter of both broadening and deepening our perceptions. The New Existentialism, having identified the reasons for the collapse of Romanticism and Existentialism, becomes a quest for instruments and exercises which may be used to extend consciousness. The New Existentialism is at one and the same time a phenomenological analysis and a methodology for human development.

One of the most important instruments at man's disposal is imagination. For Wilson, imagination is an extension of the powers of survival and an instrument of self-knowledge. It is the power to return to reality after we have become separated from it; to refocus our true values and to combat the curious erosion of our vitality that William James called 'inferiority to our true selves'. Imagination is man at work in the act of increasing his freedom.

Wilson sees the first great flowering of imagination as taking place among the ancient Greeks. The Greeks who invaded Crete and built the city of Mycenae were driven by a sense of adventure which led them to slaughter and rape in much the same way that children play at being pirates. Yet children at play do not harm each other. Their sense of achievement is satisfied, not by violence but by imagination. Four hundred years after the establishment of Mycenae, Homer recited tales of the conquest and his audience participated in the victory by a projection of their minds. Later still, when the drama was established and twelve thousand people sat in the auditorium at the foot of the Acropolis, actors in masks aided their flight of fancy and man found himself living in two worlds simultaneously – the real world and the world of imagination. Nietzsche argued that the Greeks expressed an overwhelming zest for life through their drama.

One of the most powerful forms of imaginative endeavour available to man is the novel. Samuel Richardson, whom Wilson regards as the father of the English novel, spoke of imagination as *substitute experience*. Wilson comments:

> The strange thing about substitute experience is that it is, in many ways, preferable to the real thing. If I am hungry, daydreaming about food will not fill my stomach; it will only make me hungrier. Yet if I am frustrated and bored, and I set the imagination to work, the daydream can provide the same inner satisfaction as actual experience. A frustrated vicar's daughter elaborated a daydream in which she had a love affair with a handsome gypsy. Her novel does not strike us as the daydream of an inexperienced spinster. It has *its own* reality; and it has a quality of intensity that surpasses everyday experience. The feelings evoked in us by 'everyday reality' are fairly limited. Emily Bronte had created the means of evoking a whole new range of feelings. In a sense, she had created a new reality.[25]

Wilson has been tempted to argue that science fiction is one of the most interesting literary forms of the twentieth century. He sees a healthy sign in the fact that, whereas many of the great books of the world – including *The Iliad, Oedipus Rex, Morte d'Arthur, Romeo and Juliet, Paradise Lost, Faust, Moby Dick, the Brothers Karamazov* and *Saint Joan* – have taken tragedy as their theme, science fiction represents a return to the fantastic world of endless possibility. Science fiction, in fact, seems to touch one of our deepest needs; some mythic, Jungian, deeply human requirement for a voyage beyond ourselves. Wilson summarises the nature of the genre thus:

> Science fiction sprang from the progressive beliefs that are the essence of science. The spirit of science is a spirit of enterprise; it follows naturally that writers should ask themselves how far the human race can advance through enterprise. It is natural that the first type of science fiction should be portraits of Utopias. It is also natural that space travel should be the next possibility to engage its attention. Cyrano de Bergerac's two novels about

a voyage to the moon and a voyage to the sun were published about 1660. One of Poe's best stories tells how one, Hans Pfaal, travelled to the moon in a balloon. Jules Verne was one of the first seriously to apply his imagination to the problem of space travel; his moon-voyages are shot out of an enormous canon. Shortly after this came Wells and his first novel, *The Time Travellers*.[26]

What happens as a novel is read – whether a tragedy, a romance or a fantasy – is, not that the reader is physically transported into another external world, but that he enters profoundly into a universe within himself. This is of the utmost significance to the Outsider for what he desperately seeks is an escape from the confusing outer world and a meaningful retreat into himself.

> Truth is subjectivity, and is therefore to be achieved by becoming concentrated in oneself. Ordinarily, when a man concentrates on a problem, he only retreats into the conscious area of his brain, the reasoning area. But there are deeper areas – the areas where all the past is stored up, the area from which those sudden bursts of complete ecstasy flood up into the consciousness. By lowering himself down into himself, as into a deep mine-shaft, man discovers the source of the secret life, the well-spring of life-ecstasy which drives him on in spite of the difficulties of the external world. All life is a struggle to reach this inner power, and to assimilate the endless complexities of the outer world, which sap the energies and destroy the appetite for life.[27]

For contemporary man, with a kaleidoscope of images stored within his head – the endless memories waiting to be triggered, the images carefully collected over a lifetime – and a multiplicity of stimuli bombarding him through an endless interaction with the world and the mass media, there seems to be no limit to the power of the imagination to help him soar beyond the trivial. Yet, in an unrelenting obduracy, man submits to a tendency to close his mind to all of this evocative magic and remains stranded in a stultifying boredom.

Wilson has placed considerable emphasis on the contribution of Georgei Ivanovitch Gurdjieff to an understanding of the extended mind. Gurdjieff, born to a Greek father and an Armenian mother in 1873, travelled extensively from an early age. He spent three months in a monastery in the northern Himalayas where he learnt many of the concepts which were to become central to his thinking. At the turn of the century, he was back in Russia where he married a lady-in-waiting to the Tsarina. He began teaching what he had learned during his travels, including his theory of Man's seven centres – physical, intellectual, emotional, instinctive, sexual, higher intellectual and higher emotional. Gurdjieff taught that a study of these centres would soon disclose that we spend most of our waking time in a kind of sleep. Wilson has called his book on Gurdjieff, *The War Against Sleep*.

Yet there are moments, Gurdjieff recognised, when we do seem to be almost fully awake: moments in which we experience a real sense of freedom. These moments are not simply illusions. They seem to be brought on by crisis or intense excitement, both physical and mental. The most notable of these were aimed at what he called 'self-remembering', which was an awareness of the self while remaining aware of what the self was doing. Thus, one might look at a painting and then become aware of oneself looking at the painting – but simultaneously, not as successive awarenesses. Self-remembering, claimed Gurdjieff, aids in the capacity to recognise the mechanical nature of so many of the responses we might otherwise think to be genuine and spontaneous.

For Gurdjieff, the automatic or, in Wilson's terms, 'robot' functioning of the 'human machine' lay in its 'moving centre' which had to be disciplined. He devised a whole series of exercises which were aimed at this discipline. These were based on Eastern dances he had observed in his youth and involved extraordinarily complex movements with both hands, both feet and other parts of the body doing different things at the one time. Gurdjieff called these dances 'the Work'. Their intent was to develop the range of the body's possibilities. Through the extension of physical functions, he reasoned, might lie the extension of mental functions.

Gurdjieff set up his Institute for the Harmonious Development of Man at Fontainebleu where he had many prominent students, including the novelist Katherine Mansfield. He insisted that he himself was not to be idolised and that his teachings were not to be accepted blindly. He challenged people to test his ideas for themselves and accommodate them only if they proved to be of real value. Fontaineblel was closed down in the late 1920s and

Gurdjieff resumed his travelling, visiting the United States on two occasions.

Gurdjieff's basic theory may be explained by the image of man as a computer. The resources of this computer are more complex, more sophisticated than anyone can imagine and yet we use this computer to add up our shopping bill! If we are ever going to utilise the capacity of the computer, we shall have to study it. But, bearing in mind that the computer is not something removed from ourselves but is indeed *us* – that we are engaged in self-study – we should ensure that we are fully concentrated and fully alert.

Needless to say, Wilson sees poetry as a means of extending consciousness. The poet is a person who experiences sudden glimpses of what G. K. Chesterton called 'absurd good news'. W. B. Yeats expressed such a glimpse:

> My fiftieth year had come and gone.
> I sat, a solitary man,
> In a crowded London shop:
> An open book and empty cup
> On the marble table-top.
> While on the shop and street I gazed,
> My body of a sudden blazed;
> And twenty minutes more or less
> It seemed, so great my happiness
> That I was blessed and could bless.

Yeats was a prominent member of the mystical order, 'The Golden Dawn' and before that had been a member of the Theosophical Society, founded by Madame Blavatsky. His involvement in these societies opened his mind to a range of mystical theories, including the belief that the soul is made up of a number of different personalities. While these personalities could never be disassociated from each other, neither could they be unified. Here we are close to the eternal paradox that confronts the Existentialist.

As a part of his mysticism, the Irish Yeats accepted the world of 'little people' playing tricks on unsuspecting humans. He wondered whether fairies are not the gods of the earth. Thus, he peopled his 'land of heart's desire', but this was in an endeavour to escape, not from the totality of reality, but only from the shattered reality that he detested. He considered himself and his fellow poets as human beings living in a world that was full of sub-humans who accepted their daily drudgery, not in resignation, but because they could see no higher reality open to them.

Although he never doubted its existence, Yeats lamented that the essential reality seemed beyond our grasp. Standing by a waterfall he had known and loved as a child, he reflected:

> I would have touched it like a child
> But knew my fingers could but have touched
> Cold stone and water. I grew wild,
> Even accusing Heaven because
> It had set down among its laws:
> Nothing that we love overmuch
> Is ponderable to our touch.

A great deal of Yeats' poetry is written in this mood. Much of it is nostalgic, reflecting a sense of defeat, self-pity and cynicism. In his later years especially, he seemed to lose interest in the ideas that had surged through his mind as a young man. He celebrated physical recklessness and was preoccupied with the physical. Late in life, he underwent surgery which had the curious effect of increasing his sexual energy so that much of his final work is highly sensual in nature. His last years seemed those of a weary man who will not let himself die but lacks the courage to live. Yet there are times when he manages to throw off his reductionist pessimism. In *Under Ben Bulben*, he asserted

> Know that when all words are said
> And a man is fighting mad,
> Something drops from eyes long blind,
> He completes his partial mind,
> For an instant stands at ease,
> Laughs aloud, his heart at peace.

It is this notion of 'completing the partial mind' that interested Wilson. It is the hallmark of great poetry. The contribution of the poet lies in his capacity to expand his vision beyond the limitations that seem normal to the common man; to leap beyond ordinary human values to universal values. As Wilson says,

> the poet himself remains a symbol of the most important thing about human existence – an evolutionary aspiration.[28]

One of the greatest temptations facing the poet is to separate his intuition from the insights he derives from science. The philosopher, Alfred North Whitehead, insisted that such a division – into 'artistic truth' and 'scientific truth' was a dangerous 'bifurcation of nature'. Whitehead spent his life arguing that there was a continuum in which the two could be coupled together. Yet, as Wilson points out, philosophy and science address generalities while art and religion concern themselves with the individual. Religion and art celebrate man as being of infinite worth: science and philosophy seem to present him as a worm. It seems, then, that the notion of an existential philosophy is a contradiction in terms. Wilson sees the resolution of this apparent dilemma in the concept of evolution – of complexification – and he gives this concept a central place in his New Existentialism. He argues that we must see intentionality as being evolutionary. We must recognise that man is entered upon the next stage of his evolutionary journey. It was given its impetus by Newton, encouraged by Romanticism and is to be furthered by a new sense of purpose.

The New Existentialism has also been called 'Evolutionary Existentialism'. Certainly, Wilson believes

that the answer is to be sought in the idea of evolution, as described by Shaw, Wells or Sir Julian Huxley. The objection is that evolution is too impersonal to replace religion; that it can never satisfy the personal needs in the same way as Christianity, for example. But is this entirely true? What man has lost in religion is something that, by the nature of his evolution, he was bound to lose anyway – the sense of being a mere creature whose only business is passive obedience to a master. If this was the price that man paid for his sense of 'belonging' in the world, then it was too high. With the collapse of the old religious dogmas, man has gained a new kind of freedom; he has become more adult than his forefathers. It is objected that he has lost the feeling of individual purpose, of being part of a meaningful scheme – in short, the feeling of having a kind of direct telephone to God in prayer and worship. This, say the objectors, is the thing that science can never replace.

Yet what if science *could* replace that sense of individual meaning, the feeling of having a direct telephone line to the universal purpose? For this is precisely the aim of evolutionary phenomenology: to change man's conception of himself and of the *interior forces* he has at his command, and ultimately to establish the new evolutionary type, foreshadowed by the Outsiders.[29]

This helps explain Wilson's evaluation of George Bernard Shaw as the greatest European thinker since Dante.

There were two George Bernard Shaws. The first was an intelligent, stimulating but fundamentally reserved Irish novelist and playwright. The second was a mischievous persona of the first who identified himself as GBS and who built an extraordinary public image as an eccentric. The first emulated the great dramatic feats of Shakespeare on the English stage: the second denounced Shakespear (the spelling was a deliberate attention-seeking device) as an unsophisticated peddlar in undeveloped ideas. Wilson argues that it is contemporary philosophy's loss that, by and large, it is the second Shaw who is most widely recognised, for if we delved below the public man, we would find the finest mind of the twentieth century and an important guide through the existential malaise that incapacitates modern man.

Shaw spent his early years in Dublin but by the time he had reached twenty he had come to hate that city, which 'confused the noble and serious with the base and ludicrous'. When a man of serious bent, such as Shaw, finds himself cut off from intelligent intercourse with his fellow men – when his fundamental questioning is met with a derisive rebuttal by his acquaintances – he has but two choices. He may forget his questions and his dreams or he may take decisive action. Shaw moved to London and in so doing, became an Outsider.

In London, Shaw lived in isolation. He went frequently to the theatre, seeing the opera *Carmen* again and again. In concert halls, he fell deeply under the influence of Mozart. He spent his days, like Wilson, writing in the British Museum where he produced five novels. One of these, *Immaturity*, is chiefly autobiographical. It is written in a largely unromantic style with little effective dramatisation of the events it describes. It tells a story but contains few psychological insights. The best of his novels, *An Unsocial Socialist*, written when he was twenty-seven, offers the first sign of his incipient Romanticism. In the Introduction to *Immaturity*, he wrote:

The truth is that all men are in a false position in society until they have realized their possibilities and imposed them on their neighbours. They are tormented by a continual shortcoming in themselves; yet they irritate others by a continual overweening. This discord can be resolved by acknowledged success or failure only: everyone is ill at ease until he has found his natural place, whether it be above or below his birthplace. . . . Besides, this finding of one's place may be made very puzzling by the fact that there is no place in ordinary society for extraordinary individuals.[30]

Thus Shaw had two careers. According to Wilson, he became the greatest playwright of his age when he made a total commitment to a purpose. During his early life he engaged in many false starts. His novels failed to reach a wide audience. His involvement in the socialist movement known as Fabianism was little more than an outlet for his artistic frustration. It was not until he came to see himself as an agent of the evolutionary force that he began to find his own legitimate way forward. It was as if the whole of his early career had been a preparation for a critical advance.

In his plays, Shaw began to investigate the question of defiance of authority. Again and again he placed on the stage two strong characters and engaged them in a conflict of power. The relationships between Vivie Warren and her mother in *Mrs Warren's Profession*, between Dick Dudgeon and General Burgoyne in *The Devil's Disciple* and between Caesar and Rufio in *Caesar and Cleopatra* are all based on a struggle for superiority; a rebellion of one against the authority of the other. Wilson sees that in this, Shaw is addressing a major problem.

The Outsider is not necessarily the rebel but the rebel is undoubtedly a most important type of Outsider. The rebel attempts to assert that existence comes before essence, that Will comes before authority. In another form, this existentialist theme is presented in Bergson in the opposition between 'open' and 'closed' religion. Open religion is the inspired religious insight of the prophet and saint; closed religion is the ritual and law of a Church. And all forms of this opposition are present in Shaw's work. (*Saint Joan*, for instance, is about open and closed religion). It is not too much to say that all Shaw's central themes are existentialist.[31]

Shaw believed that life itself was an evolutionary drive. Its central characteristic was what he called the Life Force; a power that drove it through obstacles towards its own fullness. At a casual reading it is possible to conclude that Shaw saw the Life Force as simply intellect. Certainly he believed that without intellect, life drifts dangerously in the direction of death. But he knew that man must evolve as a whole – that is, emotionally and intuitively as well as intellectually. The real nature of the Life Force is that it is a sense of conscious purpose.

Shaw puts into the mouth of one of his characters, Don Juan, the following:

I tell you that as long as I can conceive something better than myself I cannot be easy unless I am striving to bring it into existence or clearing the way for it. This is the law of my life. This is the working within me of life's incessant application to higher organization, wider, deeper, intenser self-consciousness and greater understanding.[32]

Wilson comments:

The 'higher form of life' that Don Juan strives to create is the Nietzschean Superman. Shaw felt obscurely that man is on the threshold of a higher form of life; either that or the Life Force may scrap him and try something new. He was right, but not wholly. Man is always on the brink of a higher form of life when a civilization reaches its stage of decline. The decline is a challenge to raise the standard of conscious life; otherwise it must smash. Man evolved from the ape by developing a religious consciousness. He then evolved from the mere superstitious tribesman by developing his reasoning power. Before he can develop to a still higher stage, he must restore the religious consciousness; nothing else will hold society together. And while religion means 'closed religion', mere ritual and superstition, then reason makes its existence impossible. Religion must become what the Outsider understands by it: a body of truth about man's purpose and relation to God. For a whole civilization to think in Outsider terms would probably mean the total disappearance of Insiders. And the price of failing to meet the challenge need not be the scrapping of the human race: it may mean only the scrapping of all that we understand by civilization.[33]

The foregoing is not an attempt to provide an exhaustive treatment of the New Existentialism. In an essay of this length, it is impossible to do justice to the philosophy of Wilson. What has taken him over eighty books to express cannot be even adequately summarised in thirty pages. Perhaps all that can be achieved is an indication that his thought is a profoundly important contribution to the history of philosophy.

There has often been a misconception that Wilson is nothing more than a synthesizer of other people's ideas. It is certainly true that his thought has encompassed almost every major thinker in the history of Western thought but he has done more than collate that thought into a body of knowledge. He has challenged it, intensified it and forged it into his own intelligent, personal statement about the situation in which modern man finds himself. His philosophy *is* Romanticism; it *is* Existentialism: it *is* a New Existentialism that untethers the human mind and points it in the direction of its own fulfilment.

Charles R. Fall, one-time Professor in the Philosophical and Social Foundations of Education at the State University of New York at Buffalo, spent his teaching career insisting that the greatest educational need of our age was for a new definition of education. Nor, he argued, was a useful definition likely to be forthcoming from within the ranks of professional educators. He understood that great challenges, great renewals, usually come from outside. If education is to be renewed, he insisted, then it is to philosophers, sociologists and artists that we must look, rather than to teachers and professional educational administrators.

This indicates another important sense in which Wilson himself is an Outsider. He emerged, suddenly, in the middle of the twentieth century, as a profound challenge to the prevailing mythologies and established philosophies. By all rights, given his biographical background, his social beginnings and the temper of the times in which he grew up, he should have been lost in a despairing worldview. We may suppose that he had a desire to escape from his social milieu by an intellectual effort – but this would have driven him towards a formal education rather than into a lifetime's work of philosophical contemplation and writing. He is outside schooling; outside academia. Perhaps it is because he refused to submit

himself to the stultifying misconceptions of the formal classroom
that he was left free to achieve great insights and see the outline
of a solution to mankind's greatest needs.

Wilson stood outside the prevailing British philosophy of Logical Positivism, as expounded by professional philosophers such
as A. J. Ayer, with its argument that anything that cannot be
reduced to logic can be dismissed as meaningless. In a real sense,
despite his attraction to them, he stood outside Romanticism and
Existentialism as they were being propounded in his early years,
until he was certain that they could not destroy him. For this was
the most uncommon fact about Wilson: he knew his own value
as a human being. He understood that the fundamental task confronting any individual is the preservation of his own existential
integrity.

It is necessary to repeat here the point made in the Introduction
– that this chapter does not contain the 'philosophy' of Wilson.
The most useful philosophies are not catalogues of ideas, neatly
separated into categories: they are meaningful patterns that reveal
connections, interactions and mutual interdependencies in which
a sense of wholeness is indicated. This chapter – this book – must
be read with this in mind.

In what was arguably the most perceptive and intelligent review
printed at the time of the publication of *The Outsider* – although
he had the enormous good sense to wait over six months while
he digested the contents of a book that refused to disclose its
wealth to an overnight reviewer's browsing – Sir Oswald Mosley,
writing as 'European' in his journal *The European*, stated:

> Mister Wilson writes: 'It is the Outsider's belief that life aims
> at more life, and higher forms of life'. At this point, this
> interesting thinker and gifted writer reaches towards that decis-
> ive movement of European thought which began, perhaps,
> originally with Heraclitus and evolved through philosophers,
> prophets and poets such as Goethe combined in his own genius,
> until it touched thinkers like Shaw and Ibsen in the modern
> age. This remarkable young man may end as the saint whom
> he suggests in his last line may be the Outsider's goal, or worse,
> much worse, as just a success: yet the fact will remain that at
> this point he touched reality.[34]

Wilson can, perhaps, be paid no higher compliment than this.

3

The Psychology

DURING his visit to the United States in 1964, Wilson was invited to attend a meeting of the American Psychoanalytical Society. At the meeting, Charles Savage, Assistant Professor of Psychiatry at the Johns Hopkins Hospital and Director of Medical Research at Spring Grove State Hospital in Baltimore, Maryland, delivered a lecture under the title, 'The Analysis of an "Outsider" '. In the lecture, Savage, using the terminology of Freud, pointed out that internal tension between the ego, the id and the superego was extremely common. He referred to Wilson's Outsider as a man who felt this tension deeply within himself. Savage went on to point out that many people deal with this inner tension by redesigning the world; by establishing a utopia through such mechanisms as writing or preaching. Usually, he contended, these utopias rely heavily on the projection of infantile fantasies. As an example of such handling of inner tension, Savage reminded his audience of W. B. Yeats, who 'planned a mystical order that should buy or hire a castle, and keep it as a place where its members could retire for a while for contemplation and where we might establish mysteries like those of Eleusis or Samothrace'.

Savage proceeded by presenting the case history of one of his patients who had set about creating an international movement which believed that unlimited, universal access to hallucinogenic drugs would produce the Internal Freedom that was the panacea for human suffering. The group began modestly, with a weekly totemic feast at which members ate their fathers, who had been transubstantiated into peyote, and possessed their mothers ritualistically. Eventually, the patient presented for pychoanalytical assistance and Savage reported that week after week, 'he reenacted the Oedipal situation'. According to Savage, 'the anal component of the drug experience could be noted in the hoarding and burying of drug supplies in the earth'. The peyote he took, Savage told his audience, was an 'incorporation of the body of Christ' – the patient had resigned from a theological seminary just prior to becoming a drug user – as well as an 'incorporation of the breast' – a 'representation of the fusion with his mother during nursing'.

Savage's patient completed psychoanalysis, then went on to complete his studies. Eventually, he travelled overseas. Savage concluded that 'analysis had led to some relief of depression and castration anxiety'.

Asked to respond to Savage's paper, Wilson commented that he was flattered that his concept of the Outsider had been used in this way. Yet he confessed to a measure of confusion. He pointed out that for fourteen years he had been developing a phenomenological and *non-Freudian* interpretation of the Outsider's problems and that he could not understand how these phenomenological notions could be connected with the Freudian division of the human mind into ego, id and superego. Commenting on Savage's patient, Wilson suggested that, in his view, 'the best treatment would have been a careful exploration of his creative potentialities and an attempt to persuade him to embark on creativity'. While admitting that he did not know the patient, Wilson expressed the view that the basic problem may not have been the feelings of guilt that were in evidence but the patient's mental laziness 'in his attempt to avoid the responsibilities of his intelligence'.[1]

The foregoing is not intended as a comment on the value of psychoanalysis nor on the psychological theories of Sigmund Freud. It is certainly not intended to belittle Charles Savage, who demonstrated in his lecture a laudable knowledge of some of the most fundamental literature of our age and a mind that is searching for synthesis. It is intended, however, to demonstrate that the psychological theories of Wilson are not to be interpreted in Freudian or any other established psychological terms because they are unique to Wilson and cannot be grasped outside the context of his total philosophy.

The true roots of Wilson's psychology are indicated in an

account, by Tolstoy, of an experience he had in his forty-fifth year. He describes it thus:

> Something very strange began to happen to me. At first I experienced moments of perplexity and arrest of life, as though I did not know how to live or what to do. . . . Then these moments of perplexity recurred oftener and oftener. . . . I felt that what I had been standing on had broken down, and that I had nothing left under my feet. What I had lived on no longer existed, and I had nothing left to live on.[2]

There are still those today who would speak of this experience as a symptom of a 'nervous breakdown'. Wilson saw in it the characteristic experience of the Outsider whose very identity is threatened by a sense of meaninglessness and contingency. It is a psychological problem only in a narrow sense. In its full ramifications, it is an existential problem. Wilson's psychology springs from his understanding of the limitations of Existentialism and his resolute attempt to identify a New Existentialism. More precisely, if we regard Wilson's philosophy as both the diagnosis of the disease and the prescription for its treatment, his psychology is the medication itself, working to relieve the symptoms but also engendering positive health.

While it must be acknowledged that *The Outsider*, *Religion and the Rebel* and, indeed, all his early works are profoundly important *psychological* texts, it will be the more common view that his first real venture into an existential psychology was *New Pathways in Psychology*. Certainly it was in this work that he provided us with the most comprehensive statement of his reasons for rejecting the psychology of Freud and that he acknowledged his affinity with the psychology of Abraham Maslow which stimulated him so much and led to his enunciation of a uniquely Wilsonian psychology.

When the nineteenth century ended, the treatment of disorders of the mind and personality was still largely primitive, chiefly because of the persistence of many medieval attitudes. Charcot, Freud's teacher, had done some notable work in the field of hypnosis but no one had yet earned himself the title, 'the Father of Psychology'. The intuitive theories of William James, who was born just fourteen years before Freud, were very much in evidence and Wilson notes their importance.

Despite the fact that he grew up as an heir to a sceptical tradition initiated by men such as Hume, Comte and Darwin, James had something of the mystic about him. This may have been due to his father, who was much influenced by Swedenborg. But the mysticism remained hard-headed and at heart James was persuaded by the rigours of science. As Wilson reminds us, he coined the term 'tough-minded' to indicate a person who strives for logical precision. James spent his early years in a dynamic family environment. His father was unusually intelligent and well-versed in literature. The other children, three brothers – one of whom was the novelist Henry – and a sister, were all bright and helped to stimulate his curiosity and his creativity.

In his late twenties, James suffered a breakdown. It seems that this may have been caused by a dilemma of the intellect as much as by anything else for James found intense difficulty in reconciling the prevailing notion of materialistic determinism with his own inclination to believe that an individual has an independent reality which entails a capacity for self-determination. It has been suggested that he resolved the dilemma – and regained his health – by reading the essays of C. B. Benouvier. Following his recovery, he decided against the notion of being an artist and accepted an appointment as an instructor at Harvard University.

Twenty years after his breakdown, James published *The Principles of Psychology*, a book which demonstrates his extraordinary insights and which guarantees him a place in the annals of psychology. The book is essentially a description of a world that has two dimensions. The first of these is the given reality that each man finds about him. The second is the world that an individual carves out of the first, as a sculptor may carve a statue out of granite, and makes his own. For James, the highest possible level of life lay in the union of these two worlds and it is his contention that they are united in an act of *effort* on the part of the individual. Wilson comments:

James has actually stumbled on the concept of intentionality, yet he fails to make proper use of it. Let me suggest briefly what I mean by 'proper use'. The question of effort applies particularly to matters involving meaning. If, in the middle of a general conversation, someone lifted up his hand and said urgently, 'Listen', everyone would make an effort of focusing the attention, listening intently. That is to say they would deliberately *put more effort* into attention. In order to grasp meanings, I must 'focus' – concentrate, 'contract' my attention muscles. Perception is intentional and the more energy (or effort) I put into an act of 'concentrating', the more meaning I grasp. . . .

James is not yet ready for these (insights). . . . He accepts that the correct procedure for the psychologist is intro-spection. . . . He rejects Hume's notion that consciousness is a series of 'states' linked together like beads, and insists that it is more like a stream than a string of beads. (James is responsible for the phrase 'stream of consciousness'.) But his analysis never carries him far into the realm of values and free will.[3]

Wilson contends that the best of the many invaluable psychologi-cal insights of James are to be found, not in *The Principles of Psychology* but in the many shorter essays that complement his major publications. Two instances must suffice. In *On a Certain Blindness in Human Beings*, he expresses his essential creed: philo-sophy must never lose sight of the *richness* of perception that permits a monk to listen intently for fifty years. In *The Energies of Man*, he presents his view that human beings need *stimulus* to get the best out of themselves.

The psychology of William James is of the highest significance to Wilson. It is a pity that in the space available here, it cannot be expounded any further. It must suffice that we have acknow-ledged that James foreshadowed Maslow in perceiving that con-sciousness has an intentional quality. This is the centre from which all his other ideas radiate. In the chapter, *Towards a Psychology of the Will*, in *New Pathways in Psychology*, Wilson sets out the full range of concentric circles in brilliant clarity. The entire chapter must be read by anyone who hopes to comprehend the foundation upon which Wilson builds his theory of the mind. Here, we can do no more than quote its final paragraph which is Wilson's summary, not, it must be emphasised, of his own ideas, but of those of James:

There is something *wrong* with 'normal' human consciousness. For some odd reason, we seldom get the best out of it. The main problem seems to lie with our sense of values, which only seems to come alive in moments of great excitement or crisis. Otherwise, it snores hoggishly, and we only live at half pressure. The trouble seems to lie in the co-operation of the conscious and subconscious mind. If you keep up a certain conscious straining, you will 'let loose subconscious allies behind the scenes'; this happens most noticeably in religious experience. We are certainly capable of a far broader and deeper sense of reality than the one we are accustomed to. The fascinating area, for psychology, lies in this realm of 'values'; and this in turn seems to be a matter of the collaboration of the conscious and subconscious parts of the mind – a collaboration that, ideally, would be *directed* by the conscious mind and *powered* by the subconscious. The conscious mind must learn to understand the subconscious – not only how to call its bluff when it shams fatigue, but how to make the best possible use out of it.[4]

Jamesian psychology was not to achieve the central place in the clinical psychology of the first half of the twentieth century that it deserved to occupy. By and large, it was swept aside, as was most other psychological theory, by the doctrine of Psychoanalysis, introduced by Sigmund Freud – and perhaps one of the five most influential scientific dogmas of the past five hundred years. Notwithstanding its influence, however, Wilson rejects the psychoanalytic theory out of hand and sets his own understanding of the operation of the human mind over against it. We need to understand something of what that theory states and something of the man who espoused it.

Freud was born in Freiberg, Moravia in 1856, to Jewish parents. His mother was twenty years younger than his father who had married before and had fathered two children by his first wife. Freud was one of seven children by the second marriage. His eldest step-brother was the same age as his mother so that, in some respects at least, he might have thought of her as a sister. Certainly, his relationship with his mother was very close and she exerted a profound influence upon him. She provided him with a very positive self-image and encouraged him to believe that greatness awaited him.

Throughout his lifetime, Freud offered very little public account of his life – even his autobiography seemed to raise more questions about him than it answered – and it was not until his friend and student, Ernest Jones, published his definitive biography that a truly accurate portrait of the man became available.

Jones reveals that Freud was intensely emotional – in his relationship with his mother, with his nephew and, later, with fellow psychologists such as Breuer, Adler, Jung and Otto Rank. His relationships were characterised by a strange ambiguity, for they fluctuated regularly between a passionate attachment and chilling resistance. He acknowledged that 'an intimate friend and a hated enemy have always been indispensable for my emotional life'.

The young Freud was abundantly clever. He had an insatiable curiosity and was committed to the scientific investigation of experience. He spoke seven languages fluently, including English, and used this fluency to gain entrance to the cultures of the countries in which they were spoken. When his family moved to Vienna, he found himself in the intellectual capital of Europe and the location served him well. After toying for a while with the idea of joining the army, he decided to commit himself to the life of the intellect.

At the age of seventeen, he entered the Faculty of Medicine at Vienna. For eight years, he studied medicine, philosophy, biology and zoology. He engaged in research into the nervous systems of crayfish. After completing his degree, he began a four-year courtship of a girl named Martha Bernhays, finally marrying her in one of the most satisfying relationships of his life. It was during this courtship that he studied in Paris under the world's best-known nerve specialist, Charcot, who was to point him in the direction that would lead to his name becoming a household word throughout the world.

Charcot had developed the work of the discredited Mesmer, who had introduced a theory of 'animal magnetism', and of Mesmer's student, the Marquis de Puysegur, who had stumbled across the phenomenon of hypnotism. Charcot applied the findings of Mesmer and de Puysegur to his study of hysteria and concluded that this common complaint could be induced by activities within the 'unconscious' mind. Charcot was also of the view that sexuality plays a significant role in the onset of hysteria. In the theories of Charcot, Freud found the focus for his life's work.

Two other profound influences on Freud must be acknowledged. He had studied under Ernst von Brucke in Vienna and had been taught by that authority that all forces acting within the human organism are 'physical-chemical' in nature. Where such a cause cannot be identified readily, it is the responsibility of the scientist to apply a 'physical-mathematical' method until the cause reveals itself. This mechanistic approach to science was attractive to Freud.

He was also inclined towards the German Romanticism of Friedrich von Schelling who had spelled out a body of belief called 'Naturphilosophie'. Here, nature is seen as being controlled by forces, such as good and evil, which are diametrically opposed to each other. Human consciousness is merely a reflection of the fundamental turmoil created by this opposition and pervading everything. 'Naturphilosophie' contended that the scientific method and empirical investigation could reveal little of the reality that lay cradled in the universal conflict. Intuitive speculation was regarded as a more appropriate instrument for examining life's secrets.

Freud managed to reconcile these apparently contradictory notions of a mechanistic science and 'Naturphilosophie' and traces of both are readily visible in his work. That work is so well known, with so much of its vocabulary having passed into the language, that there is no need here to do more than provide the simplest outline.

Freud posited the existence of *das Unbewusste*, the unconscious; a level of the mind which lies below everyday consciousness. By and large, information finds its way into the unconscious through a process that he called 'repression'. Repression is a defensive mechanism, the purpose of which is to protect the person against the flood of unpleasant memories that threaten to burst the retaining walls of consciousness at every opportunity. Despite this protective function, however, it is dangerous, because it has a tendency to permit those unpleasant memories to surface in disguised forms; forms which render the person emotionally unstable. Because they are disguised, the individual cannot recognise the cause of his discomfort and is thus prevented from dealing satisfactorily with it.

It was at this point that Freud associated his ideas on the mechanism of repression with Charcot's theory that in hysteria there was commonly *la chose sexuelle* – a sexual factor. He concluded that the area of experience an individual was most likely to repress was the sexual. The most common cause of repression, in fact, was a sexual trauma, either real or imagined. This conclusion led Freud to the central notion in his theory of psychoanalysis: that of the *libido*.

The libido is the central energy that drives life. It is essentially sexual in nature and consists of three stages – the anal, the oral and the genital. The genital stage is the stage of fulfilment and maturity in which the personality is properly primed, physically, emotionally and intellectually, for the reproduction of the species. Essentially, mental illness is a failure of the personality to achieve this genital stage. It becomes 'fixated' in either the anal or the oral stage and expresses itself in behaviour that is emotionally and socially immature.

Freud vested enormous significance in the libido, arguing that anxiety is essentially repressed libido; a denial of the energy that seeks to surge through our lives. When he was consistently challenged on the theory, he made several minor concessions, introducing the notion that the libido is complemented by two other driving energies – *Eros*, the life instinct and *Thanatos*, the death instinct. He refused, however, to abandon the theory altogether. Before he died, he was to argue that the libido theory could be used to explain not only some aspects of human behaviour but also some aspects of human culture, particularly the institutions of the armed forces and the Christian Church. His final theory, that of the tripartite nature of the human mind – id, ego and superego – was essentially an attempt to bolster his theory of the libido.

Freud's dogged insistence on the libido theory was to shatter many of his professional relationships. He pleaded with his colleagues to support him, writing to Carl Jung: 'My dear Jung, promise me never to abandon the sexual theory.' But it was a theory so flawed with inconsistencies and patchwork logic that Jung found he could not support it. Jung concluded that it failed to take account of the 'mystical' nature of much of life: Adler divorced himself from it – and from Freud – on the grounds that it ignored the impact that the environment had on personality. Wilson too, finds himself unable to support it.

Freud says he looks inside himself and finds the swirling forces of the subconscious. *Whose* subconscious? According to Freud, it is simply *the* subconscious, an impersonal force. He, Sigmund Freud, is the superficial ego, the face that looks at him out of the mirror. This superficial ego *thinks* it has opinions, makes decisions; in reality, it only reflects unseen forces. Its 'rational' judgements and actions are really expressions of these inner forces. Man's only chance of freedom is to understand these forces and come to terms with them. Man is a tiny rider on a gigantic black horse. But again we must ask the question: Whose horse?[5]

In considering Wilson's philosophy, we noted his identification of the *Robot*. The Robot may, in some respects, be equated with Freud's 'unconscious': but there is a significant difference between our relationship with our robot and Freud's relationship with his unconscious. In our lowest moments, the Robot can rob us of a sense of immediacy but in our highest moments, the robot is not 'driving' us: it is working with us. We merge with the Robot and 'he' enhances us. In Freudian terms, 'the unconscious forces are far more completely at our command than in everyday consciousness'. Thus, when we play a piano in this state, it is as if the piano is an extension of ourselves and the music we produce is more sublime than any we thought we were capable of producing. While Freud has the chaos of the unconscious dominating us, Wilson has our consciousness carefully selecting the extent to which we will accept the abundant assistance that the Robot is continually offering to place at our disposal.

Wilson comments perceptively on the relationship between the theory of psychoanalysis and the personal history of its creator:

> Freud is a member of a large Jewish family unit and his father is old enough to be his grandfather – underlying the patriarchal role. He is emotionally obsessed with his much younger mother. He is a person of strong emotions but has difficulty in expressing them. He possesses a definite homosexual leaning which appears in relations with various close friends – relationships which veer between love and hatred. . . . A man of strong sexual impulses, he nevertheless remains a virgin until he is thirty. It is not until he is in his mid-forties – towards the end of the century – that he overcomes the tendency to emotional ups and downs and gains a degree of security. And even so, the emotions continue to run strong under the somewhat rigid surface. Because his emotional patterns remain unchanged, he is inclined to relive the pattern of events of his past, in different settings, with different individuals. In due course, all these strictly personal patterns were stated in the form of generalities and applied dogmatically to the rest of the human race.[6]

Notwithstanding his rejection of the central Freudian notions, Wilson does acknowledge his importance in the history of ideas. He recognises that Freud was the first to grasp the intensity and the complexity of the unconscious and that he was a trail-blazer in terms of recognising the urgency of the sexual impulse. Wilson recognises that there was a 'poetic' quality at the heart of Freud's science. Perhaps, in the final analysis, his theories were the result of the fact that he spent the largest part of his life in a clinical setting, surrounded by people who were profoundly sick.

Wilson offers an important insight into Freudian theory when he points out that it was developed in an age of relative security and confidence. It was, nonetheless, a period in which people were largely dominated by a sense of 'taboo' and convention that led many of them into a state of hysteria. Essentially, this took the form of a 'fixation' between a mature personality and its adolescent antecedents. Modern society, however, is categorically different. It is marked by wars, revolutions and an escalating rate of change which shatter the sense of security and place individuals on the threshold of despair. Existential *angst* is the prevailing disease. The individual senses not simply a personal but a universal problem. His own condition is somehow inextricably bound up with the human condition. Schizophrenia is more common than hysteria in our society and while some elements of the Freudian therapy might have been able to address the prevailing ailments of the turn of the century, an Existential psychology is required to redress the psychological maladies of today. And central to that psychology must be an attempt to comprehend not simply the individual but the totality of the human condition.

In turning to the psychologies of the disciples of Freud who finally came to reject his approach, Wilson reveals his skill in recognising and presenting the positions they adopted.

Adler had never fully subscribed to the sexual theory of Freud although the two had been very close. One of the key ideas held by Adler was that human beings are inferior to animals in terms of their physical capacity and have compensated for this by developing the brain. All life, in fact, is an attempt to redress this inferiority: life is a will to power. Thus, for Adler, if sex plays a part in the development of neurosis, it is because it is often a significant hurdle confronting the will to power.

Adler developed a psychology that was aimed at the 'affirmative unfolding of the organism'. He fully recognised that man is an evolutionary animal and believed that neurosis represents a frustration of the evolutionary drive. Unlike Freud, he was less interested in tracing the origins of neurosis to the patient's childhood than in trying to understand its meaning – the objective towards which it was directed. Adler understood that every individual creates a particular 'lifestyle' which is fundamentally a basic sense of meaning and that neurosis occurs when the creative urge that drives that meaning finds itself thwarted.

There was another significant difference between Freud and Adler. While the former had considered his psychology a pure science that was almost mathematical in its precision, Adler had a highly developed sense of society and a strong desire that his work should benefit society. This external reference gave Adler a degree of creativity that was lacking in Freud. Adler was, in a sense, more practical than Freud. Certainly, his psychology was more practical. He believed that mental disorder was due to a collapse of the capacity to assert oneself over and against reality. It was a retreat into fantasy or depression which compensated for this sense of weakness. For Adler, the healthy man was epitomised by Dostoevsky's Mitya Karamozov who, despite being a prisoner in a mine in Siberia, could console himself with the certainty of his own innocence. Thus, Adler recognised the importance of the will in making a person either ill or healthy. Wilson points out that in this respect Adler was a forerunner to Maslow and Victor Frankl. Yet, even at his most positive, – and it is again Wilson who makes the point – Adler never quite escaped Freud's negativity. At his healthiest, man is still only compensating for a fundamental inferiority that he never fully escapes.

Freud had hoped to hand on the mantle of psychoanalysis to Carl Jung who had been a long-term colleague and a close friend. Jung, however, found it necessary to establish a boundary between his own thinking and that of his mentor. Perhaps the essential difference between the two men was Jung's inclination towards the occult. Certainly, Freud was concerned about this aspect of his friend and admonished him that psychology must be resolutely defended 'against the black tide of mud – of occultism'.

Freud saw the spiritual as repressed sexuality. For Jung, it was one of the most interesting aspects of human experience. He was first attracted to it through his study of dreams and myths. These, he convinced himself, were not essentially sexual but *racial*; that is, they were *primordial images* or – to give them the name that is most commonly associated with Jung – *archetypes*. It was through dreams and myths that human beings retained contact with a universal dimension of themselves. Thus, Jung found himself with an understanding of the unconscious that was in marked contrast to that of Freud. For the former, the unconscious was a swirling ocean of unpleasantness; of mortal dangers and death-inducing fantasies. For Jung, the unconscious was the seat of a vast trove of riches; the repository of everything fine that civilisation had produced and which could be called upon to enrich human experience.

Predictably, from Wilson's point of view, Jung's major contribution to psychology was his theory of individuation – self-realisation. Jung understood the personality as being driven forward by the archetypes in the collective unconscious. Yet he did not go far enough. He did not understand that the unconscious is basically passive; that, even though it might be more powerful than the conscious mind; it is still very much at the dictates of that conscious mind. Wilson provides a powerful analogy that both elucidates and suggests an advance on the Jungian position.

We might compare the two (conscious and unconscious) to a husband and wife team in which the wife has tremendous untapped energies and potentialities. But she is married to a feeble and passive husband. And she has been brought up to believe that the woman is supposed to be docile and obedient. So because the husband never calls upon her untapped resources, she fails to achieve any kind of self-realisation. The answer is not for the wife to leave the husband or try 'to do her own thing', but for the husband to recognise that if he can galvanise himself out of his feebleness and laziness, they can transform both their lives.[7]

It was, of course, Jung who introduced the notion that every man has within himself, an *anima* – a female aspect – and that every woman has a male within herself – an *animus*. It is these aspects of the respective male and female psyches, rather than the everyday person, who recognises and responds to the archetypes that throb within. It was also Jung who developed the theory of psychological types which identifies the *introvert* and the *extrovert*. While not under-rating the value of this classification, Wilson suggests that it is in a direct line with the Elizabethan notion of four *humours*

– that is, that it reflects a tendency to be reductionist in its treatment of the influences at work on the human personality.

In treating the Jungian revolt against Freud, Wilson comments that it was

> a revolt against narrowness. 'Freud's teaching is definitely one-sided in that it generalizes from facts that are relevant only to neurotic states of mind: its validity is confined to these states'. This sentence, which sounds like Maslow, is actually from *Modern Man in Search of a Soul*. Like Maslow, Jung was interested in the psychology of man's evolutionary faculties: his creativity, his religious and artistic intuitions, even his 'occult powers'. But it was impossible, in the Freudian climate, to take the decisive step: to *start* from the point of view of the artist or mystic, in which the centrally important fact is the creative energies themselves.[8]

Jung regarded himself as a phenomenologist. He regarded his own attempt to free himself 'from all unconscious and therefore uncriticised assumptions as to the world in general' – a position that Wilson regards as being the essence of phenomenology – as setting him apart from Freud. The complexities upon which he tried to impose an order were not philosophical abstractions but psychological states of the human mind. He described four 'functions' that we use to interact with the world. These are sensation, thinking, feeling and intuition. Thus, when we wake up from a sleep, the first experience that comes to us is a sensation of the room and its various contents. Then we think about where we are, recognising that the room is a strange hotel room. We then react to the room, deciding whether it is pleasant and comfortable or cold and uninteresting. This is feeling. Finally, we engage in an unconscious assessment about people who might have occupied the room before we did. Jung saw the first two of these functions as rational and closely related. The other two are irrational.

Jung uses these four functions to explain neurosis. He points out that individuals tend to develop one or more of the functions more extensively than the others. This is because we select a function as being our basic attitude towards life and the more we use it, the more it develops. The individual who develops the thinking function to a high degree will tend to suppress the feeling function. The person who develops sensation will probably feel little need to develop intuition. However, difficulties begin to emerge when the unused functions begin to atrophy. Jung used Freud's term *libido* to refer to *all* psychic energy – as distinct from the purely sexual – and he argued that the four functions needed to be employed. Where one develops to the detriment of another, there is a psychic imbalance which expresses itself as neurosis.

Wilson regards this theory of functions as an illustration of Jung's inclination towards reductionism. It seems very much like an attempt to make reality fit into a preconceived idea. Wilson contrasts it with the tendency of artists like Dostoevsky and Walt Whitman to see something unique and splendid in every human individual. But the biggest problem with the theory is that it directs attention away from the essential ingredients in an existential psychology – those of *meaning*, 'newness', the will to power.

In his detailed analysis of Jung, *Lord of the Underworld*, Wilson find him somewhat enigmatic. Jung was a romantic and while this, of itself, does not create a problem, his persistent refusal to acknowledge his romanticism led him into intellectual cul-de-sacs from which he never quite extracted himself. Some of his writing is so committed to the scientific genre, while trying to express the ineffable, that it can become confusing. He might have made an even greater contribution had he acknowledged more that he was as much a poet as a scientist.

There was also a degree of emotional immaturity in Jung. He was profoundly influenced by his own sexuality and was somewhat promiscuous. When he became involved with a woman named Antonia Wolff, his wife Emma confided desperately in Freud. Jung's private life became a temporary chaos which might well have governed his interpretation of Freud's work: certainly it probably influenced Jung in his rejection of Freud's theory on sexuality.

Wilhelm Reich is one of the most controversial of Freud's disciples to have broken with him and Wilson has scrutinised his life and work with considerable interest in his study, *The Quest for Wilhelm Reich*. It is doubtful, in fact, that Reich ever escaped from the influence of Freud, for his whole life and work seems to have been significantly influenced by sexual matters. When he was thirteen, he found his mother in bed with his tutor and betrayed her to his father. We can only speculate on the effect that her subsequent suicide had upon him. What is certain is that after he broke with Freud, he continued to occupy himself with sexual theories, including his understanding of the function of the orgasm and his statement of a 'sexual politics'. Here we can do no more than note a single comment on Reich's significance for Wilson.

Reich *was* a misunderstood man of genius; he was also a touchy egoist who became his own worst enemy. He was a man of profound and important insights who was also capable of embarrassing intellectual naivety (such as his notion that human aggressiveness could be blamed on the desire for private property). He is a complex human being who craved simple answers to the mysteries of the human mind. There was something almost Shakespearean about the tragedy of his life – the flawed strength that became self-destructive, the powerful spirit undermined by rage and suspicion.

In short, what kept drawing me back again and again to Reich was the fascination of the strange no-man's-land between genius and insanity, greatness and paranoia, self-belief and self-deception. For the same reason, I have always been fascinated by that other paranoid man of genius, August Strindberg – and, to a lesser extent, by the brilliant and vitriolic Frederick Rolfe who, with typical self-aggrandizement, preferred to be known as Baron Corvo.

While I brooded on this, and tried to get it down on paper, it struck me suddenly that I had stumbled on an important basic insight, one that applies to all human beings, not just the dominant few. It is this: that every one of us is a mixture of two elements, which could be labelled 'personality' and 'impersonality'; but in each one *the proportions are different*. We are all interested in ourselves, in achieving our ambitions. But we all have other interests that attract us for non-personal reasons: ideas, music, poetry, books, nature, science. We say they take us 'out of ourselves' – meaning out of the *personal* self. Even the least intelligent human being has certain non-personal interests – if only a newspaper crossword puzzle, or the fortunes of the local football team. But in men and women of talent, the dichotomy is particularly obvious because talent involves self-expression – that is, expression of the two aspects. We could picture them as the dark and light side on one of those Chinese symbols of yin and yang. The dark side is yin, the impersonal, the receptive; the light side is yang, the personal, the ambitious, the self-assertive.[9]

Wilson was busily expounding an 'Existential Psychololgy' as early as 1967, in his contribution, 'Existential Psychology: A Novelist's Approach', to Bugental's *Challenges of Humanistic Psychology*.[10] Here, after examining the significance of his concepts of the 'robot' and the 'St Neot Margin' to a psychological theory, he turns to the concept of freedom, which he calls 'the orgasm experience'. He does not limit himself to the sexual orgasm but refers to the whole range of experiences – music, poetry, a magnificent sunset – which awaken us to a sense of sharpness and wholeness. Essentially, what happens in the orgasm experience is that freedom comes gushing out from within us as water comes gushing from a fully soaked sponge when we press our finger into it. The orgasm experience – freedom – is achieved when the 'mechanical threshold', the robot, is pressed down so that it ceased to perform the act of 'living' for us.

The French novelist, Stendhal, who was highly attracted to women, was frequently embarrassed by the phenomenon known as *le fiasco* – detumescence at the point of sexual penetration. Wilson explains this phenomenon by pointing out that it is an example of intensity vanishing before it reaches its objective. *Le fiasco* is the opposite of the orgasm experience.

What is important to note here is that freedom gushes out from *within*. Consider a man who retires from work at his sixty-fifth birthday and retires to the countryside. Within a year, he is dead. Wilson suggests that his death is caused because he has allowed himself to become dependent upon external sources of stimulus and never comes to the realisation that by taking account of an internal intentionality he could remain in touch with the myriad experiences that serve to keep his interest – and therefore his body – alive. Because the sixty-five-year-old neglects this lesson, the countryside soon comes to bore him – to deprive him of a sense of immediacy, and he begins to question the value of his surroundings and eventually of his life. Ultimately, this life-devaluation becomes life-destructive.

In this context, Wilson draws attention to the work of Rubenstein and Best who experimented with the species of worm called planaria. The researchers set out to train planaria to travel down a plastic pipe and choose between a left and right fork, one of which led to water, which they need to live. Many of the planaria learned to choose the correct branch but then a strange thing happened. The successful planaria 'refused' to make the correct selection. They seemed, apparently, deliberately to choose the wrong fork, and, rather than retrace their steps, they remained stationary until they died. Rubinstein and Best concluded that this behaviour was due to a kind of 'boredom'; that the worms which had learned to select correctly became disenchanted with their ability and chose not to use it.

This behaviour was changed by the researchers when they made the 'training' more difficult. They now used two tubes, one of which was rough inside and the other smooth – so the planaria could feel the difference with their stomachs – and in one tube the water was down the lighted fork, while in the other it was down the dark fork. The planaria were transferred from tube to tube in between experiments. This task was far more difficult to master but the small percentage of worms who mastered it *never* regressed – they could do it a thousand times without becoming 'bored'.

Wilson concludes from this experiment that when an organism is forced to make a considerable initial effort, it will retain and utilise the product of that effort much more frequently than it will use the product of a more minimal effort. In other words, the quality of our ongoing energy and our capacity to solve problems, is conditioned by the amount of *effort* we put into it. The sixty-five-year-old retiree could extend his life in the country simply by putting more effort into it. Life-devaluation is a product of laziness.

But it is with his introduction to the ideas of Abaham Maslow that Wilson's psychology begins to round itself out and that his unquestionable importance as a psychologist in his own right becomes apparent. The two made contact in 1959, when Maslow wrote to Wilson after reading his third publication, *The Age of Defeat*. They immediately recognised that they had basically similar concerns. There can be little doubt that from the time they met, until Maslow's death, they were mutual intellectual stimulants to each other, both deriving benefits from the evaluations of each other's work that passed regularly between them.

Maslow differed from most of the psychologists who preceded him in one important respect. He decided that instead of studying sick people, he would turn his attention to healthy people. When he did this, he found that healthy people all experienced periodic feelings of extreme well-being. Maslow called these feelings 'peak experiences'. It must be understood that peak experiences are not some dramatic, mystical experience: they can be almost commonplace. Thus, a young mother clearing the breakfast table, might suddenly notice the sun shining through the window and feel a sense of total security and warmth; a sense of certainty that life is wonderful. This is the peak experience.

In dealing with peak experiences, Maslow made an interesting discovery. He found that when he spoke to his students about peak experiences and they continued to speak about them among themselves, they began to *experience* them with an increasing degree of regularity. What is important about the peak experience, apart from the sense of pleasure it provides, is the fact that it frees a person from the prison of the immediate environment. It allows a sense of self-value to emerge and thus gives the individual a new sense of strength.

For Maslow, the sense of valuing was extremely important. He argued that the human personality is developed as it passes through a *hierarchy of needs*. At the lowest level of this hierarchy, the personality has a basic need for food. If this is not satisfied, the personality will deteriorate rapidly towards death. Where it is satisfied, a second level of need emerges; the need for shelter. When this second need is satisfied, the third basic need – the need for acceptance by other people – emerges. The fourth need – and the highest that most people ever get to satisfy – is a need for self-esteem; for a positive acceptance of one's inner self as a decent human being. Yet, argued Maslow, there remains yet another need; a need which only begins to emerge when all the others below it have been satisfied. This highest need Maslow calls the need for *self-actualisation*.

Self-actualisation is that state of being in which a personality has arrived at the point of control over its own life. It is a state in which the individual acts, not from the point of view of a vested self-interest but for the sake of others, for mankind as a whole. It is a state in which the individual desires to perform altruistic acts for the sake of the value that is intrinsic to them. Maslow illustrates it by referring to a woman who was a very successful mother, who, when her own children were grown and off her hands, adopted a number of orphans in order to provide them with a better quality of life. Having an untrammelled understanding of her own personality and a clear idea of those functions she performed well, she turned her energies to the functions of a foster-mother as an expression of her self-actualisation.

Wilson points out that, from a psychological point of view, the Outsider might be regarded as a person who has not yet achieved self-actualisation. He is focused on his own identity and is constantly concerned about it. He knows that there is something more to himself that he has yet to discover. He has a measure of self-doubt and his environment presses in upon him uncomfortably. Yet, the Outsider remains an important figure in an existential psychology for he is a reminder that the basic human problems lie, not in social organisation or even in interpersonal relationships – although they do find expression in these – but in the individual. The Outsider's discontent may be an expression of 'dis-ease' but it is also an indication that man is capable of higher things. Wilson writes:

> If you had an absolutely ideal society with enough material goods for everybody, it would obviously still not guarantee universal happiness. In point of fact, as a student of crime, I have always recognized that one of the worst consequences of an increasingly comfortable civilization is the soaring crime rate.[11]

The clinical significance of the peak experience became immediately apparent to Maslow and he applied it in an attempt to treat alcoholics. He began with the assumption that many, perhaps most, alcoholics were extremely intelligent and that their drinking was a response to the overwhelming sense of boredom they experienced in the face of a world that failed to stimulate them. Maslow asked his patients what it had been that *had* stimulated them before they became dependent upon alcohol. He then administered a psychedelic drug and, while they were under its influence, exposed them to the stimulus they had mentioned – music, beautiful painting, an actor reading lines from their favourite drama. These stimuli produced the peak experience again and again and when the patients began to realise that such experiences could be produced without recourse to alcohol, they began to master their dependency upon it. Maslow found that he could achieve something like an 85 per cent recovery rate for alcoholics by using this method.

Oddly enough, Maslow believed that an individual could not induce the peak experience at will. His work with alcoholics had shown that it could be induced deliberately by another person, but not by one's self. Almost certainly, had he lived long enough to continue his work, he would have come to reverse this opinion, for Wilson has shown that peak experiences can be self-induced through simple exercises. Thus if we 'clench' our mind in an act of total concentration on something and then suddenly relax our attention, and if we repeat this exercise over and over, we will reach a point where it actually becomes painful. Wilson insists that if we persist with the exercise, pushing our way, as it were, through the pain, we shall find ourselves passing into the peak experience. For Wilson, *clenching* is an important concept.

Most of the time, our experiences are in a state of 'disarray'. We allow them to lie scattered all around us and pick and choose among them as a child might select a particular toy from among the twenty that lie strewn on his bedroom floor. Even those we select scarcely become 'real' to us most of the time. It is as if there is a leak in our attention and we never become fully aware of the object we hold in our hands. Clenching is a closing of the fingers around that object. It is a firmer grasp on experience. It is a sudden increase in the 'pressure' of consciousness so that we feel experience more completely. It is the flexing of the muscle of consciousness so that it is strong enough to bear more intensity of experience. Clenching is the act by which we prevent life from 'slipping through our fingers'. Wilson illustrates its significance:

> Crisis so often brings the sense of 'absurd good news'. It causes consciousness to clench convulsively, making us aware that it has 'muscles' and that these muscles can be used to transform our lives. Nothing is easier than to verify this statement. All that is necessary is to narrow the eyes, tense the muscles, make a sudden powerful effort of clenching the mind. The result is an instantaneous twinge of delight. It vanishes almost instantly because the 'muscle' is so feeble. But we know that any muscle can be strengthened by deliberate effort.[12]

It is a major contribution of Wilson that he has distinguished between two types of peak experience. Maslow acknowledged that his thinking about the human mind was somewhat akin to Taoist and Zen religious philosophies in so far as it was focused on the 'serenity experience'. Thus, Maslow's peak experience is essentially a *passive* experience. It takes the form of being 'overcome' with a sense of wellbeing; of being 'flooded' with joy. Wilson contrasts this type of ecstasy with the type experienced by Nietzsche on the hilltop named Leutsch, when, with a fierce thunderstorm raging and the frantic bleating of a goat being prepared for slaughter ringing in his ears, he suddenly felt within himself a feeling of tremendous energy. This is the type of peak experience that came to Nijinsky and which led him to write, 'I am God! I am God!' This is not in any sense passive: it is an active self-assertion that almost defies external reality.

A gestalt psychologist named Kamiya allowed some of his research assistants to see the alpha rhythms of their own brain by showing them on a screen. As they watched, they began to experiment and soon found that they could affect the rhythms and increase their intensity. When the waves reached a certain level of intensity, the people who were controlling them passed into what they described as a state of bliss. This is the peak experience that Maslow recognised. Wilson's 'clenching' has the capacity to produce the more active variety; the kind that moves beyond a present contentment and into an experience of 'the further reaches of human nature'.

Maslow applied his theory of the hierarchy of needs to social issues, including the sphere of organisational management. In a world where people are workers in an institution, a company or some other form of social organisation, professional or vocational satisfaction has a significant role in determining the degree of self-esteem available to the individual. A work-force divided rigidly into managers and workers will not satisfy everyone's need for self-esteem. What is required is a managerial structure which will permit individual growth through co-operative effort. It is not a matter of the management dispensing welfare to the workers. What is required is an opportunity for all to give expression to their creative capacities.

Wilson acknowledges the significance of Maslow thus:

Maslow saw human nature as *naturally* self-transcending. Healthy, satisfied people seek naturally for wider horizons, for the 'far' rather than the 'near'. Freud was unable to see beyond ego-satisfaction: it seemed plain to him that all urges are directed to this end. He would have said that for a human being to perform any action *not* directed at ego-satisfaction would be as illogical as a hungry man slicing up a steak and then putting it into the mouth of the man sitting next to him. But Freud had simply got his phenomenology wrong. The ego is not simply a stomach craving food; it would be more accurate to compare it to a man's whole physical organism. *Some* needs will be satisfied by eating and drinking, others by walking or swimming, others by making love, others by playing games of skill, and so on. And the needs of the psychic-organism are as various.

Maslow's 'holistic' model of the psychic organism led him to three major conclusions:

(1) Neurosis may be regarded as the blockage of the channels of self-actualization.

(2) A *synergic* society – one in which all individuals may reach a high level of self-satisfaction without restricting anyone else's freedom – should evolve naturally from our present social system.

(3) Business efficiency and the recognition of 'higher ceilings of human nature' are not incompatible; on the contrary, the highest levels of efficiency can *only* be obtained by taking full account of the need for self-actualization that is present in every human being.

This outlines Maslow's achievement, and it is enormous. Like all original thinkers, he has opened up a new way of *seeing* the universe.[13]

In the end, however, Wilson is forced to conclude that Maslow does not go far enough. In the first place there is, as we have seen, the problem of the *passive* peak experience which may leave a man happy but fails to address the absolute question of the realisation of full human potential. But a more serious concern for Wilson is Maslow's uncertainty in the face of the mechanism of self-actualisation. 'It is a great mystery to me', Maslow wrote towards the end of his life, 'why affluence releases some people for growth while permitting other people to stay fixated at a strictly *materialistic* level'.[14] In this sentence, Wilson detects an inadequate phenomenology. Maslow is 'confessing' that he has not recognised the significance of Husserl's notion of intentionality.

Had he done so, he would have realised that the difference between those who use affluence creatively and those who are destroyed by it, is that the former use the grasping function of consciousness to interpret affluence creatively. In the final analysis, Maslow did not appreciate the fact that the most critical thing about man is what he does with his freedom.

If Maslow represented a watershed in the development of Wilson's psychology, another was provided in the work of Julian Jaynes who expressed his ideas in a volume entitled *The Origin of Consciousness in the Breakdown of the Bicameral Mind.*

Jaynes expounded the view that our ancestors, even those as recent as the writers of the Old Testament books, did not possess what we today call 'self-consciousness'. They looked out at the world through their eyes and simply registered the nature of their environment. They were, according to Jaynes, incapable of looking within themselves and recognising an essential self. They had *no* inner self. Whatever sense of purpose these men had, originated outside themselves for they could never think in terms of 'Today, I shall stroll towards the mountain'. For them, purpose was given by an outside agency; perhaps the chief of the tribe or clan. More often than not, they thought of this source of purpose as simply God. It was God who told them to perform this action or that and it was their business to obey. They were governed, as it were, by a form of auditory hallucination.

Jaynes based his theory on the work of a scientist named Roger Sperry, who had done extensive work on the human brain. The brain is in fact an organ with two identical halves, each being a mirror image of the other. It has long been known that the right half of the brain controls the left side of the body and the left side controls the right. It has also been long recognized that the right side controls our capacity to draw, to make images and to engage in intuitive speculation: that it is in fact responsible for the artistic component of our personality. By contrast, the left side of the brain controls language, mathematics and our ability to engage in logical exercises: it is responsible for the scientific component of our personality. It is as if we have an artist and a scientist living within our head in separate compartments of our brain.

The two halves of the brain are connected by a network of nerves which is called the *corpus callosum*, and in the 1930s it was discovered that when the corpus callosum was severed and the two halves of the brain disconnected from each other, strange things began to happen. The patient becomes two distinct persons. Thus one patient tried to undo a button with his right hand while the left hand tried to restrain him. Another tried to hit his wife with one hand while the other hand sought to hold it back. A patient who was shown a pornographic picture with the left eye, blushed heavily but when asked why she was blushing, could give no explanation.

What has become clear from studies of split-brain patients is that the person you call yourself lives in the left side of your brain, while another self, largely unrecognised, lives in the right side of your brain. This has been clearly demonstrated, even when the two halves of the brain remain in contact with each other through the corpus callosum.

Jaynes advanced the theory that auditory hallucinations among primitive man originated in the right side of the brain. It sounded in the left brain as if coming from afar. There are some interesting common observations which suggest that the right brain *does* pass on messages to the left brain. When we have an exciting day ahead of us, most of us are able to tell ourselves that we should wake at a given time the next morning so that we miss nothing of the excitement. We do not have to rely on the alarm clock, which is the usual trigger for the left brain. Our right brain tells us to wake up and we do. We might be walking along a country road, absorbed in the beauty of the undulating hills that surround us, lost, as we say, in thought. Suddenly we look up and find ourselves in the path of an approaching car. We had not seen it before nor had we heard it. Something made us look up. Something warned us. What could it have been? Almost certainly, it was the other side of our brain, which had remained on the lookout for us while we took a mental holiday and enjoyed the view.

For Jaynes, then, primitive man had a bicameral (two sided) brain. This determined both the way he saw the world and his interaction with it, until an event took place which had a profound influence upon him. It changed, not merely his understanding of the world and of his place in it: it transformed *him* by creating within him a self-image; a self-consciousness. This cataclysmic event was the invention of writing, which took place about 10,000 BC.

It is the purpose of writing to store knowledge and provide for the retrieval of knowledge. But writing can achieve these ends only if those who use it are systematic about their approach to it. It must be catalogued and cross referenced. It must be translated before foreigners can have access to it. It must be taught from generation to generation so that its meaning remains unchanged and the original message is preserved. Writing, because it is a *visible* symbol of an authority 'out there', beyond ourselves, encourages the development of a critical faculty. Writing, in fact, introduced a human need for a new complexity which undermined man's bicameral nature.

Wilson spells out two of the consequences, identified by Jaynes, of this breakdown of the bicameral mind:

> The first sign of this 'change of Mind', says Jaynes, can be found in Mesopotamia. Around 1230 BC the Assyrian tyrant, Tukulti–Ninurta 1 had a stone altar built and it shows the king kneeling before the *empty* throne of the god. In earlier carvings, the king is shown standing and talking to the god. Now the king is alone; the god has vanished. A cuneiform text of the same period contains the lines:
>
>> One who has no god, as he walks along the street
>> Headache envelopes him like a garment.
>
> Headache is the result of nervous tension, of losing contact with the intuitive self. And when a man suffers from stress, he reacts to problems by losing his temper. And it is at this point, according to Jaynes, that cruelty first becomes a commonplace in history. It is in the Assyrian carvings of about this period that we first see illustrations of men and women impaled, children beheaded.[15]

Wilson recognises that modern man is dominated by the left brain. Today he is under the influence of scientific method, rationality, and logic. He is schooled to accept that he cannot survive without an organised body of knowledge which can only be obtained at a significant cost. This is, up to a point, as it should be. The left brain *is* and *is intended to be* the controller.

In responding to Jaynes' theory, Wilson does *not* take the view that while contemporary man is entombed in the left side of the brain, his salvation lies in his movement into the right side. The problem lies in the fact that the two sides of the brain have been allowed to remain separated from each other. In fact, Wilson advocates that what is necessary is an harmonious relationship between the two sides. He provides two symbols of this relationship working at its best. It is like a tennis game between two equally matched players, each testing the other out in a fierce sporting contest by producing their best shots in order to ensure that the standard of the game is never brought in question. Again, the two sides of the brain must cooperate as fellow workmen each on one end of a cross-cut saw, pushing and pulling in unison in order to bring down the mammoth tree that stands in the way of a major highway that is to be built.

Wilson has told how he goes to his study each morning to commence his day's typing. Some mornings, his fingers are cold and the keys of the typewriter refuse to respond at the normal rapid rate. Ideas will not come. The last sentence seems to be incapable of connecting with any new sentence with which he might follow it. Yet, on such mornings, he persists and types on. Eventually, something happens. His fingers and his mind begin to relax and the ideas begin to flow. What has happened is that the left brain has worked on, declaring to the right brain that it is ready. At last the right brain throws an idea. The left catches it and transposes it into print. 'That's right,' says the right brain, and throws another. 'Good,' says the left brain and again sets it down. Before long, Wilson finds himself under the influence of what we commonly call 'inspiration'. Intuition may originate in the right brain and typing skills may be remembered in the left brain but creative writing is the product of both acting in concert.

In a brief monograph entitled *The Laurel and Hardy Theory of Consciousness* Wilson presses home the need for a cooperative endeavour by both sides of the brain.

It seems to me that the relation between consciousness and unconsciousness is like the relation between Laurel and Hardy in the old movies. Ollie – consciousness – is basically the boss. Stan takes his cues from Ollie. If Ollie looks cheerful, Stan is positively ecstatic. Stan *always over-reacts*.

So, if I wake up on a rainy Monday morning, and think gloomily, 'How am I going to get through this boring day?', the unconscious mind begins to feel depressed. An hour later we feel miserable and exhausted – *because the unconscious mind controls our vital energies*. This confirms our feeling that this is 'one of those days', so Stan becomes more depressed than ever. . . . In short, there is a build-up of negative feedback.[16]

The notion of 'negative feedback' derives from the work of Victor Frankl whom many would regard as the founding father of existential psychology. In the early years of the Second World War, Frankl was working on a manuscript entitled *Existenz-Analyse*. When he was interned in a Nazi concentration camp, his manuscript was lost. His wife, his parents and his brother were all slain in the Jewish pogrom and it would have been easy for Frankl to resign himself to death. Yet he persisted. It was the rewriting of his manuscript that saved him for it provided him with a sense of purpose that made the conditions of the camp endurable. Upon his release, he spread his psychological insights far and wide, predominantly through his book, *From Death Camp to Existentialism*. Frankl's psychology can be summarised in three important notions.

In the first place, Frankl recognised that physical as well as mental health is directly related to a sense of purpose. So direct is this relationship, that a composer in one of the camps, who dreamed that it would be liberated on a particular day, lived enthusiastically until that day arrived. He was shattered by the fact that the prison did not fall into allied hands and he died the next day. Frankl insists that life needs goals in the future towards which it can direct itself. Where such goals do not exist life is no more than what he called 'provisional existence.'

Secondly, Frankl was fully aware that while goals were essential, they were not enough of themselves. Purposive consciousness does not depend upon recognized goals so much as upon an attitude of mind. When Jewish prisoners disembarked from their train at Dachau station, they were noted to be smiling broadly. This they could do because Dachau had no chimneys and thus their attitude towards the camp was dramatically altered. It is the attitude, linked with the goal, that makes all the difference to the quality of life. Wilson provides the analogue of a water skier linked up with a speedboat. The skier, the speedboat and the link are all important if there is to be any real forward movement.

Finally, Frankl recognised 'the law of reverse effort'. He records the case of a book-keeper patient whose fingers cramped up every time he went to enter figures in his journal. He turned to Frankl because he was terrified that his condition would lead to the loss of his livelihood. Frankl sent him home to write *as badly* as he possibly could. Soon, the patient returned to advise that he was cured. The cramps had been caused by anxiety. Frankl simply removed the anxiety and thus created a change of attitude which produced the healing.

The notion of reversed effort becomes clearer when it is linked to Wilson's idea of *preparedness*. Preparedness is the energy that builds up in Tom Sawyer's friends as they watch him painting the fence. Had Tom simply asked them to take over his brush, they would have refused because they had not built up within themselves a desire to paint. As Tom painted, and spoke of the delicious responsibility that was being exercised in the work, his friends convinced themselves that it was the most important thing they could possibly do at that time. Frankl cured a student of stammering by telling him to go away and stammer as much as he could. When the student *prepared* to stammer, he could not do it because *stammering is a product of unpreparedness*. Preparedness is the solution to boredom, for, like stammering, boredom is also a product of unpreparedness.

Intentionality is, of course, preparedness. It is a *dynamic* openness to intensified meaning.

Wilson sees the close relationship between the theory of Frankl and that of Maslow:

> Frankl's basic position is identical with Maslow's, as can be seen in his assertion, 'Meaning sets the pace of being. Existence falters unless it is lived in terms of transcendence towards something beyond itself'. And in *The Will to Meaning*, he writes: 'Existence falters unless there is a *strong idea*, as Freud puts it, or a strong ideal to hold on to. To quote Albert Einstein, "the man who regards his life as meaningless is not merely unhappy but hardly fit for life".'[17]

Wilson reviews the work of all the major existential psychologists of the past fifty years, including Binswanger, Moss, Assagioli, Rollo May and R. D. Laing. He notes that there is a particular thread that runs through all of them and which separates them from the earlier psychologies of men like Freud, Jung and Adler. It is that they adopt a more down-to-earth approach to the problems of mental illness. They also approach their patients from a different perspective. It is as if they commit an act of deliberate self-identification with them: as if they are acknowledging that they are addressing their own human condition as well as that of their patients because all men are subject to the same essential predicament. They have discarded dogmatic statements in the enunciation of their theories and have embraced a more generous, *hypothetical* method of enquiry.

By way of illustrating this new approach to the application of psychology, Wilson borrows a story which is told by the novelist, Irving Wallace in his book, *The Sunday Gentlemen*. It concerns Larry Cassidy, a young man reared by a dominant father and a mother who was totally submissive. Cassidy had a very high IQ but by the time he had reached his late teens he had gone into a state of permanent depression. It was so severe that he was ruled ineligible for the armed forces. For a long time he resisted his condition as strongly as he could, working in the newspaper trade and leading a near bohemian existence. When his mother died, he sank into a sense of intolerable boredom. He became inactive and could not hold food in his stomach. When he married, it was as if nothing significant had happened in his life. When a psychiatrist told him that his mind was like a telephone exchange in which all the wires had become entangled, he became even worse, certain that he was an irreversible mental case. Eventually, on a trip to Arizona, he had an attack of terror, and frightened his fellow travellers by screaming that he wanted to be killed. The attack led to his hospitalisation and the performance of a prefrontal lobotomy – the separation of the thalamus from the frontal lobes of the brain. After a subsequent twenty years in hospital, Cassidy discharged himself and married a second time, but he remained a five-year-old adult.

Wilson comments that existential psychology as practised by Frankl or Maslow, could probably have saved Cassidy from most of his misery – and from the surgeon's knife. What is abundantly clear is that he was not helped by a Freudian approach to his problem. Wallace himself wrote that Cassidy had a strong Oedipal complex which was manifested in the fact that he had married a woman who was several years older than himself!

Existential psychology would have recognised that Cassidy's basic problem was that he had allowed himself to slip into a *habit of passivity*. His romantic pessimism contrasted with his high intelligence and he resolved the battle by surrendering. He had written to his brother, expressing his view on the futility of life in a letter which was 'brilliantly written, terribly logical but practically unanswerable'. What he needed was sympathetic assistance in helping to find answers to his own questions about the meaning of life. He needed to have his consciousness *directed* in a quest for purpose. In the final analysis, says Wilson, the psychiatrists who administered insulin, electric shocks and finally the surgeon's knife, were wasting their time. They were not dealing with a failure of the brain but with a failure of the creative urge. This can be restored, not by surgery but by recourse to an intentional phenomenolgy.

In the final analysis, any psychotherapy – and the psychology which underlies it – is an attempt to help a human being identify a suitable self-image. This self-image must involve a high degree of self-esteem and of creativity. It must be free of all self-deception.

Wilson has argued that the difference between neurosis and psychosis is quantitative rather than qualitative. He points out that this is often overlooked because a neurotic seldom develops into a psychotic and psychotic diseases such as schizophrenia usually emerge without any preliminary neurotic stage. But both are consequences of a broken *will*. Wilson illustrates this by recounting the story of the novelist Margaret Lane.

Lane experienced a mild form of schizophrenia which lasted a little over a year. She had just given a very difficult birth to a child and for weeks afterwards she was physically exhausted. Her physical condition affected her emotional state and she found herself to be over-sensitive. In this state, she read John Hersey's account of the dropping of the atomic bomb on Hiroshima and passed into a state of acute depression. She felt nothing towards her new child although she did all the mechanical things that were necessary for its well-being. She experienced typical schizophrenic symptoms, such as perceiving the grass as being blue. It ended when she was in a field and suddenly noticed the intensity of colour in a blue flower. She knew that the dullness through which her mind had filtered everything for a year was beginning to lift. After a few more days, she was back to normal. Wilson comments:

In schizophrenia, a state of emergency is declared. The Robot takes over most of the vital functions. And, like an accountant taking over a bankrupt business, *he* doles out energy. But the realm of the Robot is the unconscious, which is also the realm of dreams. This explains schizophrenic hallucinations and distortions. With the Robot in charge, dreams are allowed to stroll in and out of the conscious mind. And they appear to challenge the real world, to possess a self-subsisting reality. . . . One of the most interesting observations to arise out of all of this is that when the mind falls below a certain energy-level, its capacity to receive meaning drops abruptly. And so, although schizophrenia is an altogether more serious illness than neurosis, its milder forms occur every day to almost everybody. You might say that your sense of meaning is suddenly cut by half; a grey, chill wind seems to blow in the mind. But then, like a water cistern, your energy tank refills and life appears normally pleasant and meaningful again.[18]

It would be difficult to overemphasise the significance of this statement for it takes us to the heart of Wilson's psychological concern. He writes:

This brings me to my central point, the point I have explored, analysed and reiterated since *The Outsider*. *Human consciousness operates at far too low a pressure for efficiency.* This has always been so – which explains why philosophers and poets have always taken a tragic view of human existence: 'All is vanity', 'It is better not to have been born', 'Misery will never end', 'This dim vast vale of tears'. But balance against that the whiskey priest's recognition that it would have been so easy to be a saint, or Raskolnikov's assertion that he would rather live on a narrow ledge for ever and ever than die at once. It also explains why vital men seek out challenges and welcome war. 'I have no life except where the swords clash'. The state of intensity, of concern, of seriousness, brought to bear by the whiskey priest on the point of death, is the correct operating pressure for the human mind. At lower pressures we are uneconomical to run. Our powers are wasted.[19]

When all is said and done, psychology becomes a matter of choice. The individual can choose between becoming a whisky priest or a saint. He can operate at a low level of intensity or he can increase that level. What he needs to do is to exercise his freedom. Wilson highlights the basic proposition of an existential psychology as follows:

> Man's freedom is a reality – a reality that makes a difference to his physical, as well as his mental health. When Frankl's prisoners ceased to believe in the possibility of freedom, they grew sick and died. On the other hand, when they saw that Dachau had no chimney, standing out all night in the rain seemed no great hardship; they laughed and joked. The conclusion deserves to be stated in letters ten feet high. In order to realize his possibilities, man must believe in an *open* future; he must have a vision of something worth doing. And this will not be possible until all the determinism and pessimism that we have inherited from the nineteenth century – and which has infected every department of our culture, from poetry to atomic physics – has been dismissed as fallacious and illogical. Twentieth-century science, philosophy, politics, literature – even music – has been constructed upon a *weltanschauung* that leaves half of human nature out of account.
>
> Man is not naturally static; his mental energy, like his blood, was intended to be kept moving. His mental being must be understood as something essentially dynamic, forward-flowing, like a river. All mental illness is a result of damming the river.[20]

The last thirty years have seen a plethora of existential psychologies being developed. Some of them have already given notice that they will project themselves into an extended future and make a major contribution to the future of mankind, while others have disclosed the symptoms of a world-weary incapacity. Not all of these existential psychologies will approach every, or even any, patient in exactly the same way. Yet every genuine existential psychology will have at its centre, the Maslovian idea of self-actualisation, whether called by that name or by some other. It is the indispensable characteristic of a genuinely *existential* theory of psychology.

Yet the notion of the peak experience is, of itself, not sufficient. Wilson's central contribution to an existential psychology is his insistence that the key to mental health lies in our learning to understand the phenomenology of the peak experience. This, he claims, is the psychological equivalent of the quantum theory, and psychotherapy will not earn the right to call itself a science until it has performed this task. From a psychological point of view, meaning-perception holds the key to our continuing evolution as a species. Wilson closes his *New Pathways in Psychology* with the following passage:

Man controls his physical environment by means of his physical powers. He controls his inner world by means of his mental powers – 'intentions'. His future evolution depends upon increased ability to use 'intentions', these mental pseudopodia that determine his thoughts, moods, ideas, emotions, insights. The intentions do not create ideas or insights; they only *uncover* meaning. They could be compared to the blind man's fingers that wander over Braille. But this image fails to bring out the most important aspect of the intention: their power to *penetrate* into meaning.

. . . Take a picture – perhaps some coloured photograph of a landscape. Look at it slowly and carefully, thinking of the eyes as projectors of needle-like intentions. An ordinary glance at the picture seems to reveal most of its meaning. But after this first glance, treat the picture as a record of hidden meanings, waiting for the needle of light to search them out and recreate them in all their richness. We soon become aware that intentions *are* fingers that are capable of probing into meaning, uncovering meanings that are already present in coded form. We are living in a world of infinitely rich meaning and we possess the equipment for 'playing it back'. The chief obstacle is our ignorance of the purpose of the equipment and of the meaning waiting to be decoded.[21]

It is clear that in such a world as that depicted here, the Outsider would find himself very much more comfortable. Equally, mental illness would be virtually absent. Indeed, the common man would be transformed into the kind of 'superman' that Nietzsche imagined and human evolution would take its next giant step forward. Wilson gives us a glimpse of such a world in his profoundly important work, *Access to Inner Worlds*:

As soon as we induce states of inner certainty (based on a sense of purpose), we begin to observe their effect. We become less accident prone. Some sixth sense helps to steer us clear of trouble. Interesting coincidences begin to occur. (When I become subject to these synchronicities, I know I am in good health). We may begin to have flashes of precognition; the telephone rings and you know who it is before you answer it. You know that a letter from a long-lost friend will arrive in the post. In short, the right brain seems to control certain paranormal powers and is willing to place them at the disposal of the left. The *Kahunas* assert that the 'higher self' can control the future; and everyone who has experienced moods of relaxed self-confidence knows that curious inner certainty that nothing is going to go wrong.

The most interesting possibility remains the prospect of unlimited 'access to inner worlds'.[22]

The existential psychology that Wilson embraces is one of the most exciting theories ever to have been created by the human mind. It is the product of an alert intelligence cooperating with a sharp intuition. It has about it a sense that it is as much given as created. It provides a satisfying explanation of the path we have traversed in the past; of our present experience of frustration and of the way forward. It makes all other psychologies appear inadequate because it is a profound synthesis of the best that each of them has to offer. It is unique in that it celebrates man – whether in his highest or his lowest moments – as a miracle of nature.

4

The Sexology

THE 'Outsider Cycle' was completed in 1966. Despite the vagaries of the critics, the volumes sold reasonably well and there were a significant number of people who considered them to be fundamentally important in the context of any intelligent examination of the human condition. Yet, there was an apparent anomaly about the cycle. Why was it, many wondered, that a series of books purporting to address fundamentally philosophical questions, should contain a volume that discussed the origin of the sexual impulse?

Wilson, of course, had already given notice of a profound interest in human sexuality. It had been present in his journals – a fact that the daily press had found invaluable in the days following the horsewhipping incident – and his first novel had painted a horrifying portrait of a sex killer. But what did all of this have to do with philosophy? Even many of his ardent readers were a little puzzled when Arthur Barker announced *The Origins of the Sexual Impulse*.

The real prelude to the book, however, was to be found, not in a journal or even in the novel. Wilson had set the foundation for his examination of sex as a component of human experience in the very first paragraph of *The Outsider*, when he introduced Barbusse's hero who was totally involved in the wind-blown skirts of women as he watched them on the bus. 'It is not a woman I want', he confides to the reader, 'but *all* women.'

It is critically important that we understand this statement to which Wilson draws our attention. On a simple level, we might understand it to mean that Barbusse's hero wants to sleep with one woman after another until he has exhausted every woman in the world. But Barbusse and Wilson are pointing to another level of human need. Barbusse's hero does not necessarily want *every* woman: he wants *all* women – he wants to penetrate into the heart of the secret that is represented by the opposite sex. To the extent that he is an outsider in this first view that we have of him, it is because he feels himself excluded from *half of the mystery of life*.

Not the least interesting aspect of *The Outsider*, when it is read in retrospect, is the fact that it deals with a wide range of historic personalities who demonstrated a greater or lesser degree of conflict within themselves over the matter of their own sexuality. Thus, the later life of T. E. Lawrence is to be understood in terms of the effect that an act – or at least an attempt at an act – of sodomy was to have upon him. Nietzsche was to die of syphilis. H. G. Wells wrestled, not too energetically, against his own promiscuity and James Joyce was an acknowledged panty fetishist. They are all there, in *The Outsider*, representing a series of case studies in the struggle of human beings to come to terms with their own sexual drives.

But Wilson simply hints at these drives in his first book. He has his mind on other matters; on the question of the broader boundaries that give definition to the Outsider and on the intensity of man's discomfort in the face of his *total* experience. And the same can be said of *Religion and the Rebel* where we meet such individuals as the sexually shrunken Kierkegaard and the homosexual Wittgenstein. Again Wilson points but does not linger because he is in pursuit of those 'religious' sensitivities that will lead man in the direction of his own well-being.

The first direct indication we have, within the Outsider Cycle, that Wilson is at work on a comprehensive sexology comes in *The Strength to Dream*. In the sixth chapter of that work, entitled *Sex and the Imagination*, he deals with the lives of Maupassant, Wedekind, D. H. Lawrence and the novel *Sanine* by Artsybashev. The very title of the chapter gives us a clear indication of Wilson's philosophical approach to sexuality. The chapter makes it crystal clear that sexuality, in association with imagination, is a powerful form of intentionality. This statement is in itself a summary of Wilson's sexology.

Before turning to sex and its relationship to imagination, it is worth noting that when Wilson wrote his essay in *The Strength to Dream* he was thirty-one years old. The point is noteworthy because it demonstrates Wilson's capacity to *think* his way through his own experience at an early age. At thirty-one, most men are riding the crest of sex, indulging in it as a form of the highest enjoyment. Intellectual evaluation of their behaviour is generally far from their minds but for Wilson, the act of sex was inseparable from the fact of sex and the latter had to be comprehended if the condition of man was to be understood. By the time he was thirty-two, he had completed *The Origins of the Sexual Impulse* and had created one of the most intelligent, sensitive and healthy views of human sexuality ever published. These adjectives sound strongly emotive but they have been selected carefully and a thorough reading of his sexology will find that they have a great deal of justification. At the very least, Wilson's understanding of sexuality serves to demonstrate the inadequacy and the intrinsic dangers of the theories popularized by Freud and which still largely dominate our understanding of ourselves as sexual beings.

In *The Strength to Dream*, Wilson takes us into the world of sexuality through the fiction of Guy de Maupassant.

The work of Maupassant is fully concentrated on sex. It would not be too much to say that he perceived of life through a 'sexual centre' which he located within himself. His early work was based on the realist tradition and it seems that he is reluctant to get to the point of his preoccupation with the sexual. His first novel, *A Woman's Life* offers an account of a marriage between an innocent woman and a man whom her imagination endows with all of the masculine charms. Her innocence is affronted early in the marriage, soon after she becomes pregnant, when her husband is exposed as a mean, pathological philanderer. With the death of her husband, who is killed by a jealous husband, the woman devotes herself to the life of her son but there is little joy in this act of devotion because the son proves to be as wanton as his father. The story suggests Maupassant's prevailing early view of women; that they were to be pitied – but used.

The later Maupassant however, managed to free himself of this element of pity, and his books took on a degree of brutality. One of his stories deals with a Frenchman who is staying with an Eastern potentate who offers him his two small girls as bedmates. Not being a paedophile, the Frenchman prefers to play innocent games with them, and when he leaves he gives them a number of his possessions as presents. He later hears that both of them have been accused of stealing from him, and executed. When one reads this story, it is Maupassant's indifference to the plight of the children that lingers in the mind. In fact, Wilson argues, Maupassant's 'detachment' is little more than an inadequate mask for approval. *Bel Ami* follows the social elevation of a scoundrel who builds his fame and fortune on the misery of the women he abuses – and Maupassant seems to sit in the margin of each page nodding his approval. In much the same way, he seems to derive pleasure from the plight of a man whose wife betrays him. Sex may be important to Maupassant but fidelity certainly is not.

Towards the end of his career, Maupassant underwent a literary revolution. While his middle works are filled with a note of confident male sexuality and optimism, his later novels reflect something of a 'defeat-complex'. His final novel centres on a male character who is demented by an invisible horror. The change was undoubtedly due to Maupassant contracting the syphilis which was later to drive him insane and lead to his suicide. But, Wilson comments:

> even without syphilis, the seeds of madness were already present in Maupassant's mental make-up, in the *Weltanschauung* of a man who could declare that cruelty and violent death are as much the order of nature as love and beauty. Morality, after all, is a direction that we give to the world, a kind of grain that we profess to see in the wood of experience. Without some such conviction, there can be no evolution of the personality, for there is *no sense of purpose on which the will can take its stand*. Maupassant's early works are full of a sense of purpose but it has not been put there by Maupassant; it is simply a reflection of a supremely healthy living organism. Like Van Gogh, he is affirming without knowing why, affirming in spite of misery and death. But Maupassant never used his brain, he never tried to gain permanent possession of this knowledge by turning it into ideas and convictions. So when his sickness robbed him of it, he had nothing; there was nothing he could do in his work but imitate the old gestures.[1]

There is, then, a *cerebral* factor in healthy living. One must use one's brain to discover a process of affirmation. One must have ideas and convictions. One must have a mental purpose. Once again we are in the realms of Wilson's philosophy of intentionality. But, it must be understood, in this philosophy, thinking is not enough. 'Thinking too precisely upon the event' is Hamlet's disease and it is more common than we might suppose. If we are to find genuine affirmation – of ourselves, of the world – then we must turn to additional capacities of the mind.

In the conclusion to his essay on *Sex and the Imagination*, Wilson points out that few 'visionary' writers place much significance on human sexuality. This, he speculates, may be due to the fact that the visionary is intent on escaping from this world and entering into new vistas. Yeats took a lifetime of dedicated self-discipline before he could bring himself to admit sex as a profoundly important human experience. But on the contrary, a genuine understanding of sex flows from a rich experience with the opposite sex. Writers such as Rabelais, Robert Burns and Synge, who reflect a healthy attitude towards sex, are unconcerned with the visionary experience. They are 'this-worldly' and given to its full pleasure. Thus is set out the basic contradiction in man's attitude towards his own sexual nature: or, at least the basic contradiction about sex that exists in the mind of the Outsider – who is a visionary by his nature, but a visionary who experiences his sexual drive as a pressing need. Central to the sexual theory that Wilson goes on to develop is a synthesis between these two positions: a resolution of the sexual paradox that bears in upon the Outsider.

The key to Wilson's synthesis is an activity of the human mind that complements thinking. For Wilson – and the New Existentialism that was being formulated – the solution lay in man's imagination.

It is the relationship that Wilson detects between sexuality and human imagination that accounts for the appearance of *Origins of the Sexual Impulse* within the Outsider Cycle. The book opens with an explanation that, in writing *Introduction to the New Existentialism*, which he did simultaneously, Wilson saw that the way forward for Existentialism lay in the application of that essential characteristic of consciousness that Husserl had called intentionality. Since imagination was a powerful form of applied intentionality, and since the most dramatic and powerful form of imagination in modern man seemed to be demonstrated in his sexuality, a treatment of sex was unavoidable. It was, in fact, so critical that it could not be contained within a single chapter of the book on the New Existentialism and thus the book of the origins of sex was necessary.

Wilson begins his work on the foundations of sexuality with an examination of sexual tension. He contends that

> the basic activity of all living organisms is the discharging of various forms of tension and the act of discharging leads to a temporary broadening of consciousness. A starving man, for example, feels a physical tension which is discharged by the act of eating and the discharge of the tension is accompanied by a sense of affirmation of life.[2]

There can be no doubt that the sexual has its physical centre in the sexual organs and that sexual demands are demands of those organs. Yet it is equally clear that the physical component in sex is complemented by a mental factor. A man or a woman may suddenly find themselves being stirred physically by a simple impression made upon the mind by the sight of a member of the opposite sex or by reading a passage in a book. Barbusse's character is sexually stirred by the sight of a woman's skirt being blown about her legs. The sexual impulse is based on a tension that is both physical and mental and the presence of the mental tension is critical since, when it is introduced, it brings with it the capacity to extend the physical beyond its normal limits.

The discharge of tension is a form of heightened consciousness. When we release the buildup of tension within ourselves, we achieve a sense of participating in the evolutionary drive: it is as if we have propelled ourselves forward into a more vital and energetic form of our own being. And what is most significant about the sexual urge is that it provides us with the shortest and most rapid means of the discharge of tension. Nabokov's character, Humbert, masturbating against an unaware Lolita, expresses the consequences of his action thus:

> All of a sudden a mysterious change came over my senses. I entered a plane of being where nothing mattered save the infusion of joy brewed within my body. What had begun as a delicious distension of my innermost roots became a glowing tingle which now had reached that state of absolute security, confidence and reliance not found elsewhere in conscious life. With the deep, hot sweetness thus established and well on its way to the ultimate convulsion, I felt I could slow down in order to prolong the glow.[3]

It is clear that Humbert is engaging in something profoundly more than a physical act. Here he is involved mentally, existentially and is in touch with a dimension of his own being that is not normally available to him. Nor should we allow any moral judgement we might make about the act in which he is engaged, to prevent us from grasping the *positive* quality of the heightened consciousness he has discovered.

Humbert's experience discloses an essential characteristic of the sexual impulse. It is fundamentally impersonal. The feeling that comes to Humbert is almost independent of Lolita. It is true that Humbert uses her body but he might just as well have been using any girl's body – or even his own hand. In a real sense, he is alone with himself: he is engaged in an encounter with himself. His everyday self has encountered a higher self which it instantly recognises as being somehow more authentic than itself. And yet there is a sense in which Lolita is important in herself because in using her, Humbert is gratifying a need to assert himself over against her. Sex is impersonal, not in the sense of being 'indifferent' to others but in sense of seeking to subject them to a will to power.

Wilson speaks of this sense of power that is associated with sexuality, as 'the Coolidge effect'. There is an account of the American President, Calvin Coolidge, visiting a farm with his wife. Taken on separate tours of the property, both found themselves, at different times, being shown a chicken pen. As she looked at the pen, Mrs Coolidge asked her guide if the rooster copulated more than once a day. 'Dozens of times,' was the answer. 'Please tell that to Mr Coolidge,' said Mrs Coolidge. When the President reached the pen, the message was passed on to him. 'And does the rooster choose the same hen every time?' he asked. 'Oh, no,' came the reply, 'a different one each time.' 'Tell that to Mrs Coolidge,' was the President's response.

In his autobiography, *A Pagan's Hosanna*, Philip de Bruyn recounts how one afternoon he watched a girl walking along a beach. He experienced a desire for her and reflects on that desire:

> The trouble was that I knew it was unsatisfiable. I might get to know her and persuade her to sleep with me. But that would not satisfy what I felt *now*; it would only be a carbon copy of this desire to lay her on the warm sand, remove her bathing trunks, and *take* her with an instantaneous fusion of bodies.[4]

The sexual impulse is an urge to conquest. This is the explanation for the male propensity for promiscuity. But again, moral judgements should not blind us to the importance of this insight. No matter what judgement we might pass upon an individual's sexual behaviour, the point to be noted is that it springs from a fundamental thrust that would drive human beings forward towards a higher realm of existence.

Wilson observes that there might be a difference in character between male and female promiscuity. In the male, it emerges as a will to power. In the female, however, it might be more correct to see it is as being

> due to a perverse kind of rebelliousness, an almost self-destructive urge, the need to defy society with an obscene gesture.[5]

Be this as it may, however, it is to be noted that an act of rebelliousness, or a defiant gesture against society, are in themselves a form of self-assertion. Thus, in both the male and the female, the sexual impulse has the nature of an attempt to assert the individual; to promote the integrity of the person. Far from being 'an almost self-destructive urge' female promiscuity seems to have the same quality as male promiscuity – an attempt to grasp more life, more reality.

The forward thrust that Wilson sees in the sexual impulse is not to be understood as being confined to sex. It is also the hallmark of all great art.

> The works of idealistic writers – poets and philosophers – move towards climaxes that attempt to make life appear meaningful. There are plenty of climaxes in Casanova and [Henry] Miller, but they are only satisfactions of ordinary human appetites, and they leave nothing behind. Since they view life as nothing more than a procession of their desires and biological processes, they naturally have no more moral sense than a fox in a poultry farm.[6]

The sexual tragedy of our age is that humanity has at its disposal a powerful instrument of self-projection which is used as a toy. Faced with the complexity of contemporary life and overwhelmed by a sense of incapacity in its midst, humanity uses its sexuality as a consolation. This is what Eliot understood when he described life as simply 'life, copulation and death'. We often copulate in an attempt to deal with an overwhelming sense of boredom. In fact, the copulative act has the potential to drive us through our boredom into a life of fulfilment. Yet it is not the act itself that has this capacity: It is the removal of the limitations on our consciousness that we experience in the act that is all important. Wilson expresses this notion as follows:

> Of all human instincts and desires, the sexual instinct is the one that most transcends man's *conscious* awareness of himself and his purposes. It is almost as if man carries a 'separate self' around with him of which he is usually ignorant.[7]

Yet, it must be emphasised, this is not to be understood as a mystification of sex.

> The sexual impulse has an important factor in common with all other human impulses. It is not somehow unique, belonging to a different order. Although a man may have less understanding and control of his sexual impulses than of, say, his desire for financial security, this is not to say that he is a puppet, a slave in the hands of a force that is completely inscrutable. The sexual urge is unlike most other human drives in only one important respect: it is by far the shortest and easiest route to release of tension and heightened consciousness. It satisfies both man's purpose and nature's.[8]

It is in the context of this approach to sexuality that Wilson understands the response made by the schoolboy to the question, 'What do you want to be when you grow up?' 'A sex maniac,' says the boy. What saves this response from absolute horror is the notion that it expresses a desire for assertion and ongoing development. It is an answer based on an intuitive understanding that sex can lead to a 'bursting through' the limitations of ordinary consciousness. If we perceive of the boy's 'mania' in this sense, his objective becomes not only less offensive but even acceptable. And this insight makes it possible to grasp the nature of every sexual perversion.

Tolstoy argued that the sexual act should be dedicated to the procreation of children. Few people in today's world would be willing to accept such a limitation for they understand that sex can produce a profound sense of satisfaction that transcends the purely hedonistic. But if the end product of the sexual impulse is the orgasm, it follows that a definition of perversion must take into account, not the end but the means by which that end is achieved. Wilson illustrates this argument with reference to *Lolita*: Nabokov's *Lolita* is about the feeling of underprivilege rather than about sexual relations with a nymphet. Humbert's passion for Lolita is only the passion of modern man for the forbidden. Humbert seems to contain the seeds of most of the sexual perversions, with the exception of sadism. He indulges in masturbation on park benches, while peering up the skirts of little girls who raise their knees to adjust roller skates – a form of voyeurism – and later uses the pressure of Lolita's leg to induce an orgasm: his original plan with Lolita is not to seduce her, but to drug her with sleeping pills and use her as a passive sexual object, without actually violating her; this is certainly a close relation to necrophilia.[9]

Humbert's sexual impulse is concentrated on the means rather than the end. He fails to comprehend what it is that he is seeking in the sexual act and thus his frustration continues because the means on which he is focused do not have the capacity, of themselves, to satisfy him. This is the essence of perversion: a delusion that human sexuality is an end in itself. The task confronting humanity is not to adjust to its own sexuality but to adjust to life itself. When this adjustment is made, there will be no need to invest our frantic energy in fetishes and other forms of sexual perversion. In a helpful image, Wilson speaks of perversion as an excessive revving of the engine of a motor car when it is out of gear.

The contrast between Wilson's understanding of human sexuality and that of Freud, is thus clear. If the mind is represented as a circle, Frued made a dot in its centre and called it the libido – human sexual energy. Perversions were represented by other dots made between the centre and the circumference, their distance from the centre depending upon the 'severity' of the perversion. Fellatio might be closer to the centre than homosexuality. Psychoanalysis was the process of drawing back into the centre dot all the dots which surrounded it. Wilson, however, would place his 'sexual dot', off centre in the circle. Thus a dot between it and the nearest point of the circumference could be drawn back, through the 'sexual dot' into the centre of the circle. For Wilson, human sexuality is simply an element of human experience which must be 'centred' together with all others if an individual is to be whole.

In the final chapter of *Origins of the Sexual Impulse*, Wilson develops his 'theory of symbolic response'. He reminds us, in accord with his phenomenology of intentionality, that there is no reality outside man that is independent of the mind that grasps it. The human mind *gives* reality to the objects surrounding it and this includes sexual objects. Further, the mind endows these objects with the capacity to respond. The instrument that man's mind uses to endow this reality and capacity to respond is imagination. Thus Wilson can write:

> A man whose imagination has lost its vitality might lose interest in a woman in the very act of making love to her. Where sex is concerned, there is no 'object'; only a symbol clothed with reality by some inner purpose. When this symbol corresponds to a living woman, we call the desire 'normal'.

It is of paramount importance to an understanding of the sexual impulse, to realise that the inner purpose we have bestowed on our sexual partners is essentially based on the idea of otherness. Sex is fundamentally a penetration of the alien nature of another human being. In the sexual act, man is violating a taboo. In recognising this we gain further insight into the nature of perversion. If man's sexual satisfaction depends on the violation of a taboo, it follows that the more taboos that are defied, the greater the satisfaction.

The theory of symbolic response is readily illustrated in the sexual act. In the very act of making love, an individual knows that he is in proximity to something he cannot touch. He knows that what he is experiencing does not emanate from his sexual partner but that she is its 'vehicle'. Yet even this does not get to the heart of the matter for his experience is finally independent of the partner. It is an ineffable experience that corresponds to the sense of the sublime that came to Wordsworth when he saw 'unknown modes of being' as he looked at a hill over Windermere. Yet the hill is simply a compound of earth and grass. What Wordsworth did with the hill – and what man does in the sexual act – is to read it as a statement of meaning.

The theory of symbolic response . . . asserts that except for 'consciousness' there would be no response from the world. Science continues to investigate the world 'out there', and believes that one day, when it has enough facts and formulae, the universe will be 'explained'. The theory of symbolic response declares that even when every inch of the universe 'out there' has been mapped and compressed into formulae, the key will still be missing, for the key is 'in here'; is an inner purpose that imposes responses on the outside world.[10]

This is the heart of Wilson's sexology. Sex is not to be explained in terms of 'facts'. If it is to be comprehended, it must be by synthesis rather than by analysis. Its 'meaning' is not to be sought in externals. It does not even rest upon a response to something 'out there'. Its centre is an interior purpose that is cooperating with the evolutionary drive. Sex points us beyond civilisation. Our sexual energy corresponds to the beauty we see in the hill: both evoke our finally becoming human.

Meaning is not a thing in itself. Meaning points to relationships. In the sexual act, brimming over as it is with meaning, the fundamental relationship is *not* between the participating partners but between the individuals they are and the individuals they are striving to become. According to Wilson, 'sex is a projection of the evolutionary intentionality'.[11]

In the work of the German novelist and playwright Frank Wedekind, Wilson finds a sexual mysticism that hints at something of his own view of the sexual impulse. In his short story, *The Burning of Egliswyl*, Wedekind records the history of a young man whose first sexual encounter takes place at the invitation of a young woman, when he is nineteen. News of his sexual initiation is conveyed by the girl to her friends and they pursue the man with a view to their own satisfaction. He meets their needs and enters into a life of intense sexual activity. Eventually, when he is invited into the room of a chambermaid named Marie, he finds himself impotent. In a blind rage at his predicament, he sets fire to the village. Wedekind has him tell us: 'I howled and shrieked like an animal in a slaughterhouse. And all I could see was flames.' He is arrested and placed in prison where, from time to time, he experiences fits of madness and has to be placed in a straitjacket.

In the man's wild dance around the burning village, Wedekind has provided us with a dramatic symbol of the power of sex. At a first reading, it seems that Wedekind is arguing that sex is a destructive force in which mankind is enveloped but, placed in the context of his whole literary production, it becomes clear that the story is concerned with sex as an elemental force that is intended to drive us forward. It is destructive only to the extent that we misunderstand its nature. In an essay entitled 'On the Erotic,' Wedekind speaks of 'flesh having its own spirit' and of the sexual act as a 'gymnastics of the spirit'. It is clear that for Wedekind, the sexual impulse was full of purpose. Far from being a tender passion, it had an explosive force that could destroy the walls within which man finds himself enclosed. Wilson summarises Wedekind's work thus:

> Altogether, Wedekind is unique. As an artist, he may lack the warmth and humanity of D. H. Lawrence but his sexual vision is in every way clearer. No other European writer has paid such homage to the sexual urge. He exalts it, not as the 'solar plexus' or the 'dark force' but as the most naked expression of the power house, the force of life. Spiritually, Wedekind is Nietzsche's twin brother.[12]

In his important book, *Sex and the Intelligent Teenager* – a title which should never have been allowed to go out of print – Wilson has provided us with a brief but useful history of sex. He points out that for primitive people, there was no essential relationship between sex and childbearing. Sex was simply a pleasurable interchange between people and by and large each was free to couple with whomever they wished. A sense of tribalism minimised the presence of jealousy and what today would be called promiscuity was then regarded as the norm.

This primitive sexuality began to alter with the emergence of imagination. As men began to dream, so there emerged models for social organisation and tribes began to establish hierarchies. The more sophisticated members of the tribe demanded preferential treatment and began to define a territory for themselves that included a harem of women to whom access by others was denied. With the complexification of mental activity, sex became a heightened function and since it was the male who acquired knowledge – the woman was regarded as the home-keeper – male homosexuality became more apparent. The Greek aristocracy was a male enclave which shared mathematics and philosophical notions and it seemed entirely appropriate that they should share their bodies. Wilson points out that the Hebrews, subjected as they were to a repressive religious sense, had strong taboos against homosexuality. The absence of science and art from their culture was matched by an unimaginative sexuality.

With the emergence of an aggressive Roman empire, sexuality took on an assertive nature. In many ways, the erect penis served as a symbol of the Roman world – a representation of coarse vitality and a powerful urge to dominate. Sexuality lost the sophisticated, spiritual character that it had for the Greeks. Homosexuality remained prominent but it lost its idealistic rationale and became a means of satisfying a crude lust. Yet the Romans fiercely defended the institution of marriage. In an age when children were important to the development of the empire, the woman was jealously protected and adultery was regarded as a serious crime.

With the rise of Christianity, the human attitude towards its own sexuality underwent a revolution. Christianity was the creation of an age and a people which were deeply discontented. Roman oppression and materialistic values were the central facts of Jewish experience at the time. The old religion was proving to be inadequate in redressing their plight. So pessimistic were they that they thought in terms of the end of the world and the central fact about Christianity was its eschatology – its theory that God was about to destroy the world and reward the faithful. In preparation for this, sexual licence was to be brought under control and life 'purified'. The message of Jesus was a tract for the times.

Following George Bernard Shaw, Wilson sees historic Christianity as the product of Paul of Tarsus. By elevating Jesus as the son of God and developing a doctrine that Jesus was the 'Christ' who had died to save mankind, Paul was ministering to a prevalent need. A belief in a Christ made it easier for people to face the backlash that came from Rome and to accept their fate as martyrs in the Roman coliseums. It was Paul who gave Christianity much of its anti-sex content, in a puritanical crusade against the phallic component of Roman and other religions. It was probably also the case that Paul himself shared his people's negative and repressive attitude towards sex.

With the embrace of Christianity by Constantine in AD 312,

the sexuality that had been suppressed by Jewish Christians began to re-emerge. Sex and religion began to intermingle as they had done earlier. Women entering convents became 'brides of Christ' and there can be little doubt that many of them in fact became the equivalent of temple prostitutes. It was an unhappy alliance that was to lead eventually to witch-hunts and other sexual aberrations that were chilling in their intensity.

Wilson sees Christianity as a dead religion but he does not underrate its value. The Christian doctrines had the effect of enriching the human mind by directing it towards higher values and models for personal development. It was largely through his experience of Christianity that man came to learn that it was possible to change human character and social structures so that the evolutionary drive is facilitated. It was also largely as a result of Christianity that man came to understand that in a fully human world, there had to be a correspondence between the world at large and man's inner experience.

Wilson sees a close relationship between the contemporary world and that into which Christianity was introduced. Now, as then, there is a fundamental discontent with the quality of life. The prevailing values are recognised – privately if not publicly, as being inadequate in terms of satisfying the most fundamental human needs. The times are sadly 'out of joint' and there is a deep desire for renewal. Just as Jesus appeared in what was called 'the Kairos' – the 'fullness of time', so Wilson argues that our age is ripe for a new religion but it is not a revised Christianity that he advocates. He uses the word 'religion' to mean a new set of ideas, of standards, of values, that will continue the thrust forward that was provided two thousand years ago by the ideas that are associated with Jesus.

Our age is characterised by a breakdown in morality that is akin to the collapse of values in the Roman world. The abuse of human sexuality is one of the most prevailing *symptoms* of this breakdown. With the emancipation of women, they too are being drawn into the sexual malaise. All are swept up in the sexual revolution. Sexual aberration and sex-related crime are proliferating at an astonishing rate. Yet, Wilson tells his young readers, the central fact about this proliferation is the fact that it is symbolic. The cause lies outside the sexual impulse itself. In pointing to that cause, Wilson writes as a critic of the future looking back at our own age.

Their civilization had become so complicated that they didn't know whether they were standing on their heads or their heels. They were too clever and well-educated to be kept in place by priests and kings, but all their cleverness did not give them *a sense of purpose*. And the main thing we notice about them is that they seemed at a loose end – strangely bored and exhausted. In 1914 they had one of the greatest wars in history – nearly nine million people died – and you would have thought that this would really have woken them up to the advantage of a sense of purpose. But no, it only made them plunge into an orgy of forgetfulness – the jazz age. The same thing happened again a mere twenty-five years later. A half-insane power maniac, already suffering from venereal disease, set out to conquer Europe. This time the total losses were fifteen million. When the power maniac was defeated the whole world went wild with delight. You would have thought – *now* their civilization will become really great. *This* will turn them into serious men with a purpose. But no. The politicians went on squabbling. The new jazz age was the television age, the age of *Lolita* and James Bond, of heroin and marihuana. Violence, suicide, insanity, sex crime reached a new height.[13]

Wilson notes that in the Communist countries, particularly Russia and China, where there is a dominant social purpose, traditional sexual standards are much better preserved than in countries that have turned away from, or failed to recognise, a sense of purpose. The United States may be pervaded by violence, crime, drug abuse and sexual aberration, primarily because it lacks a unifying sense of purpose such as it had two centuries ago when it was struggling to establish itself as a nation.

In Japan, where the social order is everywhere present, sexuality is taken for granted. Masturbation is not associated with the sense of guilt that tends to be attached to it in English-speaking countries. A Japanese father may well take his pubescent son to a brothel as a birthday gift to mark his becoming a man. Because of the openly available sex, pornography is not a social problem in Japan. The postwar Americanisation of that country has had the effect of introducing a degree of prudery but nonetheless the culture remains fundamentally free in sexual matters. If there is a sexual tension, it is largely within the Japanese male who is regarded as the keystone of the family and who feels himself under some pressure to fill his role with a high degree of honour. Where emotional immaturity exists in Japan, it is not directly related to sexuality but rather to interpersonal relationships, among and across the sexes, in which social status must be acknowledged and preserved.

Sexuality in Sweden reflects much of that country's culture. A highly advanced society, Sweden has a low unemployment rate. Its penal code is advanced to the stage where most of its prisons are open. There is virtually no censorship and sexually explicit literature has long been freely available. There is a casual approach to sex and one of the standard jokes of the culture is 'That was nice. What's your name?' Yet Sweden has the highest suicide rate in the world. This, contends Wilson, is to be explained not in terms of sexual abuse, but in terms of the level of comfort that prevails. Without a purpose that steels the will, boredom arises and when the common divertisements, such as sexual activity, no longer contain the element of interaction with an alienness that keeps the mind alive, the boredom produces a self-destructive urge.

Wilson's brief history and cultural overview of sex serves his philosophic purpose well. It illustrates that sexuality is not the central fact about man but that man adjusts his attitudes towards his own sexuality in response to the circumstances in which he finds himself. A preoccupation with sex has the effect of diverting man from his more fundamental responsibility: to identify a purpose to which he can commit himself. When such a purpose is identified, sexuality fits into place in the total scheme of things. Sexuality, in itself, is best understood as an indication that man may project himself forward into a fuller state of being.

Before leaving *Sex and the Intelligent Teenager*, it is worth noting that in its final chapter, 'Sex and the Future', Wilson firmly ties the sexual impulse to the evolutionary drive. He reports the case of one of Maslow's patients, a young woman who had been forced to give up college in order to help support her family. She took a position in an ice-cream factory where the pay was good and the work easy. Over a period of months, however, she became more and more depressed without knowing why. She ceased menstruating. It was when she began to feel suicidal that she was referred to Maslow. Had he been a Freudian, Maslow would have dealt with the sexual symptom – the failure in menstruation – and helped her to identify a sexual problem. Maslow, however, took a different approach. He simply suggested that the girl enrol in an evening course. Within a week of resuming study, the symptoms of her 'illness' disappeared. Maslow's prescription was based on his certainty that the sexual drive is not the central unifying force in an individual's life. Human beings have a more fundamental need for knowledge – for participation in the evolutionary drive. Wilson summarises what he has tried to say in his advice to teenagers:

> What I have suggested . . . is the logical next step [to Maslow's insight]. I have tried to show that the sexual drive itself is not a mere instinct of self-preservation. It goes far beyond that. It is part of man's 'poet-drive', his 'god-drive'. It cannot be understood except as part of this urge of man to become something more than man. And the sexual sickness of our own time, the increasing tendency to promiscuity and sexual violence, cannot be understood except in the light of this strange need to become more than man.[14]

Wilson first heard of Charlotte Bach in the autumn of 1971, when she posted to him a manuscript with the title *Homo Mutans, Homo Luminens* – Man the Changer, Man the Lightbringer. The manuscript set out an extraordinary thesis on human sexual aberration, particularly that aspect of it known as transvestism. Wilson wrestled with the manuscript and realised that it set out a profound insight into the relationship between sex and evolution. He arranged to meet Charlotte and learned something of the story of her life. She had been born in Hungary, from which country she fled to England following the Communist takeover in 1948. In her new homeland, she set about compiling a dictionary of psychological terms but as she worked her way through the sexual perversions she realised that there was no adequate understanding of what precisely constituted perversion. She had read *Origins of the Sexual Impulse* but had chosen to reject Wilson's theory of symbolic response. In an attempt to solve her problem, she consulted with as many sexual 'perverts' as she could find.

Charlotte's research led her to develop a theory of sexuality in which each person is a compound of the male and the female, much as is suggested by Jung in his theory of the anima and the animus. But Charlotte went further than Jung. She argued that every male has a deep desire to become a woman and every woman a deep wish to become a male. The individual can respond to this desire to be the other by either resisting it or accepting it. Those who resisted, Charlotte called 'denialists' while those who accepted were designated 'asseverationists'.

Charlotte contented that this basic dichotomy led to a classification of human sexuality into eight distinct categories. These ranged through the male positive denialist to the female negative denialist. What Charlotte believed she had achieved was a complete systematising of sexual behaviour. Further, she was convinced that there was zoological evidence that supported her theory. She read Desmond Morris' account of the male stickleback, which changes colour and pretends to be a female in order to gain sexual recognition. Significantly, when the stickleback engages in this 'aberration', there is an interference to the reproductive system of the species and a consequent strengthening of the more dominant strain of stickleback. Charlotte was convinced that human sexuality was essentially an instrument of evolution.

Charlotte took one further step. After reading an account of shamanism by Mircea Eliade, she was persuaded that the objective of evolution is to rise above both the male and the female, i.e., above sexuality. Such a condition was the essential characteristic of the shaman and religious mystic. In great artists such as Beethoven, Michelangelo or Leonardo, the opposing sexual tension had been built up to a point where it expressed itself as a powerful creative urge that produced great music or great painting. 'Perversion', for Charlotte, was the condition in which these opposing forces either refused to acknowledge each other or retained a mutually hostile attitude towards each other.

There was something in Charlotte herself that puzzled Wilson. Having worked to comprehend her sexual theory, he found that he could not locate her within it. She did not fit into any of the categories she had identified. The truth became known upon her death from cancer of the liver in 1981. She died in her home and when her corpse was taken to the morgue and undressed, it was discovered that her brassiere was padded and that she had a penis. Charlotte Bach was the *alter ego* of Carl Hajdu.

Under the guise of Charlotte, Hajdu had written an autobiographical novel entitled *Fiona*. The novel revealed the following facts. Hajdu had been born in Budapest in 1920 to a working-class background. He was an intellectually precocious child whose sexual awakening came comparatively early. He began masturbating at ten and had his first full sexual encounter with a prostitute when he was fifteen. He demonstrated a criminal tendency by regularly engaging in acts of theft from stores and elsewhere. After an unsuccessful period in the Budapest University, Hajdu joined the Hungarian army and, following a collaboration between the Hungarians and the Germans, was attached for a period to the German SS. There is every likelihood that during this service he killed a young soldier, who had stopped him to check his papers, by shooting him in the back of the head as he walked away. Hajdu was almost executed when he was suspected of aiding two English soldiers but was saved by the end of the war. In 1947 he was again in trouble with the Communist authorities – the reason is obscure – and served a period in prison. The following year, he left Hungary, travelling through Austria to England.

Hajdu's transvestism had begun following a normal sexual encounter. After having sex with a girl, he lay on the bed watching her make coffee. He covered himself with the girl's silk dressing gown to keep himself warm but soon found that the touch of the silk had a sexual effect. A year later, he began dressing in female underclothes and masturbating with, he was to write later, 'a hitherto unexperienced intensity of personal involvement'. Soon, female underwear was an adequate substitute for a girl herself.

Hajdu remained capable of sex with women. In London, he married a woman named Phyllis after she became pregnant to him. In 1964, he set up an apartment in Mayfair and began a life of aggressive sexual seduction. He had a prolonged affair with a woman he called Fiona but eventually she left him because of his promiscuity and he returned to his wife. Phyllis, however, was to die shortly afterwards in an operating theatre. When his stepson was killed in a motor accident a week later, Hajdu underwent a mental collapse which was to change him into Charlotte Bach. Yet he never completely surrendered himself to Charlotte. He worked as a male journalist named Michael Karoly and one of his prized possessions, which he showed to many of his friends and which was published in an early 1988 edition of London's *Private Eye* magazine, was a photographic montage which showed Charlotte and Karoly together, striking the pose of a married couple.

Hajdu, as Charlotte, isolated himself in his Highgate flat and began to run up considerable debts that were eventually to lead him to serve another short term in prison. There is no account of his incarceration but it would be useful to know how he protected himself in the prison environment and what personality he projected to his fellow prisoners.

In addressing – and evaluating – Charlotte Bach's theory of sexuality, Wilson writes:

> Charlotte's theory is in entire agreement with Goethe's statement that the eternal feminine draws us upward and on – or, rather, that the conflict between the eternal feminine and the eternal masculine draws us upward and on. Her theory of evolution can be compared to Newton's theory of gravitation. Newton accounted for the movement of heavenly bodies by assuming the existence of a force called gravity. . . . In Charlotte's theory, the opposition of the male and female is the force of gravity. And because we are alive and kicking – the kicking is especially important – the conflict produces evolution.
>
> This was not all – not by a long way. Charlotte came to believe that alchemy – with its basic emphasis on the male and female principles – was an ancient knowledge system based on the same recognition; but since the ancients knew nothing about Newton or Einstein or cybernetics or displacement activities or neotony, they had to express their intuitive insights symbolically. Jung was correct, she believed, in seeing alchemy as the repository of an ancient wisdom (although he failed to grasp what it is all about). The 'philosopher's stone' is the capacity for the eight-hour orgasm and for even higher mystical experiences. When man learns to understand his own dual nature, he will also learn to use it to power his own evolution, exactly as he uses an electric current, which alternates between positive and negative, to light his cities. When he understands the cause of his self-division, he will learn to control his polarities to create intensities of mind which modern man only glimpses in the sexual orgasm.[15]

Wilson is not pursuaded by the theory of transvestism propounded by Charlotte Bach. He points out that in a complex civilization, there is an artificial heightening of sexual desire. Thus, young people are attracted to the opposite sex well before the social mores are willing to condone their initiation into sexual experience. In such a situation, the sexual energy spills over. As the psychologists would say, a displacement occurs. Objects – female underwear, a glossy magazine photograph, even the lyrics of a salacious popular song – are invested with a sexual character that has the capacity to gratify our sexual needs at least temporarily. And the more intense the displacement, the more compelling its attraction for us. Wilson reminds us of the gluttonous Dr Johnson, who spilled food over his chest in a frantic effort to scoop it into his mouth. Johnson explained to Mrs Thrale that his behaviour was a result of the scarcity of food when he was a poor student. Displacement of the sexual desire produces a more frantic level of response.

Yet Charlotte's theory does highlight an important aspect of sexual experience. Wilson concludes:

> It seems to me that her insight into human evolution is fundamentally sound. According to Darwin, man has climbed the evolutionary ladder because of the pressure of circumstance; starvation and misery have prodded him on from below. This is obviously true to some extent. But Charlotte recognizes that he has also been 'lured' on from above, by a pressure of a desire for what might be called 'the ideal sexual experience'. We all observe that the reality of sexual intercourse is far from perfect; yet that does not convince us that sex is a greatly overrated occupation. Every time a man glimpses a pretty girl pulling up her stocking, he catches a glimpse of what might be called the 'primal sexual vision'. It is unfortunate that there seems to be a certain disparity between us like a will-o'-the-wisp, luring us into tormented effort. It can lead novelists to write novels, poets to write poems and musicians to write symphonies.[16].

In his attempt to understand Carl Hajdu, as distinct from Charlotte Bach, Wilson makes use of his theory of criminality. Hajdu's essential characteristic was the personality streak that is found in the criminal mind. The relevant image, in this context, is provided by Dostoevsky. Dostoevsky's fiction reveals what many critics have called an 'obsession' with guilt and shame. The internal evidence of his novels suggest a possible cause, for again and again they deal with the theme of paedophilia. In *The Possessed*, Stavrogin recounts how he seduced a young girl then did nothing to prevent her suicide. In *Crime and Punishment*, Svidrigailov has also raped a child who then killed herself. In his 'confession', Stavrogin acknowledges that he once stole from a poor clerk for the purpose of discovering whether he could feel a sense of shame. Perhaps Hajdu belongs to this same category. Having possibly killed a man, and having lived the life of a kleptomaniac and sexual deviant, perhaps his behaviour is to be understood as an attempt to expiate his sense of guilt and shame. Like Dostoevsky, he sought to utilise his self-disgust and division as an instrument of creativity, but while Dostoevsky produced literary master-pieces, Hajdu could bring into existence nothing more than a pathetic – albeit interesting – Charlotte Bach.

The Misfits is subtitled *A Study of Sexual Outsiders* and this subtitle helps to place the work in Wilson's *œuvre*. It is clearly a volume that belongs to the Outsider cycle for it deals with the same problems and solutions as are detailed in that cycle. In its treatment of Lord Byron, it exposes the inadequacies of Romanti-cism and highlights the need for a new treatment of human misery and grandeur. The theme is by now a familiar one and can be recapitulated simply.

In our common experience, our senses reveal only the world of the immediately present. That is to say that we see only a part of the real world. To compensate for this limited view, we supplement our senses with the faculties of memory and imagination. Memory evokes our past for us and when the present is dull or too threatening, we can escape from it into yesterday. Imagination takes us into other times and other places, even our own future, so that it too complements the picture we have in our minds of the present. It is as if, through memory and imagin-ation, we can be in two places at the one time. Wilson illustrates this with a picture of a man sitting beside a fire in a warm room, looking through the window at the driving snow falling outside. Without leaving the room, he can travel through the storm to meet a friend or to grasp an idea that lies recorded in a book in a library miles away. What is important here is that the journey through the snow is not just imaginary; it is *real*. It is a demon-stration of what Pierre Janet called 'the reality function'. It is only when this reality function is fully invoked that we experience ourselves as being fully alive and happy.

Our fundamental problem lies in the feeble strength of our reality function. We allow ourselves to be trapped in the present – in an awareness of what is merely present. This is nowhere more evident than in our sexual experience. Byron seduces a woman and in so doing concentrates on the act of possessing her. Immediately he has completed the act, he experiences a sense of frustration because he has not satisfied the reality principle. Thus he proceeds to another woman – and another, all the while failing to grasp what is there to be grasped – a far more efficient reality function that would burst into a sensation of perpetual delight and satisfaction. Sexual restlessness is an expression of a feeble imagination; a failure to stimulate the reality function. And it is based on the error of believing that the reality function can be produced by something 'out there' – by a woman, or a feminine undergarment. The reality function takes place within us or it does not take place at all. As Wilson points out:

> Barbusse's Outsider is more stimulated by watching a girl undressing through a hole in the wall than in going to bed with a real woman (admittedly a prostitute). De Sade and Byron needed the smell of 'forbiddenness' to enjoy sex. Brothels often cater for men who have a fixation on schoolgirls or nurses or governesses. All are attempting to achieve erection – not just of the penis, but of the reality function – through a kind of play-acting. We seem to be dealing with a laughable absurdity, a kind of schoolboy howler.[17]

This interpretation of sexual behaviour exposes the reason for the collapse of Romanticism. It simply lacked a vital reality function. In the final analysis, it did not believe its own dream and allowed itself to fall back into a waking consciousness that was pervaded with problems and pain. The world that was 'too much with' the Romantics could have been transformed into a living paradise through the cultivation of a highly developed reality function. This is the message of our sexual experience and this is the task for contemporary man. This is, at the one time, the objective and the nature of the evolutionary drive.

In a determined attempt to make his point, Wilson reiterates it over and over, using different images and allusions:

> It comes back to Dr Johnson's remark that when a man knows he is to be hanged in a fortnight, it concentrates his mind wonderfully. Sex also concentrates the mind wonderfully and that is why civilized man is so obsessed by it. It enables him

to 'savour every fraction of an inch', not merely of the act of sexual intercourse but of living itself.

But that, of course, only underlines the basic problem: that after coitus, man becomes sad, because he quickly returns to his unconcentrated and defocussed state. In sexual excitement, it is as if the spirit itself becomes erect, and becomes capable of penetrating the meaning of life. Normal consciousness is limp and flaccid; its attitude towards reality is defensive. This is what Sartre called 'contingency', that feeling of being at the mercy of chance. And this is the problem that in *The Outsider*, I had called 'original sin'. [Man's] endless sexual encounters are an attempt to escape his sense of contingency.[18]

There is perhaps no better example in the twentieth century of the failure to grasp the nature of the sexual impulse, than that provided by the behaviour of Paul Tillich. Tillich, a religious socialist who was driven out of Germany when he began to be critical of the rise of the Nazi party, is arguably the most important – and impressive – theologian of our age. His monumental *Systematic Theology* is a deeply moving statement of Christian faith but it is also one of the most profound expressions of sustained intellectual effort ever written. Its central argument is that man is in a paradoxical situation which can only be redressed through a series of correlations. Because it is a Christian argument, it insists that the ultimate correlation that must be achieved is that between existential man and God through Jesus as the Christ. Tillich displays a profound insight into the human predicament and a resolute passion in his quest for human wholeness.

In the United States, where he settled after fleeing from Germany, Tillich was a revered figure on theological campuses. There were critics who believed that he had produced a theology that was too closely associated with Existentialism and psychological theories, but even his opponents were willing to acknowledge that he represented a formidable intellectual integrity.

Eight years after his death in 1965, Tillich's wife published an account of his life which revealed a man who had not been recognised by the public at large. Paulus, as his wife called him, had spent a lifetime tormented by an intense sexuality. He collected hard pornography and hid it between the leaves of religious books while he read it. He was thoroughly promiscuous and pursued women with an undeviating intensity. Hannah, his wife, was fully aware of his philandering and was shocked at the length to which her husband was prepared to go in denying what she knew to be true. When she actually watched him with one of her female friends and later challenged him with his infidelity, he denied it with such vehemence that Hannah wondered whether she had actually seen what she had.

Hannah sought to help Tillich. At one stage, in order to encourage him to confront his immature need, she actually offered him a pornographic magazine. Tillich flew into a rage at the suggestion that he should want such a thing. What Wilson has told us about 'alienness' helps us understand this tantrum. What Tillich sought was the forbiddenness of sex. Sex in the open was totally unsatisfactory to him. Wilson evaluated Tillich's behaviour as follows:

> Does this mean that Tillich's religion was a fraud? No one who has read him could believe that. It means merely that he kept his religious beliefs and his sexual obsessions in separate compartments. The adult part of him wrote books to show how the existential misery of fallen man can be abolished through Jesus as the Christ: the childish part seduced his students and the wives of friends, and had screaming tantrums on the floor if he was found out. There was no real attempt at 'individuation', at growing up, because he found the two compartment system pleasant and convenient. He was convinced that indulging the naughty child in himself made no difference to his philosophy – he probably told himself that he could think even better after a little adultery. Yet his attitude is bound to raise doubts in the minds of those who wish to assess his importance as a thinker. Is it not, for example, inevitable that a man who cannot keep his hands off his female students will emphasize human helplessness and man's inability to resist sin, and throw the whole burden of salvation on Jesus as the Christ? Such reflections, at all events, raise doubts about Tillich's reliability as a spiritual guide and teacher.[19]

Tillich's predilection for 'dirty books' provides an opportunity to comment on Wilson's attitude towards pornography. He expresses it in an essay entitled 'Literature and Pornography' in Alan Bold's *The Sexual Dimension in Literature*. Wilson begins his essay with two quotations; both descriptions of the sexual act. In one sense there is little to distinguish between them. Both are realistic attempts to describe the bodily functions and the mental sensations that accompany them. In both cases, the female is essentially submissive. In both the essential pleasure seems to be the prerogative of the male, although there is a stirring of desire in both females. The first passage is taken from Lawrence's *Lady Chatterley's Lover* while the second is from a famous German novel called *Josephine Mutzenbacher*. Neither passage contained any language that could be considered offensive, yet Wilson defines the Lawrence extract as literature while the other he calls pornography.

The essential difference between the two passages becomes apparent when Wilson tells us that while the first deals with partners who are sexually, if not socially, equal, in Constance Chatterley and the gamekeeper Mellors, the second passage involves a man and his daughter. Instantly we are aware that in the second passage we are in the realm of 'alienness', the forbidden. The first is a description of a mutual search for sexual realisation: the second is an account of abuse.

In fact, Wilson contends, there is an even more fundamental distinction between the two passages that has to do with the intention of the writer. Lawrence is attempting to give shape to a profound human condition. He is artistically engaged in a sensitive examination of the roots of his own being. He is exposing himself to his reader in an endeavour to highlight some aspect of the universality of the sexual urge. The author of the second passage has no such objective. The passage has been written to titillate the sexual urge. It is written with the express purpose of facilitating masturbation. This is what makes it pornographic. While literature *may* excite lust, it has a higher purpose. Pornography does not. Wilson rejects it by comparing it with another form of abuse.

> The real objection to pornography can be seen if we transfer it to another field. Let us suppose that some writer of extreme political views – say, a hatred of all immigrants – wrote a series of books in which the hero walks around the streets, continually losing his temper with the objects of his dislike and inflicting various forms of punishment on them. 'His hand shot out and grabbed the old woman by the throat. Her scowl changed to an expression of terror. Slowly, inexorably, his steely fingers closed, until her face became purple and her eyes stuck out like

marbles. "I'll teach you to insult a good patriot", he murmured softly, and his knee crunched into her crotch'. We would all agree that a book that contained dozens of episodes like this – whose whole aim was to give expression to rage and disgust – would be socially injurious. No one denies that it can also be injurious to bottle up anger and frustration. But to systematically allow it full expression would be negative. By encouraging people to engage in this kind of daydream, it would damage their adjustment to reality; it would incubate paranoia.[20]

Wilson has identified another essential component of pornography. It is in its very nature, an association of the sexual energy with violence of one sort or another. At one level, it points to a violation of the physical being of another person. This is why, in pornography, the sexual detail is critical. The writer and the reader dwell on the 'quivering flesh' and the dimensions of the male organ because they are the heart of the violation. At a further remove, pornography deals with sadism and with masochism, with leather belts and chains because they represent weapons that effect submission. Yet further out is the violent sexual act that ends with murder. In the final analysis, pornography is based on a confusion about the essential nature of the sexual impulse.

In an important essay which serves as the Introduction to Robert Ollendorff's book, *Juvenile Homosexual Experience*, Wilson provides a useful study of the relationship between individual sexuality and the society in which it exists. Ollendorff, a brother-in-law and in many ways an intellectual colleague of Wilhelm Reich, developed a view of what he called 'the sick society'. In such a society, neurosis is passed from person to person by a kind of magnetism. Social mores prohibit the expression of a natural sexuality among adolescents, at the very time when it is at its most powerful. As a consequence, many young people direct their sexuality towards members of the same sex and the roots of homosexuality are established. Homosexuality, then, which Ollendorff correctly identified as being much more prevalent in the modern world than society seems willing to admit, is a product of 'conditioning'. Because it works at the point where the sexual energy is most insistent, it is embraced as a suitable form of behaviour for the remainder of the individual's life. The fundamental problem of homosexuality does not lie, then, in itself but in the fact that it prevents the individual from continuing a pattern of normal sexual growth. It is very likely a product of an authoritarian society, epitomised in a repressive father figure, who make the life of the growing adolescent more difficult than it need be. The answer to the problem, suggests Ollendorff, may lie in a 'children's liberation movement' which leads to a more responsible attitude towards the emerging sexuality of the pubescent child.

The concept of children's liberation must be clearly understood. It is not a movement aimed at the abolition of school and the institution of four Christmasses each year. It is an attempt to facilitate the 'further maturation of the personality, mentally, physically and biologically'.

It is easy to see why Ollendorf's theory should appeal to Wilson. It is concentrated, not on a Freudian notion of repression or the dominance of a libido but on a positive view of the development of personality.

> When Ollendorff analyses these [social] factors, he induces an odd feeling of optimism, for you sense that he feels they are absurdities. . . . In fact, you may feel that some of his ideas are too simplistic to provide a solution to the problem – for example, children's rights; but somehow, that is not of ultimate importance. What is important about Ollendorff is his sense of reality, the intensity with which he raises questions and demands an answer, the feeling of being engaged in the constructive discussion of major problems, the sense of intellectual boldness.[21]

The essence of Ollendorff's psychology of the homosexual is the assumption that human beings are not fundamentally violent, criminal or perverse. It is Wilson's contention that in generally recognising this fact, man will have moved a long way forward towards the healing of the sick society. For Wilson, Ollendorff's work is a demonstration that a healthy mind can be established and sustained through an intelligent idealism.

Inevitably, in the minds of some readers, Wilson's sexology will suggest a mysticism. In fact, in its examination of sexually different human beings, *The Misfits* reveals that sexual misfits themselves are close to a form of mysticism. By and large, what they are attempting to achieve is a bolder, fuller, richer grasp of life. The quality of life that Nietzsche called 'Dionysian' is at the heart of the sexual impulse. The Australian musician and sexual masochist, Percy Grainger, did not distinguish between his athleticism, his Nietzscheanism, his sexuality, his sado-masochistic urges and his Dionysian lust for life. These were not separate elements for him but part and parcel of the one force that drove him forward. Thus he could write:

I love being driven like a beaten slave to sex, art, activity, sensuality. No freedom for me – give me the brutal tyranny of some relentless blind urge, and I don't mind being mashed up between two or three grinding away at once if I get the chance.[22]

And Wilson comments:

So when Grainger thought of warriors charging into battle, or of healthy bodies diving into cold water, or of tremendous natural forces, he experienced what he valued above all: the feeling of a vital current that raised him to a higher level of vitality. His sadism was in fact a kind of mysticism. But this insight makes us instantly aware that this is the essential key to *all* sexual aberrations. They are all an attempt to achieve a higher level of vitality. It is as if a man felt like an underpowered electric light-bulb that scarcely gives off enough light to read by; but then, in certain moments, the bulb blazes with a radiance that lights the darkest corner of the room. Understandably, those who have experienced it feel it to be worth any sacrifice.[23]

But to say that sexual aberration is a form of mystical experience is simply to comprehend it, not to justify it. Mystical though it might be, perversity is an immature sexual response. It is comparable to the greedy child who thrusts his hand into the bowl of sweets and tries to scoop up every last one. It is an exaggeration of the attempt to satisfy the need. And, in the final analysis, the sweets churn in the stomach until it has to expel them in an act of violent rejection. The human body was not intended to endure overlarge doses of sugar.

It was the mystic poet, William Blake who wrote:

Five windows light the cavern'd Man: through one he
   breathes the air;

Through one hears music of the spheres; through one the
    eternal vine
Flourishes, that he may receive the grape; through one can
    look
And see small portions of the external world that ever
    groweth;
Through one himself pass out what time he please; but he
    will not
For stolen joys are sweet and bread eaten in secret pleasant.

Man's fifth sense – the fifth window – is imagination. For those
individuals in whom it remains dormant and uncultivated, there
is a profound deprivation of the most stimulating aspect of human
experience. When man develops his imagination, as he did in the
invention of drama and in the novel, the *whole* of his world
becomes open to him. One of the most profound problems facing
man in the modern age, is his refusal to let his imagination have
free rein. We are still apt to believe that 'stolen joys are sweet';
that 'bread eaten in secret [is] pleasant'. We close ourselves up
and try to satisfy ourselves with that which reaches us through
the four physical senses. This is what is at the heart of contemporary sexual confusion. Whereas a person like de Sade indulged in
daydreams which were lurid but essentially harmless because they
remained dreams, modern man has continued to dream of sexual
conquest but has taken the additional step of converting his most
bizarre dreams into reality and turning to actual rape and other
forms of personal violence to assuage his need for more.

It is central to the sexology of Wilson that infinitely more is
there for the taking: but not through rape or the deliberate abuse
of another human being. The component that we recognise as
being absent from our experience is available to us through our
imagination; through an imaginative grasp of our own potential.
In Wilson's terms:

This is the real significance of the imaginative revolution that
is the subject of *The Misfits* . . . In sexual ecstasy the misfits
(discussed there) caught glimpses of a godlike consciousness.
They made the simple and obvious mistake of thinking that
the key to such states lay in the sexual urge. But even before
the age of Romanticism, the work of de Sade had made it clear
that it is not so. The sexual urge derives its strength from the

body and the emotions, and is not powerful enough to lift us to a new level of conscious awareness. This can be achieved only with the aid of the intellect. Those who have attempted to use sex as a rocket fuel to escape the body's gravitational field have always come crashing back to earth. *This* is the real objection to the Charlotte Bach theory of evolution. Even allowing for the 'ritualization' of deviations, it still remains an inadequate mechanism for evolution.

When, on the other hand, we grasp the full significance of the imaginative revolution, it becomes clear that this provides a basic mechanism for evolution. If, for example, we regard the peculiar behaviour of the stickleback – the male performing the female courting dance – as a crude attempt to use imagination to overcome frustration, then we can also see that such an ability has an evolutionary value; a creature that can 'let off steam' in this way is fitter to survive than a creature that goes half mad with frustration.[24]

When careful consideration is given to the effort of individual researchers to understand human sexuality, it becomes clear that they have remained too close to their own sexual experience to be able to achieve a truly objective view. In the final analysis, this might not matter as much as we think. At this stage in our development, the attempt to understand may be more important than the theories that are developed. It is only in comparatively recent times that humanity has achieved the tools that make the examination possible. Intelligence is at our disposal in a way that it never was before. Our scientific techniques are more advanced. Our powers of observation are more highly developed. We are learning more and more about the power of introspection and more and more of the nature of the human mind. But above all, we are beginning to comprehend that our imagination is one of the most important instruments we have at our disposal for delineating our own essential nature. We are only now beginning to understand that we are not imprisoned in a meaningless world but free to explore the furthest reaches of our own nature.

What makes our situation even more exciting is the newly acquired evidence which suggests that what we are currently leaning about ourselves will pass easily into universal consciousness. Following the work of William McDougall in the 1920s and that of Rupert Sheldrake more recently, there is reason to suppose that new knowledge acquired in one generation becomes an intrinsic awareness in the next. This theory of 'morphic resonance' – with its contention that learning jumps across space and time through a process that is akin to an iron bar picking up the electrical field of a coil of wire and converting it into a magnet – is an important reassurance to any forward-looking species but it is also a challenge to the existing generation to address its problems as intelligently as it can, for in so doing it is contributing to the ongoing evolutionary purpose. An appreciation of our own sexual nature is a pressing necessity.

Man need not be unduly concerned that he experiences his sexual nature as an inner tension. It is precisely because it is a tension that it has the capacity to direct us beyond ourselves. We may think of our sexual energy as a new language. When a child wrestles with the task of learning a language, he finds it difficult and confusing. As the learning advances and there is a measure of control over the language, the child experiences a sense of achievement and excitement at his capacity to express himself. The analogy suggests that when humanity has learned to use his sexuality wisely and well, it will provide him with new means of projecting his real self-image upon his world. Wilson contends that we are at a point in history that is close to the 'feedback' point. The long struggle that we have had with our sexual tension may be about to reward us by thrusting us forward into a fuller life. When we have come to realise that the ultimate pleasure is not in the act of sex but in the very reality of living, we shall know that we have arrived.

5

The Criminology

OSCAR Wilde observed that while most men live in the gutter, there are some who gaze up and see the stars. Wilson's theories on murder and the criminal mind, which are so developed as to warrant being called a 'Criminology', are to be understood partly within this context. They are expounded in a series of books which are at the one time both terrifying and stimulating, beginning with his three volumes of case histories, moving through his study of assassins and culminating in his monumental, *A Criminal History of Mankind*.

Wilson's first major reflection on crime was entitled 'The Faust Outsider' and was written as a chapter for his first book, *The Outsider*. Because of the size of the completed manuscript, however, Victor Gollancz decided to discard this particular essay but fortunately it has survived, at least in part, as an appendix to the *Encyclopedia of Murder*. This fragment makes it clear that Wilson saw that the character type he had described in his first book, was, under a particular set of conditions, capable of the most heinous crimes. The Dostoevsky creation, the killer Stavrogin, was at but a small remove from Barbusse's character, in *L'Enfer*, who spent his time in a voyeuristic observation of life as it unfolded in the hotel room next to his own. Both have a full comprehension of William Blake's contention that it is better to 'murder an infant in its cradle than nurse unbridled desire'.

Wilson has always been fascinated by murder. As a child, he read the *True Detective* magazines that were handed down to him by older members of his family. His interest was not a morbid attraction; rather, it was a challenge to his intellect which wrestled with the question of why humanity should treat its own kind so brutally. He wondered about what it was that could turn one man into a savage, ruthless killer while his neighbour lived a normal life, fully adjusted to the social mores. It was a question that demanded an answer if an adequate understanding of what it meant to be a human being was to be achieved.

For most people, murder is such a horrible act that it is too dreadful to contemplate. We shun it as we turn from vermin, preferring to pretend that it does not exist or that, if it does, it belongs outside the range of our proper interests. Wilson does not enjoy murder but, acknowledging that a murder is committed somewhere in the world every minute of the day, he refuses to close his mind to it. He is convinced that its study is essential to a complete comprehension of the human condition.

Wilson's first major statement of his theory of murder was published in an essay entitled, 'The Study of Murder', as the introduction to the *Encyclopedia of Murder*. He points out that whereas murder in past centuries was essentially a moral issue, in recent times it has become a psychological and sociological matter. For him, however, it is an existential problem. To begin with, he had assumed that human beings could be divided into two groups; one composed of people like Bertrand Russell, who were rational and a second which was made up of emotional, unthinking people. As he developed, however, he came to see that there was a more important dichotomy. Human beings could be divided into those who could take their everyday existence for granted and encompass it easily and those who, like Van Gogh and Nijinsky, wondered if the suffering and tragedies of life finally outbalanced all great human achievements.

For Wilson, the process by which civilisation develops is a humanisation of our environment. The highest social order is a form of freedom in which human beings escape from the dehumanising forces that dominate a more primitive social order. The highest order of men, it therefore follows, are those who struggle for freedom, especially among the comfortable appurtenances of a developed society. And this provides us with the essential clue that leads to an understanding of the criminal mind.

The criminal is the man who cannot feel at home in his social order but is equally incapable of grasping a measure of freedom. Instead of persisting in the struggle to escape from the sense of meaninglessness that pervades him – which is precisely the ongoing struggle in which the Outsider is engaged – or transmuting his anger into a creative act such as the writing of a poem or a symphony, he succumbs to grasping at any easy solution and gives vent to his frustration in an act of crime. Just as all great art is a bringing to consciousness of a new area of existence, so crime is an attempt to create a new and more meaningful life-space. Viewed from Wilson's point of view, murder is essentially a cry for freedom. For him,

> murder is the meaninglessness of life become dynamic, a dramatization of the hidden futility of life. It is the human act, with all its inherent values, placed upon the microscopic slide where it cannot dissolve into the featureless landscape of all other human acts. The study of murder is not the study of abnormal human nature; it is the study of human nature stained by an act that makes it visible on the microscopic slide.[1]

Murder is also about values.

> (My *Encyclopedia of Murder*) could be regarded as a series of exhibits in a lecture on the meaning of Existentialism. Each case represents fairly clearly, by implication, the way in which a murderer *sees* the world. It is almost as if you could fire at every murderer the question: 'What is the value of life', and get from him the answer in quite precise physical terms: ten pounds, a snub, my wife's infidelity, a broken engagement, etc. And no doubt many murderers in the death cell change their estimate radically, and feel, like Raskolnikov, that they would prefer to live on a narrow ledge forever rather than die at once.
>
> Murder confronts us with this act of decision about the value of life more directly that most human acts.[2]

This existential theory of murder is dramatically illustrated by the murder committed by Nathan Leopold and Richard Loeb in Chicago in 1924. Leopold and Loeb were students at the University of Chicago. It appears that they had a strange relationship which may have been homosexual. Leopold certainly was infatuated with the charm of Loeb while the latter was greatly impressed by Leopold's intelligence. Both came from very wealthy homes and wanted for little. They spent much time discussing the philosophy of Nietzsche and subscribed to his theory of the Superman, with whom they considered themselves to belong, outside the restrictions of any ethic or law. They bolstered their sense of contempt for restrictive codes of behaviour by engaging in several petty crimes but these did not assuage their sense of boredom. Finally, they contracted with each other to commit the perfect murder. Towards the end of May, they picked up a friend of Loeb's younger brother named Bobbie Franks. Once they had him inside the hired car, they struck him repeatedly over the head with a heavy metal chisel so that his skull sustained four fractures. He was then conveyed to a railway culvert where his head was held in swampwater to ensure his death. Hydrochloric acid was poured over his face so that it was badly disfigured. The corpse was pushed into a drainpipe and the entrance covered with weeds.

There was an attempt at a ransom demand but before it was paid the body was found and identified. A pair of glasses were found near the culvert and these, together with the ransom note, were traced to Leopold. Confronted with an accusation by the police, they broke down and confessed, each accusing the other of striking the fatal blows. Despite an impassioned defence by the celebrated attorney, Clarence Darrow, they were convicted and sentenced to jail. Leopold was set free in 1958, long after Loeb had been killed in a prison brawl in 1936.

The luxury in which both murderers lived lowered their threshold of satisfaction. Their intellectual pursuits, fuelled by dreams of a higher level of existence, completed their frustration. Instead of accepting the challenge to develop themselves, they settled for a violent act that exposed their inadequacies to the world. The values they held were not high enough to embrace the sanctity of life. They had no regard for Bobbie Franks and ultimately they had no substantial regard for themselves.

In 1961 Wilson had catalogued three distinct classes of murder. The first of these was the type described above; murder that is committed as a result of a narrowness of the lives of the murderers. This narrowness is accompanied by an absence of imagination, a deficiency which robs murderers of one of the most powerful means of escaping from the narrowness that closes in on them. The second class of murder is comparatively rare. It is the murder occasioned by a thwarted vitality. It is the fullest extension of the behaviour of the juvenile delinquent for whom all adventurous pathways are closed and who vents his spleen in a petty crime such as breaking into a house. Finally, there are those murders which are the product of sheer brutality and total insensitivity to suffering. Although he also mentioned other categories such as sex crime and motiveless crime in 1961, it was not until later that he developed his ideas on these. They will be considered below.

Thus there is no 'typical' criminal mentality but this does not mean that many murderers do not have a range of characteristics in common. These include a degree of stupidity and insensitivity. Frequently, murderers are weak people and many will be judged to have been the victims of bad luck. Many of the worst murderers are accomplished liars and have a long history of petty crime. It seems that crime begets crime. Prolonged exposure to a criminal environment seems to taint the individual: even members of the police force and the judiciary seem prone to its influence.

There are, however, many murderers for whom this description would be quite inadequate. Some are intelligent and, in many respects well-disciplined. The case of Robert Irwin, although in some respects bizzare, illustrates this class of murderer. In New York, in 1937, Irwin murdered the mother and sister of his girl-friend. Prior to the murders, Irwin had been preoccupied with a notion that he called 'visualising'. It had struck him that before a sculptor could create a piece of sculpture, the work had to be visualised in the artist's mind. For Irwin, the function of imagination was to allow a man to close his eyes and 'see' whatever he wishes to see – the text of a Shakespearean play or some past experience. Irwin decided that castration would enhance his visualising powers. He almost bled to death after an attempt to perform the surgery on himself. Soon after, he committed the murders. One of the most interesting statements made by Irwin was made to the psychiatrist called on for his defence, Frederick Wertham. He told Wertham:

the life force . . . uses every living organism for its purpose of prolonging the race until we finally reach a stage of perfection in which we can rise above the material world. Every organism, upon reaching maturity, sacrifices itself to the task of reproducing. In other words, the driving force in back of our lives, which can be used for other purposes, we sacrifice to the task of reproduction. I realized that if I could once bottle that up without her [his girlfriend], I didn't need her. It's a great deal of fun to monkey around with a woman. It's a great deal of fun to have five dollars and spend it. But if by forgoing the five dollars you will later get a million dollars . . . [3]

Some murderers are aware of a higher self and a higher humanity. They are also aware of the value of discipline. For them, however, something goes wrong and they find themselves unable to utilise their self-discipline in the interests of their higher self. Nor is it justifiable to argue that what went wrong in Irwin's case was that his sexuality interfered. As Wilson points out, a man who can attack himself with a knife in order to free his imagination is not a total slave to his sexual impulses.

It is to be acknowledged that there is something disturbing and repulsive about Irwin's behaviour. Yet it becomes comprehensible when we remember what George Bernard Shaw said about the criminal – that we judge him by his worst moments while we judge the artist by his best. Wilson argues that the real difference between the two is not, finally, a difference of personality or circumstances but a matter of choice. We are presented with a choice, not only in the rich and full moments of consciousness but also in the darkest and worst. Making the right choice when we are feeling psychologically defeated has the effect of redirecting us towards a healthier state of mind; making the wrong choice sets us on a course that is ultimately self-defeating. We are constantly on the knife-edge of choice – a choice between instantaneous gratification or the satisfaction of our long-term interests. Living means constantly being required to select between impulse and purpose. Invariably, the murderer makes the wrong choice and the inevitable chain of events is set in motion.

It is certainly true that just as a great poem or symphony gives us a sense of the endless potentialities of human life, so murder makes us clearly aware of what might be called 'original sin'. All men live in a limited and short-sighted way, but the great artist and the saint reject the limitation that their senses and their lives impose upon them; they refuse to be defeated by the limitations of everyday consciousness, to betray the god in them by behaving as dwarfs. The murderer formally signs a pact with triviality as black magicians once signed a pact with the Devil. And his pledge of allegiance is the ultimate crime – ultimate because it cannot be undone. [4]

In the human personality there are, according to Wilson, two compelling forces which he calls Force T (for tension) and Force C (for control). Force T is aroused when we experience frustration and the greater the level of frustration, the more intensely we experience the impact of Force T. If the front doorbell rings while we are engrossed in reading, we are mildly annoyed; Force T awakens. If we answer it and it rings again ten minutes later, Force T is intensified. A third ring has Force T positively bristling within us. Yet Force T is not entirely a negative emotion. It is produced by any challenge with which we are confronted and without it we would probably be incapable of recognising danger. What is most interesting about Force T is that we often experience it as an energy within ourselves which is seeking an escape. A mild degree of Force T will seem to leak out of us; a more powerful amount will explode from us.

By contrast, Force C is a counterbalance to the destabilising Force T. It is a focusing of our energy on a resolution of the problem represented by Force T. Force C is the power to return to the book we were reading when the doorbell rang and resume our reading as if the interruption had never occurred. In its simplest form, Force C is a kind of patience.

Human beings spend most of their waking hours in responding to both these forces. The healthy individual achieves a more-or-less permanent state of balance between them. Weak human beings are more likely than the healthy person to be under the control of Force T. Wilson reminds us that Beethoven was capable of bursting into a raging anger – but he was also capable of producing the most sublime music. It is the man who cannot submit his Force T to Force C who is most likely to enter a life of violent crime. Wilson goes so far as to express the view that Force C is the most important thing about a human being.

In *Order of Assassins*, Wilson makes a fundamentally important distinction between the murderer and the assassin. He reports that an analysis of sixty-two murders conducted in 1912, produced the following classification: twenty were the product of emotional quarrels; thirteen were attributable to alcohol; nine involved jealousy over a woman; four followed arguments over money; three were due to negligence; one to race antagonism; while five took place during robberies and there were two cases of infanticide, leaving the remaining five as the product of 'general causes'. An analysis of contemporary murder would probably produce similar results although there would certainly be a marked increase in the number of murders relating to sex. More significantly, perhaps, whereas the 1912 study showed that murders were generally related to family quarrels or to a need for money, both involving strong emotional factors, modern murder has come to acquire a strong cerebral factor. In the United States, between 1940 and 1954, crimes of violence increased by 35 per cent but in three years – 1968 to 1970 – the increase rose to over 50 per cent and the most significant feature of this 'explosion' is the increase in 'resentment crimes' by men who had an intelligence level that was well above the norm. Wilson prefers to call such killers 'assassins' rather than murderers.

The Assassins were a Moslem religious sect who killed as a matter of conviction. Their name derives from the popular super-stition that they always killed under the drug hashish but, while they certainly took the drug, it was not the primary cause of their violence. This flowed from an intellectual conviction that by killing the enemy of their leader, they could enter into Paradise. Some even believed in murder as a religious duty. The historic order of Assassins was established by Hasan ben Sabbah, whom Wilson describes as having the religious fervour of St Augustine and the political astuteness of Lenin.

Little is known of Hasan's early life. He was a devoted scholar of high intellect and given to a deeply religious devotion. He was attracted to the intellectual force and mysticism of an heretical sect called the Ismaili, which had founded the city of Cairo, and joined forces with them in 1072. After three years in the court at Cairo, he travelled extensively, proclaiming the Ismaili faith. In 1090, Hasan acquired the castle of Alamut. For the remainder of his life, he studied, wrote treatises and planned the extension of his authority through conquest. He was a strict authoritarian who gave orders that his own son should be killed for drinking wine. Hasan's abiding hatred was directed towards the Turks who were personified for him in the person of the Nizam Al-Mulk. Hasan called for a volunteer to murder the Nizam and when the feat was accomplished, Hasan celebrated. 'The killing of this devil is the beginning of bliss', he declared – and we may conclude that he meant the expression to be taken literally.

'The Old Man of the Mountain', as Hasan was known, rep-resents an important defiance against established order. Wilson writes:

Men came together into cities for protection; not from wild animals – for that purpose villages were as good as cities – but from their fellow human beings, the dispossessed who found it easier to rob and rape than to work. When the marauders were caught, they were treated with unprecedented ferocity (after all, it was not long ago that the bodies of highwaymen were allowed to rot on gibbets in England). A ruler might be cruel and arbitrary; but he was also the law-giver and protector, the foundation stone of social stability. By sending out his fanatics to murder viziers and princes, Hasan was touching a nerve of deep insecurity. It was as if – for example – some modern terrorist organization held society up to ransom by threatening to bomb school nurseries. The Assassins produced a feeling of outrage by doing something that simply 'wasn't done'. It is difficult for us, in our comparatively stable and law-abiding society, to understand the feelings aroused by the Assassins in a society where stability was newly-acquired. They seemed to threaten a return to chaos and violence. They were creatures of nightmare.[5]

It is in this sense that Wilson sees many modern murderers. They set themselves against the established order for the sake of asserting themselves. Like the Thugs who succeeded the Assassins in India, they kill for the sake of murder itself rather than for the sake of the robbery or the rape that accompanies it.

The novelist John Cowper Powys has a passage in one of his novels which captures something of the universal quality that many modern murderers might associate with their crime. Describing the motivation of a sadistic character named Mr Evans, Powys writes

The nature of his temptation was such that it had nothing to redeem it. Such abominable wickedness came straight out of the evil in the heart of the First Cause, travelled through the Interlunar spaces, and entered the particular nerve in the erotic organism of Mr Evans which was destined to respond to it. He saw his soul in the form of an unspeakable worm, writhing in pursuit of new, and ever new mental victims, drinking new and innocent blood.[6]

Commenting on this passage, Wilson writes:

What is important is that we recognise the *autonomous* nature of this urge to destroy, which seems to be as basic as the sexual or territorial drive. For whatever reason man *is* capable of experiencing a morbid involvement in the act of destruction, as if some deep erotic nerve had been touched by a craving for violence. And, like the sexual impulse, this destructive impulse has the power to blind him to everything but its own satisfaction. The future becomes unimportant or non-existent; all that counts is fulfilment of the need for violence.

And it is the presence of this impulse, this 'worm of destruction', that distinguishes 'assassination' from the ordinary murder case. It can always be sensed underneath the apparent motive for the killing, whether it is sexual, or political, or simply a general resentment against society.[7]

In 1811 there occurred a series of murders which have become known as the Radcliffe Highway murders. On 7 December, Timothy Marr sent his servant out to purchase oysters. When she returned to the house, she found the entire family brutally murdered. Timothy Marr, his wife Celia, their infant and the apprentice had all been battered with a sledgehammer, which was soon found in one of the bedrooms. A fortnight later, a nearby family, the Williamsons, was also slain brutally. They had been struck by an iron bar and their throats had been slashed. A lodger in the Williamson house, John Turner, caught sight of the murderer then fled by climbing out of his bedroom window, using a rope made from his bedclothes. Turner attracted a crowd which rushed into the house to see the murderer crouched over the fourteen-year-old daughter of the household. He fled through a rear window, scrambled up a muddy bank and escaped.

Subsequently a young Irishman named John Williams was charged with the murders. During the morning on which they had occurred, he had returned to his room and shouted to his room-mate to snuff out the candle that was burning. Later, his boots and socks were found to be covered in mud and much of his clothing stained with blood. A knife was found hidden in a mouse-hole. In his house there was a tool box that was of the type to hold a sledgehammer.

Williams committed suicide in his cell before he could be brought to trial. There has been much speculation as to his guilt and a substantial body of evidence suggests that the real murderer might have been a man named Ablass, a companion of Williams who had a history of violent behaviour. There is even a suggestion that Williams was murdered in jail with the connivance of the warders.

The English literary figure, Thomas de Quincey, wrote an essay on the Radcliffe Highway murders in a book entitled, significantly, *Murder Considered as One of the Fine Arts*.

Whatever the motive and whoever the culprit, these murders were committed with lunatic savagery. Such was their ferocity, in fact, that talk about motive becomes ridiculous. The very nature of the murders assumes the central importance. They fascinated de Quincey because the killer was obviously attracted to violence for its own sake.

The murders committed by the members of Charles Manson's 'family', at Manson's behest have this same characteristic.

Even after . . . Manson had been sentenced, there was a feeling that nothing that had been said explained what actually had been done. There were strange justifications, arguments about the sick society derived from de Sade or Marcuse; but nothing that could be identified as a sufficient motive. It would have created a sense of psychological relief if a prosecution psychiatrist had been able to show . . . that Manson's delusions of grandeur were due to venereal disease. But it was precisely this kind of certainty that never emerged. The American public found the Manson case particularly frustrating because he seemed to be arguing according to some non-linear logic. He was innocent; not because he had nothing to do with the murders but because society was guilty . . .

One thing is clear: if we accept the distinction between assassins and murderers, then . . . Manson . . . belong(s) with the assassins. The ordinary murderer commits his crime *looking over his shoulder*. He hopes not to be caught: if he is caught he will hang his head and acknowledge his sense of guilt by saying, 'It's a fair cop'. The assassin peers down his rifle with a sense of justification felt by a headmaster as he canes an insolent pupil or a hangman as he released the trap. He is punishing society. He feels that he is *in the right*.[8]

In *Order of Assassins*, Wilson sets out an interesting contrast between the way a Freudian analyst might see Charles Manson and the way in which he might be regarded by a Maslovian. The dual analysis takes us to the heart of Wilson's theory of murder. Freud developed the theory that man has a powerful death urge to which he gave the name *thanatos*. In *Beyond the Pleasure Principle*, he argued that sadism is an expression of this basic urge for self-destruction. When the energies that are implicit in *thanatos* confront the life instinct (which includes the sexual impulse) the life instinct tries to redirect them towards other people. In Freudian theory, Manson was locked in an internal battle between his *thanatos* and his life drive. He reached the point where the *thanatos* was beginning to take over. In the hippie communities of San Francisco he sought to revitalise his life instinct by engaging in excesses of sexuality. But this was not a redirecting of the death wish towards others; it was a compounding of his problem since excessive preoccupation with sex works against the creative process. In establishing a 'family', Manson was trying to ensure greater power for his *thanatos*, but the destructive impulse grew until it eventually manifested itself in the murder of Sharon Tate.

Maslow's theory of self-actualisation provides an alternative interpretation of Manson's behaviour. Manson was, in fact, a frustrated self-actualiser who could see no way forward. Lower levels of his need had not been satisfied and this fact prevented him reaching the further boundaries of growth. His childhood had lacked any sense of family security and during his teens his sexual urges were never satisfied. Suddenly, with the creation of his 'family', there came a sense of security and access to sexual expression. The shackles that had held him were suddenly cut and he began to develop at an accelerated pace. Overnight, as it were, he was confronted with a need to satisfy the highest of his urges, the urge for self-esteem which could have been met had he been able to actualise himself. But growth through the hierarchy of values is best achieved at a gradual pace. A sudden projection through a number of stages may expose a lack of preparation for the next. It is not enough simply to meet each need as it presents itself; each must be consolidated before the next can be fully appreciated. An accelerated forward thrust will result in psychological exhaustion – a form of life failure.

Manson's earlier poems and songs make it clear that he was not prepared for the satisfaction of his highest needs. Wilson comments:

Having ascended the 'hierarchy of values' at top speed, Manson was brought up with a bump by lack of training and preparation. He simply had no capacity for inner-direction, for working alone: the crowd of admirers was essential to his well-being. The states of disorientation produced by drugs were no help either. The 'vicious streak' that becomes apparent during the final year is the result of exhaustion and frustration at the creative level – the level of self-actualization. In this state of confusion and emotional fatigue, Manson did what most people do in that situation – reverted to an earlier stage of his development, the prison stage of anti-social resentment.[9]

Wilson is not so naïve as to suppose that a personality as complex as that of Manson can be explained in terms of a single psychological theory. Yet he remains convinced that the key to an explanation lies in the human quest for freedom.

One of the most dramatic illustrations of the creative utilisation of the human urge to advance is provided by the work of Dan MacDougald, an American lawyer who was asked to assist in an argument between a group of farmers and government authorities over the over-filling of a dam. What puzzled MacDougald was the fact that the government officers simply did not seem to hear the case that was being put by the farmers, who were losing crops and animals in the consequent flooding of the valley below the dam. Closer investigation showed, in fact, that the officers were not simply not hearing; they were actively refusing to hear the case made against them. MacDougald soon came to realise that this 'editing out' is a commonplace among human beings – indeed that it is essential, since our senses are bombarded with such a range of sensations that we would be driven insane if we allowed them all to register simultaneously. In fact, MacDougald discovered, the Harvard psychologist George Miller had performed experiments which indicated that we all register no more than seven 'bits of information' at any one time. Thus, it seemed, the government officials were not editing out their antagonists' arguments as an act of wilful stubbornness. They were defending themselves against input that exceeded the amount they were capable of handling.

What, in fact, the government officials were doing was akin to what a cat had done in an experiment conducted at Harvard University. An oscilloscope was fixed to the cat's aural nerve so that the oscilloscope needle swung when a bell was rung within the cat's hearing. However, when a mouse in a cage was placed in front of the cat and the bell was rung, the needle did not move. The cat had effected a 'blotting out' of the sound of the bell as it gave its full attention to the mouse. MacDougald concluded that the officials had chosen to concentrate on the argument for the increased dam level and in so doing they shut out all counter-arguments.

MacDougald extrapolated, from the argument between the farmers and the authorities and his own interpretation of it, a theory regarding the rehabilitation of criminals. He suspected that they had become so focused on negative views of themselves and of the world that they were incapable of receiving any 'good news'. They were responding negatively in a world that was itself basically negative.

MacDougald reasoned that a man's attitudes are reflected in his use of language, particularly in the meanings that are attributed to words. Thus words such as 'love', 'neighbour' and 'responsibility' are of paramount importance. MacDougald found that a significant number of criminals had an incomplete or even a contradictory understanding of the meaning of these words. In an experiment with prisoners at the Georgia State prison, he began by accepting that they possessed a high degree of intelligence and challenged them to come to grips with their own essential natures, rather than the everyday person they felt themselves to be. He worked assiduously at helping them examine the meaning of the words they used. He spent much time talking with them about the meaning of words such as 'love', 'happiness', 'friendship' and 'forgiveness'. He related their language to their goals. Where they blamed 'life' for their predicament, he suggested that their problem stemmed from an incomplete view of themselves and a whole range of negative values. MacDougald's results were spectacular. Within a matter of weeks, sixty per cent of the prisoners he had worked with showed a noticeable improvement in their behaviour within the prison. Follow-up studies eighteen months later revealed that the improvement had been sustained. The Yonan Codex Foundation, which was the name MacDougald gave to his Institute, found that it could train prisoners to review their own language and use it to assess and then improve their behaviour. These prisoners in turn were able to teach others to do the same so that the programme had a rapidly expanding efficiency. In one example, two prisoners who were opposed to each other to such an extent that one came close to killing the other with an iron bar, were encouraged to talk together over a cup of coffee and discuss their differences. The result was that the antagonists became friends. Given the opportunity, human beings are more likely to engage in creative acts than in destructive ones.

On the surface, this all sounds ridiculously simplistic. But the whole exercise becomes of major significance when we analyse what has taken place. MacDougald's programme led the two prisoners to look at the nature of what was happening between them. They saw that their relationship ignored the concept of forgiveness. When this concept was introduced the relationship began to change. The would-be assailant saw that his intended victim was his neighbour and that any attack upon him would inevitably have negative consequences for the attacker. Once this was understood, the need to attack was brought under control. The prisoners responded to insights which are commonplace to the vast majority of human beings but which they had previously chosen to ignore, perhaps because the search for relief from insecurities and inconveniences which had dominated their earlier life had required their total attention and energy. They learnt that human beings can often get what they want by contracting with each other for it and that a criminal 'grabbing' is essentially an immature approach to satisfying their needs. Further, they came to realise that they were not trapped in a criminal destiny; they had the capacity to transform themselves into socially acceptable individuals.

Wilson is indebted to the science-fiction writer, A. E. Van Vogt, for another concept that is of major significance to his theory of crime. In 1954, while researching a novel, Van Vogt visited numerous courtrooms and sat listening to evidence. Many of the cases he heard were divorce cases and as he reflected on them he came to see that a great many of the men figuring in the actions were of a particular type. Van Vogt set out the characteristics he observed in them and soon had the outline of what he called 'the violent man' or 'the right man'. Essentially, 'the right man' is preoccupied with a need for self-esteem. He must feel that he is 'somebody' and the worst disaster that can befall him is to lose face. Thus he can never admit that he might be in the wrong. He is intensely jealous of his marital partner and the least suggestion of infidelity on her part is likely to enrage him. He, on the other hand, has the right to be as promiscuous as he wishes. He sees no contradiction whatever in this dual standard of behaviour. When it is challenged – indeed, whenever any of his patterns of behaviour or ideas are challenged – he is capable of becoming violent and can even commit murder.

The 'right man' lives in a world of adolescent fantasy. He is a human failure whose self-image is totally dependent upon how others see him. To challenge him is to reject him and he is incapable of living in isolation. He depends upon adulation and congratulation. When, as often occurs, his wife deserts him, he collapses into the frightened adolescent he has been trying to outgrow. He will plead with her to return since he needs her to assure him that no matter what he does, she regards him as the centre of her universe.

The central fact about the 'right man' is that he seems to have made a decision that in one area of his life he will allow himself to be out of control. When his emotions explode in a rage, he feels he is entirely justified. There can be no peace for him until the rage is fully spent. Any action undertaken in that rage is intended to assuage his inner tension. But paradoxically, the sense of justification increases the rage and thus he is caught in a vicious spiral. Wilson argues that

> this tendency to allow our emotions to reinforce our sense of justification is a basic part of the psychology of violence and therefore of crime.[10]

Wilson has borrowed from Sigmund Freud the name 'magical thinking' to designate this practice of using an emotion to convince oneself of the truth of something that the intellect knows to be untrue. He illustrates it by referring to Patrick Byrne, a labourer who killed several women in Birmingham in 1960, decapitating one of them because, as he said, he wished to 'get his revenge on women for causing him sexual tension'. Here, there is no logical connection between the problem and the proposed solution. It is easy to understand that magical thinking, a common characteristic of the 'right man' may well account for a very large number of murders.

It would be a mistake to suppose that all 'right' people are in fact male. Wilson argues that although 'right women' may not be as common as 'right men', they do indeed exist. He points to

Elizabeth Duncan who contracted two criminals to murder her daughter-in-law because her son had married her despite his mother's express injunction against the wedding. When the killers had completed their side of the contract, they returned to Duncan for payment. She promptly reported them to the police, accusing them of attempted blackmail. Eventually, the three were executed by gas.

The *Encyclopedia of Modern Murder* treats only twelve female killers. At least one of those, Lindy Chamberlain, who was convicted of slaying her infant daughter even though she insisted that the child had been taken by a dingo in the Australian outback, is widely regarded as being innocent and has in fact been released from prison and is seeking total exoneration. Yet one of the women discussed in the book provides a further interesting example of the 'right' woman.

In February 1980, Blanche Wright was walking down a street in New York with a companion named Robert Young, an escapee from a hospital for the criminally insane. As they passed two men, Marshall Howell and his bodyguard, Sam Nevins, Young pulled out a gun and shot Howell. As he attempted to fire a second shot, his gun jammed. Nevins, in turn, fired at Young who was killed instantly. Nevins fled but Wright now drew a weapon of her own, walked to the dying Howell and shot him in the head.

Shortly after, police called on Young's aunt and there met a woman who fitted the description of Young's accomplice. To begin with she vehemently denied having anything to do with the killing but when she was taunted by the police for not drawing her gun early enough to save Young's life, she became indignant and was soon insisting that it was her bullet that had killed Howell. Eventually, it was discovered that Wright and Young were contracted killers who had been responsible for several other murders. What is interesting in Wright's case, of course, is the anger she displayed when it was suggested that she was responsible for her partner's death. Her self-image as a 'right' person led to her conviction and imprisonment.

The problem of 'right man' behaviour is closely associated with dominant people. Wilson has long been convinced that at any one time five per cent of the human population is dominant – that is, they have a measure of 'vital energy' which sets them apart from the other ninety-five per cent. This is not a form of philosophical elitism; it seems to be supported in both animal and human communities by biological evidence. The Chinese discovered during the Korean war that if the dominant five per cent of prisoners in prisoner-of-war camps were separated from the others, the number of escape attempts was substantially reduced.

In fact, five per cent of the human population represents a vast number of people – three million in England alone. This poses a considerable problem since there is not enough room in a society for such a large number of leaders. Inevitably, then, many of the dominant five per cent will experience a degree of frustration since they cannot advance at the rate generated by their self-image. This problem is described by Wilson:

> large numbers of these dominant individuals develop into 'right men'. In every school with five hundred pupils, there are about twenty-five dominant ones struggling for primacy. Some of these have natural advantages: they are good athletes, good scholars, good debaters. (And there are, of course, plenty of non-dominant pupils who are gifted enough to carry away some of the prizes.) Inevitably a percentage of the dominant pupils have no particular talent or gift; some may be downright stupid. How is such a person to satisfy his urge for primacy? He will, inevitably, choose to express his dominance in any ways that are possible. If he has good looks or charm, he may be satisfied with the admiration of female pupils. If he has some specific talent which is not regarded as important by his schoolmasters – a good ear for music, a natural gift for observation, a vivid imagination – he may become a lonely 'outsider', living in his own private world. (Such individuals may develop into Schuberts, Darwins, Balzacs.) But it is just as likely that he will try to take short-cuts to prominence and become a bully, a cheat or a delinquent.[11]

Wilson has made an interesting observation in relation to dominance as a factor in criminality. It seems that in cases of murder involving a pair of murderers, one of the two usually exerts a high degree of 'control' over the other. It will be recalled that in the Leopold and Loeb case, both had a strong fascination for each other but it became clear in the courtroom that Loeb was the dominant partner and that he exerted a profound influence upon Leopold. Myra Hindley, one of the Moors murderers, was virtually totally submissive to her partner Ian Brady. Brady seems to have relished his authority over her and she, for her part, considered him a brilliant intellectual to whom obedience in all things seemed entirely appropriate. Her acquiescence to his every whim made it easy for him to lead her into petty crime and then into the total horror of murder. In a relationship between a high dominance male and a medium- or low-dominance female, the male is likely to derive as much satisfaction from the power he exerts over his partner as from any other factor, including sex.

The late nineteenth century saw the introduction of the sex murder. Wilson believes it had its beginnings with the crimes of Jack-the-Ripper, in whom he has had a long-standing interest.

In large part, Jack-the-Ripper was a product of his age. Wilson describes a Victorian world in which insensitivity was rampant. There was a flourishing industry in pornography, which was produced by way of a compensation for the prevailing prudery. Sex becomes more and more associated with furtiveness. Victorians expressed their earthy emotions directly. Sexual conquest of women by men was a common preoccupation. Victorian women were on the verge of a new emancipation which was beginning to fuel the flames of the 'naughty Nineties'. The Ripper drew many of these strands together in his violent crimes.

The quest for the identity of the Ripper has occupied an extensive group of professional and amateur criminologists for a century. While the search is certain to continue, it must remain doubtful that his identity will ever be known; but in a real sense it is not his identity that is important. What is needed is an understanding of his personality and his motive. Wilson has addressed these issues in a penetrating essay in *Jack-the-Ripper: Summing Up and Verdict*.

Wilson believes that there are two types of sexual murderer. The first is the man who suffers from satyriasis – an insatiable desire for sex. This is instanced by Christopher Wilder, a millionaire American businessman who went on a rampage across the United States, picking up women who were raped, tortured with an electric probe and finally killed. Wilder committed suicide as he was about to be arrested. Such was the intensity of his sexual urge that he could not satisfy it with the prostitutes he so easily could have afforded. He had to 'embellish' his sexuality in an attempt to satisfy it and in the process he became a sadistic satyr.

The second type of sex murderer is the man whose ego has

been distorted by frustration. It is to this category that the Ripper belongs. Wilson sees him as an introverted, unattractive man, having no ready access to normal sex so that he becomes embittered. He kills in a frenzy of frustration. Such crimes as this man commits are probably rehearsed mentally for years in advance in fantasies about sex in which the victim is seen as being passive and submissive. Wilson quotes James Melvin Reinhardt, writing on a teenager who had murdered an eight-year-old boy, as a typical description of this type of sex murderer:

> I gathered from conversation with him that his nature was such as to derive an overpowering satisfaction out of the contemplation of cruel acts upon another person. A combination of very bad training and a somewhat abnormal physical appearance had, in my opinion, helped to cut him off from normal social life and to shut him within himself. His ego is the sort that demands cruelty, and he found a great deal of ego satisfaction in an abnormal sex act involving the infliction of cruelty on a relatively helpless creature.[12]

Jack-the-Ripper murdered in response to a need for total dominance over his victims. For him, the assertion of dominance was associated with violence. The stabbing and slashing he inflicted were expressions of a totally perverse sense of power. Nor was his power exerted simply over the prostitutes he murdered. It is clear that he followed the daily press reports of his exploits with great interest. He sent letters to the police, boasting that they would never catch him. He gained satisfaction out of watching society shudder at his acts.

Since the outbreak of the sex crime with the Ripper, there has been a steady increase in its occurrence. In 1916, twenty-four petrol drums were found on a Hungarian farm, each containing the body of a woman preserved in alcohol. The murderer, Bela Kiss, had been known to frequent red-light districts. He had apparently lured his victims to his farm by advertising for female companions. Between 1927 and 1944, a German named Bruno Ludke murdered no less than eighty-five times. Ludke had been arrested for sexual assault in 1936 and the court had ordered him to be castrated. Although the operation was performed, it seemed to have little effect on his appetite for sexual violence. In 1946, William Heirens of Chicago was arrested for the murder of a six-year-old girl. Subsequent investigations found that he had killed at least three other women. Hierens, after committing one of his murders, wrote on a wall, 'For Heaven's sake catch me before I kill more. I cannot control myself.' At his trial, it was learnt that he had tried to lock himself in his own house to prevent himself killing again but he left the house by crawling along a gutter.

The cases of Ludke and Heirens serve to illustrate the role imagination has to play in some sex crimes. The killer's sexuality is heightened by his imagination until it takes on an intensity that is both morbid and compelling. Wilson sees imagination as a key to the very emergence of sex crime.

> It is clear . . . why sex crime suddenly made its appearance in the second half of the nineteenth century: it was due to a combination of imagination – fed by the new habit of novel-reading – and of frustration due to Victorian prudery. Suddenly, sex was no longer the down-to-earth occupation it had been for Cleland and Boswell; it had become something to brood about and gloat about. Baudelaire remarked that unless sex was sinful then it was boring and meaningless; what he meant was that, in the crucible of the imagination, sex could be turned into something that was at once wicked and delicious.[13]

The consequence was inevitable:

> Sooner or later, the 'imaginary' sex crime was bound to be translated into reality.[14]

In 1914, the French novelist André Gide published a novel entitled *The Vatican Cellars*, in which a young man pushes a fellow traveller out of the door of a moving train. Wilson sees the anecdote as an anticipation of the emergence of a whole new class of murder – the motiveless killing that seems to be perfectly illustrated by the case of the teenage American, Robert Smith, who walked into a beauty parlour in Arizona and ordered five women and two children to lie on their stomachs on the floor. One by one he shot them in the back of the head and later gave as his explanation, the statement: 'I wanted to become known; to get myself a name.'

Wilson finds part of the explanation for motiveless killing in an argument put forward by the English novelist, Brian Marriner. Marriner points out that for the major part of social history, the individual has undertaken a passive role. He has conformed, stoically, to everything that nature and his fellow man has thrown at him. In recent times, however, in response to programmes of universal education, this passivity has begun to give way to a degree of self-assertion. The individual has come to believe that he has certain rights which he should take for granted. Most of us have learnt to *react* to the stimulus of our environment. What characterises the motiveless murderer is that he has reacted in an immature manner. He has concluded that other people are responsible for his predicament and closed his mind to the possibility that he himself may be the source of his greatest discomforts. From such a position, it is but a short step to an act of violence against the 'enemy'. Such an explanation certainly seems to make sense of the action of Robert Smith.

According to Wilson

there is a basic desire in all human beings, even the most modest, to 'become known'. Montaigne tells us that he is an ordinary man, yet that he feels his thoughts are worthy of attention; is there anyone who can claim not to recognize the feeling? In fact, is there anyone in the world who does not secretly feel that he is worthy of a biography? In a book called *The Denial of Death*, Ernest Becker states that one of the most basic urges in man is the urge to heroism. 'We are all', he says, 'hopelessly absorbed with ourselves'. In children we can see the urge to self-esteem in its least disguised form. The child shouts his needs at the top of his voice. He does not disguise his feeling that he is the centre of the world. He strenuously objects if his brother gets a larger piece of cake. 'He must desperately justify himself as an object of primary value in the universe; he must stand out, be a hero, make the biggest possible contribution to world life, show that he *counts* more than anyone else'. So he indulges endless daydreams of heroism.

Then he grows up and has to learn to be a realist, to recognize that, on a world scale, he is a nobody. Apparently he comes to terms with this recognition; but deep down inside, the feeling of uniqueness remains. Becker says that if everyone honestly admitted his desire to be a hero, and demanded some kind of satisfaction, it would shake society to its foundations. Only very simple primitive societies can give their members this sense of uniqueness, of being known to all. 'The minority groups in present day industrial society who shout for freedom and human dignity are really clumsily asking that they be given a sense of primary heroism'.

Becker's words certainly bring a flash of insight into all kinds of phenomena, from industrial unrest to political terrorism. They are an expression of this half-buried need to *be* somebody . . . There was a weird, surrealistic air about Charles Manson's self-justifications in court; he seemed to be saying that he was not responsible for the death of eight people because society was guilty of far worse things than that. Closer examination of the evidence reveals that Manson felt that he had as much right to be famous as the Beatles or Bob Dylan . . . : in planning Helter Skelter, the revolution that would transform American society, he was asserting his primacy, his uniqueness.[15]

Here we have the beginning of an argument for a re-evaluation of the place of the individual within our societies. Certainly we have an insight into the turmoil that must rage in the mind of the dominant personality who is denied the realisation of his potentialities.

It is a commonplace to say that all murder is tragic. Yet usually, when this is said, it is the victim that the speaker has in mind. Murder is also tragic in terms of the murderer. With typical sensitivity, Wilson points out that

reading about . . . Manson and Brady (*et al*) leads to a recognition that they are not laboratory rats, driven to violent behaviour purely by social pressures. They are free individuals who have *decided* to kill by following a certain thought process. It is because the thought process is magical – because it contains a fallacy – that they end as killers. Magical thinking . . . is the attempt to avoid the effort of self-control at all costs, based on the spoilt child's assumption that he deserves 'freedom', and that all his desires ought to be satisfied more or less immediately. All of which suggests that the motiveless crime since 1960 reflects an increase in magical thinking. Long-term solutions demand a deeper understanding of the nature of magical thinking.[16]

Two sets of events following the infamous 'Black Dahlia' case, in which Elizabeth Short was murdered in Hollywood in 1947, prompted Wilson to another important insight. In the first place, in the twelve months following the murder, there were six more in Los Angeles. It is generally accepted that these were not committed by the Black Dahlia murderer but were imitations of that crime. Then, over the next nine years, the police received twenty-eight 'confessions' to the original crime. Wilson sees both the imitations and the confessions as expressions of an emotional participation in the murderer's experience. But he sees more in them than this. They express 'an irrational desire for self-destruction' which has its origin in a lack of purpose that produces a feeling of self-disgust. In the final analysis, they reflect a life-rejection that is the hallmark of all murder.

As long ago as 1964, Wilson was arguing that murder is in fact a symptom. No matter how repulsive we might consider the deliberate taking of a human life to be, we have yet a greater horror to face; the general breakdown of all that is ennobling about human life. Wilson writes:

> Murder is only a small part of the problem. It would be interesting to know how many of the men involved in the great train robbery were in some way driven to crime – by social causes – and how many *chose* it in the same way that Leopold and Loeb chose to murder Bobby Franks, as an obscure gesture of rebellion or bravado. For in any kind of highly organized and fairly affluent society, a kind of mental strain based on boredom and unfulfilment is bound to result in various criminal acts. One of the major problems of our society is that too many people are too intelligent to accept religion, but not intelligent or strong-minded enough to look for acceptable alternatives; in the same way, many people are strong-minded enough not to want to be 'organization men', but incapable of seeing beyond an act of protest. These situations produce a sense of being 'between two stools', lacking real motive; a sense of mental strain is produced that may find its outlet in violence, or in organized anti-social behaviour. Periodically, some appalling case involving hooliganism or sadism makes us aware that there is a great deal of this state of mind to be found in our society – as in the A6 murders, or the case of the teddy boys who kicked a man to death for a few shillings. We then realize that there are thousands of young people who feel no kind of

responsibility towards society, but only a kind of slow-burning resentment. *This* is the problem.[17]

In *A Criminal History of Mankind*, Wilson has produced a panoramic view of the criminal that will remain of inestimable value for a considerable time. The central argument of the book may be summarised thus: despite the fact that man seems always to have been a killer of his own kind, murder has sociological, psychological and existential characteristics which make it capable of being understood and once it is properly understood it may well be possible to eradicate it from human experience. The book is a description of murder from its earliest days to the present, in which changing nuances in its nature are noted, a variety of possible causes are identified and steps towards its eradication are proposed. Some of its data will be hotly debated and some of the conclusions will ultimately be rejected but there can be no doubt that it is a profoundly important contribution to the science of criminology.

Wilson was prompted to write *A Criminal History of Mankind* when he rediscovered an essay by H. G. Wells entitled *Mind at the End of Its Tether*, in which the novelist expressed his opinion that:

> Since 1940 a tremendous series of events has forced upon the intelligent observer the realization that the human story has already come to an end and that *Homo sapiens* as he has been pleased to call himself, is in his present form played out.[18]

Wilson concluded that Wells had adopted this view because he had failed to admit the violence that had played such a large part in human history. The horrors of the Second World War brought this in upon his mind with such force that he was overwhelmed by a sense of pessimism. Wilson determined not to submit to such a defeated world-view and to examine the nature of the violence until it could be understood. He states:

> What I wanted to show is that if you put crime back into its central place in human history, it makes human history far more horrific. Wells seems to think that man was rising on the stepping-stones of his dead self to higher things. I wanted to show that this is not so, but that even so, even when you put

crime back into its central place, there's still plenty of cause for optimism: That you can face the worst about human kind that can be faced and still emerge optimistic about it.[19]

It is impossible to do any justice here to *A Criminal History of Mankind*. It treats a broad canvas of human criminality, ranging from the tribal killings of primitive cavemen, through pre-Biblical atrocities, Greek and Roman human sacrifices for religious purposes, medieval brutalities, Western and Eastern patterns of murder and into contemporary fields of a new barbarism. It must suffice to note that Wilson's examination of the history of murder provides a solid basis for the conclusion that there is an over-riding pattern – and that the pattern belongs within a greater whole. We can pause only for a glimpse at how Wilson uses the crime of Nero to demonstrate his criminology.

The Emperor Nero came to power in AD 54, at the age of seventeen. Among his predecessors, Marius had been paranoid, Tiberius an embittered sadist and Caligula insane. Nero was none of these things. On the surface, he was a talented young man who had a strong desire to be admired. Wilson points out that if there was a visible weakness in his personality, it was the 'sheer intensity of his naive egoism; he found himself inexhaustively interesting'. He gained early endearment from his people by trying to imitate his great-great-grandfather, Augustus and flooding them with extravagant gifts. But his self-image gradually overtook him. He played his music on every available occasion, entering competitions in which the judges invariably awarded him first prize because they could not afford to offend him. A year after he assumed office, he had a poisoner named Locusta murder his half-brother, Britannicus, the son of Claudius and Messalina, whom many thought to be the rightful Caesar. Nero's difficulties with his own mother, Agrippina, were temporarily brought under control when he began an incestuous relationship with her. This did not last, however, and when the old bitterness was revived, he decided to be rid of her. An attempt to drown her was unsuccessful, so he provided himself with another opportunity to kill her by claiming that she had planned his death. He sent his ex-tutor to her bedroom and she was put to death by the sword. When he was congratulated on his escape from his mother's 'death plot', Nero allowed himself to be persuaded that the emperor could do no wrong and that he was impervious to all harm. He argued that his mother had died of her own hand after her plot had been uncovered. It is likely that he actually believed this account of her death – in an early instance of 'magical thinking'. In this state of mind, his murderous amusements were unbridled. In an effort to marry another woman, he accused his wife Octavia, of adultery. One of his friends made a public 'confession' that he had committed adultery with Octavia and she was exiled to an island where she suicided. Her husband finally submitted totally to his murderous passion and it is impossible to say how many died at his hand. In an attempt to account for his reign of murder, Wilson writes:

The lesson of Nero is very simple. He makes it possible to see that criminality is basically childishness. He was not a particularly 'evil' man – he completely lacked the kind of misdirected resentment that characterizes most real criminals, from Alexander of Pherae to Carl Panzram. But because he became Caesar before he had time to grow up, he was totally subjective, completely self-absorbed. He saw other people as slightly unreal: to him, in fact, the whole world was slightly unreal. So, when he wanted something, he simply grabbed it. When someone stood in his way, he 'removed' him. Because of his childishness, this came as naturally to him as killing mice to a cat.

In Nero, we can see the basic problem of human development: the moment human beings are released from the pressure of necessity they seem to go rotten. And if that is so, then there is something self-defeating about the very idea of civilization, since its aim is to release us from necessity. It seems to be a vicious circle. Man is brilliant at solving problems; but solving them only makes him the victim of his own childishness and laziness. It is this recognition that has made almost every major philosopher in history a pessimist.

Yet although this is the truth, it is not the whole truth. As we examine human history, we realize that man also seems to possess an instinctive counterbalance to this natural drift towards criminality. In its most basic form this seems to consist of an intuitive certainty that this narrow world of the personal ego is *not* the whole world – that something far greater and more interesting lies beyond it. This excited feeling of the sheer *interestingness* of the universe is inherent in all poetry, music, science, philosophy and religion. When we read of great men – an Alexander or a Frederick II – dying in a state of world-weary pessimism, we feel that they have somehow allowed themselves to become blinded by fatigue and allowed their senses to close. Somewhere along the way, they have missed the point. And when the conquerors and criminals have wreaked their havoc and left the scene, the sense of magic and mystery flows back like a tide and sweeps away the wreckage, leaving the beach smooth and clean again.[20]

A Criminal History of Mankind did not evoke the critical response it so clearly deserves. Among the all too few reviews published, Laurie Taylor protests that here, once again, is Wilson's familiar technique of 'slapping together findings from a whole variety of sources as though they constituted a logical argument'.[21] John Moses contends that 'new evidence, backed by rigorous research, has never been one of Colin Wilson's strengths. His accounts of history seem more often than not to be based on anecdote rather than analysis.'[22] For Gordon Hawkins, the book demonstrates that Wilson 'has the ability to ricochet from the particular to the general and make sweeping generalisations without worrying about tiresome details like educing evidential support. But the theoretical edifice that he erects on the foundation of his magpie assemblage of facts and ideas is more like a movie than a solid building.'[23] Yet even Taylor is forced to concede that 'Wilson really does have fascinating ideas about the nature of those modern unpredictable acts of violence where the older motives of greed and sexual passion will not serve; the gratuitous crimes which Dostoevsky regarded as an anguished, fevered expression of individuality'.[24] We are left to choose between an imposed need for an established logic and the depth of intuitive insight that many have claimed to be Wilson's genius, or at least to bring these into balance.

No study of Wilson's criminology would be complete without a reference to his novel *The Killer (Lingard* in the United States). In the same genre as Truman Capote's *In Cold Blood*, which recorded the murder of the Clutter family in Kansas in 1959 through the eyes of the murderers – Richard Hickock and Perry Smith – *The Killer* present a composite portrait of the sadistic, sex killer. Based on a number of murderers, including Peter Kurten, Peter Manuel, William Heirens and Hans Van Zon, a

Dutch killer who claimed at least four victims, the first probably being a woman named Elly Hager-Segov whose throat was cut in 1964, this stark work reveals the complexity of the murderer. Wilson has deliberately set out, in this powerful novel, to match the clinical realism achieved by Berg, Kurten's prison psychiatrist who wrote a brilliant study of his patient. Wilson, in fact, narrates Arthur Lingard's story through the eyes of a psychiatrist, Dr Kahn. While not pleasant reading, *The Killer* provides an essential insight into what it is that might drive a man to murder.

The Killer contains a great deal of precise detail about Arthur Lingard's life. Wilson is convinced that murderers should be studied in great detail for the cause of their behaviour must be uncovered if we are ever to eradicate murder. As an Editorial Adviser and contributor to the ninety-six volume part-work, *Crimes and Punishment*, Wilson argued for the inclusion of contributions from as many different countries as possible. He notes that while some countries do have a considerable archive on their murderers, others do not. But it is not the clinical case-history of a police officer that is needed; it is the life story of the murderer seen through the eyes of a psychologist, or, perhaps more importantly, of a novelist. Such studies would almost certainly identify a whole range of personality problems and behavioural patterns related to murder which have been unnoticed to date and which would provide some possibilities for exercising a measure of control over the rapidly expanding occurrence of murder.

Wilson's latest criminological volume, *Written in Blood*, looks at crime from the other end of the spectrum. His interest in the criminal mind is, of course, shared by those responsible for detecting criminals and in this fascinating volume, Wilson studies the methods used in detection, ranging through simple intuition and the application of the science of ballistics to psychological profiling and genetic fingerprinting. In an important postscript to the book, Wilson explains precisely why he considers the study of crime to be as important as the study of philosophy or religion. After identifying Dickens' Scrooge as an example of MacDougald's 'negative blocking', discussed earlier in this chapter, Wilson goes on:

Now it is obvious that we are all in this position, to some extent – for, as Wordsworth says, 'shades of the prison house begin to close around us' as we learn to cope with the complexities of existence. So we are all in the position of the criminal. But criminals do it far more than most people – to such an extent that when we read of a man like H. H. Holmes (a late-nineteenth-century American murderer), we can suddenly see that he was an idiot to waste his own life and that of his victims. As strange as it sounds, studying criminality has the same effect on most of us that the ghosts of Christmas had on Scrooge – of making us more widely aware of the reality we ignore.[25]

Wilson summarises his interest in murder and his philosophy in relation to it, thus:

In moments of crisis, man becomes aware that he possesses a far higher degree of freedom than he ever realized. In a sense, the problem of murder is implicit in Auden's lines:

> Life remains a blessing
> Although you cannot bless.

We are all subject to 'the great mystery of human boredom', which is the most common form of eclipse of the 'blessing'. But on the point of being shot, Graham Green's whiskey priest suddenly realizes that 'it would have been easy to be a saint'. Raskolnikov realizes that if he had to stand on a narrow ledge for ever, in eternal darkness and tempest, he would still prefer to do this than die at once. Even the American gangster, Charlie Birger remarked as he stood on the scaffold: 'It is a beautiful world, isn't it?' We deny this freedom during every moment of our lives, except in these brief flashes of vision. But it is by far the most interesting possibility that human beings possess. And this recognition is the basis of my own philosophical vision, the central problem of all my work. We are like poverty-stricken Indians whose land is rich in oil; one day, someone is going to learn the technique of sinking wells. It will be the most important thing that has happened in human history.

Murder interests me because it is the most extreme form of the denial of this human potentiality. Life-devaluation has become a commonplace of our century. We talk glibly about social disintegration, about our moral bankruptcy, about the depth of our sense of defeat, and existentialist philosophers have been the chief exponents of this kind of pessimism. It may therefore sound absurd to say that every time I contemplate murder, I feel an odd spark of optimism. But it is so. We can accept boredom and philosophical pessimism as somehow inevitable, like the weather; but we cannot take this casual attitude towards murder. It arouses in us the same kind of morbid interest that the thought of fornication arouses in a puritanical old maid. If the old maid were at all analytical, she would see this morbid interest as proof that sex cannot really be dismissed as nasty and disgusting; we do not feel morbid interest in a beggar covered with sores, or the carcass of a dead rat. Her morbid interest is an inverted form of the recognition that sex can be man's most vital insight into his secret potentialities. And if a murder case arouses this same sick curiosity, it is because we instinctively recognize it as a denial of these secret potentialities of freedom. Our interest in murder is a form of stirring in our sleep.[26]

Criminologies and psychological interpretations of the murderer abound in our age and this is to the good. The more we study personalities crippled by boredom, insensitivity and an inadequate value structure and the more we discern about the underlying causes that create them, the more likely we are to reverse the current explosion in crimes of violence. Yet psychological and sociological studies and even the current holistic approaches, although important, may not be sufficient of themselves to effect the breakthrough we need. It may be that the problem will succumb only to an existential analysis. It is difficult to think of anyone who has done more than Wilson in providing a panoramic view of the problem of crime or more intelligent and promising suggestions for its resolution.

6

The Occultism

WITH the publication of *The Occult* in 1971, many readers believed that Wilson had redirected his interest to a new field. They interpreted the appearance of the volume as an indication that he had ended his wrestling with existentialist ideas and had turned to a more popular form of thinking and interacting with experience. Many thought he had abandoned his principles and settled for the acclaim of a more receptive press. For many, this suspicion was fuelled by his admission that he had been attracted to write the book as a means of solving his financial problems. So much for the romantic notion that insists a writer should forgo all monetary considerations for the sake of his art or idealism!

It is inconceivable that the author of The Outsider cycle would not have proceeded to an investigation of the mysterious world that lies beyond the boundaries of our established sciences and our intellectual preconceptions. The very term *Outsider* implies an incapacity to remain restricted within such parameters. The Outsider is outside the prevailing myths of his age, no matter how respectable the form in which they present themselves.

In fact, *The Occult* was written in direct response to an invitation from the United States publishing house, Random House. Nor did it represent a new departure for Wilson. His earlier work is strongly marked by expressions of interest in the fringes of the scientific method. In his very first book, he had dealt with such figures as William Blake, William Butler Yeats and Sri Ramakrishna, all of whom had represented a challenge to traditional ways of thinking. In *Religion and the Rebel*, he had entered the worlds of Jacob

Boehme, Blaise Pascal and Emanuel Swedenborg and considered various elements of their philosophies which could only be described as expressions of an occultism. Indeed, the writing of The Outsider cycle had been punctuated with the writing of *Rasputin and the Fall of the Romanovs*, a study of one of Russia's most enigmatic figures.

It is important, in discussing Wilson's occultism, to have in mind a clear definition of what he means by the term *occult*, for in popular usage it has an element of threat and arouses a measure of apprehension and fear. For Wilson, the word simply means *the unknown – the hidden*; the vast amount of potential experience that lies beyond the acknowledged boundaries within which man is permitted by his culture to interact with the world of nature and of his perceptions.

Predictably, *The Occult* received a mixed reception. The anonymous reviewer in *The Times Literary Supplement* wrote of it,

> Mr Wilson should stick to fiction, or take the thirty odd pages on Faculty X and develop a coherent theory without the occult allies, which far from being supporting guns are more like damp squibs, bringing weariness and scepticism about the whole claim to possess latent powers which enable men to reach beyond the present.[1]

Alan Hull Walton, however, writing in *Books and Bookmen*, asserts

> Wilson's approach is that of the careful scientist, convinced of the reality of unusual facts and happenings previously dismissed by the strict materialists as due either to imagination, or inexplicably on the basis of superstitious misinterpretation . . . [It] is by far and away his best book to date and worthy to be placed on the same shelf alongside William James. F. W. H. Myers' monumental, *Human Personality* (in its complete two-volume edition) and Frazer's *Golden Bough*. And it has something of the thoroughness and erudition of Havelock Ellis's celebrated *Studies*.[2]

The Occult has at its centre one of Wilson's most important concepts. He calls it *Faculty X*. This he defines as being the human capacity to reach beyond the here and now into the realm of the unknown in such a way that further human potential can be realised. For the present time, Faculty X remains crudely undeveloped but its growth is a vital necessity if man is to project himself further along the evolutionary path. Faculty X is both a freedom *for* development and a freedom *from* the restrictive patterns of thought and behaviour which constitute a limitation on growth. Thus, in a person in whom Faculty X is operative, there is a capacity to register subtle vibrations in the network of experiences that comprises living whereas, in a person devoid of Faculty X, a sense of boredom might screen out those nuances. Where the vibrations are felt, there is a connection made to meanings which already exist in the scheme of things. Faculty X is a focusing on a broader, richer reality which surrounds, but which is invisible to, those who fail to cultivate it.

Once again Wilson is on an assault course against the human propensity to submit to a sense of boredom. He quotes Richard Wilhelm, who pointed out that the primary meaning of the Chinese symbol of the *Yin* is 'the cloudy, the overcast'.[3] Wilson asks whether there can be a richer representation of dullness and boredom than this and then relishes the notion that the Yin is complemented by the *Yang*, which Wilhelm interprets as a 'banner waving in the sun'. The Yang is the moment of vision, the point at which there is a proclamation of what G. K. Chesterton called 'absurd good news'.

The final chapter of *The Occult* is called 'Glimpses'. It contains a record by a friend of R. H. Ward, the author of *A Drug-Taker's Notes* which takes us, simultaneously, into the heart of the process by which this absurd good news breaks in upon us and into something of the content of the good news itself:

> Last night, as I was walking home from the station, I had one of those strange experiences of 'rising within myself', of 'coming inwardly alive'. . . . A moment or so after I had left the station, I was attacked by indigestion. I thought to myself, though I suppose not in so many words, 'I could separate myself from this pain: it belongs only to my body and is real only to the physical not-self. There is no need for the self to feel it'. Even as I thought this the pain disappeared; that is, it was in some way left behind because I, or the self, had gone somewhere where it was not: and the sensation of 'rising up within' began.
>
> First there is the indescribable sensation in the spine, as of *something mounting up*, a sensation which is partly pleasure and

partly awe, a physical sensation yet one which, if it makes sense to say so, is beginning to be not physical. This was accompanied by an extraordinary feeling of *bodily lightness*, of well-being and effortlessness, as if one's limbs had no weight and one's flesh had been suddenly transmuted into some rare substance. But it was also, somehow, a feeling of living more in the upper part of one's body than the lower, a certain peculiar awareness of one's head as . . . the most important and intelligent of one's members. There was also a realization that one's facial expression was changing: the eyes were wider open than usual: the lips were involuntarily smiling. Everything was become 'more', everything was *going up to another level.*

I found that I could think in a new way. Or rather, it would be more accurate to say that I could think-and-feel in a new way, for it was hard to distinguish between thought and feeling. *This was like being possessed of a new faculty.*[4]

Wilson identifies this *new faculty* as Faculty X. Nor is it as rare as those who have not experienced it may judge it to be. Hindu theories of *kundalini* may well explain the mounting feeling in the spine and the Jungian theory of alchemy may help towards some explanation of the transmutation into a rarer substance but when one has rationalised all the detail, the whole is left untouched. Ward's friend – and there is no suggestion that he was under the influence of a drug – seems to have broken through into a new dimension of perception in which he experienced himself as existing in a more intense form.

Perhaps the most important single statement in *The Occult* is a brief parenthesis in which Wilson defines philosophy as *the pursuit of reality through intuition aided by intellect.*[5] This definition represents a complete reversal of our way of thinking and places some of the criticism directed at *The Occult* into perspective. In his review of the book on 21 October 1971 (source unknown), A. S. Byatt refers to it as 'a half-intellectual book', which deals with 'a subject where it is necessary for argument to be consequential or abandon the form of argument'. But logic as we apply it stops short of the mounting feeling in the spine and the transmutation experienced by Ward's friend. Even *kundalini* is an unscientific concept. And this is Wilson's real problem: to elicit sense in an intellectual climate which seeks to impose upon him a restriction to diagnostic tools which are inadequate to the task.

In 1968, five years before *The Occult* was published, Wilson wrote a short essay which was published by Lawrence Ferlinghetti's City Lights Books in San Francisco – a work which was later substantially expanded and published by Hutchinson in London.[6] In this essay 'Poetry and Mysticism', Wilson addressed the question of the vision of the poet which often produces insights which defy the limitations of formal language and normal perceptions. It is the poet who provides us with the most immediate contemporary form of the mystical experience.

For Wilson,

> personality is a distorting glass that lies between man's inner reality and the reality of the outside world. In the poet, this distorting mechanism suddenly vanishes; the inner and the outer world face each other directly, with no distorting glass between them.[7]

When this glass is removed, the poet has a more complete vision of the world. At such times, there is frequently a feeling of exultation, of ecstasy, which generates itself in the language of poetry. Significantly, one of the most common elements of the glass that distorts is the intellect. The poet, Louis Singer, was one evening waiting in his room for a visit from a medium's 'control'.

> Now, in the quiet of my room, I waited for her visit with relaxed mind. Of course, nothing happened. I next decided to experiment with a candle. I lighted it and kept it under observation. The flame burnt undisturbed. With mind relaxed I watched it, hoping against hope for one of those mystic 'breezes'; but none came. However, suddenly I smelt a beautiful perfume that I had not observed before. In the state of passivity I smelt it without any doubt whatever. I rose and tried to find it. There was nothing in my room to account for it. Finally I followed my nose. It led me from the top of the house to the basement where the bath was situated. There I found the cause – a piece of scented soap. Here then was my first concrete lesson. In the passive state, when the power of intellection is fully suspended, the senses become hypersensitive. Normally I could not have smelt the soap; abnormally I could.[8]

Viewed from one point of view, Faculty X is the extension or widening of consciousness that has been a preoccupation of Wilson from the very beginning of his literary career. It is consciousness focused on the beyond – no matter in which direction that beyond extends and no matter how remote its boundaries might be.

When a poet is overwhelmed by the superb beauty of an Indian Summer, it frequently happens that something 'bursts' inside him. Something within longs to be expressed and struggles vigorously, even painfully, to shape itself in language. In such moments, the poet comprehends the profound richness of life and the petty concerns and activities, even the ambitions of ordinary men, seem restrictive and absurd. It is this heightened awareness that forms the heart of Wilson's theory of the occult.

In *Strange Powers*[9] Wilson directed his attention to three particular exponents of Faculty X. These are Robert Leftwich, Eunice Beattie and Arthur Guirdham. Leftwich seems to have had a wide variety of powers that cannot be explained in ready terms but his most dramatic expression of Faculty X lay in his dowsing ability. Wilson argues that in its simplest form, there is nothing spectacular about dowsing: Leftwich himself contended that magnetic fields were the key. The dowser picks up a magnetic field in much the same way that a radio picks up electrical signals and transfers them into sounds on the radio. Wilson believes that Leftwich's power emerges from his capacity to project himself, through what might be called a *superconsciousness* into a state of profound receptivity. Wilson noted that

> Robert Leftwich is a non-passive personality: in fact he is a highly active personality, whose psyche has always exerted a definite pressure on the world, in the form of curiosity, expectancy, interest. Such pressure is like water: it finds its way into cracks and enlarges them.[10]

In his attempt to explain the strange capacities of Leftwich, Wilson turns to the concept of 'superconsciousness', which, he believes, was first developed by Aldous Huxley. Just as the subconscious is that part of consciousness which operates below the threshold of consciousness, so the superconscious is that part of consciousness which operates above the threshold. If this concept is accepted, it might well be expected that the superconscious might have a more extensive range of faculties than normal consciousness. In *The Unexplained*, a short essay on the paranormal, Wilson writes:

> Clearly, the 'superconscious' is a valuable hypothesis in explain-ing all kinds of 'occult' phenomena. But it should be clearly understood that we are not positing some strange supernatural faculty. A hawk can see many times further than a human being, and in that sense, its 'sight' is above that of a human being. The salmon finds its way back over many thousands of miles to its home rivers by a highly developed sense of smell – but a sense of smell that works at *that* distance might well be regarded by human beings as a 'superconscious faculty'. There is nothing supernatural about the lightning conductor's powers. We are speaking, then, of faculties that we all possess to some extent, but which in most of us are blunted. If you use a cut-throat razor for sharpening pencils, it would soon become as blunt as an ordinary penknife. It seems likely that we possess many faculties that are intended to be razors but have become blunted by the repetitive, everyday use we put them to.[11]

Eunice Beattie is a woman who speaks, in more stereotypical occult language, of movement through emotional soul levels to a psychic level. Wilson acknowledges that he finds her somewhat more enigmatic – and more puzzling – than Leftwich yet he remains convinced that she possesses strange powers, particularly the power to produce what appears to be automatic writing. For Wilson, she demonstrates his thesis that man's forward journey entails a necessary inward exploration.

Arthur Guirdham was convinced that he was a reincarnation of a Cathar 'priest' named Roger de Grisolles, who had lived in the Montsegur area of France in 1243. Guirdham expounded to Wilson his theory that instances of reincarnation, which he was convinced he had uncovered, related, not to sick and overly sensi-tive human beings, but to healthy active people who had an abundance of what might be called more than average energy. Once again, we are in the realm of the extended self. Guirdham reminded Wilson of the thesis of Harry Edwards, expounded in *A Theory of Disease* that disease is often due to the degree to which a person is preoccupied with his or her own personality.

In *The Outsider*, Wilson had made it perfectly clear that he was a steadfast opponent of the determinism and reductionism of contemporary science. It concerned him greatly that the two most prevalent philosophies of the day, Logical Positivism and Linguistic Analysis, considered questions relating to the nature of human freedom as being unworthy of consideration. Personalities such as Leftwich, Beattie and Guirdham provided him with some basis for maintaining his thesis that the quest for human freedom is the ultimate objective for all philosophy. The occultism they represented was a playground for human potentialities and thus it was an arena within which freedom might be explored.

In Wilson's mind, magic is a great deal more than a childish escape from the boring trivialities of everydayness. Magic, for him, is the universe of actuality that lies beyond the boundaries we have drawn about ourselves and within which we have contracted to limit our experience. Magic is the science of the future. Thus, whereas we have a wider spectrum of colours than that available to our forebears, future man may have at his disposal another twelve colours of which we have no present knowledge – or no readily available capacity to experience.

In fact, there is an intrinsic connection between magic and evolution. Primitive man may well have possessed faculties which today are regarded as fantastic. He may have preserved his animal instincts for telepathy in the form of a sixth sense – demonstrated in part by an intuition of danger. Other powers that many people are willing to attribute to cats or dogs but not to human beings, may have been at his disposal. As civilisation developed, man's need for these powers may have appeared to diminish. Unused, they atrophied. Yet their remnants may well remain within the reach of modern man and it may be that from time to time there is a 'regression' – a regression which from one point of view might be regarded as a dehumanising agent but which, from another point of view might appear as a transcendence of the human condition – a leap forward. His subscription to the latter view forms part of the foundation for Wilson's contention that civilisation has tended to make mankind too soft for his own good. Primitive man, confronted with a life-threatening danger, rapidly focused all his defensive powers to address the enemy; contemporary man surrenders himself to indulgent pleasures and has no need to bring the full range of his powers into a sharp focus. Support for this thesis is readily provided in times of war or social calamity, when individuals and groups raise themselves to heights of human achievement they otherwise would have regarded as being beyond them.

In an important sense, what Wilson has achieved is a 'demythologising' of the occult. He insists that there is no fundamental distinction between a rational commonsense and those powers that are resident in primitive man and in many animals. So-called magical powers may be in operation all about us but we fail to recognise them because we no longer have any pressing need to call upon them to protect us. Occult powers may be available to us upon demand, provided we free our minds of a recently acquired prejudice against them.

While Wilson's 'Outsider' is not necessarily an occultist, and *vice-versa*, it is interesting to note Wilson's contention that the individual wholly immersed in a society is likely to be distracted and self-divided. The individual who avoids losing himself in the crowd – and this is one of the characteristics of the Outsider – operates with a measure of single-mindedness and this single-mindedness is a fundamental prerequisite for the capacity to experience the occult. Given Wilson's contention that only about five per cent of the populace are Outsiders – that is, preserve themselves from the danger of total submission to society – it is easy to understand the common failure to acknowledge the nature of the occult. Yet for those who have access to it, it is the most significant part of their lives. Thus Wilson accepts it easily, although he readily confesses to being personally 'inept' at its practice.

P. D. Ouspensky was an adept in the occult. Wilson writes of him:

At fourteen, Ouspensky [was] plunged into a state of ecstatic excitement by a book on physics, because it [was] a contact with the world of the impersonal. But science is a dead end for an imaginative youth; he doesn't want to end up injecting guinea pigs in Pavlov's laboratory. He has a feeling that all the ways of life offered by the modern world lead him in the opposite direction from the way he wants to go. In moments of depression he is inclined to wonder if this craving for distant horizons is not some odd illusion; 'the desire of the moth for the stars'. But an instinct led [Ouspensky] to search persistently in books on magic and occultism: later, the same instinct led him to wander around in the East, searching in monasteries for 'esoteric knowledge'.[12]

Wilson continues:

> This sense of 'meanings' that are not apparent to ordinary consciousness is experienced by everyone at some time or another. One may ignore such hints for years, until some event brings them all into focus; or the 'focusing' may happen gradually and imperceptibly. Science declares that life began with the action of sunlight on carbon suspended in water and that man has reached his present position by a process of natural selection. In that case, the laws of human existence are physical laws and can be found in any textbook of science. But there occur moments of absurd certainty that seem to transcend the usual laws of probability.[13]

One of the most persistent examples of the manifestation of Faculty X cited by Wilson is the story told by Proust, in *Swann's Way*. Proust describes how, one morning while seated in a café, he dipped a madeleine biscuit into his tea. This simple act triggered a memory of his childhood in Combray where his aunt often used to give him such a biscuit. As the memory flooded into his mind in the tea shop, Proust records:

> an exquisite pleasure had invaded my senses . . . And at once the vicissitudes of life had become indifferent to me, its disasters innocuous, its brevity illusory. . . . I had now ceased to feel mediocre, accidental, mortal.[14]

The major part of *The Occult, A History of Magic*, is essentially a catalogue of such moments, particularly when they are allied to the application of an energy which is not to be explained in current scientific language. Wilson recounts story after story of individuals who escaped the contingencies of everydayness and found, at least momentarily, a new domain in which to exercise their budding powers. Personalities such as Simon Magus, Albertus Magnus, Cornelius Agrippa, Paracelsus, Helvetius, Swedenborg, Mesmer, Casanova, Cagliostro, the Count of Saint Germain, St Martin, Mme Blavatsky, Rasputin, Crowley and Daniel Dunglas Home, all provide tantalising glimpses of the human mind which has snapped the tether that ties it to an all-too-present reality and soars into the future reaches open to it.

Here, a single account must suffice.

Emanuel Swedenborg is today best regarded as a theologian and belongs, properly, to the history of religion rather than to the history of magic. Even so, Wilson describes him as the 'greatest occultist of the eighteenth century'.[15] His biblical works will appeal only to a very small circle of contemporary readers yet they do reflect a man with a deeply serious mind who was much given to a consideration of fundamental philosophical pursuits. Many of his views appeared to be eccentric to his contemporaries. One morning he awoke from sleep convinced that his hair was full of small snakes which were a parting, malicious gift from a group of Quakers who had recently died. Such delusions and such accusations may suggest that Swedenborg was paranoid. He was given to having bizarre dreams and often went into ecstatic trances. In one dream he was picked up by the wind and flung down on his face before a figure of Christ. Frequently, in trances, he visited Heaven and Hell which he described – perhaps with some profundity – as being states of mind. Much of his writing may now be regarded as pietistic yet even a casual reading will confirm that it does have an intriguing inner consistency that embraces an extremely broad domain. Even his most odd assertions – such as that all the planets are inhabited and that the inhabitants of the moon speak with an energy generated in their stomachs rather than with air from their lungs – have a logic similar to the logic of a modern science-fiction novel. For Wilson, what is most interesting about Swedenborg's imagination is that it is obviously very highly developed. It is this keen imagination that might account for the fact that when, on 19 July 1759, a huge fire broke out in Stockholm, Swedenborg, who was three hundred miles away at the time, was able to announce it to his friends. He was also able to tell them the precise duration of the fire and that it had burnt itself out just three houses from his family home. His account was verified two days later when a messenger arrived from Stockholm with an account of the blaze.

In 1761, Swedenborg was asked for assistance by a widow who had lost a receipt for a silver tea service for which she was certain her husband had paid prior to his death. Two days later, Swedenborg informed the widow that the receipt was to be found in her husband's bureau. The widow explained that the bureau had been searched, at which Swedenborg directed her to a secret drawer. The drawer did indeed exist and it did contain the receipt. Swedenborg, when pressed for an explanation, insisted that he had been told of the location by the deceased husband. He never wavered in this explanation.

On one occasion, Swedenborg, at a court reception, was in discussion with the Queen of Sweden, who asked if he had had a conversation with her brother, the Prince Royal of Prussia. The fact that the Prince was deceased is clear evidence that the Queen had heard of and had at least tacitly accepted Swedenborg's strange powers. Swedenborg replied that he had not conversed with the Prince, upon which the Queen requested him to do so. At a meeting two days later, Swedenborg reported to the Queen that he had now had a conversation with the Prince who wishes to apologise for his failure to answer the Queen's last letter to him. He wished to answer it now through Swedenborg. When Swedenborg uttered the response to the letter, the Queen was stunned and, referring to the content of the response, tremulously whispered, 'No one but God knows this secret!'

In his assessment of these stories, Wilson writes:

> E. J. Dingwell, in a penetrating article on Swedenborg, points out that the evidence for these three incidents and for certain others of a similar kind, is confused and conflicting. This may well be so but, unless we intend to dismiss all these stories as fabrications or at least exaggerations, there is no point in dwelling on minor differences between versions written by various witnesses at different times. There have been many other mediums who have performed similar marvels. If the basic proposition of [*The Occult*] is correct – that the occult faculty is latent in everyone and can be developed by anyone who really wants to – then it is likely enough that the . . . stories are fundamentally accurate. Swedenborg had the first important qualification for acquiring second sight and/or mediumship: lack of self-division, a whole-hearted obsession with 'things spiritual'.[16]

The beginning of an answer to the charge that Wilson is naïve in attributing occult faculties to Swedenborg, rather than dismissing him as a crank under the influence of some religious fervour, lies in our approach to science. If we contend that science is a closed body of knowledge which precludes anything new entering into human experience, then Swedenborg must be discarded as an aberration. But such a view of science is obviously absurd. No one would contend that there are not new insights awaiting the acknowledgement of science. If we admit one possible new insight, we are forced to admit the possibility of an endless variety of new experiences. The occult may be regarded simply as the realm of experience that has not yet been catalogued by science. The strange happenings of today or even yesterday may well become the established processes of tomorrow. If we read the events of Swedenborg's life and the substance of his philosophy in this context, we are likely to experience a sense of awe at our own undiscovered potential.

In her review of *The Occult*, Joyce Carol Oates sees Wilson as a sceptic.

> His inclination towards scepticism keeps him from uncritically endorsing most of what he reports and a typically English kind of understatement runs through the book. I did a double-take when reading his dismissal of ghosts as real enough but too trivial to spend much time on – 'Their chief characteristic appears to be a certain stupidity, since a tendency to hang around places they knew in life would appear to be the spirit-world's equivalent to feeble-mindedness.'[17]

When Wilson turns from occult personalities to occult movements, as he does in part 3 of *The Occult*, he retains a high measure of objectivity. In his consideration of the phenomenon of witchcraft, which flooded Europe in the seventeenth century and which remains vitally in evidence today, Wilson begins with the observation that mankind seems to have an innate need to create other worlds. In the nineteenth century, a whole range of novelists, from Balzac and Hugo through to Dickens and Trollope, worked energetically at this craft. They were, of course, preceded by such men as Cervantes, Chaucer, Boccaccio, Malory and Rabelais but these did not have a wide audience, being recognised and read largely by scholars and the other privileged people who had learned to read. All of these writers were engaged in the business of transcending themselves and their world by creating fictional characters and setting them adrift in a 'new' world – in the setting of the novels they created. In the seventeenth century, the human imagination had less scope for expression than it has today.

Wilson sees the rise of witchcraft as a response to this need to create new worlds. He likens it to a vitamin deficiency. Witchcraft arises when the prevailing culture ceases to provide an avenue to the higher reaches of the human mind. Where the creative urge is frustrated by a limiting social order, alternative means of expression are found. The contemporary re-emergence of the witch's coven may represent a challenge to our prevailing cultural mores by suggesting that they are too restrictive.

In the novel *The Fiery Angel* by the Russian novelist Valeri Briussov, Wilson finds a useful treatment of the phenomenon of witchcraft. Wilson wrote an extensive introduction to the English translation of this novel, published by Neville Spearman in 1975. He regards it as a remarkable work in which Briussov, using in part events from the actual trial of Sister Maria Renata von Mossau who was beheaded as a witch in 1749, makes a concentrated attempt to explain the meaning of witchcraft. The conclusion he reaches is very much in accord with the world view of Wilson; that the powers of the mind are more powerful than is commonly accepted and that these powers can be set into action by *symbols*. In the novel, the central character, Rupprecht, responds to a crown placed on the head of The Seated One – the Devil. The crown emits a moonlike glow. Wilson sums up the book a being a *tour de force* in abnormal psychology, in which the characters become engulfed in the fantasies that their own subconscious minds have formed. It is notable that these fantasies frequently have a considerable sexual content.

If traditional witchcraft was designed to satisfy sexual craving and the need for alternative, less punitive worlds, modern witchcraft appears to have a different intent. With a more permissive sexual environment and a whole range of artistic devices available for sojourns into other times and other places, modern witches are more concerned with the search for an appropriate liturgy. They seek a form of worship that facilitates a right relationship with the 'supreme powers'. Their interests are attuned to a desire to cooperate with the unseen forces that promote self-discovery and human well-being.

The movement known as Spiritualism had its beginnings on 31 March 1848 with strange rapping sounds that occurred in the home of the Fox family in Hydesville, New York. The movement rapidly spread across the United States and Europe, attracting to itself some of the most notable charlatans of modern times but also some of the most interesting men and women in recent history. Among a large field of candidates, perhaps the most notable, and typical, is Daniel Dunglas Home. Wilson collates a considerable body of evidence that discredits Home and there can be little doubt that some of his feats were the product of a deliberate attempt to deceive. Charles Darwin referred to him as 'that scoundrel Home'. The poet Robert Browning flew into a rage at the very mention of Home's name. Yet he was the subject of numerous scientific tests and again and again he passed these with considerable credit. In March 1871 he was investigated by the renowned physicist, William Crookes. The expectation of the scientists of the day was that Crookes would thoroughly expose Home as an unmitigated fraud. In fact, Crookes, while admitting that his rational mind made it almost impossible to accept the evidence, was forced to conclude that he could not denounce Home's demonstrations of fire-handling, elongating objects or levitation.

According to Wilson, it is the sheer amount of the evidence that finally exonerates Home. Thousands of people, at one time or another, served as his audience. Sometimes, tied with ropes and in full view of his audience, he was able to lift tables and chairs several inches off the floor without touching them. Again, the mind is inclined to reject the evidence as either mischievous or intentionally deceptive – but we must remember that the mind operates according to a set of preconceived, socially induced notions that make it difficult to accept the evidence.

In the chapter 'The Realm of Spirits' in *The Occult*, Wilson deals, apart from the feats of Home, with materialisation of spirits, table-rapping, seances, communication with the dead, dreams, apparitions, poltergeists, thought-photography, ghosts and reincarnation. Nor is this list exhaustive. He collects what must be the most extensive set of case histories representing these phenomena available in a single volume anywhere in the English language. At the very least they make compelling reading but, of course, the question is whether they mean more than this.

Wilson summarises his position thus:

We may consider all this [spiritualism] absurd, but then, the whole subject of the occult is full of 'absurdities' that offend the logical mind and yet cannot be dismissed as fantasies. Our position in the world is absurd: life seems solid and real enough but the moment we try to pursue any problem beyond a certain limit, it vanishes into a misty realm of ambiguities. We are enmeshed in dreams and illusions and the strongest character-istic of the human race is stupidity and short-sightedness. . . . The only thing that emerges with any certainty from the study of spiritualism and occultism is that our normal, sane, balanced standpoint is built upon quicksand, since it is based upon a commonsense view of human consciousness that does not cor-respond to the facts. Perhaps the only valid criticism of spir-itualism is that it would be better to learn to grasp the facts of human consciousness before we concern ourselves with the facts about the 'other world'.[18]

In 1972, Wilson began working on a series of articles under the collective title *Crime and Society*, for the partwork, *Crimes and Punishment*, for which he worked on the editorial board. Almost a hundred articles of about three thousand words each were involved and considerable pressure was applied by the publishers, who wanted to meet demanding deadlines. As he worked on these articles, Wilson suffered what he calls a series of 'panic attacks'. Several times he awoke in the middle of the night in a cold sweat with his heart pounding and his mind racing. He arose from bed and tried to calm himself but to no avail. The attacks went on intermittently for several weeks and Wilson thought he was having some kind of nervous breakdown. Desperately, he contemplated the symptoms, trying to find an explanation. Eventually, however, he began to realise that a mental concen-tration on the attacks themselves only seemed to increase their ferocity. What was required was a measure of objectivity. Thus he tried to step back from himself and observe what was happen-ing. In so doing, he realised that the attacks were the product of a 'juvenile' self which was reacting indignantly to the pressure of work that had required total attention. Wilson countered the attacks by calling on a more purposive, more 'adult', self. When he concentrated his attention on the purpose at hand, it had the effect that a schoolmistress has when she walks into a room of yelling children and claps her hands: everything is instantly brought back to a state of calm order.

Reflecting on this experience, Wilson came to the realisation that human beings have within themselves, a whole range of 'selves' and that these selves are arranged in a hierarchy, or ladder. 'The Ladder of Selves' became the title of the introduction to his second major work on the occult, *Mysteries*.[19]

Reflecting on the ladder of selves, Wilson recalled William James' observation that a musician might play a musical instrument for a considerable period of time with gradually increasing virtuosity until at last he reaches a stage where the instrument seems to be playing him. What has happened is that a higher self has taken over the playing. The application of ever-increasing effort or an increase in concentration has the effect of passing the activity in which we are engaged on to a higher self in much the same way that a football is passed from player to player in a football match. Inevitably, the question arises: is Faculty X a characteristic of one of our higher selves which is lacking in our lower levels?

While searching for an answer to this question, Wilson reflected on the phenomenon of dowsing. He had observed dowsers detect underground streams with a divining rod and had heard that a pendulum could be used over stone circles to determine the date at which the circle had been formed. He believed that primitive man, who had this capacity, seemed to believe it to be a gift of a beneficent spirit. Wilson, however, concluded that the answer lay in one of the higher selves having access to the information that was being sought and making it available through the medium of the rod, or the pendulum.

If we all possess higher selves which are able to perform more sophisticated functions than those available to everyday consciousness, why do we not live at the highest possible level of self? The answer is simply that we have trained ourselves to accept a measure of boredom as being the norm. It is as if we have gone to sleep while watching television: while we sleep, the programme, with its capacity to transport us to other times and other places, continues but we are no longer aware of it. How can we awaken ourselves? Wilson writes:

> If [occult] powers depend upon our 'higher centres' then there are two ways of establishing contact: either clambering up the ladder, or through some form of short circuit that connects the higher self and the everyday self without the everyday self being aware of it. The first is Gurdjieff's way; the second

Rasputin's. Faculty X seems to be a combination of the two; a flash of extended awareness without the surge of energy.[20]

Apart from its relationship to the awakening of our occult powers, the theory of a ladder of selves has profound implications for a philosophy of human existence. It provides a possible explanation for the sense of meaninglessness which is endemic within twentieth century man. Surrounded by a panorama of astonishing variety and richness, we live on the bottom rung of the ladder so that our view is restricted. Inevitably we become bored with the puny environment our vision extends to, like a child whose sense of wonder at a particular toy gradually drains away as the hours pass. But once we begin to ascend the ladder, the sense of meaning expands and our sense of self expands with it.

It may be that the ladder-of-selves notion provides the explanation for hypnosis. In the hypnotic trance we may simply move up – or down – the ladder and gain access to more – or less – developed insights than those which are lodged within our normal consciousness. Perhaps, too, the theory holds the answer to the perplexing riddle of multiple personality.

In 1877, a young French boy, Louis Vive, was attacked by a snake. The experience caused him to pass into a state of deep shock. Normally, Louis was a well-adjusted child who knew his place and was moderate in his behaviour. The child who came out of the trance, however, was decidedly different; he was verbose and given to expounding radical political theories. Moreover, he was paralysed on one side of his body. This second Louis was interchangeable with the first who had retained his personality but was paralysed on the opposite side of the body. Physicians found that they could transfer the paralysis from side to side and with each movement of the paralysis there was a switch between the two personalities.

Wilson points out that there is a sense in which we all possess multiple personalities and suggests:

it is arguable that the phenomenon of multiple personality is so baffling, simply because most of us are blinkered by a mistaken notion about the permanence of the present 'me' – in exactly the same way that we think the present moment is far more permanent and unchangeable than it actually is. If human consciousness was powerful enough to grasp the reality of our lives, we would recognize that personality is as permanent and as real as a column of smoke rising from a bonfire. We all experience different selves according to our circumstances and whom we happen to be talking to. Assertive people make us feel ineffectual; gentle people make us feel strong; admiring people make us feel admirable; contemptuous people make us feel contemptible, and so on.[21]

In *Mysteries*, the second volume in Wilson's Occult trilogy, Wilson continues his survey of occult phenomena, directing his attention to, among other things, ghosts, giants, ley-lines, precognition, alchemy and elementals. No matter what attitude one has towards the occult, it is impossible to doubt that the trilogy constitutes the most comprehensive assemblage of case histories on the occult ever drawn together.

In *Mysteries*, Wilson deals extensively with the theories of Tom Lethbridge who, in 1957, retired from Cambridge University, where he had had a distinguished career as an archaeologist, and settled in Devon to pursue his interest in dowsing. Lethbridge, who had been Honorary Keeper of Anglo-Saxon Antiquities at Cambridge, did not consider himself an occultist but he did have a long-standing interest in dowsing which was probably associated with his academic profession – which was based on recovering historical evidence from underground. Lethbridge indulged his interest and gradually discovered a fascinating aspect of this ancient art.

Lethbridge dowsed with a pendulum – which can be made simply, with a button or a bead tied to a length of string or chain. It operates by ceasing to swing and beginning to revolve in a circle over particular objects. Lethbridge found that his pendulum began to circle over coins which he had placed under cushions in his lounge room. It also circled over coins placed in secret locations by his wife. Then Lethbridge began to experiment with the length of the string of his pendulum. Winding it around a pencil, he lengthened it or shortened it and found, to his astonishment, that different lengths caused the pendulum to circle over different substances. If the string was 22 inches long, the pendulum circled over – that is, located – silver. If it was 30½ inches, it located copper. Over several days, he confirmed that sulphur, aluminium, gold, milk, apples, oranges, alcohol, sand, garlic and diamonds all responded to particular lengths or rates. Many objects had the same rate but those which grouped together seemed to be linked also by a curious logic. Thus 22 inches was the rate for lead, silver, sodium and calcium which are all grey or greyish. Further, items within the same group could be distinguished by a discrete number of circles made by the bob of the pendulum.

On one occasion, Lethbridge wondered if he could determine a rate for truffles – a culinary delicacy which grows in forests. He separated some truffles from a tin of pâté, in which they had been used as a flavouring agent. He concluded that truffles did have a rate – 17 inches. A few days later, while walking through a wood, Lethbridge set his pendulum at 17 inches and within half an hour had uncovered a small plant. The South Kensington Science Museum, to which the specimen was sent, identified it as an exceedingly rare type of truffle.

But there was more astonishment ahead for Lethbridge. Persisting with his experiments, he found that human emotions also have a rate which responds to the pendulum. He set the string at 40 inches and thought about something that had made him angry. The bob began to circle. Some stones which Lethbridge had collected at an Iron Age Fort named Wandlebury Camp also responded to 40 inches. Lethbridge concluded that they had been thrown in anger during a battle at the fort.

The rate for life, Lethbridge discovered, was 40. He lengthened the string beyond 40 inches and became convinced that he was measuring objects which existed beyond death. This claim seemed to be supported by the fact that he could not find a rate above 40 for time. In the light of these findings, Lethbridge wrote.

From living a normal life in a three dimensional world, I seem to have suddenly fallen through into one where there are more dimensions. The three dimensional world goes on as usual but one has to adjust one's thinking to the other.[22]

The final paragraph of his book, *A Step in the Dark* reads:

Our earth life compares with the larval stage (of an insect) and contains time and movement. The next stage is like that of a chrysalis, which remains for a while apparently dead and completely inert. Then comes the stage of the perfect insect, when time and movement not only return again, but are much accelerated. Here we must stop until more work is done: but at least we can leave this study with a greater conviction of the survival of the individual human mind.[23]

When he was a student at Trinity College, Lethbridge saw a ghost. As he was leaving the room of a friend, he passed a porter who was entering the room. Lethbridge greeted him but there was no reply. When he asked his friend, the next morning, what the porter had wanted, his friend insisted that no one had entered the room. It was only at that point that Lethbridge realised that the man had been wearing, not a porter's uniform, but some kind of hunting habit.

Ghosts appeared somewhat regularly to Lethbridge. Living next to his home in Devon was a woman who was widely regarded as a witch. She told him that she had the ability to travel outside her body – the phenomenon is widely attested and is known as 'astral travel'. One day in 1959, Lethbridge noticed the old woman as he looked through the window of his home. She was outside the gate of her own home and was accompanied by another woman who was dressed in what seemed to be a fashion of a generation earlier. Later in the morning, as he walked past her house, he met the witch and asked about her visitor. The old woman responded with the comment, 'You're seeing my ghosts now.'

There were also experiences of what Lethbridge called 'ghouls'. At the bottom of a stairwell in a school, he had witnessed what he describes as 'a strange, icy presence'. He writes of it:

There was more to it than cold. It was actively unpleasant. I have only met such a sudden cold in Melville Bay on the west coast of Greenland, when the motor boat in which I was sitting passed from sunlight into the shadow of an iceberg. At one moment the sun was streaming onto you and you were enjoying the glittering beauty of the bergs; at the next, an icy hand seemed to grip the whole of your body. This feeling at the bottom of the stairs was much like that but there was a feeling of misery with it too.[24]

Lethbridge recalled this sensation at the foot of the stairs in 1961 when, with his wife Mina, he visited Ladram Bay. As he stepped on to the beach, he experienced a sense of having walked through a blanket into a fog of depression and fear. Mina walked on towards the other end of the beach. Within a few minutes, however, she returned and expressed a desire to leave the place as she felt decidedly uncomfortable and frightened. Later in the day, Mina recounted her experience to her mother who commented that she herself had had a similar experience at the same place five years earlier. Five days later still, they returned to the beach. Immediately upon reaching it they felt the same sensation but as they neared the exact spot where they had stood on their earlier visit, Mina noted:

> Here the feeling was at its worst. It was so strong as to make me feel almost giddy. The nearest I can get to a description is that it felt not unlike one feels with a high temperature and when full of drugs. There was definitely a sensation of tingling to accompany it.[25]

On a nearby cliff to which she had wandered, Mina felt another unpleasant sensation, as if someone was trying to push her over the cliff.

Reflecting upon these threatening places which he called 'ghouls', Lethbridge made the observation that they always seemed to occur very close to water or heavy dew in the air. He concluded that, just as a stone seemed to be capable of 'containing' the emotions of a man who had thrown it hundreds of years ago, so water was also capable of recording human emotions. Thus Lethbridge suspected that ghouls and dowsing were closely linked. They both suggest the existence of a field of energy that surrounds objects and places and which can, perhaps, be measured. Indeed, it is one of Wilson's working hypotheses in *Mysteries*, that such field forces abound in the world about us and that all 'psychic' phenomena are to be explained in terms of individuals somehow interacting with such a field.

At the conclusion of his extended treatment of the theories of Lethbridge in *Mysteries*, Wilson writes:

> When I settled down to the systematic study of Lethbridge's books, it became clear that they fall into four groups. There are the books on archaeology and primitive religion, and the books on pendulums and related matters. *Legend of the Sons of God*, that remarkable anticipation of the findings of Erich von

Daniken and John Mitchell about 'visitors from other worlds' and the magnetic forces of the earth, belongs in a group of its own. The same is true of the final (posthumous) book, *The Power of the Pendulum*, in which he seemed to be about to embark on a new line of enquiry about dreams and the nature of time.

I must admit that, as I picked my way among his strange theories, I was reminded of some of the weird cults described in Martin Gardner's *Fads and Fallacies in the Name of Science*. Yet the shrewdness and humour – and a breezy willingness to admit that he may be quite wrong – remained basically reassuring.[26]

In another place, Wilson passes this judgement:

Between 1961 and his death in 1971, Lethbridge wrote ten books, all of them fairly short (about 150 pages). In these, he described in detail the progress of his investigations. These books, I believe, form one of the most fascinating records of 'paranormal research' of the twentieth century.[27]

One of the most central movements in the history of the occult is the practice of alchemy. Albertus Magnus, a thirteenth-century scholar who was canonised by the Catholic Church as recently as 1932 and who was a teacher of Thomas Aquinas, produced a considerable literature on this 'ancient art' and Wilson devotes a large section of *Mysteries* to an examination of it. Alchemy's 'lesser work' consists of the extraction of the essence of plants and vegetables for medicinal purposes. This essence, called 'the life principle' or 'mercury', could be distilled by placing the plant or vegetable in alcohol. By a complicated process of further distillation, the mercury thus obtained could be transformed into what was called 'the stone of the vegetable kingdom', which was itself a primitive form of 'the Philosopher's Stone'.

The production of the Philosopher's Stone itself was regarded by alchemists as the Great Work. While this task is commonly understood as the transmutation of a stone into gold, it was in fact a much more significant work. The Philosopher's Stone was a substance alchemists believed could be produced, with divine assistance, from particular raw materials which had to be submitted to chemical processes. (The historic value of alchemy may well lie in the fact that its chemical experiments provide much of the foundation upon which modern chemistry is based.) Alchemists believed that the world was pervaded by a universal spirit which united everything. The Stone was a physical compression of this spirit which became an elixir. When added to ordinary metals, it had the capacity to transform them into gold. But, much more significantly, this elixir, when swallowed as a medicine, had the capacity to cure a wide range of ailments. And here we come to the heart of alchemy. Neil Powell, a researcher into alchemy, writes:

Alchemy is extremely complicated. It is based on the practical skills of early metal workers and craftsmen, on Greek philosophy and on Eastern mystic cults that sprang up in the first centuries after Christ and influenced so much of magic and occult thought. It must be remembered that when alchemy flourished there was no dividing line between science and magic. Ideas such as the influence of the planets and the effect of certain numbers or letters on people's lives might today be regarded as superstitions. At that time they were perfectly acceptable to those who were making the kind of accurate observations about the material world that paved the way for modern science.

Long before the beginning of alchemy, gold was regarded as the most valuable metal. Its possession indicated wealth and power, and it was prized for its beauty. Known as the most perfect metal, it soon acquired symbolic meaning. It came to stand for excellence, wisdom, light and perfection. For serious alchemists, gold had both a real and symbolic significance, which at first seems confusing. The reason is that alchemists embarked on two different and difficult quests at the same time, and success in one meant success in the other. The first aim is the one that most people know about. The alchemist was attempting to find a way of transmuting, or changing, ordinary metals into the most perfect metal, gold. The second aim is less well-known but was far more important. The alchemist was trying to make the soul progress from its ordinary state to one of spiritual perfection.[28]

Wilson acknowledges that:

Alchemy is puzzling because it seems to stand in a different category from other branches of the paranormal such as psychometry, radiesthesia, telepathy and so on. Most paranormal faculties are passive: they work best when the mind is tranquil and they take place without any conscious effort. Alchemy is active, an attempt to produce transformations in the composition of matter. And alchemists maintain that it is not a purely chemical process; it involves a parallel transformation in the mind of the alchemist.[29]

Central to the notion of the Philosopher's Stone was the idea of the reconciliation of opposites. Indeed, the Stone itself has been described as being a compound of fire and water, masculine and feminine, stone and not-stone. The twentieth-century psychologist, Carl Jung, noting that many of his patients reported their dreams by using symbols that were common to alchemy, spent a considerable amount of time studying the art. His study supported his theory of a 'complete self' in which all conflicting and opposing elements of an individual life were reconciled to each other in such a way that the final product was something greater than the sum of the parts. Once again, alchemy pointed the way to a higher self.

Reflecting on Gurdjieff's notion that the body is a form of alchemical machine which transforms food into the energy we need to live, Wilson realised that sex is also an alchemical art. On one level, we understand the sexual act as a physical act but an analysis of the range of pleasure we derive from that act provides a clear indication that something more than the body is involved. Intercourse engaged in purely at the physical level, seldom satisfies us. In some profound sense, the act is fully pleasurable and fully satisfying only when the mind is intimately involved. Wilson argues that all sexual aberrations, including rape and sadism, are attempts at compensation for a normal sex act that no longer produces a feeling of satisfaction.

Sex is a means of awakening our highest intensities: it is a form of ascent on the ladder of selves. It is a transmutation of our physical existence into a heightened consciousness. Sexual alchemy is a form of Faculty X. In Tantrism, a branch of Hindu religious philosophy, the universe is composed of two basic elements, the male which is called Shiva and the female which is called Shakti. These forces come together in sexual energy which the Tantrist seeks to move up his spine through a series of centres known as *chakras* until they reach the brain and produce a state of intense illumination or enlightenment.

Alan Hull Walton, in his review of *Mysteries*, called 'Colin Wilson's *Magnum Opus*' ('Great Work'), interestingly enough points out that Wilson is insatiably curious as to why a majority of scientists seem reluctant to explore the vast array of evidence of the paranormal that has been accumulated over the centuries. Wilson addresses this question specifically in the chapter, 'The Curious History of Human Stupidity'.

In 1632, Pope Urban VIII picked up a book entitled *Dialogue on the Two Chief World Systems*. Something in the first few pages annoyed him and the annoyance developed as he read on until he was in a rage of indignation. What had offended him was the fact that the author of the book, Galileo, had broken a promise which he had made to the Pope some time earlier while the book was being written. Galileo had promised that while he would use the theories of Copernicus about the heliocentricity of the universe, he would stop short of supporting them as being true. Further, Galileo had promised to include several suggestions the Pope had made on the text. As he read the book, Urban saw that the corrections had not been made and that Galileo was in fact giving his whole support to Copernicus. The end result of the Pope's rage was that Galileo recanted – although with an ambiguity that enabled him to retain some self-respect.

The clash between Galileo and Urban is probably the most widely known example of the almost universal clash between established orthodoxy and new ideas. History provides dozens of examples, involving Goethe, Lamack, Darwin and others and Wilson has catalogued many of them with careful thoroughness. In attempting to explain this resistance by authorities, Wilson draws on the psychology of Abraham Maslow. Maslow had pointed out that men have a fundamental need for self-esteem and once it has been acquired, they are prone to defend it vigorously. Part of one's self-esteem is related to the body of ideas one holds as being 'true' and when these ideas are challenged, the tendency is to protect them vigorously – so vigorously, in fact, that objective truth becomes endangered in the process. What begins as a natural reaction becomes a bold arrogance.

There may well be a problem with the very thought processes that mankind brings to bear on the problems that confront him.

By and large, Western man uses as his intellectual analytic tool a system that has derived from Socrates and is called the Socratic method, or scientific method. Essentially, this system relies upon the intellect alone, refusing to acknowledge that intuition can provide any useful insight – or at least insisting that any insight that might be intuitive must be validated by 'reason' before it can be admitted to the established orthodoxies. But just as Socrates' disciple, Plato, had to defend the Socratic method against opponents such as Gorgias, a Sophist from Sicily, so the modern scientific method must learn to find answers to critics such as Arthur Koestler who insisted that many of the great break-throughs in human development were achieved by 'Sleepwalkers' – men who stumbled across a profound truth, not because of the evidence that pointed to it but despite the orthodoxies which concealed it. One such Sleepwalker, argues Koestler, was Galileo himself.

Yet another problem is created by the diminished value contemporary man places on ideas. It is true that there are many individuals in our world who are earnestly engaged in an evaluation of the central issues but, for the overwhelming populace, thinking is too demanding a requirement and they continue to gaze at the television set with a dullness of mind that ensures their gullibility and their manipulation.

It is a concern of Wilson that whatever will not fit into established patterns of thought is frequently rejected with a mindless foolishness. He is persuaded that a wholehearted and genuinely intelligent treatment of the evidence that surrounds us would result in insights that would project us forward on the next stage of our evolutionary journey. Nor should we be overly selective in terms of which pieces of the evidence we will admit:

> There is no reason why we should not take our clues wherever we can find them – in Lethbridge, Jung, Janet, Gurdjieff, alchemy, astrology, even ritual magic.[30]

Prior to the extensive investigation of poltergeist phenomena that constituted the research for his book *Poltergeist!*,[31] Wilson had been willing to subscribe to the theory that the poltergeist was a manifestation of the unconscious mind of an unhappy person. The phenomenon itself had been long established as a fact and it was known to be associated, frequently, with a disturbed teenager. While various researchers such as Frank Podmore had argued that they were usually due to deliberate fraud, there seemed to be no evidence to support this view. Nor, at this time, could Wilson find any evidence to support the view of his friend and fellow researcher, Guy Playfair, to whom *Poltergeist!* is dedicated, that poltergeists are caused by a disembodied spirit. A particular case, investigated by Wilson himself, was to alter his view.

In 1980, Wilson visited the home of the Pritchard family in Pontefract, a small town in Yorkshire. The Pritchards had been the centre of national attention in August 1966 when their home was visited by a poltergeist. The majority of the family were away on holidays but Mrs Scholes, Mrs Pritchard's mother remained behind with her grandson, fifteen-year-old Phillip. One Thursday afternoon, Phillip entered the lounge room to find his grandmother sitting in a chair knitting. All around her on the floor was a grey-white powder, like chalk. Thus the phenomena had started. A pool of water was found on the kitchen floor. When Mrs Scholes mopped it up, another pool appeared. A neighbour turned off the house's water supply. Still the pools of water appeared. That evening, in the kitchen, the button of the tea dispenser went in and out of its own accord and tea was sprinkled over the sink below it. A sudden crash was heard. Grandmother and grandson rushed out into the passage. A large plant, normally set in a tub on the first landing of the stairs, was lying on the floor at the foot of the stairs. The tub remained in place. In the course of the night, framed photographs were torn from walls and flung on the floor. One, a photograph of the Pritchard's wedding, was slashed, as if by a knife. The next day, the family returned from their holiday and before long they were all subjected to the poltergeist's activities. Diane, the daughter, went to her bedroom and saw a grey shadow form on the wall. The room became icy cold. As she rushed from the room, a hall-stand floated in the air towards her then pushed her down and pinned her to the floor.

The full story of the Pontefract poltergeist cannot be told here – it occupies thirty-four pages in Wilson's book. The phenomena ended almost as abruptly as they had begun. One day, Phillip and Diane were sitting watching television. Suddenly, both noticed the outline of a figure through the glass panel of the door that led to the dining-room and kitchen. Phillip crossed the room and opened the door to see the figure of a monk passing through the doorway into the kitchen. After this, the poltergeist was never seen again.

Ten years after the appearance of Fred, as the poltergeist came to be called, a researcher named Tom Cunniff claimed that the Pritchard house stood on the site of a gallows where, in the reign of Henry VIII, a Cluniac monk had been hanged for the rape of a young girl. Wilson was unable to corroborate this claim but he did find that there had been vigorous litigation within a monastery of Clunaic monks who had lived nearby.

It was while on his way to Pontefract that Wilson called in to see Guy Playfair, who advanced his theory that a poltergeist is basically a disembodied, mischievous spirit. Wilson reflected on Playfair's theory and concluded that the evidence relating to the Black Monk of Pontefract could be explained by it.

Wilson believes that the explanation may be found in an underground stream that flowed under the Pritchard house. This recalls Lethbridge's theory of water and dampness as being capable of containing psychic impressions. The evidence suggests that somehow the spirit of a monk from one of the local monasteries had insinuated itself into the force field around the house and that it had begun to manifest itself, using the sexual and emotional energy that was available, first through the adolescent Phillip who, it seems, was locked in a psychological battle with his father and then through the pubescent Diane.

In a review of *Poltergeist!*, John Grant laments the shift in Wilson's thinking on the subject.

Until very recently, Wilson not only supported the hypothesis that poltergeist events originated in the right brains of human beings, but he put forward a very good case for that hypothesis. Then, while writing this book, he was convinced by Guy Lyon Playfair that the spirits of the dead are involved. The theory seems to run that the human involvement is the production of a 'football' of psychic energy; along come some malicious spirits and they start kicking the football about. Wilson says that his conversion came about while he was investigating the Pontefract case, in which, at one point, the assumed 'focus', Diane Pritchard, was dragged upstairs by the throat. Surely her unconscious wouldn't have done that to her, he concludes. Frankly, I don't see why not. It is well known that the personalities involved in multiple-personality cases are not always kind to each other; also, the conscious mind itself is perfectly capable of the most masochistic behaviour.[32]

Notwithstanding Wilson's interpretation of the events at Pontefract, or Grant's objections to them, *Poltergeist!* provides a respectable body of circumstantial evidence that the 'noisy ghost' does appear from time to time and that a great deal of its behaviour can be catalogued. What it is and what causes it remains a subject of legitimate study.

Inevitably, a study of the occult must address the ultimate question – that of whether or not there is a form of existence after death. Wilson's contribution to this debate is contained in *Afterlife.*[33]

The question of the reality of an afterlife is best approached from an indirect point of view. Wilson spends considerable time discussing a work by Frederick Myers, the founding father of the Society for Psychical Research. The work is entitled *Human Personality and Its Survival of Bodily Death.* Wilson regards it as probably the most comprehensive work ever written on the subject of the paranormal – although contemporary judgements must surely conclude that his own 'Occult Trilogy' has now surpassed it. In fact, Myers' book does not raise the question of bodily survival of death until its final pages and then treats the subject only briefly. It is much more concerned with other phenomena which defy explanation. It opens with a lengthy treatment of what is now called 'multiple personality', proceeds through a discussion of genius and hypnosis and expands into a lengthy discussion of what Myers called the 'subliminal mind' which is, as he understands it, the crucible in which are forged those flashes of insight that are commonly called 'genius'. In an introduction to an American edition of the book, the late Aldous Huxley said of it that it is

an immense store of information about the strange and often wonderful goings-on in the upper stories of man's soul-house.[34]

Myers argued that we have very considerable powers of which our conscious mind is normally unaware. These include the power to transmit our thoughts, or even images of ourselves across thousands of miles. Some of these powers are readily apparent in men of genius. Thus, a young Mozart could play a complex tune having heard it only once before; or a five-year-old Benjamin Blyth could calculate accurately, within a few seconds, the number of seconds he had been alive. Strangely enough, these powers are also manifest in some sick people. The psychiatrist, Oliver Sacks, provides an account of twins, 'idiot savants' who had been institutionalised for several years, who played games by providing each other, within a few seconds, with the next number in a string of primes or naming the day of any date within the past or future 40,000 years.

In multiple personalities, there seems to be a 'basic' or 'real' self to which the other selves are attached. The collective personalities seem to have a 'substratum'. Thus the body may well be an instrument which responds to the demands of the personality, much like a car responds to the demands of a driver. Myers suggests that when we are physically ill, it may be the personality that is ill, with the symptoms being expressed in physical terms. Modern psychosomatic medicine knows that this is certainly true to some extent.

If the 'substratum' of personality does exist, having been created over thousands and thousands of years in some sort of Jungian 'collective unconscious', we have the beginning of an argument that it might survive bodily death. There seems to be an absurdity about the proposition that the essential self is carefully evolved and protected against the idiosyncrasies of a particular, historic personality, only to be extinguished with the death of an individual.

One of the most widely studied cases of an alleged survival is that of Dr A. S. Wiltse, who was formally pronounced dead by a doctor in Kansas in 1889. Four hours after his death, he 'awoke' on his bed and gave a detailed account of a whole series of events that had taken place. After losing consciousness, he had found himself still within his own body but was able to observe the way in which his various organs interacted with 'himself'. Gradually, he separated from his body, starting at the feet and then moving up the limbs until the head was free. He felt himself to have the shape and feel of a jellyfish. He could see his own dead body on the bed below him. As he walked out of the door, he became aware that he remained connected to his body by a 'spider's web' thread which expanded as he moved away. Outside, he felt himself being pushed along a road by an invisible force.

Ahead, he noticed three rocks. A voice inside his head told him that if he passed the rocks, he would be entering eternity. Although he was strongly tempted to walk on, he finally resisted. Suddenly, he woke up on his bed.

On the surface, this seems like a typical case of a 'near-death' experience but it must be realised that a doctor had pronounced him dead four hours earlier. There may be, of course, a rational explanation. The doctor could have been mistaken in his judgement and Wiltse could simply have dreamed everything he was to report later. Wilson, together with Myers and many others who have studied the case, concluded that it seems strange that he should have continued to dream long after his pulse had stopped.

In isolation, the Wiltse case proves nothing. Myers, however, studied numerous cases and came to the conclusion, despite his natural inclination towards scepticism, that the body of evidence did suggest, and very strongly, that there were instances of the bodily survival of death.

When William James, the pragmatic psychologist, visited Myers in 1882, he was a committed sceptic as far as psychic abilities were concerned. Soon afterwards, however, his mother-in-law told him of a woman who had been able to give an account of the James family which was astonishing in its accuracy and about which the woman could have had no prior knowledge. James went to visit the woman, a Mrs Piper, and was himself surprised at her perceptive insight into his family life. Mrs Piper gave her accounts through a medium called Phinuit and James came to the conclusion that Phinuit was an aspect of Mrs Piper's personality – that she was a 'split personality'. No matter what the explanation, Mrs Piper's feats were formidable. In the presence of James' mother, she had written a message on a sheet of paper which was handed to another person present – a Judge Frost. The message purported to be from the Judge's deceased son and the Judge declared it to be 'remarkable'. Somewhat reluctantly, James became convinced that Mrs Piper was genuine. He had her in mind when he wrote

If you wish to upset the law that all crows are black, you must not seek to show that no crows are: it is enough if you can prove one single crow to be white.[35]

In *Afterlife*, Wilson sets out what might well be an assemblage of 'white crows'. His evidence may well be uneven and, at times strained, but the effect is to make it very difficult for any serious reader to contend that the case for human survival of death is beyond contest. Perhaps his most striking evidence, which not only strongly suggests survival of death but also a form of reincarnation, is the case of Jasbir Lal Jat.

Jasbir, a three-year-old Indian boy, died of smallpox in 1954. The decision was taken to leave the burial until the next day but before it could take place, the child had stirred and begun to recover. It was several weeks before he was fully recovered but all who knew him found that he had undergone a complete change. He informed his family that he was a Brahmin, which Jasbir was not, and that he was the son of Shankar from the village of Vehedi. He refused food until it was prepared according to Brahmin custom. Jasbir insisted on his story for a whole year. He also insisted that he had lived a previous life which had ended when he had been given poisonous sweets and had fallen from a cart. Then a Brahmin woman from Vehedi visited his village which was called Rasulpur. She was instantly recognised by Jasbir as his aunt. Puzzling for an explanation, Jasbir's family decided to take him to Vehedi and were astonished when, on the way, he took the lead and led them through a complicated route to the village he had never visited before. He led them to a particular home, which he said was his, and gave a detailed account of the family, Brahmins, who lived there. He knew, not only its members but a great deal about its private affairs. The family had earlier lost a twenty-two-year old son named Subha Ram who had died of smallpox, the same disease that had caused the death of Jasbir. Astonishingly, both deaths had occurred at the same time.

Of the Jasbir Lal Jat case, Wilson acknowledges that it is more suggestive than conclusive but we are left to wonder if it does not represent a white crow.

By way of a summary of the case histories set out in *Afterlife*, Wilson writes:

> This is finally the most convincing argument for the view of life after death . . . there is such an enormous body of similar evidence to support it. There are literally hundreds of reports of 'life after death' that display the same pattern. That pattern is roughly as follows. After the death experience, which may

be accompanied by a sense of pain or suffocation, there is a sudden sensation of freedom. In many cases, the person has a sense of passing down a long tunnel and seeing a light at the end. Then he finds himself looking at his own body. This is usually accompanied by a feeling of deep peace; and a certain relief at having done with physical existence. The person may find it impossible to accept the idea that he is dead and tries to talk to other people. They ignore him – although animals sometimes seem to be aware of him. He tries to touch them; his hand goes through them. And, again and again in these accounts, the 'dead person' is met by relatives who have already died: this happens only when he acknowledges that he is dead. There seem to be many cases in which the dead person is in a state of confusion, rather like being in a fever, and fails to grasp that he is no longer alive. In that case, he may remain trapped on earth – an 'earth-bound' spirit – indefinitely.[36]

Yet, with characteristic intellectual integrity, he warns,

It is not my purpose to try to convince anyone of the reality of life after death: only to draw attention to the impressive consistency of the evidence and to point out that, in the light of that evidence, one need not feel ashamed of accepting the notion that human personality survives bodily death.[37]

Just as Wilson drew his Outsider cycle to a close with the volume entitled *Beyond the Outsider*, so he has chosen to close what must now be called his Occult cycle with the important volume *Beyond the Occult*. It should be born in mind, however, that just as volumes written after *Beyond the Outsider*, such as *Introduction to the New Existentialism* and the more recent *The Misfits*, properly belong within the cycle, so we may anticipate that future volumes will appear which will have to be placed within the Occult cycle. Nonetheless, *Beyond the Occult* rounds the cycle off while, at the same time, it introduces two important new concepts.

The first of these is the notion of levels of consciousness; a notion somewhat akin to the idea of the ladder of selves. Wilson posits a hierarchy of levels of consciousness and spells out the first seven. Level-one consciousness is the sleeping dream or the hypnogogic state. Level two is the basic level of waking consciousness. It is the consciousness of a child being driven home from a late party. He looks out of the car window but sees without seeing. Level-three consciousness has become self-aware but everything seems to be merely itself. Our own reflection in a mirror seems as if it could be of anyone. This is the level of Sartre's 'nausea'. Level-four consciousness is the consciousness we all experience every day. Wilson says of it:

> It is no longer too heavy to move: it has learned how to cope with existence yet it tends to think of life as a grim battle – possibly a losing battle. Consequently, it tends to sink back easily towards level three and to find experience meaningless and boring.[38]

These first four levels of consciousness are essentially passive but at level five, consciousness takes on a life of its own. Level-five consciousness is 'holiday consciousness'. It sees life as self-evidently fascinating and satisfying. This is the consciousness of Hermann Hesse's Steppenwolf as he sips a glass of wine and is put in mind of Mozart and the stars.

Wilson calls level-six consciousness 'the magical level'. Here, consciousness is a continuous mild peak experience in which problems seem trivial. It is what J. B. Priestley would have called 'delight'. Next on the scale is level-seven consciousness – the experience of Faculty X and the Proustian sense of the God-like. Nor, it must be emphasised, does Wilson close his scale at this point. The levels of consciousness are an open-ended hierarchy for we do not know what lies ahead.

The second important insight expounded in *Beyond the Occult* is concerned with the mechanisms by which an individual moves up or down through the levels of consciousness that constitute his being. Movement from a higher to a lower level is effected by what Wilson calls 'upsidedownness'. In simple terms, this is a state in which the essential equilibrium between intellect and emotion is disturbed and an individual is being dominated by emotion. A human being is upside-down when in a state of rage, since this is an emotional state over which the intellect is permitted no controlling influence.

The movement upward through the levels of consciousness is facilitated by what Wilson calls 'completing'. Completing is applied relationality. It is the process by which a human being builds up the jigsaw pattern of experience and sees the connections that exist between people, situations and things. Completing is the acquisition of a bird's-eye view: the objectification of our own subjectivity. The more we complete, the more absurd our rage will appear to be.

Mankind's proper attitude towards the occult should be one in which the objective is completion. Wilson writes:

> The universe seen by the clairvoyant has much in common with the universe seen by the mystic and both are bigger and more complete than the universe seen by the rest of us. The view of the sceptic is based upon a misconception: that the mystic – and the clairvoyant – is offering an alternative to the ordinary reality that surrounds us. One of Daskalos's [the adopted name of Spyros Sathi, a modern Magus] followers once objected to him, 'material reality is the only thing that I know exists. It is what I can see, touch, feel, smell.' And Daskalos replied, 'There is nothing more misleading than the five senses.' He means that our assumption that the five senses 'reveal' reality is mistaken. They only reveal the limited reality of the immediate present and this (itself) would be meaningless to us unless it was 'completed' by our minds. The senses of the mystic and the clairvoyant are like doors that will open wider than the doors of ordinary humanity. What they perceive is not an alternative reality but an extension of normal reality.[39]

Wilson's study of the occult is profoundly important. In an age dominated by an intellectual persuasion that resists even an invitation to explore the totality of the evidence to hand, his work constitutes a major challenge.

Martin Gardner, in a review of *Poltergeist!*, wrote:

> Colin's . . . six hundred page work, *The Occult* covers every aspect of [the paranormal] from ancient times to Wilhelm Reich's orgone energy and the ability of Ted Serios, a Chicago bellhop, to project thought-pictures onto Polaroid film. Colin bought it all. With unparalleled egotism and scientific ignorance he believed almost everything he read about the paranormal, no matter how outrageous. Nothing by believers escaped his notice, nothing by skeptics held his attention. *The Occult*, he once told me, outsold all his previous books put together. A 1979 sequel, *Mysteries* (667 pages), was more of the same. He

edited the twenty volumes of a lurid, worthless set called *A New Library of the Supernatural*. His own contribution to this series, *The Geller Phenomena*, is surely the most gullible book ever written about the Israeli charlatan, now thoroughly discredited in the eyes of almost everybody except Colin.[40]

Wilson is frequently criticised for being careless, inaccurate and emotive in his work. The extract from Gardner just quoted is open to the same charges. The reference to the Chicago bellhop is emotive, suggesting that a bellhop may be safely dismissed as being incapable of doing anything, let alone taking psychic photographs. The counting of the pages of Wilson's two books is also emotive, suggesting that many pages of drivel are somehow more unintelligent than one page. The word 'lurid' means 'glaringly vivid or sensational'. *A New Library of the Supernatural*, by its very subject matter, is dealing with sensational material but it is made sensational by the intellectual ethos of the age rather than by Wilson's treatment of it. 'Gullibility' is a human attribute: how can a *book* be gullible? Far from being inattentive to his critics, Wilson introduces, again and again in his work, alternative points of view and frequently leaves it to the reader to decide their relative merits.

   None of this is intended as a cheap attack on Gardner; nor is it a defence of Wilson. It is intended to demonstrate that it is easy to take the written word and show that it can contain inconsistencies and inadequacies. Yet it does contain meaning. We know what Gardner is saying and we know what his general position is. It would be satisfying to see critics discuss Wilson's theories rather than submit him to the inferior form of evaluation that is all too common.

   But there is another passage in Gardner's review that is of even greater significance. He writes

In 1966, when my wife and I lived in a Manhattan suburb, Colin came to visit us. During his stay of several days he talked nonstop, often pacing the floor while great thoughts agitated his brain. Nothing I had to say about anything was of the slightest interest to him. I recall interrupting his monologues only once. 'Colin', I said, 'it seems to me that what is bugging you the most is that you are not God'. To my amazement, he found this perceptive. Shortly after he left we received a courteous thank-you note in which he said that his visit had provided the most stimulating exchange of ideas he had had in America.[41]

When this passage was drawn to Wilson's attention, he insisted that he had been enormously stimulated by the conversations he had had with Gardner and that he had been greatly interested in everything his host had said. The agitation of Wilson's brain that Gardner observed might well have been caused by Gardner's contribution to the discussion. Perhaps, after all, it was Gardner who had the closed mind. Certainly, it seems that while Gardner was busy observing Wilson, Wilson was following the stimulating meanderings of his own thinking.

Wilson's overview of the occult world and its exploration can best be stated in his own words. He concludes:

The whole history of psychical research has been a series of demonstrations of the apparently 'absurd' powers of the human mind. For the scientist, this has always been at best an embarrassment, at worst a scandal. But it now begins to look as though this may be because he is the slave of his old-fashioned ideas of the nature of science. More than three centuries ago, René Descartes established the modern method of science and philosophy; he called it 'radical doubt'. The Philosopher, says Descartes, should sit in his armchair and contemplate the universe around him. He should then proceed to doubt everything that can be doubted. Does the sun really go around the earth, as it seems to do? If we question it, we may arrive at the truth. As to the question, 'How do you prove your own existence?', Descartes replied: 'I think, therefore I am'. And having established this apparently unshakeable foundation, he felt able to relax in his armchair and turn his telescope on the universe outside his window.

The investigator of the paranormal has no doubt that 'I think, therefore I am', but he is inclined to add the disconcerting question: 'You are *what?*' For this is clearly the question that Descartes overlooked. Who precisely *am* I? He assumed, naturally enough, that he was René Descartes; that is what it said on his birth certificate. But every mystic has had the curious experience of realizing that he is not who he thinks he is. In moments of visionary intensity, his identity dissolves and he becomes aware that he is no more than a mask. Instead, he is looking into the depth of an inner universe that bears a strange resemblance to the outer universe. And the question: 'Who am I?' can only be answered by pointing his telescope inside himself.[42]

Wilson's occultism is not an undisciplined flight of fancy or a wild speculation. It is a controlled insistence that life is more than it seems to be; that we have an extensive journey within ourselves yet to make; that we have almost certainly called ourselves 'man' too early.

7

The Critical Theory

THE literature of the early 1950s posed a considerable problem for established literary critics. Their confusion in the face of this literature is well illustrated by their response to the publication of Jack Kerouac's novel, *On the Road*, which heralded in the Beat Generation in the United States. Critics acknowledged that it was an interesting book but they tended to speak of it in terms of a literary genre which had been long established – that of the *picaresque* – the novel of the traveller in search of a fuller, richer life. The *picaresque* had been created as early as the fifteenth century, with the publication of Cervantes *Don Quixote*, which told the story of the travels of the man of La Mancha and his *alter ego*, Sancho Panza.

Yet the critics seem to have sensed that *On the Road* differed from the classic *picaresque*. It dealt with an even more fundamental quest than the search for Dean Moriarty's essential self: it hinted at the human need for an essential freedom that seemed a basic ingredient of mid-twentieth-century experience. It was this element with which the critics seemed uncomfortable, not knowing what to make of it or how to respond to it. They could recognise it but they could not write about it because they had not reflected sufficiently upon its nature.

The critics' dilemma had been foreshadowed in part by T. S. Eliot. As early as 1934, Eliot had spoken of a need for a criticism that launched itself from an ethical, religious platform. He tried to demonstrate such a criticism in his book *After Strange Gods*, which was a critical treatment of novelists such as D. H. Lawrence, Thomas Hardy and James Joyce. Wilson judges this attempt by Eliot to have been unsuccessful and attributes the failure to his refusal to expose the basis of his own religious belief in public. His 'ethical' criticism foundered on the shoal of a confusing dogmatism.

Yet Wilson recognised in Eliot's argument an important insight and he is generous enough to acknowledge *After Strange Gods* as a work of *existential criticism*. At best, however, Eliot's notion was a precursor to a new genre of literary criticism. It fails as existential criticism because, as Wilson himself points out, it does not take into account the values upon which the writers it discusses base their work. The new criticism must finally be acknowledged as the creation of Wilson and its significance cannot be overemphasised, for through existential criticism the most profound and helpful of all possible interpretations of humanity's creative endeavour become available.

The fundamental nature of existential criticism can be demonstrated easily with reference to T. S. Eliot's own work. In his early work, he spoke out against the static nature of his contemporary society and insisted that progress was to be achieved through a programme of change. He might be regarded as expressing a sociological criticism of society. In his later works, however, he argues for the renewal of society through the espousing of traditional Anglo-Catholic beliefs. In this, he might be said to be expressing a religious criticism of society. Existential criticism identifies a fundamental contradiction in these two positions in which society is challenged to effect a change and yet remain static.

Existential criticism shares the same basic concerns as the Outsider. In a real sense, it may be defined as the criticism applied by the Outsider in his finest moments. It has been noted that Existentialism flourishes in a period when values are undergoing fundamental changes. Such a climate brings the Outsider into the open and it also presents existential criticism with its greatest opportunity. As Wilson points out, Existentialism aims at identifying a new science of life and existential criticism is an evaluation of the arts from the perspective of the contribution they make to this new science. The common man will put down a book after he has completed reading it and will comment to his friend that he has 'enjoyed' it: the existential critic will inform his friend that the book has profoundly influenced his life because it has introduced him to new dimensions of meaning. This is not to argue that the novel should not amuse us.

> The novel is an impersonal form developed by men who wanted to entertain. The twentieth century writer usually has an intensely personal viewpoint to express. The struggle lies in uniting the two.[1]

It is important to distinguish between existential literature and existential criticism. *Some* literature is existential. *All* literature may be interpreted existentially. Some novels may deal directly and explicitly with the basic issues confronting man, just as Hermann Hesse deals with the question of absolute freedom in *Magister Ludi*. All novels, including Jack Shaeffer's western *Shane* – ostensibly shallow and belonging to a cult readership – can be read with a view to assessing what it has to contribute to an understanding of the status of man.

With the emergence of the great Russian novelist, Fyodor Dostoevsky, a significant theme was introduced into modern fiction. In *Crime and Punishment*, Dostoevsky retained many of the conventions of the nineteenth-century novel, including the wronged woman and the heartless landlord, but these do not provide the essential thing about the work. What lingers after the book has been read is the world in which Raskolnikov has his miserable existence – the drabness of Moscow and the futility of his experience. Dostoevsky accurately reflected the setting against which twentieth-century man was to seek his own identity. Wilson has delineated that setting very clearly as the background against which the Outsider stands out.

In *The Age of Defeat*, Wilson recounts how a sentence from De Tocqueville's study of *Democracy in America* helped him formulate one of the most critical problems confronting contemporary man. De Tocqueville had written:

> When [the American] comes to survey the totality of his fellows, and to place himself in contrast to so huge a body, he is instantly overwhelmed by his own insignificance and weakness.[2]

Wilson understood that De Tocqueville had uncovered a disease which had entered Western culture in the last half of the nineteenth century and had since spread with increasing virulence. To this disease, Wilson gave the name, *Insignificance*.

In the writings of the American sociologists, Vance Packard, David Reisman and William H. Whyte, Wilson found all the evidence he needed to support his theory of insignificance. Advanced Western cultures had turned human individuals into 'organisation men' whose primary responsibility was to serve the interests of the organisation. While Whyte thought of organisations in this context as being private companies, it soon becomes clear that they were much more inclusive than the organisations for which men worked. Welfare agencies, including hospitals, had become organisations. Schools and universities were organisations. Local and larger governments were organisations. There were signs that even the church had become an organisation. In short, society itself was an organisation which had to be maintained for the benefit of mankind, and the fodder that sustained it was the individual.

It was little wonder that in the face of organisations, individuals began to under-rate themselves. Their function was to support the organisation; not to utilise it. The teacher busied himself in securing higher grades in his class, not for the sake of his students' education but for the sake of the school's reputation. The Christian contributed more money for the building of more places of worship and that, rather than a corporate act of worship in celebration of a saving grace, became the centre of his religious duty.

Much of the so-called art of the mid-twentieth century not only reflected the idea of insignificance: it copied it. The 'movel' – the novel written in order to be sold as a movie script – emerged, devoid of ideas, except those that would appeal to a mass audience, and totally without benefit of the artist's craft. 'Pop-art' became the medium of the day, with labels from soup cans finding their way into art galleries and a cacophonous disharmony belching out what the clever entrepreneurs chose to call music. The decline in the dignity of the individual's self-image found expression in a debased art form.

It is, however, in the novel that insignificance becomes most immediately apparent. Wilson detects that in the middle of the twentieth century, the hero has virtually vanished from the novel. In his place there is the anti-hero, personified, at least for William H. Whyte, in Captain Queeg, of Herman Wouk's *The Caine Mutiny*. Queeg is the master of the *Caine* who finds his ship in the midst of a violent storm. Queeg is terrified by the storm and tries to outrun it by turning the vessel down wind. His first mate, Maryk, knows that this is inviting certain disaster and argues that Queeg should turn the ship back into the wind. The neurotic captain refuses and Maryk, with great reluctance, tells him that he is relieving him of command. Maryk is court-martialled for his 'mutiny' but the court finds Queeg unbalanced and Maryk is acquitted. What makes the story interesting for Whyte is that the attorney who defends Maryk tells him, after the trial, that he believes he was wrong and that he would have preferred to defend Queeg, for whom he thinks he could have won the case.

Whyte submitted the plot of this novel to a group of students and sought their opinion on the moral questions it raised. He was astounded when the overwhelming majority of the students indicated their belief that Maryk was in the wrong and that authority is to be obeyed simply because it is authority. Whyte concluded that their attitude was representative of the 'organisation man'. It is an attitude that takes us directly to Wilson's notion of the failure of modern literature – and of his concern for the identification of more substantial values than those which pervade contemporary Western culture.

Wilson reviews a number of contemporary novels which introduce us to a defeated hero. In James Jones' *From Here to Eternity*, there is Prewett, a young army officer who refuses to represent his company in the boxing ring. But it would be incorrect to suppose that this refusal marks him as an individual of principle. The inadequacy of his self-image becomes clear in the response he makes to his girl friend, when she asks why he intends to return to his company after an extended leave. 'What did the army ever do for you, besides beat you up and treat you like scum and throw you in jail like a criminal?' The only answer he can articulate is, 'What do I want to go back for? . . . I'm a soldier!'

The elevation of Queeg and Prewett as models of acceptable heroes is a reflection of the fallacy of insignificance. Insignificance, both in the novel and in society at large, is one of the principle problems confronting a humanity which wants to advance. It is a fundamental target for existential criticism.

A great deal of modern literature is existential in method rather than in nature. Wilson writes:

the existential method in the modern novel, the microscope that moves slowly over the surface of a chair or a wall, observes the sheen of colour on the wing of a dead fly in a glass of water. I am assuming that readers are familiar with *La Nausée* and its slimy grey stone and twisted tree roots and the other *objects* that dominate the book. This method has been carried to a strange limit by three young French novelists, Alain Robbe-Grillet, Michel Butor and Nathalie Sarraute. Robbe-Grillet derives from Hemingway in ignoring emotions and concentrating on 'the facts'. Like Hemingway, he never tells the reader, 'This character is in mental agony'; he prefers to record casual conversations, the appearance of the chair, and allows the reader to infer the agony. But he is infinitely less successful (artistically) than Hemingway, for the method demands strong, clear emotions that can make their own impact without the writer's help. Robbe-Grillet specialises in long, dull descriptions of physical objects; his attempt to keep the novel detached and scientific has simply emasculated it.[3]

The problem with this detailed observation approach to the writing of fiction is summed up, for Wilson, in W. B. Yeats' lines:

> Shakespearean fish swam the sea, far away from land;
> Romantic fish swam in nets coming to the hand;
> What are all these fish that lie gasping on the strand?

'Shakespearean fish' are a detached creation: they are the product of a premiss that is taken for granted. 'Romantic fish' are the product of introspection. More recent 'fish' are spilled on the beach as if someone had poured out a scientific catalogue.

There is, in fact, very little that is of ultimate value to be gained by a meticulous analysis of details except as that analysis points to *meaning*. Wilson points out that Robbe-Grillet and other writers of his kind use an existential method but never get to the existential substance. They describe a physical reality but seldom relate it to the question of the destiny of man. They observe and record their observation but they seldom analyse. When they do get down to questioning the meaning of an individual's life, it soon becomes clear that they are more concerned with the social dimensions of that life than with the individual value-system that it represents and reflects. To this extent, many of the *avant-garde* novelists simply extend the tradition of writers such as Flaubert.

Sartre, however, provides us with the genuinely existential novel. Sartre's pessimism posed a real problem for him in the face of post-war French enthusiasm. As compensation for this pessimism, he introduced the idea that man is free and that he is responsible for putting his freedom to good use. The fact that Sartre could not identify a satisfactory use should not be interpreted as meaning that he did not write existential fiction. Although he did write from a position of futility, there is a strong suggestion in his work that there *is* room for idealism. Sartre did have a vision: his tragedy was that he could find no way of realising it. Sartre made an honest attempt to reflect the world he saw. The problem is that the world he saw was without meaning. For Wilson,

> All art asks the same question: What is the meaning of human life? – and implicitly answers it. Its 'value-premises' may be completely hidden and taken for granted but they are present. The history of the experimental novel in the twentieth century proves that technique in itself defeats its own object – increased maturity. Hemingway and Joyce have nothing in common except their avoidance of general ideas and their technique of detachment. The reason is the same in both cases: the questions asked and the values implied in their best work are never developed.[4]

Existential literature and art as a whole, abounds, in varying degrees of quality, in our present culture. Wilson has referred to it more extensively than any other writer of the century and no one provides a more intelligent introduction to it. He argues that there is in fact, an existential 'temper' in modern literature that gives it a distinctive quality which separates it from the vast majority of the literature that preceded it. It is important to note, however, that this 'temper' is related to Existentialism rather than to the New Existentialism. It is not until the fiction of Wilson himself that we are introduced to a full fictional expression of the New Existentialism.

Nonetheless, Wilson had his precursors. Foremost among these were H. G. Wells, David Lindsay, James Joyce and Friedrich Durrenmatt.

For the medieval church, the map of the world contained no *terra incognita*. Christian faith supplied the answer to every riddle confronting the world and in the face of any unknown, one had only to stimulate religious belief and it would give a shape to the mystery. By the beginning of the twentieth century, however, the map was pockmarked with areas of the gravest uncertainty. Some men were still able to use their faith to see a vague outline but most agreed that there could be no certainty. Wilson regards H. G. Wells as one of the most successful cartographers of his age. In fact, in Wilson's view, it is one of the primary responsibilities of the artist to diminish, as much as possible, all areas of *terra incognita*.

The notion that, above all others, provides Wells with his greatness as a novelist is his conviction, expressed in *The History of Mr Polly*, that if a man does not like his life, he can change it. This change is effected by a resolute subjectivism; a self-examination and reflection of one's inner self. In his *Experiment in Autobiography*, Wells wrote:

> Entanglement is our common lot. I believe this craving for a release from bothers, from daily demands and urgencies, from responsibilities and tempting distractions, is shared by an increasing number of people who, with specialised and distinctive work to do, find themselves eaten up by first-hand affairs. . . . Most individual creatures, since life began, have been 'up against it' all the time: have been driven continually by fear and cravings . . . and they have found a sufficient and sustaining interest in the drama of immediate events. . . . But with the dawn of human forethought and with the appearance of a great surplus of energy in life such as the last century or so has revealed, there has been a progressive emancipation of the attention from everyday urgencies. People can now ask what would have been an extraordinary question five hundred years ago. They can say: 'Yes, you earn a living, you support a family, you love and hate, but – *what do you do?*'[5]

This, points out Wilson, is a cry for less involvement in the external world and a greater participation in the pleasures available to the inner man.

Wells confessed that he had no desire to continue his life unless he could devote himself to his 'proper business'. Wilson interprets this confession as follows:

> Self-enjoyment is synonymous with purposeful evolutionary activity of the intellect and the senses: and the notion of a living creature capable of absolute self-enjoyment is the notion of a man-god, no longer plagued by tiresome necessities over which he has no control. When a man commits himself to this definition of meaning, the 'value of life' ceases to be a matter of material symbols, comparable to a bag of sugar on the grocer's scales and therefore limited by the consciousness and the physical aims of the individual; it becomes instead a function of the limitless realm of the intellect and imagination, of the creative will.[6]

It is easy to imagine Wells, then, as the author of *Men Like Gods*. In this novel, Wells gives an account of a group of motorists on a country road who suddenly find themselves 'transported' into a new world in which nudity and telepathy are the norm. Wells peoples his Utopia with representative characters including a priest, a politician, etc. He parodies these characters in an attempt to express his criticism of the real society of his age. Yet, although the people of Utopia are happy and free, Wells fails to breathe real life into them. They remain unconvincing as gods. In a similar manner, Wells wrote *The Food of the Gods*, in which a group of people eat a particular food which transforms them into giants. Again the novel fails to realise its full intent of depicting a race of supermen. The giants are attacked by the rest of society, which wants to destroy them. In another Wells' novel, Mr Polly, having left his wife and set himself up as an odd-job man, is only a symbol of happiness and freedom; the truth is that he is just as unfulfilled at the novel's close as at its beginning. One has only to recall that at the end of his life, Wells wrote his essay, *Mind at the End of its Tether*, to realise that his vision was unable to surmount the final horizon beyond which lay ultimate fulfilment.

Wells was intensely interested in imagination. He envisaged a new man in whom there exists a highly developed imaginative consciousness, as well as an observational and reflective consciousness. For Wells, the man with a highly developed imagination was as advanced in comparison to the common man as the first amphibian was advanced in comparison to fish. Yet it must be acknowledged that the vision of Wells is essentially scientific. There is no doubt about the value that he placed upon imagination but, in the final analysis, he believed it was science that would fire imagination beyond its last barrier. In fact, he perceived of himself as a 'world-betterer' rather than an artist and his whole intellectual activity was posited on the notion that common sense and science were the keys to the future.

There is one particular characteristic of Wells which may explain his failure to reconcile his vision with his personal reality. He was a promiscuous individual who spent much of his time in pursuit of middle-class young women. He kept the mantlepiece of his home adorned with photographs of his mistresses, a decoration which seems not to have worried his wife – at least not to the point where she felt she had to leave him. Wilson is puzzled that Wells, while having ready access to these women, and thus a wide range of experience, failed to learn from this experience and bring his sexual impulse under control. Hoopdriver, the central character of Wells' early work, *The Wheels of Chance*, meets a young woman who is fleeing from her husband in the company of a young man who wishes to seduce her. Hoopdriver seizes the opportunity to indulge himself and after spending time with the young woman, whom he manages to extricate from the young man who was with her when he met her, leaves her with the promise that he will work to make himself worthy of her. In one form or another, Hoopdriver reappears again and again in Wells' novels. He takes on the persona of Kipps and that of Mr Polly. Wilson recognised this trinity – Hoopdriver, Kipps and Polly – as a composite self-portrait by Wells and it is this observation that leads him to comprehend Wells' sexuality and his failure as an artist. Wilson explains:

> Promiscuity always raises a problem: someone is bound to get hurt. Each new conquest involves getting rid of the old one, or at least a certain amount of deception. On most kindly and intelligent people, this exercises a certain breaking effect. Besides, experience-hunger, like any other appetite, can be satiated; as a man gets older, he outgrows the old urgencies. But the most basic reason that creative people tend to outgrow promiscuity is that it spoils the self-image; sexual desire, after all, is based on desire to explore the forbidden: it is a first cousin to the criminal urge. Besides, there is a certain incongruity in

the thought of a philosopher spending his days in pursuit of the opposite sex. That Wells never outgrew it suggests some curious fault or deficiency in the self-image mechanism.[7]

In a personal taped interview with Daniel Farson, Wilson declared that 'the purpose of art is to praise life. It must be difficult', he argued, 'for any man with a twist in his personality, to praise life'.[8] After all the critical evaluations have been written, it may be this perspective of Wilson that best explains the ultimate inadequacy of Wells as an existential novelist.

In the Scottish fantasy novelist, David Lindsay, Wilson sees, 'the struggle of a man of genius to express a sense of values that is fundamentally mystical'.[9] Lindsay was born in London but spent most of his youth in the highlands of Scotland, which provided him with the inspiration for the stark and stunning landscapes he created in his fiction. His work was never widely accepted in his lifetime and even the novel he considered his masterpiece, *Devil's Tor*, was virtually ignored. As a consequence of this critical dismissal, Lindsay became more and more depressed and in the remaining fifteen years of his life published nothing else.

Lindsay was astonishingly incompetent as a writer. His prose is clumsy and laboured and his language, which at times reaches considerable poetic heights, is more often pitched at a level of competence that could be matched by any reasonable journalist. Yet Wilson rates his first novel, *A Voyage to Arcturus*, as the greatest imaginative work of the twentieth century.

The novel centres on Maskull, who travels to a distant star called Arcturus. The star has strange creatures, bizarre animals; but what is most remarkable about it is its landscape – and the fact that it is home to the devil, who bears the name 'Crystalman'. What becomes clear as the reader follows Maskull, is that the mountains and valleys he traverses represent a real world; a higher form of reality that lies behind and beyond the world we experience from day to day. Lindsay is arguing that we can enter this world through putting ourselves in touch with sublime landscapes. Crystalman is the spirit of triviality and banality.

Lindsay developed a theory of fiction in which he divided novels into two classes. There are novels which describe the world and there are novels which seek to explain it. His own work belongs clearly in the second category. In *A Voyage to Arcturus*, he shows us two worlds – the everyday world and the world of the fully developed human being. When we look at ourselves in the common world, we see a distortion of ourselves. It is only when we look at ourselves in the sublime world that we can come to identify our essential nature.

In *The Haunted Woman*, Lindsay created a symbolic house that has much the same character as the landscape in Arcturus. Isbel Loment finds herself in a house which has two levels. But in fact the two levels are different worlds, the lower being the real world and the upper being something altogether different. Upstairs, the view from the window is vastly different from the view through the downstairs window. Upstairs, everything is a hundred years older than anything downstairs. Upstairs, she meets her host, Henry Judge and the two realise that they love each other. Downstairs, they scarcely feel anything for each other. The notes they write to each other upstairs become indecipherable downstairs. Upstairs is another dimension that is altogether more real.

When Isbel sees her reflection in an upstairs mirror, she sees what she would be if she could come to her full stature as a human being. It is, of course, the life that she lives downstairs that makes it impossible for her to achieve this ideal.

In his posthumously published *The Violet Apple*, Lindsay uses apples, grown from seeds of the apple eaten by Adam and Eve, as symbols of the two worlds. When the apples are eaten, they reveal the world of the sublime, in much the same way as it exists upstairs in *The Haunted House*. In *Sphinx*, the reality that underlies our common experience is symbolised by the dream. The novel's chief character, Nicholas Cabot, is attempting to create a machine which will correctly record dreams. Lindsay elaborates on the theme that dreams may indicate to the conscious mind things that lie deeply buried in the unconscious.

It seems that Lindsay is pointing out that the society in which we live somehow prevents us becoming ourselves. This was abundantly the case for Lindsay himself. He was, generally speaking, a pedantic man who was constantly embarrassed and uncomfortable in his social relations. Before he had begun to write, he had endured what was for him the agony of working in insurance. He married a woman eighteen years younger than himself, suggesting that he might have been uncomfortable with women of his own age. It is interesting to note, in this context, that many of his main characters are women. Lindsay read Nietzsche and

Schopenhauer and spent hours listening to the music of Beethoven. It was not until he escaped from the pressures of London, where he worked, to Cornwall, that he found himself able to settle down to writing. He seems to provide evidence for Wilson's observation that there is a clear relationship between the mental disposition of the recluse and the writing of fantasy. Wilson has written:

Lindsay himself had no idea of what sort of person he wanted to be. All he knew was that he didn't much like the kind of person he was: the rather stiff, reserved Scot, who found it incredibly difficult to address even close friends by their Christian names. So, to some extent, these books of Lindsay spring out of his own frustration, his sense of not being able to express the person he basically felt himself to be. His marriage to Jacqueline (strongly disapproved by parents on both sides) and his decision to throw up his safe job and become a writer, both demonstrate this deep dissatisfaction. Nietzsche, a philosopher Lindsay deeply admired, talked about 'How one becomes what one is'. It was a secret Lindsay never discovered.[10]

Why, then, does Wilson rate Lindsay so highly? The answer lies in the nature of his struggle. Wilson summarises that struggle:

The man of artistic genius attempts to create a kind of road to another level of reality; he wants to travel vertically rather than horizontally. Lindsay likes to use the image of some immense stairway, symbolised by the rising chords at the opening of Beethoven's Seventh Symphony. And he likes to speak of this 'other reality', this *real* reality, as the 'sublime'. . . . Lindsay expresses his own basic view of the world as a deep conflict of good against evil: not conventional good against conventional evil, but a cold and sublime reality fighting for its life against a sweet and cloying beauty that masquerades as goodness.[11]

Lindsay's literary endeavour was directed at an attempt to evoke that other world which offers an alternative to the present world with its misery and suffering; its unreality. In this, he belongs to a noble tradition that stretches back into the history of writing. Like most others in the tradition, however, he was defeated by the reality of this world which was 'too much with him'. In the

230 Colin Wilson: The Man and His Mind

final analysis, he must be judged, not by his success or his failure as a writer, but by his attempt to challenge the human imagination to reach out towards a higher reality and it is on this criterion that Wilson regards him as one of the most important novelists of the first half of the twentieth century.

James Joyce centred his fiction on the idea of what he called 'epiphanies' – moments of experience when we seem to grasp the 'whatness' of a place or situation so that the most common object becomes radiant. The ephiphany is akin to a photograph which captures every nuance of the object photographed so that we comprehend it in its every aspect. Joyce set out in his novels to present his readers with a whole series of epiphanies. In the newspaper office scene in *Ulysses*, the room is depicted as if through the lens of a camera, with a number of 'stills' being provided: cameos of this and that element serve to convey the total confusion of the office. As the characters leave the office, Stephen Dedalus provides the basic epiphany. He tells of two elderly women who go out one day to see Nelson's Pillar. There is nothing to their visit, which ends up with their spitting plumstones through the fence around the pillar. The point is that real life is not composed of great dramatic moments but is made up of common experiences which are themselves as real or as unreal as we allow them to be.

Joyce's fiction is, in one respect, the quintessential fiction of the twentieth century. It is a fiction which protests at the limitations human beings confront: a statement of dissatisfaction with the seeming paucity of what life has to offer. It is, in Wilson's term, a 'complaint addressed to human destiny'. Clearly, however, in the light of the women spitting plumstones, the problem lies, not in the external reality, but in the way in which we perceive that reality.

Joyce began to write fiction at the turn of the century, when he was twenty years old. His chief interest was autobiography and in *Portrait of the Artist as a Young Man*, he set out to show himself as the intellectual hero. His manuscript was rejected twenty times and he threw it on a fire from where about half of it was rescued by his mother. Disgusted with Ireland, he moved to live in Trieste, where he reworked his text on Stephen Hero and wrote his set of stories *Dubliners*, in which he exposed the social and cultural drabness of the city from which he had retreated. In the completed *Portrait* we are introduced to a very determined young man who seems almost fanatical in his quest for literary success. It becomes clear that Joyce was virtually obsessed with the need to become an artist-outsider.

His grand attempt at discovering himself was poured into the writing of *Ulysses* and it succeeded to the extent that it did introduce him to the entire literary world.

In general terms, a novel is a form of 'wide-angled consciousness' which broadens our vision. In *Ulysses*, however, Joyce reversed the process and focused our attention on the detail of our living. The novel records events that take place in a single day. Its setting never extends beyond the boundaries of the city of Dublin. It gives an account of the actions and thoughts of people who are so common that they might be our next door neighbours. Joyce placed a magnifying glass before the reader's eye and brought into focus the minutiae of daily life.

Yet it would be incorrect to argue that *Ulysses* has no plot. Its plot is the determined effort of Stephen Dedalus to become an artist. This effort is counterpointed by the presentation of Leopold Bloom, a likeable enough fellow but a man without ambition or artistic vision. Stephen is the artist in an unfriendly world who is forced, again and again, to protect his artistic vocation by choosing between compromise and integrity. The plot of the book consists of his development of a resistance to conformity. In the powerful brothel scene, he thinks he sees the ghost of his mother rising through the floor and asking him to mend his ways. '*Non serviam,*' he responds. 'I will not serve.'

Ulysses is, in a sense, the first of the Freudian novels in the sense that it deals with sex in a public manner which would have been impossible before Freud. Bloom is a pantie fetishist and a masochist. The sex in the novel is earthy, sensual. It becomes another statement of Stephen's defiance; a ready embrace of anything that moves beyond the established mores.

Joyce projected himself as the antithesis of the established literary circle. While his contemporaries acknowledged the wisdom of Plato, he preferred the hard-headed philosophy of Aristotle. He opposed the celebration of Shakespeare as the greatest of Elizabethan writers, preferring Jonson. His contemporary fellow writers were all concerned with expressing ideas in their novels. He argued that ideas were of no significance to the true novelist. When there was talk about *Ulysses* ushering in the end of the novel, he encouraged such talk, insisting that the book represented the next stage in the development of the novel. And all of this takes us to the heart of his work. In fact, Joyce was the supreme egotist. *Ulysses* is a statement of self-affirmation by a man who felt himself to be under-rated by the world. Wilson has written of him:

> The truth may well be that Joyce was a religious man who had lost his faith and turned art into a substitute religion. Like all religious fanatics, he was inclined to distrust the intellect and despise mere ideas. But it was this dislike of ideas which fitted in so well with the 'existentialist' temper of the period, that did most damage to the cause of the novel, and literature in general. Ideas are the result of man's mental activity as he confronts problems. The atmosphere of ideas tends to be optimistic because a man would not bother to think unless he hoped to solve the problem. The writer who declares that ideas are unimportant has committed himself to an attitude of pessimism. Joyce only deepened the pessimism that had settled on the novel since Flaubert.[12]

According to Wilson, Joyce made a fundamental mistake in his attitude towards ideas. In rejecting ideas and insisting that the novel should be about 'reality', he failed to realise that the way we see reality is itself an idea and the task confronting the writer is to develop that idea as far as possible. To refuse to do so is to guarantee a negative view of life and art.

This then, is the strange contradiction about Joyce. While he clearly set out in his writing to strengthen his self-image, he ends up as a pessimist. Wilson finds the answer to this paradox in the fact that it is not enough for an artist to ask what he wants to *be;* he must also concern himself with where he wants to go. Joyce succeeded in developing a strong self-image but he burnt himself out in the act. It is notable that in the latter years of his life, he constantly spoke of the Dublin of his youth and his final work, *Finnegan's Wake*, never in Wilson's opinion, rises above the level of an experiment with language. There was so much of Joyce invested in *Ulysses*, that there was insufficient of the artist left to continue producing great literature. Wilson believes that he became a victim of the conflict between the idealistic artist and a materialist society.

Wilson has described Friedrick Durrenmatt as the 'heir to the existential tradition'. At a cursory glance, Durrenmatt seems to be little more than a student of Franz Kafka but a more careful examination discloses that he belongs to a much broader literary history and in fact represents a watershed in the fictional treatment of existential ideas.

In Durrenmatt, there is a sense of joy in life and a measure of success in living. This is illustrated in one of his early stories entitled *The Tunnel* in which a young man, a student, is travelling in a train to his university. The student wears darkened glasses and has cotton wool in his ears. It is as if he wants neither to see nor hear the world. As he sits in his carriage, the train enters a tunnel and he waits for it to emerge at the other end. Time passes, however, and the train continues travelling through the tunnel, on what appears to be a downward slope. Eventually concerned that the tunnel seems to have no ending, the student wends his way to the driver's compartment – only to find it empty. He returns to the guard's station and discusses their plight with him. The guard is anxious and afraid but the student accepts his situation, advising the guard to take comfort in the fact that they are in the hands of God and are going *down* to meet him. The student is not simply resigned. He is able to embrace the horror of his existence with a kind of faith.

The central concern expressed by Durrenmatt in his novels is with the inadequate quality of the standards which prevail in the modern world. He sees a sense of betrayal and revenge as the most prevalent contemporary value and he challenges it in everything he writes. This is made perfectly clear in his play, *The Marriage of Mr Mississippi*. Florestan Mississippi is an inhabitant of a mythical country who considers it his mission to re-introduce the law of Moses with its notion of an eye for an eye. He preaches that not only the guilty party, but both members of a marriage in which adultery has been committed, should be put to death. In his travels, he meets Olympia who has murdered her husband because of his adultery. Mississippi acknowledges that it was his own wife with whom Olympia's husband has slept and confesses that he too has killed his spouse – and by the same method as that used by Olympia to rid herself of hers. In a perverse logic, Mississippi proposes that he and Olympia wed, in an expiation of their crimes. The play ends with their mutual death.

There are many interesting stage innovations in this play. One of these has some of the characters addressing the audience directly about a number of matters, including the purpose of the play-wright who wrote the play, i.e. Durrenmatt himself. One of the characters tells the audience that the play has been written to examine the question of 'whether the human mind is able to alter a world which *merely* exists'.

In another play, *An Angel Comes to Babylon*, one of the characters makes a speech in which he enunciates what Wilson believes may be regarded as Durrenmatt's central personal position as an artist, thinker and man:

> I love an earth that exists in spite of everything, a beggar's earth, unique in its happiness. . . . An earth that I subdue over and over again, intoxicated with its beauty, in love with its image.'[13]

The most significant of Durrenmatt's works, however, is the novella, *A Dangerous Game*, in which we are introduced to a travelling salesman, Alfred Traps. His name is a magnificent symbol of the nightmare in which he is to find himself. Traps' car breaks down and he seeks refuge in a country home. The situation is almost a parody of the plight into which the travelling salesman falls in a thousand smutty jokes but this gives no indication of the horror in which he will be involved.

Traps' hosts for the night are four gentlemen, all associated with the legal profession. One is a judge, two are barristers and the fourth is a retired hangman. The four entertain Traps at a sumptuous dinner and during the course of the meal, suggest that he might like to join them in a game – a mock trial in which the Judge assumes the bench and the two barristers take opposing sides with respect to the accused. The accused is, of course, Traps. A 'crime' is invented: Traps is charged with the murder of his boss, Gygax.

The trial proceeds through what must be some of the most carefully controlled logic in the modern novel. The prosecuting attorney builds up his case and Traps tries to rebut it. Yet every time he opens his mouth his defence attorney shudders, for every word he speaks is a further indictment of his behaviour. No, he insists, he did not murder Gygax – but he must admit that there were times when . . . Finally, Traps is so enmeshed in Gygax's death – by heart attack – that there can be no doubt that he was its cause. At the end of the trial, Traps is insisting, not merely that he is a murderer but that he is a master criminal. He demands that he be executed. The hangman sits at the table, silently.

The evening meal breaks up. The four hosts are delighted with the game. It is the best they have played in years. The five men prepare for bed but little do the hosts realise that when he gets to his bedroom, Traps will hang himself.

Wilson does not like Durrenmatt's ending. He believes that the internal logic of the story demands that Traps should be hanged by the hangman. But the hangman is within Traps rather than outside him. In any event, the end result is the same. Traps has been punished for his crime and the game has been played out in full.

On this economically written and powerfully evocative story, Wilson has written:

> Here the meaning is very plain. Traps lives the same pointless, futile life as the rest of us. Suddenly he sees himself as a super-human criminal – not a man whose life is dominated by chance, but one who has guided himself step by step with immense certainty. He prefers this new vision of himself; it frees him from his futility. He is like a lunatic who wants to believe that he is Christ. And if believing this involves carrying out on himself the sentence of death, then he prefers to die.[14]

Wilson believes that Durrenmatt has found a way forward from the despairing fiction of Sartre and Camus. In his work, he has shown us how we might address the disorder of our lives. He uses the same existential tools as Sartre, including the idea of inauthentic existence and self-deception but he also brings to bear a sensitive intuition and a high degree of optimism in the manner of Shaw. The existential situation that exists in *The Tunnel* ignores nothing of the horror of life, yet the horror is softened by the possibilities that remain open to man as he confronts it. By the time he had come to write *An Angel Comes to Babylon*, Durrenmatt had embraced, consciously or not, the Shavian philosophy that suffering will end when men bring their trivialities and self-preoccupations under control. He represents the beginning of a move in the direction of the New Existentialism in fiction.

The existential temper of the modern novel finds its most complete expression in the *bildungsroman* which Wilson regards as being the natural medium of the existentialist as the artist-philosopher. In what he admits is a dogmatism, he has even said that the *bildungsroman* is the only serious form of literary art in the twentieth century. Among the greatest examples we have, he lists *Wilhelm Meister, The Brothers Karamazov, The Ordeal of Richard Feverel, The Magic Mountain, Demian, A Farewell to Arms, Immaturity* and Sartre's *Chemins de la Liberté.*

The German word *bildungsroman* is a compound of the two words *bildung* – education, formation, growth, foundation – and *roman* – novel. Thus it is a novel which treats of the growth, education or development of an individual. This is not to say that it is a novel about school or even about the series of events that make up the life of a young man. What is of concern are those basic events and influences by which the boy becomes a man – reaches the threshold of a genuine maturity. By its very nature it is a reflection of Hesse's idea that 'man is a bourgeois compromise' – that is that 'man' does not exist; that there are only individual men.

Hermann Hesse understood life as an ongoing period of perplexity, made up of boredom, doubt and misery. He considered that the moments in which we manage to achieve ecstasy are few and far between. It is as if we can have them only by first paying the price in ennui and suffering. Thus, in order to live in this world, a man needs the moral rectitude of a saint and the will-power of an accomplished artist. These attributes can be acquired only when the individual moves beyond the world of the physical and enters the world of the mind. The life of the mind is a pilgrimage in spiritual perception. It is precisely this pilgrimage that Hesse's character Emil Sinclair undertakes in the *bildungsroman, Demian.*

Young Sinclair knows two worlds. The first is the world of order; a home life that is based on precisely prescribed duties, a mother who is always in her place and in which there was an appropriate mix of guilt and pardon. Sinclair's other world is the world that exists outside home; the world of prisons, slaughterhouses and burglaries – in a word, the world of chaos. The task lay in reconciling the two. The task begins in earnest when Sinclair goes to school and meets a fellow student named Demian. It is Demian who offers him an interpretation of the biblical story of Cain and Abel which challenges Sinclair to the depth of his soul. Demian suggests that the traditional picture of Cain as a brutal murderer may be a falsification. What if Cain had been responding to a noble urge to assert himself when he slew his brother? Sinclair hears the challenge but he is unable to rise to meet it. Here is the first suggestion of Hesse's major theme, that in order to experience the heights, man must first descend into the depths. Order comes out of chaos. Wilson understands Hesse thus:

> The conclusions of *Demian* are clear. It is a question of self-realisation. It is not enough to accept a concept of order and live by it; that is cowardice and such cowardice cannot result in freedom. Chaos must be faced. Real order must be preceded by a descent into chaos. This is Hesse's conclusion. In theological terms, the fall was necessary; man had to eat of the fruit of good and evil. . . . In refusing to face evil, Sinclair has gained nothing and lost a great deal; the Buddhist scriptures express it: those who refuse to discriminate might as well be dead.[15]

In one of his earliest stories, *Disillusionment*, Thomas Mann has the narrator meet a stranger in a square in Venice. Without warning, the stranger launches into a discussion with a question. 'Do you know what disillusionment is? Not a small miscarriage in small, unimportant matters, but the great and general disappointment which everything, all of life, has in store?' He then goes on to recount how everything he has experienced has been a disappointment. When he was a small child, the house in which he lived caught fire. He watched it burn, while all the time thinking, 'so this is all. This is a house on fire.' So complete is his disillusionment with the promises of life that he awaits death, expecting that when it comes he will again be forced to ask, 'So this is all there is?' In this simple story, Mann is confronting the question of meaninglessness.

In Mann's masterpiece, *The Magic Mountain*, we are introduced to a young man who journeys to a sanatorium to visit his tubercular cousin. He finds a strange attraction within the sanatorium and is not at all unhappy when it is discovered that he too has the disease and must remain within the hospital. The wards have a warmth about them; they offer a security. They are a form of protection, not for the outside world against the disease but for the patient against the outside world.

During his stay in the sanatorium, Hans Castorp engages in long philosophical discussions and intimate personal reflections which constitute the very heart of this *bildungsroman*. As a consequence he undergoes a heightening of his sensibilities. He acquires the insight and temperament of an artist. He is happy and quite content to let the world pass him by. It is the outbreak of war that brings him to the comprehension that he cannot remain where he is but must re-enter the world, with its harshness, its brutality – but also with its action.

Unlike Hesse, Mann is interested in ideas and enthusiastically follows them wherever they lead. He sees ideas as vital rather than static and a reading of *The Magic Mountain* leaves one exhilarated, enthusiastic for life. It is clear that Mann knew a great deal about the individual man but he understood that the individual exists within a society from which he cannot finally retreat. In consequence of this understanding, Mann argued that 'in our time, the destiny of man presents itself in political terms'. There can be no doubting the attraction of a quiet hospital ward as a haven in the midst of a barbaric and violent world but in the end, hospitals are for people who are ill. The healthy man discovers, with Hans Castorp, that his place is in the real world and that his responsibility is to make as great an impact upon that world as he possibly can.

Wilson states his understanding of the *bildungsroman* as a literary *genre*, as follows:

> The *bildungsroman* sets out to describe the evolution of the hero's soul; it is fictional biography that is mainly concerned with its hero's reaction to ideas, or the development of his ideas about 'life' from his experience. The *bildungsroman* is a sort of laboratory in which the hero conducts an experiment in living. For this reason, it is a particularly useful medium for writers whose main concern is a philosophical answer to the practical question: What shall we do with our lives? Moreover, it is an interesting observation that as soon as a writer is seized with the need to treat a problem he feels seriously about in a novel, the novel automatically becomes a sort of *bildungsroman*. The *bildungsroman* is the natural form of serious fictional art, no matter how short the period of the hero's life that it treats.[16]

This then, is the world of existential fiction. It hones its language and its stylistic techniques and addresses the fundamental questions of human existence with a relentless insistence. It demands that life surrender its secrets and provide a way forward for all those clambering to escape from contingency and misery. It tries itself to become that way, testing the ground here and there to see if it is safe. It follows existing highways, cuts its way through overgrown, discarded pathways and even forges tracks in the undergrowth in an endeavour to gain access to life. If it fails, we should not discard it, for the very attempt that it represents is a large part of the solution it seeks. If, as Wilson suggests, the Outsider is the genius in embryo, the existential novelist is the midwife. It will be a bloody birth at which he attends; a birth wracked by parturitional pain and piercing cries. Yet it will issue in a new man and a new dimension of life.

As we have seen, existential criticism is not simply criticism of existential literature. In *The Strength to Dream*, Wilson included a note on the need for existential criticism as well as a sample of how it might be applied to the work of Aldous Huxley. We shall consider this sample shortly. In fact, the whole of the book and the criticism that permeates all of Wilson's early books is existential and it is possible to be precise about what he means by the idea of an existential criticism.

All great art is, according to Wilson, an attempt to teach people to take themselves and their lives more seriously than they do. It is a recognition that we all suffer from what he calls 'experience hunger'. We need more experience if we are to develop: so long as we settle for the minimal range of experience that is our common lot, we will remain stunted. The great painting, the great poem, the great symphony and the great novel are all forms of substitute experience that enable us to recognise some of the dimensions that are missing from our lives. They provide us with both an image of what we are yet to become and something of the stimulus we need to become it. Existential criticism is an evaluation of literature and art from the point of view of clarifying that image and intensifying that stimulus.

Great art opens up new dimensions of human freedom. It creates landscapes and epochs that lie parallel with the real world and into which we may enter through the use of our imagination. But the essential freedom offered by art is freedom from our petty self-image. It confirms within us the notion that we *do* have a 'truer' nature; that we need not succumb to our worst self-images. Existential criticism is a magnet that attracts all the iron filings of freedom that lie buried between the words of a novel or the brush strokes that constitute a painting and present them to us as a solid, real possibility.

Wilson points out that 'a novel derives its power from the novelist's struggle with a problem'. It may well be true, as Sartre argues, that every individual who reads a novel, in fact rewrites it. Yet the one thing we are obliged to leave intact is the problem with which the work concerns itself. We may allow the problem to transfer from the consciousness of the novelist through the characters and events of the novel to our own consciousness but we must not diminish it or try to resolve it in a facile solution. Existential criticism admits the problem and contemplates it courageously, knowing that it is more valuable than most of the 'solutions' others have applied to it.

In his novel *The Roots of Heaven*, Romain Gary tells of a group of soldiers, imprisoned in a prisoner-of-war camp. Their captors seek to brutalise them; to break their spirit and make them totally submissive. Faced with this threat, one of the prisoners, Robert, introduces a game to the camp. He tells his fellow prisoners to imagine that they have in camp with them a beautiful young woman. This woman shares their dormitory but she does not share their bed. In fact, she is the model of all womankind. The prisoners are to behave in front of her exactly as they would behave in front of a real woman for whom they had the greatest respect. If they undress for bed, they must be sure that they do it outside her presence. If they swear in her hearing, they must apologise. As the game is played, the prisoners develop a higher morale. They assist each other in delineating a proper standard of behaviour in front of the imaginary woman.

Eventually, the Commandant of the camp, who has noted and been concerned by this improved morale, discovers their game. Determined to outwit them, he enters their dormitory and insists that they surrender the girl to him, telling them that she will be taken to serve in a brothel for his officers. The men refuse to surrender her and the game is won. The Commandant can do nothing in the face of this imaginative force. In a rage he isolates Robert in solitary confinement but Robert has learned the trick and he retains his sanity in the dark cell by imagining himself roaming freely across vast planes in Africa with herds of elephants. In the midst of his imprisonment, he is free. On this story, Wilson comments:

> This is one of the great parables of our age. Gary has grasped the secret of the power that lies in the heart of the human mind.

Reality is *not* what happens to be most real to us at the moment. It is what we perceive in our moments of greatest intensity. And the peculiar power of the imagination enables us to cling on to this vision after the intensity has vanished. The French soldiers have not merely conjured up an imaginary sexual partner: they have succeeded in recreating something of the mystery of the 'eternal womanly', and of their deeper motives for living. The girl is no fantasy; she is a reminder of a deeper reality than the prison camp.[17]

Wilson follows on with the observation that in the light of Gary's parable, it is no criticism of a novel to say that it is unreal. 'The real question is what *depth of human need* is symbolised by the fantasy.' Existential criticism recognises the absolute depth of our need and assesses the novel in terms of its capacity to satisfy that need.

Existential criticism is not simply an examination of the content of a work of art. It is equally an assessment of the implications of that art. This is because the difference between great and mediocre art is that the former will concern itself, not simply with recording the observations of the artist but much more with aspects of human behaviour and experience that normally lie below the level of our awareness. Thus existential criticism is not a mere intellectual evaluation; it alerts intuition, imagination and vision in order to see below the surface. The existential critic is interested in the idea behind the art work.

When we talk about the idea behind a novel, we mean the author's attempt to summarise his vision of existence. Or at least, his *attitude* to his own everyday life. Is he a natural winner or a natural loser? Does he believe that human reason and will-power can improve things, or does he feel that nothing we do has much effect – that we are creatures of circumstance (a view held by many noted writers including Thomas Hardy and Somerset Maugham). Is he compassionate about human suffering, or does it touch a secret spring of sadism – a feeling of 'it serves them right' (which is what we feel in Maupassant). Above all, does he really record the surface of human existence as we all see it, or does he try to get below it? Is he a describer or an explainer?[18]

Finally, existential criticism is based on the notion that every writer has an irreducible body of ideas, however small, which constitutes a symbol of what he means by freedom. In the act of writing, he tests that kernel of freedom against the everyday world. This testing process is the essence of the creative act and its observation and evaluation is the fundamental task of existential criticism.

In applying existential criticism to the work of Aldous Huxley, Wilson begins with his personality. Huxley was a gentle and humble man who subjected himself to an intense self-discipline. By nature he was epicurean, forever seeking pleasure – which meant the absence of pain. The early Huxley was given to intellectualising and he derived a great deal of self-satisfaction from his mental prowess. He had a strong dislike for bodily functions and seems to have had an ambiguous approach to sexuality although he had a liking for the writing of D. H. Lawrence. In this context, it is interesting to note that in almost all of his novels, there is an instance of rape. He had an enduring passion for the past. Later in his life, Huxley became concerned about social problems and believed that he had found an answer to many of these in his 'perennial philosophy' which was largely religious in nature. It was this stance that led to him being described as 'almost saint-like'.

In examining Huxley's literary style, Wilson finds many weaknesses. He is given to repetition, which interrupts the flow of his plots. He uses the exclamation mark to excess, with the result that much of his work has a feminine quality. He is clearly influenced by Proust but deviates from the French writer by interrupting time sequences and 'twisting' time in strained chronologies. He might be judged a better essayist than novelist although this is not to suggest that his novels do not contain some remarkably successful examples of powerful prose.

The central concern that Huxley addresses in all his work is introduced by Philip Quarles, in *Point Counter Point*. Philip states:

> Being with Rampion rather depresses me: for he makes me see what a great gulf separates the knowledge of the obvious from the actual living of it. And oh! the difficulties of crossing the gulf. I perceive now that the real charm of the intellectual life . . . is its easiness. It's the substitution of simple intellectual schemata for the complexities of reality. . . . It's much easier

to be an intellectual child or a lunatic than a harmonious adult man.[19]

The 'harmonious adult man' is Huxley's ideal for humanity. In *Point Counter Point* he introduces us to two men who are searching for maturity and wholeness. Philip is one of these; the other is Spandrell. Their common problem is that they know they are living an inauthentic existence – a life of Sartre's 'bad faith'. Philip deliberately sets out to seduce a woman he does not want – just in order that he might experience the sense of having conquered her. Spandrell goes even further. His attempt to revitalise his authenticity takes the form of a murder when he kills a political figure. Finally, instead of allowing this action to awaken him, he chooses suicide.

Huxley makes it clear that he considers Philip's and Spandrell's problem as a lack of intelligence. They attempt to solve their problem without any recourse to logic. Philip, Huxley's mouthpiece, does think but his intellect is so uninspired that it puts his marriage in jeopardy. He and Spandrell obey their emotions rather than reason. And this highlights a weakness in Huxley himself. He is ambiguous about his own feelings and oscillates between them instead of wedding them to his intelligence.

Brave New World is, ostensibly, a study in the communist myth that man can be bettered by social control. It presents us with men who are unable to act of their own volition. Huxley seems to have accepted the fact that reason and common sense are finally inadequate of themselves to rejuvenate a debilitated man. The novel exposes the meaningless nature of so much of contemporary life. Its central character rebels against the prevailing social order, but only to a limited extent. He never comes to grips with his own personal deficiencies. It is as if Huxley is admitting that he does not know how to create the harmonious adult man.

In a collection of essays, *Ends and Means*, Huxley complements the theme of his novel *Eyeless in Gaza*. In the novel, he moves in the direction of a religious mysticism, with its central character expressing a sense of responsibility towards his fellow men. In the collection of essays, Huxley states the case more strongly: the way forward lies in abandoning universal scepticism and embracing a faith.

Wilson sees this basic treatment of Huxley's work as being as far as 'literary' criticism can go. It identifies the writer's objectives and passes a judgement on the extent to which he has realised them. Existential criticism takes one more, critical, step.

> It is by considering the general 'unsatisfactoriness' of all Huxley's work that literary criticism attempts to expand into existential criticism. One reason for this sense of 'something lacking' [is] Huxley's attitude to the physical world, which is never far from that of Sartre in *La Nausée*. It takes very little to disgust him. One has only to compare the death scenes in *Point Counter Point* or *Eyeless in Gaza* with Tolstoy's death of Count Bezukhov in *War and Peace* or Trollope's death of the bishop in *Barchester Towers*, to realise that Huxley is always too near the borderline of 'nausea'. And yet, to have a dim appreciation of the physical world is not necessarily a disadvantage to a writer, as we can see in the case of Dostoevsky. Unfortunately, although he is serious, Huxley never takes himself *that* seriously. He can never escape a tendency to do intellectual cartwheels and handstands: he can never escape his own frivolity.[20]

The work of Aldous Huxley makes it clear that there is a legitimate need for an existential criticism. In the final analysis, what constitutes the failure of Huxley's characters is the 'dilution of their vital force by thought'. Any approach to these characters or to the world-view and art of their creator which is based on a pure intellectualism, is bound to meet with a similar failure. Literary criticism is largely an academic exercise that helps us place a work in a literary heritage and genre and in so doing it is of considerable value. But it is insignificant when compared with the capacity of existential criticism to lead us through a work of art to a profound life-affirming truth.

It is not Wilson's intention that existential criticism should be limited to fiction. Certainly it can be applied to poetry and to music.

According to Wilson, the 'secret' of the poet is his capacity to overcome the limitations of his own personality in an act of what Wilson calls 'promotion'. Promotion is the capacity to forget oneself in the act of identifying a higher self. It is achieved, frequently, by role-playing. The poet acts out his ideal self with the result that it gradually becomes the real self. One of the most successful self-dramatisers in the world of English poetry was Rupert Brooke.

Brooke was born into the upper-middle class, in Rugby. He was an extremely handsome young man who enjoyed his social privileges without letting them distort his self-image. He thought of himself as a poet. In a letter, written at school, he wrote:

> I'm enjoying everything immensely at present. To be among 500 people, all young and laughing, is intensely delightful and interesting. . . . Wonderful things are happening all around me. Some day, when all the characters are dead – they are sure to die young – I shall put it all in a book. . . . The rest are only actors; I am actor and spectator as well.[21]

It is clear, then, that even at school, Brooke had the temperament of the romantic. When he was twenty, he wrote:

> Swiftly out from the friendly lilt of the band,
> The crowd's good laughter, the loved eyes of men
> I am drawn nightward; I must turn again
> Where, down below the low untrodden strand,
> There curves and glimmers outward to the unknown
> The old unquiet ocean. All the shade
> Is rife with magic and movement, I stray alone
> Here on the edge of silence, half afraid,
>
> Waiting a sign. In the deep heart of me,
> The sullen waters swell towards the moon,
> And all my tides set seaward.
>   From Inland
> Leaps a gay fragment of some mocking tune,
> That tinkles and laughs and fades along the sand,
> And dies between the seawall and the sea.

Here is to be felt the sense of expansion, of limitlessness, of promotion. It is as if Brooke is feeling himself being *evoked* by a force he but dimly comprehends. He is tremulous in the face of this evocation of something fuller, yet he continues to gaze upon it as if unable to leave his vantage point.

Brooke died before his twenty-eighth birthday. This has led many to regard his poetry as simple juvenilia. Yet, as Wilson points out, his poems reveal a complex, interesting, self-critical, humorous and intensely alive personality. It cannot be argued that Brooke remained totally immature. In fact, he was more competent than many older and better poets in his capacity for promotion. At one time, he was lying on the earth, contemplating the evening sky and brooding on women and death.

> Then, from the sad West turning wearily,
> I saw the pines against the white north sky,
> Yet beautiful and still, and bending over
> Their sharp black heads against a quiet sky.
> And there was peace in them; and I
> Was happy, and forgot to play the lover,
> And laughed, and did no longer wish to die;
> Being glad of you, O pine trees and the sky!

It might well be that this is not great poetry; indeed that it *is* typical of the immature romantic – yet only at a shallow reading. Wilson comments:

> This is the fundamental poetic experience: being more-or-less self-absorbed and egotistic, and suddenly awakening to the real experience of the external world. The immature and self-dramatising Rupert Brooke vanishes; the senses open. It is the 'negative capability' that Keats regarded as the fundamental quality of the poet, the opposite of what Heidegger called 'forgetfulness of existence'. It was this quality that Brooke continued to develop until his death, and that is found in his best poems. It is the pure poetic experience, the sudden forgetfulness of personality. Personality is a distorting glass that lies between man's inner reality and the reality of the outside world. In the poet, this distorting medium suddenly vanishes; the inner and the outer world face one another directly, with no distorting glass between them.[22]

Brooke's war poems have been subjected to considerable criticism, with many critics, including Louis Macneice, dismissing them as being too sentimental. But this may be to miss the point. For Brooke, the war was like the pine trees against the northern sky. It directed his attention away from himself and towards a world that was full of vitality.

In a real sense, Brooke's poetry has the quality of the *bildungsroman*. It all has to do with the experience of growing up. It concerns itself with the central issues of youth – with the dream of making love, with unrequited love, with the enticement of the horizon and with the tragedy of death. As Wilson points out, Brooke's poetry reads in part like a juvenile diary; full of intimate observations and youthful 'secrets'. Yet it has a certain wisdom that properly belongs with innocence.

If there is any sense in which we can speak of a mature Brooke, it must be acknowledged that his maturity came late. He never outgrew the youth's understanding of love and it seems that he remained sexually frustrated up to his death. Certainly he could make fun of his attempt to love:

> I dreamt I was in love again
> With the One before the Last,
> And smiled to greet the pleasant pain
> Of the innocent young past.
>
> But I jumped to feel how sharp had been
> The pain when it did live,
> How the faded dreams of Nineteen-ten
> Were Hell in Nineteen-five.

As Wilson points out, 'the feminine element is as important to the poet as water is to a plant'. This feminine element remains fundamentally unfulfilled in Brooke. The women he interacted with were, generally speaking, staid middle-class virgins who could give him little hint of the full range of the feminine element that would have enriched his poetry.

Yet, it might be argued, Brooke embraced the feminine element in a far more fundamental way. The following passage, too intrinsic a unity to try to abbreviate, demonstrates this, just as it demonstrates his capacity for promotion. Writing to a friend, Ben Keeling, he states:

Do not leap or turn pale at the word Mysticism. I do not mean any religious thing or any form of belief. I still burn and torture Christians daily . . .

It consists just in looking at people and things as themselves
– neither as useful nor moral nor anything else; but just as
being. At least, that is a philosophical description of it. What
happens is that I suddenly feel the extraordinary value and

importance of everybody I meet, and almost everything I see. In *things* I am moved in this way, especially by some things; but in people by almost all people. That is, when the mood is on me, I roam about places – yesterday I did it even in Birmingham! – and I sit in trains and see the essential glory and beauty of all the people I meet. I can watch a dirty, middle-aged tradesman in a railway carriage for hours, and love every dirty, greasy, sulky wrinkle in his weak chin and every button on his spotted unclean waistcoat. I know their states of mind are bad. But I'm so much occupied with their being there at all, that I don't have time to think of it. I tell you that a Birmingham gouty Tariff Reform fifth-rate business-man is splendid and immortal and desirable.

It's the same about the things of ordinary life. Half an hour's roaming about a street or village or railway station shows so much beauty that it's impossible to be anything but wild with suppressed exhilaration. And it's not only beauty and beautiful things. In a flicker of sunlight on a blank wall, or a reach of muddy pavement, or smoke from an engine at night, there's a sudden significance and importance and inspiration that makes the breath stop with a gulp of certainty and happiness. It's not that the wall or the smoke seem important for anything or suddenly reveal any general statement, or are suddenly seen to be good or beautiful in themselves – only that *for you* they're perfect and unique. It's like being in love with a person. . . . I suppose my occupation is being in love with the universe.[23]

Rupert Brooke qualifies as a poet on the basis of this passage alone. In it, he demonstrates that he has transcended the triviality of everydayness and connected himself with the universal reality that gives meaning to all life. When we realise that the last years of his life were largely unproductive, we understand that the cause may well have been his inability to resolve the question of his relationship with Ka Cox so that his creative capacity became temporarily sterile. But poets do not reach a point in their lives at which they enter a stage of creativity which runs its course and then ends forever. They ebb and flow, passing through numerous creative periods and having to endure times when they cannot write a word. It is likely that, had he lived, Brooke would have resolved his difficulties with Ka Cox and resumed writing and that there would have been a progression in his ability to move from the poetry of youth to the poetry of maturity. We can never know – but in the end, it does not matter. His letter to Ben Keeling gives us the essence of poetry. Existential criticism can ask for no more than this.

Although Wilson has spent extended periods of time contributing reviews of classical recordings to magazines – including *King* and *Audio and Hi Fi,* he has devoted only one book to music – the early *Brandy of the Damned.* The title of the introduction to this volume is 'Purely Personal: On Being a Musical Eclectic' but Wilson is too much the philosopher to remain purely personal for too long. In the last sentence of the introduction, he makes the statement that 'all the essays in this volume are an attempt to write existential criticism'.

Immediately prior to this sentence, Wilson indicates the basic principles involved in applying existential criticism to music. He argues that academic criticism concerns itself with the value of a particular work of art. Such criticism concentrates its attention on the *work* itself. Existential criticism, however, refuses to separate the work from the life and personality of the artist. Thus, academic criticism would compare the symphonies of Haydn and Beethoven in terms of the variations in form and musical procedures introduced by Beethoven. It would pay no regard to the difference in the characters of the two composers. Existential criticism, on the other hand, would begin its evaluation with reference to the aggressive qualities that are the hallmark of Beethoven as a man – the intense desire to reign over the realm of the human spirit. Without due acknowledgement of this determination, existential criticism would argue, little of real significance can be said about Beethoven's music.

In the essay, 'Mozart and Beethoven: A Retrospect', Wilson treats their lives and personalities as a preparation for an evaluation of their music. Mozart is to be understood essentially in terms of his sheer genius. He was not a great man in the historic sense, nor did he possess the sharpest intellect the world has seen. Yet he was a noble soul with a quick intuition. He had the heart of a child and a simple trust in the world. He was fundamentally healthy and could relate well with other people. He was a devoted husband who loved his wife.

By contrast, Beethoven's genius was untamed. He had the morality of the superman and the restless temperament that goes with it. He pitted himself against established authorities – once, in the company of Goethe, he pushed his way through the royal family while Goethe stood aside – and even the gods. Ordinary mortals were of little value to him, except as he could use them to his own benefit. He felt no compunction about swindling his publisher. While many of his biographers excuse his behaviour on the basis of his genius, Wilson suggests that he was a neurotic, suspicious, bad-tempered individual who brought his own miseries upon himself. What redeems him, if anything, is that he recognised that he was involved in a universal struggle between good and evil and refused to capitulate to the forces of evil. Although he could find little in individuals to which he could respond, he did learn to relate to mankind in the abstract.

Two such different personalities as these were bound to produce a different kind of music to each other. In Mozart, Wilson finds an essential vitality that strains against the bonds that would contain it, yet the struggle is always controlled. It is clean, precise and delicate. Mozart wins the struggle by creating a music that belongs to a world of innocence. It is a primal music that expresses an unquenchable faith in life. *The Magic Flute* is, in fact, a hymn to life that celebrates man's most fundamental experiences of the world. This is music that is genuinely evolutionary in its design and its execution. Wilson penetrates to its centre when he writes:

> Nothing is so untrue as that 'beauty is in the eye of the beholder'. This is like saying that beauty is in the dusty window pane because cleaning it makes the garden more visible. Beauty is *out there*. The beauty is really there and if we could disconnect ourselves from our pushing humanity for a moment, I think we would dance and sing like madmen at what we could see. Well, the greatest music has the power to get through the glass in spite of the dust, to tell us something about the absolute value of life, quite apart from our bored personal preoccupations. It would be wrong to say that the content of Mozart's music is mystical, for all music is mystical in that sense, like nature. But for those who can hear, it says something completely primitive about the nature of life, something that cannot be translated into words.[24]

There is no disputing that the music of Beethoven is great. It reflects its composer's inner struggle. It points towards the age of Romanticism and has much the same qualities as are seen in

Manfred, standing on a mountain-top and shaking his fist at God. Yet, in a sense, it is precisely this which reveals its limitations. It suggest that Beethoven, like the later Romantics, was struggling against his own weakness. As assertive as it is, it fails to win the ultimate battle.

Wilson reminds us of the aphorism of Mencius: 'He who follows that part of himself that is great will be a great man: he who follows that part of himself that is little will be a little man.' Mozart followed his own genius and produced the music of genius. Beethoven pursued his own deficiencies and his music reflects the pursuit rather than the conquest. Beethoven's music is like a steel rod, plunged into a furnace to purge it of its impurities. Mozart's is the fire.

It will have become clear from the foregoing outline of Wilson's critical theory that existential criticism is not simply a reaction to art. While it may be going too far to suggest that it is a *dialogue* with art, it is certainly not too much to say that existential criticism constitutes a *challenge* to art. It is an analytical *control* which seeks to keep the artist faithful to his creative responsibility. It is a fundamental achievement of Wilson's criticism that the concept of the 'death of the hero' in the latter half of the twentieth century is being carefully examined and evaluated.

Wilson hopes for the widest possible application of an existential criticism as an aid to what he earlier called 'the existential revolt'. Today he might speak of it in other terms but the ground rules remain the same:

The existential revolt could take place on two levels: the philosophical and the creative. On the first level, it might produce its own text-books of 'irrational philosophy' to take up the problem where Sartre left it in *L'Être et Le Neant*, Heidegger in *Sein und Zeit*, Camus in *L'Homme revolte*. On the creative level, it would be a revolt against the unheroic premiss, the attempt to create heroes who possess a vision that extends beyond the particularities of environment. This does not necessarily mean a hero who carries a copy of *Man and Superman* in his pocket, but it means heroes who are closer in conception to Stendhal's Sorel, Balzac's Rastignac, Braine's Joe Lampton, Hopkins' Plowart. It is even conceivable that new, realistic Fausts, Zarathustras, Ahabs, might grow out of it.[25]

In introducing existential criticism, Wilson has done more than offer us a new *form* of criticism. He has offered us a new *purpose* for criticism – and it is nothing less than the freeing of humanity from its present bonds to pursue its destiny. In this, it shares the task of art itself.

8

The Fiction

FROM the beginning of his literary career, Wilson has regarded fiction as an important medium for the expression of his philosophy. *The Outsider*, it should be remembered, was in fact written during an interruption to his work on *Ritual in the Dark*. So intimate is the relationship between his philosophy and his fiction, that he has frequently written two books simultaneously, a novel and a non-fiction work, both dealing with the same theme. Thus *The Outsider* and *Ritual in the Dark* both portray the misery of the Outsider as he confronts his own alienation from society. The fictional Austin Nunne, although different by virtue of being a murderer, knows the anguish that stirred in the breast of Hermann Hesse and Vaslav Nijinsky. *Man Without a Shadow* was a fictional treatment of the sexual mysteries Wilson had addressed in *Origins of the Sexual Impulse*. In *Introduction to the New Existentialism*, Wilson actually outlined the basic idea of *The Mind Parasites* as an illustration of the inadequate understanding of human consciousness that interferes with the evolutionary thrust. *The Killer* is clearly a treatment of the characteristics of the murderer as spelled out in the introductory essay to *Encyclopedia of Murder* and in *A Casebook of Murder*. *The Glass Cage* deals with the differing psychologies of the criminal and the mystic, a theme that had been developed in *Beyond the Outsider*.

More recently, Wilson has continued this dual treatment – fictional and non-fictional – of the ideas that preoccupy him. *The Personality Surgeon* was the product of a man who had thought his way through the implications of an existential psychology and contemporary theories of the bicameral nature of the human brain. *The Janus Murder Case* is an expression of the consideration he had given to the psychological phenomenon of multiple personality. Niall, the central character of the two volumes of *Spider World* published to date, could have been conceived only by a writer who had comprehended the application of intentional consciousness to human experience.

It is Wilson's contention that fiction is not only an appropriate but an essential vehicle for the examination of philosophical concepts. He has said:

> For me [fiction] is a manner of philosophising. . . . Philosophy may be only a shadow of the reality it tries to grasp but the novel is altogether more satisfactory. I am almost tempted to say that no philosopher is qualified to do his job unless he is also a novelist. . . . I would certainly exchange any of the works of Whitehead or Wittgenstein for the novels they ought to have written.[1]

In his assessment of Wilson's fiction, Nicholas Tredell has correctly identified the essence of the philosophy that is expounded in his novels. Tredell writes:

> Pessimism has become modish, and it is, as Wilson constantly reiterates, sometimes the easier option. 'Facing up to the harsh realities of life' provides an excuse, a noble justification, for inaction. Nothing to be done. Wilson's novels, his whole *œuvre*, are an attempt, a virtually one-man attempt in contemporary culture, to hold up a heroic image of man, to produce a literature of celebration. If it does not altogether succeed, this is partly because our language of heroism and celebration has worn thin. It seems archaic and false. The dominant linguistic modes are pessimistic, carriers of defeat and despair. Wilson, however, believes that the writer must be prepared to work alone, unsupported by his age, fighting against its language, creating his own concepts, his own language, in the hope that they may one day become common concepts, a common language, the Everlasting Gospel of evolutionary man. Wilson is attempting to create a re-definition of man in the light of the future. Of the positive future.
>
> This is the greatest value of Wilson's novels.[2]

Although there are not many critical assessments of Wilson's novels, those that do exist tend to classify them within established genres. There are, it is argued, his detective stories, his science-fiction stories, his fantasies and so on. Such an approach faces the danger of doing him a disservice by drawing the reader's attention away from the content and towards a comparative evaluation of his work with the particular genres. Thus, to assess *The Glass Cage* as a 'detective novel', is almost certainly to relegate it to a position behind the works of such writers as Simenon and Agatha Christie who are masterful exponents of that genre. Wilson is not writing a detective story but a story which takes us to the heart of fundamental intellectual issues. This may be why it is subtitled, in the American edition, 'an unconventional tale of mystery.' In the same manner, *The Space Vampires* is only coincidentally a 'science-fiction' novel. In its essence, it is a *tour de force* – and again the publisher, this time Hart-Davis MacGibbon, is forced to say so in what is virtually a subtitle. If the attempt to classify all his novels into genres is carried to its logical extreme, it is finally left with a work such as *The Personality Surgeon*, which simply refuses to fit into any class. To describe *Necessary Doubt*, as Tredell does, as 'a detective thriller with a science fiction twist at the end',[3] is not only to strain the language but to point away from the sheer cleverness of the work.

For this reason, the following examination of Wilson's novels will avoid, as much as possible, reliance on recognised forms. It will treat the three novels that constitute the Sorme Trilogy as a single unit. The Saltfleet duo will be treated as two investigations by the unorthodox police inspector. We shall then turn to the autobiographical work, *Adrift in Soho* before examining the social and philosophical set that comprises *The World of Violence, Necessary Doubt, The Glass Cage*, and *Rasputin. The Killer, The Black Room* and *The Personality Surgeon* will be regarded as psychological works and all the remaining novels assessed as intellectual fantasies. Of course, this is to do no more than substitute one set of categories for another but it does have the advantage of avoiding the limitations that the more traditional genres might impose upon a writer – and a reader.

In *The Sorme Trilogy*, we have a classic fictional treatment of the Outsider and his struggle to move beyond himself into a state of inner peace based on accomplishment. There can be little doubt that Gerard Sorme is Wilson himself, wrestling with the intellectual, emotional, social and sexual characteristics through which the Outsider experiences his anguish. He is the observer of human experience but in a very different sense to Barbusse's observer trying to gratify his lust for life at a hole in the wall. Sorme is engaged in an intelligent search for an understanding of the human condition rather than with the immediate satisfaction of his own needs.

In *Ritual in the Dark*, Wilson deals with three basic themes. These are: the nature of the Romantic and visionary idealist, human sexuality, and the decline of religion. These themes are developed through an examination of the relationship between three characters; Sorme, Austin Nunne and Oliver Glasp. Each of these represents a variant of the Outsider. Sorme is intellectually disciplined but lacks control over his body and his emotions. Glass is in control of his emotions but not of his sexual appetite or his intellect. The murderer, Nunne, is physically disciplined but lacks control over his intellect and emotions. Thus, in these three characters, Wilson has provided us with a powerful composite portrayal of the human condition.

Ritual in the Dark is fundamentally an examination of Romantic man. There is, in Nunne, an element of the drive that we find in Nijinsky. Glasp is based largely on Van Gogh. Between them, the characters of the novel have a vision of a higher level of existence but they have no idea of how to attain it. Glasp pours his energy into artistic creation but he never finds a satisfactory sense of direction. Nunne allows his own energies to burst into violent crime and commits several murders. Inevitably, they find themselves in the same position as the Romantics at the end of the nineteenth century – bereft of hope and floundering in despair. It is left to Sorme to continue the struggle.

Much of the critical response to Wilson's first novel centred around Sorme's apparent acceptance of Nunne's murders. Such criticism fails to recognise that Wilson is dealing with the totality of the human condition. In fact, while Sorme tries to understand Nunne, he never condones his acts and at the end of the novel we learn that Sorme believes Nunne 'might as well be dead'. What Wilson is concerned with is the failure of human beings to deal with those aspects of existence which produce the murderer. While these remain unaddressed, there is little point in lamenting the acts they induce. Nunne murders because he does not recognise his own value.

John Lehmann, in his review of the book – which he recognises to be a 'philosophical essay' – argues that it is a failure. He bases his judgement on moral grounds, finding it difficult to accept what he calls Wilson's 'romanticising of Nunne, even when his suspicion that he is a murderer has almost become a certainty'.[4] But this is to miss the point that Nunne is not so much 'romanticised' as presented as a symbol of Romanticism. Judged from one point of view, murder may well be regarded as a product of the same inadequacies that led to the demise of Romanticism.

It is impossible in an essay of this length to do justice to the complexities of *Ritual in the Dark*. With its powerful evocation of the London streets of the Fifties, its rich characterisation and the authentic dialogue that carries the plot forward, it is a remarkable first novel. Like most of Wilson's fiction, it has stood the test of time and is still eminently readable. Yet, if we cannot dwell on its substance, we can identify Wilson's essential purpose in writing it. It is expressed in two paragraphs. Sorme is speaking:

> You know the Egyptians all believed they were descended from the gods? For the Egyptians, man was a sort of god, a god in exile. For the Christian Church, he was an immortal soul, poised between heaven and hell. Today he's just a member of society with a duty to everybody else. It's the steady devaluation of human beings. But that's our job, Austin, yours and mine. We're the writers and the poets. We can fight the deflation. Our job is to increase the dignity of human beings, try to push it back towards the Egyptian estimate.
>
> He began to feel excited and happy as he talked, and grateful to Nunne for releasing this sense of certainty. Nunne was listening with an expression of interest, but there was no response in his face. Looking at him, Sorme remembered his image; being burnt out inside, like a hole in a carpet. That was it. Something had short-circuited Nunne inside. His capacity to respond had been burnt out by guilt and fatigue. Nothing Sorme could say would strike any response; there was nothing to respond.[5]

It is not to be supposed that Gerard Sorme is the hero of the New Existentialism. At the time he created him, Wilson had not even used the term. Wilson like Sorme, was only at the beginning of his struggle with the negative thinking that had produced Sartre's nausea but in the passage just quoted it is clear that the foundation for an evolutionary optimism had been established. If *Ritual in the Dark* is the description of an existential problem, it is also the first step in the direction of a solution.

When we meet Sorme again in *Man Without a Shadow*, he is settled in a room in Camden Town, preoccupied with writing an account of his own sexuality. The novel is written in the first person and this has the effect of giving it a sense of immediacy. Sorme recounts his sexual adventures but it is not his intent to boast of his conquests in the sense that a Casanova or a Frank Harris might do. Sorme's interest in sex is related to his quest for self-discovery. He knows that his own sexuality is of profound significance to his development. He writes:

> I believe that, far from being 'abnormal', the intensity of my sexual impulse is a part of the total intensity that makes me what I am – an intelligent being, responding with unusual directness to the problems of modern civilisation. I watch my sexual impulse at work with a kind of amazement. I may not know why I'm alive, but something inside me does. Sex is the only power I know that can defeat the awful pressure of the present. The world looks blank and meaningless, grey, point-less, mocking my brevity and hunger with its permanence and serenity. Only when sexual desire blazes in me can I overcome its indifference; the desire turns on it like a flame-thrower; my body suddenly carries a current at thousands of volts, surging from some main down in my subconscious; I become realler than the world, harder, intenser, more lasting.[6]

It is clear, from this passage, that Wilson is writing more than a novel. He is giving expression to his basic sexology. In fact, *Man Without a Shadow* is in many ways more like a case study in an evolutionary philosophy of sex than a novel. Wilson himself supports this view in the introduction he wrote for the book.

> Is it not time that we created a new type of novel, the kind of novel that I could only dimly envisage as I wrote this one? The old novel of the Nineteenth century was like a ship out at sea, sailing on its way without much relevance to the problems of its readers; it merely took them on a voyage. The Joyce novel aimed at pure writing as Cezanne aimed at pure painting –

observation of reality where the subject counts for very little –
a stove pipe will do as well as a mountain – and the manner
everything. But when I think of the kind of novel written by
Dostoevsky and Wells, I think of a hatchet biting into a tree and
making the chips fly, not an evasion of reality or a description of
it, but an attack on it. As I describe it here, it sounds vaguely
like the 'social realism' prescribed by the Soviet ideology; but
mere social realism never bites deep enough. What is needed is
an existential realism. Like social realism, its attitude to reality
is not passive or pessimistic. In a qualified sense, it might be
called practical; it wishes to change things. What it wishes to
change I prefer to leave unstated; it can be inferred from this
book.[7]

Man Without a Shadow also reflects Wilson's interest in the occult.
One of its major characters, Carodac Cunningham, who is based
on Aleister Crowley, seeks to persuade Sorme of the power of
magic. Like sex, it too is a form of extended consciousness.
Although Sorme remains somewhat sceptical of Cunningham's
'sexual magic', he does agree to assist in magical ceremonies. The
last of these ends in a disaster when one of the female participants
is rushed to hospital, having taken an overdose of an 'aphrodisiac'.
Extracts from Sorme's diary are made public through the daily
newspapers. Cunningham flees the country and Sorme too leaves
England with his partner Diana, taking her to Ireland. Tredell
has judged this conclusion to the book as being farcical. He fails
to realise that it is no more than a fictionalized account of the
events that befell Wilson and Joy Stewart after her father had
wielded the horsewhip.

The critical response to this novel was almost universally dis-
missive. In the *New Republic*, Stanley Kauffmann wondered if it
was intended as a spoof and went on to wonder whether Wilson
himself was not a spoof – some literary pseudonym for a collabor-
ative effort by Kingsley Amis, Malcolm Muggeridge and Peter
Ustinov. The *Time* reviewer assessed it as being 'Promethean
flimflam that steams up from a painfully protracted puberty'.[8] Yet
Man Without a Shadow remains an important statement of the
philosophy of the Outsider. It reflects man in the attitude of
exploring his own sexuality and it does so with an intellectual
honesty that is all too rare in the field.

But if the critics did not like *Man Without a Shadow*, they were even less impressed with *The God of the Labyrinth*, the third volume in the Sorme trilogy. Essentially, the theme of this work is that identified in the second volume of the trilogy: the idea of the 'eight-hour orgasm' – which in itself is a symbol for the prolongation of heightened intensity. Sorme gains the capacity for such an experience through the study of an eighteenth-century mystic and roué named Esmond Donnelly and the Sect of the Phoenix, of which he was a member.

For Maurice Capitanchik, writing in the *Spectator*, the Sorme of *God of the Labyrinth* represents 'the rationalisation of a neurosis'.[9] Wilson is rebuked as 'a seeker after enlightenment who faces life with his mental eyes shut'. But such judgements can only be made when the novel is read without any reference to the total philosophy that Wilson has enunciated. No matter how unpleasant it might appear to be, the fact remains that there *is* a logic in this novel that stands the test of 'the rest of truth'. Here, the sexual orgasm is utilised as a symbol and where the reader fails to recognise this, the cost must inevitably be a misapprehension of what the book has to say.

The most severe critics rejected *The God of the Labyrinth* as pornography. Wilson had anticipated such a response and appended to the book, in its very first edition, a note on pornography. In this note he wrote:

When I read Rider Haggard as a child, I experienced both detachment and involvement. The detachment came from sitting in an armchair reading a book; the excitement from marching through snake-infested jungles with Alan Quatermain. This is the essential quality of civilised experience – detachment *and* involvement. But where sex is concerned, this notion is still not accepted. We are supposed to be either directly involved – in bed with a partner – or totally detached, as when I read a case in Havelock Ellis and murmer 'How interesting'. There seems to be an element of absurdity about this. Most adult readers have had the experience that is described by Cleland or D. H. Lawrence; and, unlike cruelty or crime, this experience is not regarded as socially undesirable. Is there really such a gulf between the subject of sex and subjects like history, adventure, sport? Is there any reason why civilised adults should not, if they are so minded, read about sex with feelings of detachment, or humour, or even a certain involvement?[10]

The God of the Labyrinth may well be one of those novels which is not understood because its readers have not yet learned to objectify their attitude towards their own sexuality. To the extent that this is true, it is an indictment of its readers rather than of its writer but the real shame lies in the loss of the insights that the book has to offer.

The Sorme Trilogy is, collectively, a *bildungsroman*. It is an account of a sustained effort by its central character to come to grips with the primary facts of his own existence. It allows us to observe a personal struggle that is being waged in the real world – in the world of crime and of sexuality. It introduces us to a character who knows that his life is there to be enriched; to be fulfilled. There is little point in speculating, with Tredell, on the consistency of the characterisation between the three novels. In each, we are confronted with a different aspect of the one person-ality as it seeks to gain control over its experience. In the persona of Gerard Sorme, Wilson has given us an indication that those who persist in the effort can facilitate their own growth. If the end result, in the character of Sorme, does not reflect true greatness, it may be because Wilson himself was still refining his own insights. In any event, Sorme displays a level of maturity that few of the trilogy's readers can match.

It should not be supposed from any of the above that Wilson's trilogy is unreadable because it is overburdened with philosophy. It is certainly true that these first three novels have a philosophical purpose and that they are best understood when that purpose is grasped but they nonetheless remain intensely interesting and readable. Wilson has argued:

The novel, like the drama, is intended to be entertainment. Provided it can hold an audience, purely as entertainment, the writer is at liberty to fill it with his obsessions. But if the obsessions come to outweigh the entertainment, he has no right to demand an audience on the grounds that he is a 'serious artist'. In-so-far as he ceases to be a good entertainer, he also ceases to be a serious artist. An artist's seriousness is not gauged simply by his capacity for strong feeling, but also by the depth of his interest in the objective world, and the attempt to reflect this in his work. A novel that is pure fact and observation may be absorbing, even if it could never be a masterpiece; a novel

that is pure subjective feeling will almost certainly be unreadable.[11]

The continuing sale of the Sorme trilogy is a clear indication that,
notwithstanding the judgement of the critics, it is acknowledged
as being acceptable literature. Many of its readers will make the
same judgement with respect to the philosophy it expresses.

If there is any sense in which Gerard Sorme is Wilson's *alter
ego*, the same can be said of Harry Preston in *Adrift in Soho*.
Wilson has said that in this short novel, he was attempting to
produce the English equivalent to the American 'Beat' novel. Yet
the novel does not blend happily with the work of Kerouac and
Holmes. *Adrift in Soho* is a *bildungsroman*. There is always a sense
of purpose about Preston that is lacking in Kerouac's characters.
It is true that there is something comic about this purpose but it
is there nonetheless. These are the frantic days that Wilson and
his friends spent in Notting Hill Gate immediately prior to the
publication of *The Outsider*.

This novel was first written as a play, *The Metal Flower Blossom*
which was commercially produced in Plymouth. The play is
lighter than the novel. It contains a scene in which a large quantity
of alcohol is 'smuggled' into the flat in a coffin, around which
the exuberant young people dance in celebration. The incident is
repeated in the novel, but without the sense of energy that it
would have provoked on stage.

Adrift in Soho is important within the context of Wilson's work.
It is a clear demonstration that he was aware of the distractions
of the Fifties. This was Bohemian London, with its enticing
invitation to enjoy the existential drift that pretends to offer hope.
As demonstrated in Daniel Farson's recent work, *Soho in the
'Fifties*[12], the bars and brothels of Soho were filled with would-
be-artists who lacked the self-discipline to commit themselves to
the obligations of their own creativity. Preston acknowledges the
invitation but finally rejects it, preferring to spend his time in the
British Museum researching the book he is writing under the title
The Nature of Freedom. In a novel that is appropriately light and
effervescent, Wilson's seriousness is carefully maintained.

What is questionable about this fictional community of Lad-
broke Road – apart from Preston himself – is that it is without
substantial values. The painter, Ricki Prelati, has a vague vision
of the world he wishes to create but he never quite manages to

get it down on canvas. When his paintings are all purchased by a rich American, there is a sense that, far from escaping the inadequate values of Soho, he has confirmed them. Prelati himself understands this. He tells Doreen:

> My dear girl, I've never had the faintest doubt that I'd be successful. When I was sixteen, I met a weird Irish painter who was supposed to have second sight. He took one look at me and said, 'You're going to be very successful one of these days'. And I replied: 'Yes, I know'. Because quite suddenly I realised I *did* know. I've always known it. It was only later that I began to realise what success can do to a man who's not prepared for it. So I determined to hold it off until I *was* prepared for it. I haven't succeeded.[13]

But this is not intended to suggest that *Adrift in Soho* is a description of life-failure. Always hovering in the reader's mind there is the energetic Preston. Bernadine Bishop takes us to the heart of the work:

> What stands out in this novel and makes it not only readable but also worth reading, is the personality of Harry. He has a fund of intellectual energy and a vigorous determination to extract the last ounce of meaning from any experience; more, he refuses to allow any experience to be meaningless. He sees to it that everything that happens to him has a didactic value or at least starts a profitable train of thought.[14]

In his first two novels, *Ritual in the Dark* and *Adrift in Soho*, Wilson set about confronting his own creative bent and establishing a measure of control over the craft of fiction. Neither can be regarded as great novels but they certainly represent an honest beginning, for they laid the foundation for a series of books which grapple intelligently with significant issues that are the proper province of the novel. The first of these was *The World of Violence*.

Written in the first person, and again clearly autobiographical in part, *The World of Violence* is an account of the development of Hugh Greene, a mathematical prodigy who rejects the possibility of undertaking study at Cambridge in favour of submitting himself to the examination of his own experience. The novel has a setting of social violence but the real drama is again an internal one, involving the identification of a set of values which are honest enough to support human growth.

One of Hugh's mentors is Uncle Sam. This larger-than-life character is the source of much of Hugh's temperament, particularly that part which deals with other people. He is, in fact, the quintessential Outsider. In a forty-page document addressed to Hugh, he provides an account of a climatic moment in his life:

> I remember pushing my way through a crowd on the platform, and suddenly being overwhelmed by a feeling that struck me as abruptly as a heart attack. It was a sudden and violent hatred of all my fellow human beings. As I stood there, surrounded by pressing bodies, loathing and contempt rose in me until I felt I was drowning. . . . I got up to the street with difficulty and as I walked through [them], all the stupidity and pettiness of humankind were present to my mind. . . . I felt as if I had been transported into a city of gigantic and hairy spiders, who perspired rottenness.[15]

We might pause to note, in parenthesis, this interesting image of a city of spiders – a clear anticipation of the later *Spider World*, which Wilson conceived and developed in discussion with Donald Seaman – a friend he had not yet met when *The World of Violence* was written!

Uncle Sam struggles with his perception of people for several years until, one day in church, he suddenly realises the cause of his repulsion. Human beings, he comprehends, are slaves:

> It seems to have struck no one that human beings are grossly exploited by God. We are expected to bear misfortune, to learn from experience, (like obedient schoolchildren), to offer thanksgiving for the benefits received; our role is in every way that of the slave and the sycophant.[16]

The contempt Uncle Sam feels for his kind is explained in terms of their slavish behaviour and their passivity. He despises them because they are a clear indication of his own failure as a human being. This insight leads him to lock himself in his attic, where he spends the next twenty years living in darkness (an anticipation of *The Black Room*) in an attempt to 'treat directly with God on behalf of my fellow human beings'. In the end, an hour before his death, he has a vision which he reports to his wife in the words, 'I have seen it'. Hugh never learns what 'it' is but it does not matter. He had learned from his uncle that the essential question is, 'What is the logical response to being alive?'

Wilson has declared that *The World of Violence* is 'a study in the contrast between the ivory tower of an intellectual and the chaotic violence of actuality'.[17] In Hugh Greene there rages a battle that is of profound significance to us all.

The existential theologian, Karl Zweig, of *Necessary Doubt* – based in part on Paul Tillich – is a ready-made vehicle for the exposition of Wilson's ideas. Zweig's interaction with Gustav Neumann, one of his ex-students, provides the novel with its basic plot. Zweig suspects that Neumann, who had earlier expressed a philosophical interest in becoming a 'great criminal', may be responsible for a number of murders. But if the plot centres on an attempt to solve a crime, the theme is nothing less than human renewal. Tredell states the case as clearly as possible:

> *Necessary Doubt* is primarily the story of Zweig's regeneration, in which the possibility of a more general regeneration of Western culture is implied. It is no mere detective hunt that Zweig is engaged on, but a quest for spiritual revival; his hunt for Neumann is a hunt for the 'New Man'. The action of the novel takes place over a cold, snowy Christmas; the wintry weather, of which we are frequently made aware, complements our sense of a certain sterility in Zweig which Wilson's evocation of his age and essential solitude has aroused. Christmas, for both pagan and Christian, is a symbol of spiritual rebirth in the heart of winter. For Wilson, it is also one of those moments when consciousness expands, and the world seems richer, stranger, more meaningful. *Necessary Doubt* could be called Wilson's *Christmas Carol*. It is the story of a conversion, like Dickens' tale, but in reverse; not to Christianity, but from Christianity to evolutionary existentialism.[18]

It is Tredell too, who points out an interesting comparison between *Necessary Doubt* and *Ritual in the Dark*. In the latter, Sorme begins in a friendly relationship with the murderer but finally comes to reject him as a human failure. In *Necessary Doubt*, Zweig at first has a negative view of a man who may be a murderer but eventually comes to accept him and share his vision.

There is, of course, one fundamental difference: Neumann is not a killer. His interest lies in experimentation with the human mind. The argument seems clear: the evolutionary drive is inextricably bound up with an ongoing modification of judgements and it loses its energy when confined within a closed mind.

Wilson has an extraordinary capacity for providing telling metaphors. A single image points to the central problem that he addresses in *Necessary Doubt*. Neumann tells Zweig:

> One day, my father put on a kettle to make coffee but the gas was very low and it took nearly an hour to boil. My father was trying to write an article for a psychological journal at the same time. Suddenly he looked up and said: 'My brain is like that kettle – it won't boil'. And in a flash it came to me: that is what is wrong with all human consciousness. The pressure is so low that it never boils. We live at half pressure. We are all psychologically undernourished because the pressure of consciousness is so low. My father was right. If his consciousness had been brighter, the article would have been written as fast as the pen could move across the paper.[19]

A series of brutal murders provides the plot of *The Glass Cage*. Here, the chief investigator is once again other than a member of the police force. In Damon Reade, Wilson draws on the internationally recognised Blakean scholar, S. Foster Damon. Reade is involved because each murder is characterised by a quotation from William Blake, written on a slip of paper and left in close proximity to the murdered victims. Wilson, in using such a device, makes it clear that this novel, like everything he writes, is designed to stimulate the intellect.

By any standard, *The Glass Cage* is a highly successful novel but it is the relationship it has with Blake's poetry that lends it its uniqueness as a work of fiction. Few contemporary novelists would dare to draw into their story the metaphysic of one of the most complex of English poets. Wilson not only manages to accomplish this but he does it with an authority that wins the plaudits of students of Blake. In a paper published in the journal *Blake Studies*, Stuart Curran writes:

> *The Glass Cage*, however disappointing to followers of Perry Mason and Ellery Queen, is a significant volume for followers

of Blake. Its major figure is not just a student of Blake, but a true Blakean, who reads his author as Blake hoped to be read, as guide and prophet to the modern world. Colin Wilson translates Blake's epic vision into a culture removed in many superficial respects from that which burdened him into art, but which has developed with uncanny accuracy into the crisis Blake predicted. Less a novel than a cultural survey, *The Glass Cage* draws on Blake to support, not the existential despair of those who have retreated into Ulro to wait for Godot, but a radical Christian humanism, beginning in existential negation of external values and ending in a faith that man can redeem himself through mental liberation. Even if the Limit of Contraction is defined by this life, the Limit of Opacity within the mind is, like the limits of space beyond, distant, indefinite, perhaps never to be attained. Wilson's England is as obscured and tortured as Blake's; the human condition he observes is sad and as deserving of compassion; his faith in the expansive redemption of continuous revolution as adamant and as humane.[20]

As Curran points out, the key to Blake, like the key to *The Glass Cage*, is the human sex drive. Curran claims that 'in fixing on sexuality as the reductive symbol of the world of generation, Blake's canon is the most probing analysis of sexual motivations in English literature'.[21] Wilson's murderer, Sundheim, whose name translates as 'house of sin', is a physically huge, bisexual Outsider whose desperate effort at self-fulfilment is finally frustrated by the inadequacy of his commitment to sex as a symbol of his innate power. Sundheim is the Outsider as criminal and his aetiology is well documented in Wilson's sexology.

> Sundhein glanced up for a moment, and grinned almost sheepishly. Then he returned to the beef on his plate, and began cutting it with powerful jerks of his knife, and shovelling it into his mouth two slices at a time. As he came towards the end of the champaigne, he began to chew more slowly, like a slated animal. Veins stood out across his forehead, and a drop of sweat trickled down from the hairline. He thrust the last of the bread into his mouth, and washed it down with champaigne.[22]

We have met this energy directed at food – and at sex – before in Wilson's psychology and we know it to be misplaced. This is the theme of *The Glass Cage*.

By virtue of its inclusion in the Reader's Digest publication *Tales of the Uncanny*, for which it was written, Wilson's novelisation of the life of Grigori Rasputin is directed at a more popular audience and is written with this in mind. Nonetheless, it contains the basic ingredients of Wilson's understanding of the enigmatic Russian monk, as set out in *Rasputin and the Fall of the Romanovs*. Rasputin is yet another Outsider figure. Wilson imagines a moment towards the end of his life. After an unsuccessful attempt to persuade Prime Minister Goremykin to recall the Duma and define a political package that might appease the rising liberals, he returned home feeling exhausted and depressed. Then,

> to calm himself, he walked along the quays of the Neva until he was facing the Gulf of Finland. The great expanse of water gradually soothed his spirit. He found himself remembering that first day in Saint Petersburg, when he stood in this same spot, looking out towards Kronstadt Island. It seemed a century ago. It suddenly struck him that he had at last achieved all he had dreamed of as a child: a position of power and intimacy with the Tzar even closer than that of the Archpriest Avvakum. The irony of the situation made him smile. He was trapped in a city that he had come to hate, and in a way of life he found deadening to the soul.[23]

Here is unfulfilled desire: or, rather, inadequate desire. Rasputin has achieved his ambition but his ambition was never sufficient of itself to thrust him forward beyond his deepest frustrations. All that remains is nostalgia and irony. The very objects of his dominance – the court, the city – close in upon him and he comes to look at himself as the one certain source of self-realisation too late. Ahead, there is only death and not even the powerful resistance he offers to it seems to have any relevance other than as a symbol of tragedy. Whatever mystical powers he may have possessed were finally of no avail. The Siberian monk represents a life of dissipated opportunity and power. Not even his religious faith could defend him. Wilson summarises his life thus:

> Compared to any of the great religious figures of Europe – Pascal, William Law, Newman, Kierkegaard – his religion is

curiously unintelligent, curiously literal and objective. This is difficult for a European to understand – for Rasputin himself was far from unintelligent. He was also monumentally self-reliant. But it was not the intellectual self-reliance of a Nietzsche. If the least grain of Zarathustra's scepticism had ever found its way into Rasputin's mind, the whole structure of his personality would have collapsed. The Tzarevitch nicknamed Rasputin 'the novik', the new man. But he was not a new man; intellectually, he was the last of the Old Believers, and it is fitting that he should have died before the October revolution.[24]

In so far as they deal with the reality of the human condition, Wilson's books have a capacity to disturb. None is more disturbing than *The Killer*. This composite portrait of a sex murderer is chilling in its authenticity. In a sense, it would be easier reading if Arthur Lingard did not become as real as he does for then, holding him at arm's length, we would be much more comfortable with him. But, of course, Wilson wants us to meet him eye to eye. Whether we like to admit it or not, the murderer is one of the characteristic individuals of our age and to the extent that we ignore him, or fail to understand his essence, we are out of touch with ourselves.

Wilson sees *The Killer* as the third volume of a criminological trilogy that includes *Ritual in the Dark* and *The Glass Cage*. Yet it seems to stand alone; a penetrating psychological study. It remains fiction but it does have a documentary element which Tredell considers to be unsatisfactory. In support of his view, Tredell argues that the 'facts' with which it deals are *too* unpleasant to be digested readily. Because the reader knows that it is a fiction, there is a tendency to avoid the 'truth'. Further, he argues, the facts do not fit into a tight structure. It is as if the work is overloaded with detail. Thus, '*The Killer* forfeits the advantages of both fact and fiction, losing the authority of the one and the form of the other.'[25]

But Graham Zellick cuts through the debate on form and identifies the most important fact about this novel:

There are, thankfully, few killers like Arthur Lingard in Britain; but there are some. The processes of the law can reveal little of what goes on in the mind of such a man, and the accusatorial nature of the proceedings is notorious in this respect. Mr Wil-

son's account is a frightening one; but it is all the more valuable
for that reason. It may be a novel, but it has something of the
classic case-study about it.[26]

The point must be made that *The Killer*, even read in isolation
from the rest of his work, reveals Wilson as a consummate artist.
The novel has a remarkable internal consistency and the inevita-
bility of the events with which it is concerned seems totally
plausible. It is a work which leads the reader again and again
to think 'If only . . .'. Lingard's crimes flow easily out of his
background, not in some simply Freudian sense but in an ava-
lanche of brutalising frustration. In reading it, one experiences an
intuitive certainty that it is right; that its depiction of the psyche
of the criminal is intrinsically useful.

But there is another point which must be made with equal
force. Those who have read nothing else by Wilson apart from
this novel, must be careful not to conclude that he is himself a
sado-masochist. The work is a statement of the problem he
addresses in his criminology and cannot be appreciated apart from
it. Then, too, all of his fiction belongs within the context of his
philosophy of evolutionary phenomenology and is impossible to
understand unless it is placed within that context. *The Killer* is
not for the squeamish: nor is it for the unintelligent. It does
not call for revulsion, nor for compliment: it demands sober
reflection.

Wilson has Arthur Lingard killed by a fellow sex-criminal
named Dooley inside a prison. On the last page of the novel, we
are told:

What happened is still not clear. The two men seemed to like
one another. They were under the supervision of a guard,
talking in the garden. The guard wandered off to exchange
words with another guard. When he looked around he saw that
Arthur was on the ground with Dooley's huge hands at his
throat. He died later without recovering consciousness. Dooley
would only say, obstinately: 'He started it'. Another prisoner
claimed that Arthur had leapt at Dooley and started pummelling
him with his fists. The cause of the quarrel, apparently, was a
pair of black panties that Arthur claimed Dooley had stolen
from his locker.[27]

It is no accident that Wilson chooses to close this disturbing examination of a pathological mind with a simple indication of the total *absurdity* of the act in which one human being takes the life of another.

The second Wilson novel to address a psychological theme directly was *The Black Room*. Here he is concerned with the phenomenon of sensory deprivation and its effect on human consciousness. The spy plot is incidental to the theme but this does not mean that it lacks pace or interest. Kit Butler's involvement in the intelligence networks of Britain and the United States, in their power struggle against the Eastern bloc, makes entertaining reading. But it is the black room itself that should occupy our attention, for it represents one of Wilson's most carefully developed philosophical symbols.

In fact, the black room is an instrument that can be used for the development of intentionality. It is, in Tredell's terms, 'the technological equivalent of the tub of Diogenes, of the cell of the medieval anchorite and of the darkened attic inhabited by Uncle Sam in *The World of Violence*.[28] Its purpose is to cut out all external stimuli in order that its inhabitant might confront his own internal reality.

In his initial attitude to the prospect of being placed in the room, Butler is convinced that he will not be able to withstand the terror of total isolation. He anticipates that his mind will crack under the tension of being focused on himself. In the event, however, his being locked in the room awakens within him reserves of concentration and self-acceptance that he had earlier known nothing about. He does experience a profound sense of crisis but rather than filling him with terror, it awakens within him a feeling that he is *capable of controlling his response*. And this sense of control remains with him when he is eventually set free from the room.

Butler continues to develop his capacity for control. Towards the end of the novel, he is strapped to an encephalograph by Stauffmann and Ehrlich of Station K, both of whom are interested in his success in the black room. As the machine takes its final reading:

Stauffmann said: 'Could you put into words how you generate that much concentration?'
Butler said: 'It's not all that difficult, once you've learned

how to do it. I'd say that it consists in summoning "energy of emergency". And I got used to doing that at the training camp.'

' "Energy of emergency". A good phrase. The important thing is that we now know that it is possible. Would you say that anyone could do it? Or is it a kind of talent, like creative ability?'

Butler said patiently: 'I've tried to explain. It is merely a matter of strengthening a muscle that everybody possesses.'

'And could you, in theory, strengthens yours even more?'

'Of course.'

Erhlich said: 'What is the theoretical limit?'

Butler said: 'That's more difficult to explain. It's the limit of your sense of meaning . . . Yes, I think I can explain it very simply. All animals possess an instinctive sense of meaning . . . that is, they respond instinctively to things. Man has developed his intellect and slowed down his feelings, his sense of meaning.'[29]

It is not necessary to quote any more of this passage. What we have is sufficient to demonstrate that *The Black Room* is an illustration of one of Wilson's central concerns; that man should accept responsibility for expanding his consciousness by grasping a more comprehensive sense of meaning.

In *The Personality Surgeon*, we are introduced to Dr Charles Peruzzi, a young medical practitioner who has to stand in for his cousin and deliver a paper at a psychology convention in London. Charles is very much an experimental psychologist who is convinced that, while traditional theories can offer some assistance, the real help his patients need is to be found in new concepts of mental and emotional processes. He bases this conviction on his observation that emotionally disturbed people are characterised by a lack of personal freedom.

Peruzzi invests in a computer to enhance video tapes which allow his patients to see a new dimension of their inner lives. What they see, in fact, is what other people see in them and with this understanding at their disposal, they are able to envisage more completely the self they wish to become. Needless to say, it is this sense of a future meaning for their lives that plays the most significant part in their personal recovery. Peruzzi seeks to help an alcoholic whose second husband has committed suicide because of his inability to control his pederastic tendencies.

Central to the theme of the novel is the contention that the human will can be fortified and that when it is, the emotions themselves become strengthened.

Peruzzi establishes a clinic in which to advance his technique. He films a number of patients in an attempt to discover more about their personalities. He reflects on the film as it is projected back on to a screen:

> He was struck by the difference between behaviour on-screen and behaviour off. Duncan Baron was the most obvious example. In private conversation he seemed almost self-effacing, and he occasionally hesitated or stumbled over a word. The moment he was being interviewed, he seemed to draw upon hidden resources. His eyes developed a curious, concentrated look, and all the hesitancy vanished.
>
> With the others, the difference was less marked but still provided some interesting insights. Lucasta, who might have been expected to radiate confidence on the screen, became oddly subdued. Jonathan, with his comedian's face and natural charm, also seemed to become unsure of himself, and he blushed at any question that seemed remotely personal. Pam, whose intense gaze suggested an underlying aggressiveness, became calm and tranquil in front of the camera, with occasional gleams of humour that seemed to transform her eyes. She began badly, blushing as she talked about her home and her parents. But when Charlie asked her about her earliest experiences of the theatre, she began to describe a pantomime horse-act, and suddenly became more animated. When she reached the climax of the story, with the horse trying to clean its teeth with a handbrush, she burst into shrieks of laughter that made everybody laugh.[30]

Wilson adds a touch of realism at the end of the novel by introducing himself. He writes of a meeting with Peruzzi and of the subsequent writing of the book.

> I began assembling material for this book. I could see that it demanded a completely different approach from my biographical studies of Abraham Maslow and Wilhelm Reich. There my main task was to place them in the mainstream of the history of psychology. In the case of Peruzzi, this would be unnecessary.

> He was a loner whose ideas owed nothing to anybody but
> Topelius [a character in the novel]. Besides, the story of the
> development of his ideas . . . was so naturally dramatic that all
> I had to do was to tell it, as closely as possible, in his own
> words.[31]

The Personality Surgeon is a well controlled fictional investigation
of the mysteries of the mind. It utilises a variety of insights,
ranging from those associated with ancient Chinese theories of
physiognomy to current applications of high technology in the
study of human illness. It is a work that demonstrates Wilson's
enthusiastic determination to break through the barriers that con-
fine consciousness.

The Mind Parasites was written in response to a challenge from
August Derleth. Derleth had been mildly offended by Wilson's
treatment of H. P. Lovecraft in *The Strength to Dream* and suggested that he should write a contribution to the Cthulhu mythos
that Lovecraft had created. Lovecraft, who was born in 1890,
imagined a fantastic world that was dominated by Cthulhu, a
gelatinous monster who lives below the Pacific ocean in the city
of R'lyeh. Together with his relatives, including Yuggoth,
Tsathoggua and Yog-Sothoth, Cthulhu constitutes the Great Old
Ones who once ruled the earth. Periodically, they emerge from
the ocean and attempt to regain control. Their exploits are recorded chiefly in Lovecraft's *The Call of Cthulhu, At the Mountains
of Madness* and *The Haunter of the Dark*. The basic document from
which Lovecraft gained his knowledge of the Great Old Ones
was yet another of his inventions, *The Necronomicon* – The Book
of Dead Names – purportedly written by an insane Arab named
Abdul Azred. Wilson himself has collaborated in the spoof publication of this primary work, writing a long introduction to it.[32]

The mind parasites are a form in which the Great Old Ones
reappear. As the title of the novel suggests, they infiltrate the
mental processes of a group of human beings. In the year 1994,
their presence is detected by a scientist named Gilbert Austin,
who discovered that they have been resident in the mind since
the Romantic Age. It is a useful exercise to reflect on the manner
of the parasite's operation.

> To destroy a man's habit circuits before his eyes is crueller than
> murdering his wife and children. It is to strip him of everything,

to make life as impossible for him as if you had stripped him of his skin. The parasites had done this, then quickly replaced the habit circuits with new ones. Certain circuits were restored: breathing, speaking, mannerisms (for these were essential to convincing people that he was the same person and in full possession of his senses). But certain habits were completely eliminated – the habit of thinking deeply, for example. And a new series of responses had been installed. We were 'the enemy', and we aroused in him boundless hatred and disgust. He felt this of his own free will, in a sense, but if he had not chosen to feel it half his circuits would have gone dead again. In other words, having surrendered to the parasites, he remained a 'free man' in the sense that he was alive and could choose his actions. But it was consciousness *on their terms* – either that, or no consciousness at all. He was as completely a slave as a man with a gun pressed to his head.[33]

Austin engages in a monumental struggle to combat the parasites and eventually succeeds, although the struggle itself makes compelling reading and should not be regarded as light fiction. In what many will regard as the climactic scene of the novel, Austin and several of his colleagues travel to the environs of the moon, and are able, by a focusing of their parasite-free wills, actually to divert it in its orbit. It is a telling symbol of the power Wilson locates in the concentrated mind.

Writing on this work, R. H. W. Dillard comments:

Wilson combines the familiar pieces of science fiction in a new way to form his own myth, a metaphor for his own vision of human destiny. His heroes commune to become a larger self; from the new perspective they are able to view other men both as apes and brothers; they form an evolutionary vanguard for the future and leave the account of their victory (the Gospel according to Gilbert Austin) behind to guide their fellow men in taking the evolutionary leap. In some ways less emotionally powerful than *Necessary Doubt* or *The Glass Cage*, *The Mind Parasites* is the fullest picture of the new hero as he can be and an apocalyptic parable of Wilson's insight into the nature of things. It and those other two novels, are meaningful examples of an imaginative and transforming art, an existential realism.[34]

The Philosopher's Stone is Wilson's second contribution to the Cthulhu mythos. Despite the popularity of *The Mind Parasites* – it has been used as the basis for a ballet by the Bauer Contemporary Ballet in the United States – *The Philosopher's Stone* must be regarded as the more significant work. It introduces Howard Lester. In fact, Wilson had clearly intended to call him Howard Newman (the symbolism of the Christian name, which means 'keeper of the soul' is as important as that of the surname) for it is this name that appears on the dustjacket of the original English edition. But Newman becomes Neumann to designate, not the central character, but the metal that is injected into Lester's brain to effect his dramatic transformation. The novel gives an account of Lester's early years when he develops under the watchful guardianship of Sir Alistair Lyell. Lyell raises Lester in the tradition of intellectual integrity and the young man learns the essentials of scientific research and enquiry. When Lyell dies, Lester commits himself to a study of gerontology for he is convinced that ageing and death are the last great barriers the human mind has to overcome. His ultimate attitude to death is that it is the result of moral weakness; of a failure of the will. Tredell points to the interesting reversal between Wilson and Shaw on the question of longevity. For Shaw, the longer one lived the more one's consciousness expanded. Wilson's theme, in this novel, is that the wider one can expand consciousness the longer one will live.

Lester is introduced to another Knight, Sir Henry Littleway, who is also interested in the possibility of prolonging life. Littleway has been impressed with the research of a man named Marks – clearly based on Abraham Maslow – who has investigated what he calls 'value experiences'. Marks' theories, however, prove to be inadequate for Lester and he sets about developing his own notion of a lengthening of life based on the intensification of consciousness. It is through the application of this theory, and with the aid of Neumann metal, that Lester escapes his intellectual limitations and enters into a higher form of life. It is at this point that the Great Old Ones appear.

Lester and Littleway, who has followed him into the enlightened state, pit themselves against Lovecraft's primitive enemy. An obscure document, the Voynich manuscript, helps them understand the nature of their opponents. In fact, they are not essentially enemies at all. In a sudden twist, Wilson has transformed Lovecraft's Great Old Ones into man's potential partner in the evolutionary thrust. Man, in fact, was created by the Old Ones in an attempt to advance themselves through the adoption of a physical form. But the advance had not been successful. The Old Ones have retreated to regroup while man struggles to develop as a separate species. If man fails, the Old Ones will re-emerge in an upward thrust. They watch our struggle, waiting for us to falter. Lester concludes that if man is to have a future:

> The Old Ones must awaken to find a society of Masters, with whom they can collaborate on equal terms. What is more, *they must be awakened by these Masters.* For nothing is more clear to me than that man will soon need the Old Ones as much as they once needed him. While the new stage of evolution is restricted to people like myself and Littleway, there will be no difficulty; we shall deal with problems as they arise. But we shall be a very small proportion of the human race. The greater proportion of the human race consists of people like Zachariah Longstreet and Honor Weiss – people who will shrink from the great step to inner freedom. There will be far too many of these people to be helped by the minority who are already making the leap. Only the Old Ones can solve the problem.[35]

It must be conceded that the end of *The Philosopher's Stone* is complex and difficult to reconcile with the early part of the novel. Glen St John Barclay, in his *Anatomy of Horror*,[36] argues that while it adds a great deal more than Lovecraft himself could ever have done to the mythos – as a consequence of Wilson's superior literary skill – it remains a less successful treatment of the elements of the myth than the short story, *The Return of the Lloigor*. Yet there can be no doubt about its theme. Wilson is persisting with the idea of a forward thrust that is the product of heightened human consciousness.

In her introduction to the United States Rediscovery Edition of *The Philosopher's Stone*, Joyce Carol Oates brackets Wilson, as one of four 'especially exciting' English writers, together with John Fowles, Doris Lessing and Margaret Drabble. Of the novel itself, she writes:

> *The Philosopher's Stone* is a peculiar, quirky, exasperating and ingenious variation on a theme by Lovecraft, one of the rare works of science fiction that uses horror not as an emotion so

much as an *idea*, the stimulus for forcing the reader to think. Wilson has said that he will leave to other writers the challenge to make people feel emotions; he believes they feel too often and think too little. It is the intention of *The Philosopher's Stone* to make us *think*.[37]

The Return of the Lloigor develops the notion of a drowned continent call Mu which is populated by 'invisible ones from the stars'. These are led by Ghatanothoa, known as the Lloigor. The very business of existing, however, has weakened the Lloigor and his subjects, so that all they can do is engage in periodic forays against the human beings who used to be their slaves. Although it stands in its own right as a successful short story, it must finally be regarded as a preliminary treatment of the theme that was to be fully developed in *The Philosopher's Stone*.

Wilson has one other short story: *Time Slip*, which was published in an anthology edited by his friend John Grant.[38] As the title suggests, the theme is time travel and Wilson uses the opportunity to express his interest in psychometry and the work of Joseph Buchanan and William Denton, whose work is more fully investigated in *The Psychic Detectives*. The story also uses Wilson's ability, together with that of his wife, to dowse with a divining rod. It is an interesting tale but raises little if anything that is not present in other works.

From one point of view, *The Space Vampires* may be regarded as a return to the theme of *The Mind Parasites*. Wilson has acknowledged his obligation to A. E. Van Vogt's novel, *Asylum*, for its inspiration. It is a novel that is full of powerful ideas and images, none of which was adequately treated in Tobe Hooper's translation of the work to the screen under the title *Lifeforce*. There is, however, a fundamental difference between mind parasites and space vampires. While the former may drain an individual of physical energy, they yet require the continuing life of human beings because they live *through* them. Space vampires live by consuming the lifeforce of their victim. When that has been extracted, the victim himself becomes a vampire and so the species is preserved and extended.

The novel centres on the intensity of the struggle between the vampires and Wilson's central character, the astronaut Carlsen, who is inadvertently responsible for bringing the vampires back to earth from outer space. Carlsen finds himself in bed with a beautiful woman in whom a feminine vampire has established herself but who has not yet been drained:

> He was aware suddenly that Selma Bengtsson's hand was resting against the back of his thigh, and that energy was flowing from it. The vampire was alert again, drinking it as a cat laps cream. Now, suddenly, he knew that she was dangerous, and that if she became hostile, she could destroy him. While her attention was distracted, he closed his mind to her. He even turned back to Selma, running his hand over her naked body, allowing a trickle of energy to seep through him. She stirred in her sleep and sighed; her open lips were a temptation, but he rejected it. He allowed himself to become heavy and sleepy. He reached down and carefully pulled up the bedclothes. Then he took the girl into his arms, and concentrated on giving her some of his own energy. The vampire lost interest; it was incomprehensible to her that anyone should give away his lifeforce.[39]

The nature of the struggle is clear. The vampires constitute a challenge to the will. Victory over them can be achieved only when an individual concentrates his energies in the white heat of personal authenticity.

By any standard, *The Space Vampires* and its percursor *The Mind Parasites* are to be judged as belonging to the finest of contemporary science fiction. This is not to suggest that they are pure science fiction for they range too widely across a range of literary forms, including the metaphysical drama, the Gothic vampire tale and the horror story that builds on the notion of psychic possession. Yet they belong on the same shelf as Robert Heinlein's *Stranger in a Strange Land*, Arthur C. Clarke's *2001: A Space Odyssey* and Olaf Stapleton's *First and Last Men*. They have earned an honoured place in the literature of our century.

The Saltfleet novels, *The Schoolgirl Murder Case* and *The Janus Murder Case*, had their origin in a projected series of twelve novels that were intended to be translated to television. They are the only two to have been produced to date but there is every likelihood that more will follow. The fact that they were designed for the more popular medium should not lead to the conclusion that they are insignificant. In fact, they are novels of ideas, one dealing with the nature of the sex crime and the other dealing with the question of multiple personality. The name of the hero detective derives from a character in one of David Lindsay's novels, *Devil's Tor*. Lindsay's Saltfleet recognises that, in coupling with Ingrid, he will produce the avatar.

The Schoolgirl Murder Case opens with the discovery of two bodies: that of Manfred Lytton in his uncle's Hampstead manor house and that of a young prostitute, half-dressed in the uniform of a schoolgirl, just outside the gateway leading to the house. Lytton was a devotee of the occult, with a particular interest in sexual magic. The murders are eventually traced to a cult killer. Predictably, for those who know Wilson's work, the key to the solution of the crimes is Saltfleet's insight into the psychology of the sexual killer.

In reviewing this work, Wilfred De'ath acknowledges that

> Wilson's great, rare value as a writer has always been his interest in ideas and even this slight work is instructive as a further glimpse into his remarkable mind.[40]

Following the publication of *The Space Vampires* in 1976, there was an extended passage of time before Wilson's next novel appeared. *The Janus Murder Case*, published in 1984, had its beginning as a stage play entitled *Mysteries*, which was produced in Cardiff, although little, if any, critical notice was given to it. There can be little doubt about its success as a gripping novel. Here, the victim is a Polish sailor but, in a philosophical sense, the centre of attention is on the murderer, who is in fact a dual personality undergoing psychiatric care. Wilson leads us through the labyrinth of her mind and provides an intelligent interpretation of the behavioural complexities that are associated with such a mental condition. At the end of the story, he evokes our sympathy, even for the personality that commits the crime, for we understand the extent to which she herself is a victim of forces that are as yet little understood. Wilson supplies a brief but useful postscript in which he reminds us of the extent to which multiple personalities occur and offers what might be the beginning of a solution to the problem with his ladder of selves theory.

Wilson's fictional *magnum opus* is *Spider World*. It is the product of a master craftsman and a mature philosopher whose intellect is balanced with a profound wisdom. Beautifully written, it raises the central issues confronting humanity in a form that is so simple and appealing as to make them immediately available for scrutiny. Although not yet complete – Wilson is currently working on a third volume, which he suggests will be as large as the first two combined – it is nonetheless sufficiently developed to stand alone and satisfy even the most fastidious reader. With its publication, Wilson's reputation as a novelist, no matter what derogatory comments may have been written of earlier works, will be finally secured.

Spider World is a genuine *bildungsroman* which traces the development of Niall (pronounced Nile), a child, when we meet him, living in a cave in the Great Desert with his brother Veig, his two younger sisters, Runa and Mara and his parents; his father Ulf and his mother Siris. A sense of foreboding hangs over the desert from the first page. Niall detects the approach of their most forbidding enemy; a balloon full of the spiders which rule this world of a barren twenty-fifth century. Rushing to the cave to escape detection, Niall waits with his family while the balloons glide silently over their dwelling. We feel the searching eyes of the spiders as they seek out their prey. It is an opening scene as powerful as any in modern fiction. It grasps the reader's attention with a force that is almost physical. It is a marvellous challenge to the film-maker's art.

With Wilson, we explore this cave that is a family's home. It is stark in its physical simplicity and yet a warmth permeates it. The full range of emotions that are shared by the family – their affection for each other, their mutual apprehension of an ever-present danger outside and their pride in the simple act of survival – all combine to soften the absence of physical comforts. The sand on the floor muffles their movement and absorbs their fear. We are clearly in a privileged position as observers of a human community that has managed to maintain its dignity in the face of mortal danger. In the figure of Ulf, we recognise a solid but compassionate symbol of authority. We feel, much like Siris and the children, that we are in his hands, and we are strangely content to be there. Wilson instils within us a quiet confidence that what we find here is ultimately secure.

Gradually, Niall learns the complexity of the non-human life forms that exist in the desert and he uses his insights to comprehend the nature of the spiders. Eventually, however, he is captured and taken to the city of the spiders, a brilliantly conceived world with its own hierarchy and social systems. Niall joins forces with a larger-than-life character named Doggins and together they address the problem of the spiders.

In the centre of the city there is a white tower in which, Niall discovers, is to be found the basic information that will ensure his success over the spiders. He penetrates the tower and finds a mysterious old 'man' named Steeg who teaches him the history of his kind. The lesson occupies thirty-eight pages of the novel and it is one of Wilson's most brilliant achievements. It reveals a breadth and depth of mind that is stunning in its simplicity and profundity. Niall travels through time and space with his tutor, Steeg, and is introduced to the climactic moments of human development. He visits Florence, Athens – and then moves out into space, passing Venus and Mars and assimilating their secrets. Niall learns the essential identity of Neanderthal man and Cro-Magnon man. He sees the secrets of the agrarian, the industrial and the scientific revolutions. He grasps the essence of his own identity as a human being.

Steeg connects Niall to a machine – the Steegmaster – and Niall lies on a couch.

He was completely unprepared for anything so inexpressibly delightful; the tingling seemed to turn into a kind of white light that suffused his whole body as if it had become transparent. . . . Quite suddenly it seemed as if a higher note of intensity sounded inside the white light, a note that was itself an intenser form of light. It rose higher and higher, and the light became as blinding as the sun at midday. All this was the prelude to an experience that lasted for perhaps five seconds.

So far, he had accepted all that had happened passively, with immense gratitude. But a point came where he became aware that these sensations were not being imposed upon him from outside. They were only a reflection of something that was happening inside. It was as if the sun were shining from below some horizon of his inner being. And then, for a few seconds, there was a sensation of raw power – a tremendous, over-whelming power rising from his own depths. It was accompanied by an insight that, for some reason, made him want to laugh. The power, the Steegmaster, the old man, even the spiders, all seemed a tremendous joke. And he, Niall, was also a joke, for he was aware that Niall was an imposter. In fact, he was an absurdity; for the truth was that he did not really exist.

Then the light faded, the sense of power diminished until it became merely a sense of pleasure, and he felt as if he was being lowered gently onto a beach by some powerful receding wave. Yet the insights remained. He knew now that the power came from inside himself.[41]

Steeg gives Niall a 'thought mirror', which he wears as a pendant suspended around his neck. It is a powerful tool of intellectual comprehension and it offers Niall the insights that are to save him again and again.

It is impossible to do justice to *Spider World* here. Suffice to say that I believe it is a novel that is destined to be regarded as one of the central products of the twentieth-century imagination. It is difficult to imagine how the third volume will sustain the sheer magic of the first two, let alone add to it, and yet when one reads the first volume of Tolkien's *Lord of the Rings*, one has the same sense that what follows must be inferior. Such, of course, is not the case.

Once again, with the publication of *Spider World*, Wilson was largely neglected by the critics but in this case the silence is clearly an indication that his work is not being judged on its own merits. By any standards, his latest novel is an artistic achievement of the highest order.

Writing in the *Australian Weekend Magazine*, John Baxter takes Wilson to task for inconsistency. Baxter argues that Wilson has failed to take his own advice for in *Spider World* he has ignored the science which he insists, in his essay *Science Fiction as Existentialism*, should inform all science fiction. It is interesting to note the passage of the short monograph that Baxter quotes:

The importance of science fiction lies in its attempt at objectivity – to convey an exciting and life-enhancing sense of the mystery of the universe.[42]

Certainly, *Spider World* conveys 'an exciting and life-enhancing sense of the mystery of the universe': to argue otherwise would be absurd. As to the sense of objectivity that Baxter – and Wilson himself – requires; it is to be found in the imaginative, intentional use of the writer's own mind rather than in the product of that imagination. To argue otherwise would be to condemn all great works of fantasy as being, in Baxter's terms, no more than 'pulp fiction'.

This resistance to Wilson's work – both his fiction and non-fiction – must be addressed. As early as 1967, Hilary Corke, writing in the *Listener*, recounted thc following parable:

> Once upon a time there was a lovely Outsider who lived wild with the badgers, undetected in the boscage of a great city's park. He possessed a jersey and a sleeping bag but nothing else except his flashing white teeth, which he kept that way willy-nilly, for he had no food except such old, hard picnicker's bones as he would find abandoned in the brakes. One day a jackal, or talent scout, happened upon him, and hurried back to report to his master at Insider's Castle, an ancient king of lions: 'Sire, Sire, I have happened upon a perfectly lovely Outsider, with a smashing set of flashing gnashers'. 'Have him to dinner,' said the king. So the Outsider came lolloping up, and was invited to stay, and stuffed his rattling belly with every kind of costly réchauffé hash-mash, and after a week his teeth were as blunt and brown and carious as the king's and the jackal's; so they kicked him out again.[43]

Reflecting on her parable, Corke concludes:

> But Mr Wilson turned out to be a much tougher egg. An Outsider of a different colour, a well-heeled Outsider, absolutely not in diplomatic relations with the metropolitan mob, he produces work after work like a powerhouse and his sales in Romania are probably terrific, though the ripples are faint enough here in Britain. And it's our loss, and it's time we forgot and forgave and began to do both him and ourselves justice again.[44]

While it must be admitted that Danial Farson is a friend of Wilson, it must also be admitted that Farson has not always provided him with the best publicity. Perhaps Farson's early debunking of the 'genius' Wilson has been redressed somewhat in his review of *Spider World*. He writes:

> This is not another in the horror genre involving predatory

animals which was started by James Herbert with his *Rats*, followed by gigantic crabs, snakes and scorpions eager to wreak their vengeance on the human race. This is on a higher level. Numerous comparisons will be made, especially to Tolkien, although Wilson spares us the *Hobbit* whimsy while acknowledging his debt. I detected echoes of H. G. Wells and Orwell's *1984* but finally all such comparisons become pointless unless they prove how little Wilson owes to anyone. This is his own, unique creation and I believe it is his masterpiece . . . it is rich in detail and argument and Wilson never indulges in obscurity or ambiguity. . . . From start to finish, he knows what he is doing and shares his enjoyment with the reader. Literary swots and pedants who have lost their youthful vision may hate this book but there is no justice if this extraordinary novel fails to become a best seller.[45]

This entire overview of Wilson's novels is almost offensive in its simplicity. In entering the world of his fiction, at almost any point, one enters the world of ideas and is stimulated. For many people, it is a foreign world, for in an age dominated by an electronic media that offers to do our thinking for us, intelligence is under attack. Wilson's fiction stands as a reminder that we retain an imagination that may yet be activated by the written word. Seen in its own right as a body of novels, his work is impressive. The creation of nineteen highly imaginative and deeply challenging stories is an accomplishment not easily achieved. Placed in the setting of a carefully developed philosophy and acknowledged as an illustration of that philosophy, the novels attain an ever greater significance. They are more than an entertainment; they are an invitation to the reader to realise something of his own potential. Wilson makes the point:

It is possible that the novel may never again play such an important part in human development as it played two centuries ago. Yet there is no reason why it shouldn't. All that is necessary is that the novelist should recognise his true purpose; not merely to reflect the 'immense panorama of futility and anarchy which is contemporary history', but to liberate the human imagination and to give man a glimpse of what he *could* become. He must learn to understand what Shaw meant when he said that a work of art is a magic mirror in which man is able to

see his own soul. And when he has grasped that, he will discover that his magic mirror has an even more useful purpose:
to reveal the future direction of human evolution.[46]

If there is any truth in this claim, Wilson has demonstrated the
essential fact about the novel. It is an instrument of the intentionality of consciousness and as such has the capacity to extend us in
the direction of our own becoming.

9

The Critical Response

FEW English writers of the twentieth century can rival Wilson in the intensity of the response they have evoked. This is not to suggest that he has enjoyed untrammelled popularity, for the relationship between Wilson and his audience as a whole has been characterised as much by ambivalence as by anything else. It has been suggested that the acclaim with which *The Outsider* was initially greeted was comparable to the reception given to Byron's *Childe Harold* on the morning it first appeared but, as we have seen, it was not long before he was subjected to critical rejection. Yet the ambiguity of the response goes much deeper than this. There is a vast readership that turns to his work again and again. This is clearly evidenced by the fact that *The Outsider* has never been out of print in English since its original publication thirty-four years ago. This would be remarkable if it were true of a novel: that it is true of a volume subtitled *An Inquiry into the Sickness of Mankind in the mid-Twentieth Century*, constitutes something of a challenge to credulity.

There is some evidence to suggest that Wilson is read by what might be called an 'underground' readership. He is not a writer who is openly and widely discussed in academic circles, although some of his works are now beginning to appear on reading lists in humanistic psychology and studies in 'alternative philosophy'. He is not the subject of learned articles in literary journals. The Secretary of the Existentialist Society in Melbourne indicated that it took him twenty years to find a person who was willing to lecture on Wilson's ideas. Yet, booksellers report that his books, both new and secondhand, move steadily from their shelves and first editions of his early works are beginning to attract premium prices. This suggests an ambiguity within the readership itself. It turns to his works but it does not acknowledge its interest publicly.

But there is a visible, public response that is largely negative. In Watkins' bookshop in Cecil Court in 1986, the writer asked for Wilson's secondhand titles. The proprietor responded that there were none currently to hand. At that moment, in a happy synchronicity, a middle-aged customer entered the shop with a case which was opened to reveal a large range of Wilson's books. The writer engaged the seller in conversation and was told that the books were being sold because 'they made my son sick'. Pressed for an explanation, the man explained that his son had confined himself to his bedroom, reading Wilson hour after hour. This seemed sufficient reason for his father to collect the books and bring them to Watkins for sale.

This anecdote touches something deep in the response to Wilson. A librarian commented that 'Wilson is a chronic depressive whose books are as grey as his mind.' Such a diagnosis serves to indicate that the librarian had either never read him or had grossly misunderstood the case he was presenting. Yet the criticism cannot be dismissed. It is representative of a considerable public response. Virtually without exception, the publication of a new Wilson title brings forth a stream of strong emotional response. It may be significant and, it must be acknowledged as being true, that the majority of this negative assessment is directed, not so much at his ideas, as at the man himself.

Wilson has addressed this problem himself. He is inclined to think that a large part of the negative response is due to the fact that people are not willing to accept intellectual or emotional challenges. If most of us are victims of the *St Neot Margin*, it will follow that we shall be more at ease with creaturely comforts than with ideas that threaten the very ground of our being – even if that ground is of itself insecure. We are the products of a culture which pays lip service to intellect but which encourages us to minimise the extent of our critical analysis of life. Then too, we have carefully constructed the emotional models with which we defend ourselves against the world and we are not inclined to question them readily.

Some part of the negative criticism addressed at Wilson can be explained in terms of a single word that appeared again and again in criticisms of his early books. Wilson, so we were told, was an *autodidact*. Even as late as 1988, with the publication of *The Misfits*, a reviewer who was largely sympathetic to the argument put forward, felt compelled to advise that it 'breathes the bracing ozone of autodidactism'.[1] 'Autodidactism' means simply, 'self-taught' but the use of the term in relation to Wilson, has, despite Burgess, a somewhat skewed meaning. In our age, education is firmly in the hands of formal institutions – schools, colleges and universities. The educated person is the person who has learned to comply with the given body of knowledge. Education is the transmission of the prevailing *mythos* from professor to neophyte through the instrument of the scientific method. In this mythos, a self-taught person is almost a contradiction in terms: an aberration.

There is, then, a resistance to Wilson's thinking that may be based on a rejection of the idea that the individual is capable of taking responsibility for his own personal development – both intellectual and emotional. Wilson's own conviction that prophets, priests and teachers do not have access to a hidden wisdom that is not available to him directly seems strangely foreign to a culture that submits itself readily to established preconception and irrational bias. Nor does the recognition, in comparatively recent years, that every educational institution operates in accord with a 'hidden curriculum', extricate us from the reality. Even those who recognise the hidden curriculum have a perverse tendency to comply with its demands. The myth that learning is the product of teaching is preserved; the arrogance of academia is perpetuated. The autodidact comprehends that there is no teaching where there is no learning. It is a lesson that our universities might well assimilate.

What many readers found exciting and stimulating about *The Outsider* was its freedom from the cant of the classroom. It was the product of a mind which had cut across the stultifying limitations imposed by the 'analytic method' and had established contact with intuitions and insights which made the dogmatisms of such a method patently absurd. It came from a mental attitude which understood what Albert Einstein meant when he retorted that it had taken him ten years to overcome the effects of his schooling. Kazantzakis has a magnificent recollection of his own childhood in school, where, one day, a fellow student named Nikolios, watching a swallow soar on the summer air outside the classroom window, could stand the monotonous grammatical conjugations of his teacher no longer and exclaimed spontaneously, 'Be quiet, Sir! Be quiet and let us hear the bird!' Wilson himself had known the absurdities of the classroom, the dehumanising discipline of the Air Force barracks and the meaningless decadence of the factory floor. But his mind – and his heart – knew another reality that he could not ignore and as he scratched in his youthful journals and typed out the manuscript of *The Outsider*, he began to give that greater reality a shape – not only for himself but for the many others who shared some vague knowledge of it. In *The Outsider* and other works, Wilson articulated for thousands of people, in a wide variety of cultures, the deep dissatisfaction they felt at the mores that were not elastic enough to accommodate their most personal vision.

Even today, an open-minded, honest reading of *The Outsider* will reveal that its author is addressing most of the essential problems confronting humanity. We must remain grateful to him that he did not allow himself to be broken by the abusive response that found expression six months after its publication. Had he done so, we would have lost the benefit of the intense struggle in which he has since engaged in an attempt to order the chaos that surrounds us. It is not to the detriment of his endeavour that he has not persuaded vast numbers of people. It is to the detriment of so many critics that they came close to the truth with which he has wrestled and chose to turn their back on it, failing to recognise that it was a call for greatness.

There is another persistent theme in the criticism of Wilson. It comes largely from women, who claim to detect in his thinking a high degree of male chauvinism. The answer to such a criticism is disarmingly simple. Wilson knows that there are female outsiders; that countless women comprehend his argument – and that they could even advance it. If women outsiders are not adequately represented in his work, it is because they have not appeared in the literature with which he illustrates his theme with the same regularity or force with which men are apparent. Nor could they, in a literary heritage which has been dominated by the male as has every other aspect of recent Western culture. Yet the fact remains that few twentieth-century writers have done as much as Wilson in espousing the essentially feminine principles that may hold the key to the human future. He frequently quotes Goethe's statement that 'the eternal feminine draws us upward and on'. There is no doubting Wilson's masculinity: there is no denying his sensitivity to the feminine – as will be immediately apparent from a reading of his text to Piero Rimaldi's photographic essay *L'amour; The Ways of Love* or his brilliant essay, *Love as an Adventure in Mutual Freedom*.[2]

It is true, of course, that in May 1956, critics such as Cyril Connolly, Phillip Toynbee and Edith Sitwell *did* recognise that the publication of *The Outsider* was a profoundly important event. They perceived that the book encapsulated something basic in human experience. In the final analysis, nothing can alter the fact that Connolly wrote:

> Mr Wilson does not write as one who believes in a particular religion but rather as an intellectual who is being forced more and more into accepting religion as the only solution to the problem of the Outsider. In other words, the anxiety and uneasiness, the sheer horror of being oneself in the modern world is not to be cured by reason or even by a study of philosophies which set out to explain them, like Existentialism; the unpleasant symptoms have to be lived through, leading to the worst, in order that the final, mystical experience may be attained. The Outsider has it within him to become a saint. Yet, though Mr Wilson is drawn to religion, and all his arrows point that way, he never departs from his standards of intellectual analysis.[3]

If Cyril Connolly came to recant his assessment of Wilson, the reason must be sought, not in the book but elsewhere. More likely than not, it was the pressure applied by the literary and academic establishment and the fickle nature of popular opinion. One suspects that if he were alive today, Connolly would be tempted to revert to his earlier assessment.

The Logical Positivist, A. J. Ayer, did have the courtesy to take Wilson seriously and maintained a persistent stance. For him, the difficulty lay in Wilson's advocacy of 'religion'.

> He suggests that the true solution to the Outsider's problem may be found in his development of a religious sense. And perhaps, for some such men, it is. But this does not put them in the right, or the rest of us in the wrong. I am sure that mystical experiences are very well worth while having. What

is quite unwarranted is the assumption, which Mr Wilson is disposed to make, that the world that the mystic inhabits is somehow objectively more 'real' than the world of common sense.[4]

But Wilson has never been concerned centrally with morality. It is not that he is indifferent to the distinction between right and wrong but he is convinced that morality will look after itself when man has developed a phenomenology which coincides with his total experience of the world. And, of course, Wilson has never contended that mysticism reflects a more 'real' world; only *another part* of the world – and this, not objectively but *subjectively*. Perhaps this misunderstanding by Ayer reflects a deficiency in Logical Positivism rather than in the position Wilson adopts.

In 1960, the Thomist theologian, Joseph C. Mihilach, rejected the Outsider thesis as being 'intriguing and original but philosophically untenable and artificially contrived'. He illustrated this 'contrivance' by reference to Nijinsky:

> One of the most pathetic sequences in the portrayal of the Outsider is the account of the personal deterioration of Nijinsky. The factors in the dancer's mental collapse are apparent, but they are sublimated in the interests of supporting the Outsider thesis. The first strong indication of Nijinsky's illness was marked evidence of religious fanaticism. He became 'intoxicated with God', constantly using the name of God in his writings and conversation. Nijinsky was raised a Roman Catholic but compromised this early training by becoming a partner in a long-time association with a sensualist impresario in order to guarantee his professional career. The strain of such a perverse relationship weighed heavily upon Nijinsky, contradicting as it did his sense of religious principle and a once healthy devotion to God. It is conceivable that psychological overcompensation for a guilt complex occasioned his fanaticism and contributed to his ultimate breakdown. With Nijinsky, there was a division of personality that undermined his existence – a division not so much between intellect and emotion as between Nijinsky and himself. The break resulted from the rape of his conscience and the betrayal of his ego.[5]

Wilson simply knows better. Of course there is no better description of the Outsider than that he is divided within himself. But, as we have seen in our brief consideration of Freud, the Outsider is not to be understood in terms of an over-compensation for guilt. The problem *is* existential rather than psychological or religious. In the act of shaking his fist at God, Byron's *Manfred* was not ultimately denying God, but affirming him. And if, as Mihalich suggests, Nijinsky did have two selves, two egos, which of them did he betray?

Perhaps the problem was not a betrayal of either but an incapacity to reconcile the two. If God *is* to be located in the brain, it must be, not in the left or in the right hemisphere, but in the *corpus callosum* – the bridge between the two.

In her brief Introduction to the Tarcher edition of *The Outsider*, Marilyn Ferguson takes us to the heart of the matter when she points out that it is Wilson's contention that the Outsider

> does not wish to accept life merely because fate is treating him well at the moment *but because it is his Will to accept*. He wants to control his responses through understanding; to build affirmation into his vision. Freedom of response is the only authentic freedom.[6]

The Outsider is not created by a diversion from Roman Catholicism or any other 'ism'; nor is he saved by a return to it. He is the product of an inadequate perception of what the world *is* and his salvation lies in the development of an intentional consciousness that grasps more and yet more meaning for itself. Wilson's catechism is recited to the beads of a relational intentionality that locates the individual in the *fullness* of the universe.

Thus it would be possible to continue with argument and counter-argument based on the vast array of reviews – over sixty have been catalogued – that assessed the merits and demerits of *The Outsider*. Yet finally, one is drawn to the conclusion that the critics did not give it the attention it deserved. They wrote about it but they did not reflect upon it. They responded to it but they did not comprehend it. They acknowledged, however reluctantly, that it *did* address the fundamental issues but they did not assimilate its treatment of them. And having thus 'dealt' with it, they put it aside to gather dust on the shelves, never really connecting it to the titles that followed and explicated it. Wilson will long remain identified with *The Outsider* but its full impact will be felt only by those who read it within the context of his full range of writing. It must be acknowledged that the number of critics who have attempted to do this is disturbingly few.

The first extended essay on Wilson was written by an acquaintance, Kenneth Allsop, in 1958. Allsop, a young journalist, novelist and nature writer, set about writing an account of what he considered to be the cultural revolt of the Fifties. He gave to his work the title *The Angry Decade*, picking up the label that had first been suggested by Leslie Paul in his autobiography *Angry Young Man* and taken up by the media to describe the group of young literati that emerged in Britain in 1956.

The Angry Decade introduces us to a Britain of the early Fifties which was still struggling to draw to an end the 'post-war period'. Allsop quotes Rose Macauley, writing in 1946, portraying the English scene as it was then but also as it was largely to remain well into the Fifties:

> The post-war period has not yet established itself. A kind of miasma, a dullness, still obscures the imaginative life of many. A young man who has spent his adult years in high tension, among perils, discomforts, fears, adventures, will not see or write of life as if he had lived at ease: he will be either toughened or sensitized. No new style is even faintly to be seen on the horizon. There has been in fact, a flight from style. The novel of the future will be in plain, uncoloured English, with no frills; the Max Beerbohm period is dead: those laurel trees are cut and we shall go no more (for the moment) into those elegant, aromatic and verbaceous woods. Those who write mannered English are all of older generations: the future of the novel is not with them.[7]

Allsop sees in the coronation of Queen Elizabeth II, on 2 June 1953, something of a benchmark that heralded the end of the post-war period. With it, the grand English ceremonial returned. The ritual, the marriage market, the persuasive English advertisement and the debutante's season all re-emerged, shook off the dust of battle and resettled themselves in the fabric of British life. Pomp and circumstance had reasserted itself. Yet, as Allsop points out, if the surface was pristine, shimmering like the radiant crystals of a kaleidoscope, below there was still a stagnation of intellect and creativity.

In his evocative study of post-war Europe, Richard Mayne reminds us that at this time Europe was not altogether free of the social dichotomy that the economist Galbraith described as 'private affluence and public squalor'. But class distinction was coming under siege in England. In 1949, Angus Wilson addressed the problem in his novel, *The Wrong Set*. Five years later, Julian Slade and Sandy Wilson staged their youthful musicals, *Salad Days* and *The Boy Friend* as statements that post-war Britain belonged to the refugees from the Establishment. Nancy Mitford, daughter of a baron, lampooned the linguistic distinction between U (for Upperclass) and non-U speech, then followed up with *Noblesse Oblige*, a work which made the distinction even less tenable.

But it was in May 1956 that the new post-war British literature was finally born. On the stage of the Court Theatre, the 'no frills' prediction of Rose Macauley was finally vindicated. John Osborne's character, Jimmy Porter, denounced the establishment in a language and a manner that led the critic Kenneth Tynan to write, 'it is a minor miracle . . . the best young play of its decade'. Two weeks later, Gollancz released *The Outsider* and the era of the 'angry young man' was upon us.

There is no need here to repeat the case against the idea of 'Angry Young Men'. It has been done over and over again, most recently and conclusively by Harry Ritchie in his 1988 study, *Success Stories*. It was a term that was born of established literary critics of the Fifties and the media and which had no basis in reality. If it is used below it is for the sake of convenience rather than for the sake of its accuracy. But ultimately, we shall have to discard it, for it is a misleading description of almost all the writers it came to embrace and none more so than Wilson.

Allsop recounts the events that engaged Wilson through the remainder of 1956 and the first half of the following year. He quotes extensively from the autobiographical introduction to *Religion and the Rebel* and from the journal entries which Wilson made available to the daily press for publication. He refers to the biting comments made by Wolf Mankowitz, who dubbed Wilson 'the midget Leicestershire Zarathustra'. But then he turns to his own evaluation which, in its very ambiguity, captures something of the permanence of Wilson's philosophy. It deserves to be quoted in full:

I believe Colin Wilson made a valuable contribution when, with the eyes and the voice of a young man of the 'Fifties, he formulated a postwar philosophical attitude in Britain by putting an original mind to diagnosing the spiritual condition of the time. His solution – or the means he proposes for reaching a solution – is not for me and I hope won't be for most other people here.

In Britain today, there is the curious placidity, the half-living that maddens Osborne and drives the Outsider further into isolation. There is no outward pressure of urgency, of crisis, of imminent terror, of being on the 'pain threshold' that the world situation might seem to justify. But is the period really so poisoned that the public who was instantly contacted by *The Outsider*, was one of hitherto unidentified, unrecognized, anti-humanists? – whose heart leaped joyfully to read 'Humanism is only another name for spiritual laziness', which is exactly the sort of slogan any sweatshop industrialist or any corporate state commissar would use as sanction for bullying and controlling?

It may indeed be true that man has long since lost most of his dignity and most of his freedom, but it would be folly, and rather frightening folly, to throw out what is left of the humanistic ideal too, for if Britain were filleted of that, you would be more likely to get a Western Germany, power-driven, disparately rich, materialistic and ruthless, rather than a whole population with 'fire in the head', lifted to a higher intensity of living.

Still – there is the situation. The excitement that Wilson's books have caused may be symptomatic of a vacuum in our society, one which sufficient intensity of 'feeling' of the wrong sort, whipped on by the shrill emotionalism of the Osbornes and the [Lindsay] Andersons, might fill with a new mystical absolutism of the extreme right wing.[8]

Here is criticism that is a 'child of its time'. It submits its subject to the exigencies of the age. It saw war as an ongoing threat; it was watchful for a revitalised Nazism and saw an incipient threat in industrialisation and political systems, suspecting them all of applying maleficent methodologies. It failed to recognise the universal issues that it needed to address. Yet, despite its limitations, it came close to the integrity of the argument it confronted. It recognised the lack of 'outward pressure, of urgency, of crisis' but it failed to recognise that this lack is in itself a form of 'poison'.

In the final paragraph of his analysis, Allsop rejects 'the heights at which Wilson sets his sights, his refusal to become bogged down in immediate surrounding questions'. He advocates the contention of Bertrand Russell that '(while) we are sometimes told that only fanaticism can make a social group effective, I think this is totally contrary to the lessons of history. The world needs open hearts and open minds, and it is not through rigid systems, whether old or new, that these can be derived'. It is clear that Allsop has confused Russell's notion of 'fanaticism' with Wilson's notion of 'passion'. It is equally clear that he has failed to grasp Wilson's philosophy, which is nothing if it is not an attempt to *extend* human immediacy and advocate openmindedness.

Leslie Paul, writing in 1965, allies himself with Allsop. Paul comments on the period thus:

If there was genius here [among the 'angry young men'], it has, with the possible exception of Osborne, dissipated and fragmented itself and one is more and more tempted to wonder what the excitement of the 'Fifties was all about. There is not one member of the school who has produced a developing body of work comparable to that of their contemporary William Golding, for example. Have they collectively the wit and range of Iris Murdoch, Doris Lessing and Brigid Brophy, also their contemporaries in age? Stand their works up against French or even German schools and they appear insular and poverty-stricken, even xenophobic. Not one of their works nor all of them collectively match the range and audacity of *The Tin Drum*. Almost at random one says that Philip Roth has more comedy and compassion, James Baldwin more anger, than any of them. Kenneth Allsop really put the whole thing into liquidation with *The Angry Decade*, two years before the decade ended. The observer in 1984, he said, will see in the 'Fifties and its writers 'a sensitive, emotional, intelligent but wretchedly neurotic society, obedient to protocol beneath the exhibitionist rebelling, and obsessively class-conscious'.[9]

In his essay on *Beatniks and Angry Young Men*, Derek Stanford in 1958 saw Wilson's emergence as being deeply symptomatic of the age. He quotes an entry from Wilson's journals and then comments upon it:

> 'How strange', [Wilson] wrote, 'that my success should have occurred along with that of Elvis Presley'. The juxtaposition certainly has meaning, though one which the author clearly did not guess at. In brief, I think the situation which led to Wilson's apotheosis can be described as a scramble for culture without a base in education. Art and thought, now, for vast numbers of the young, have become stimulants like fast driving, ice skating, or skiffle-grouping. The pursuit of the new, the latest thing, with little knowledge of that past out of which it has developed, is a note of the 'little magazine' public. Flocks of boys and girls today, in the coffee bars of London, unable to write an intelligible letter, feverishly attempted to cope with the mysteries of Kierkegaard, Alberti and Rilke. The ethos of the non-university young is insensitive but incredibly ill-informed; and Wilson, who has read all the O.K. names, appears as an heroic intellectual athlete to all these self-taught initiates with their 'digest' smattering of contemporary culture. This ardent philosophical public, most of whom have never opened the first pages, say, of Kant's *Critiques* or Descartes' *Discourse on Method*, have no power to verify an author's credentials. So when Wilson, with no by-your-leave and no subsequent justification, lumps together, as mystics of a like nature, George Bernard Shaw and St Francis de Sales, nobody sees the joke of it – the hopeless cultural perspective it reveals.[10]

What is perhaps most significant here is the intellectual elitism that is represented. Universities do *not* have a mortgage on education. Kant and Descartes are *not* indispensable purveyors of a 'necessary' knowledge base: There *are* no measures by which we might 'verify an author's credentials'. And the pursuit of the new is not simply an aberration: it is an imperative. What Stanford fails to acknowledge is that it was Wilson who directed the coffee bar set to the world of the mind. Without his impact, many of that set might have failed to recognise that it was legitimate to explore one's thoughts as well as one's feelings.

In his study of the Fifties, Peter Lewis refrains from making his own judgement on Wilson's philosophy. But he does point out that Wilson himself seemed to be an adequate example of the

Outsider type with which his first book dealt. He was hailed, suggests Lewis, not because of the philosophical argument he had developed but because he had managed to get it past the apparently overwhelming hurdles that were represented by his social background. It was Lewis who noted with real insight, that, with the horsewhip episode, the 'angry young men' suddenly changed character. Before the event, they had been a literary group, intent on applying their new-found insights to the overthrow of the establishment: after it, they were a nondescript band of coffee-house loafers who espoused the idea of free sex and, when they could not find it, engaged in undisciplined pseudo-intellectual discussion about their 'angst'. The horse-whip symbolised the retaliation of the establishment, defending its outraged honour.

> There could scarcely be a better example of how an Establishment operates. Having taken a naive and over-confident young writer at his own valuation, with one accord the literary mandarins made him a sacrificial scapegoat and reasserted their natural prejudice against anyone who had come up from the ranks. It is the unanimity which is sinister and unreal.[11]

It is Lewis also, who draws attention to the intensity of the attack on Wilson that took place in the United States, by reminding us of John W. Aldridge, who wrote in the *New York Times Book Review*: 'By less charitable American standards, Mr Wilson is quite simply brash, conceited, pretentious, presumptuous, prolix, boring, unsound, unoriginal, and totally without intellectual subtlety, wit and literary style.' It is to Aldridge's credit that he concedes 'the existential concept is one of the most, if not the most, important ideas in the thought of our time, and the most effective challenge to materialistic philosophy conceived. But', he continues, 'it is not properly served by Mr Wilson. His book is not a synthesis or an analysis but an exposition, an industriously produced primer on its subject'.[12]

In 1981, Robert Hewison produced a review of the culture of the Fifties in a volume entitled *In Anger*. Although the title might suggest that it is a study of Osborne, Wilson and the other 'angries', it has a much broader field of reference than this. It does, however, deal with Wilson and thus gives us a more modern view of his place in the cultural history of Britain.

Hewison reiterates the judgement that the appearance of *The*

Outsider symbolised the complete separation of the establishment from the new postwar generation. The emergent emphasis on the individual, in Kingsley Amis' *Lucky Jim* and in Jimmy Porter of *Look Back in Anger*, contrasted totally with the closed ranks of the established. It also represented a contrast with the conforming intellectual tradition which was a characteristic of the establishment. What emerged was a reaction to the intellectual and social rules that had been imposed from the Oxbridge set. Here was the product of the 'red-brick' university, graduating almost before the university had opened. It took the form of individual self-assertion. Charles Lumley, in John Wain's *Hurry on Down*, graduates but then refuses to 'settle down' in a conventional job.

In a real sense, the class struggle that was simmering at the time Wilson appeared on the scene was reflected in a review Amis wrote of *The Outsider*, in which he declaimed, with what Hewison calls 'university wit', 'one of the prime indications of the sickness of mankind in the mid-Twentieth century is that so much excited attention is paid to books about the sickness of mankind in the mid-Twentieth century'. This quotation also makes abundantly clear the abundant *disunity* of the 'angry young men'.

Hewison himself sees an interesting cultural aspect of *The Outsider*.

Although Wilson's ideas are more derivative than was realised, his book emphasised the decay of conventionally held cultural values and stirred the emotions of those who felt divided from the society in which they lived. Above all, the title of his book and his treatment of his theme in terms of a personality added a new and easily identified character in the chorus of disenchanted fictional characters who were voicing their dissatisfaction with the way society had developed. It was this, rather than his reactionary views, that contributed so powerfully to the myth. Many more people knew about the book than had actually read it.[13]

Hewison does not set out to make an analysis of Wilson's philosophy but his cultural analysis seems to have something of a ring of astuteness about it. The same astuteness is evident in his evaluation of the 1957 MacGibbon and Kee publication, *Declaration*:

What makes *Declaration* so typical of the new generation, whose arrival it proclaims, is its internal dissent – and the outright refusal of one of its principal spokesmen to be included at all. Kingsley Amis refused to participate with the words, 'I hate all this pharasaical twittering about the "state of our civilisation" and I suspect anyone who wants to buttonhole me about my role in society', thus remaining consistent about 1950's caution about joining anything. Those who did join – Doris Lessing, Colin Wilson, John Osborne, John Wain, Kenneth Tynan, Bill Hopkins, Lindsay Anderson and Stuart Holroyd – represented a [broad] spectrum both socially and politically. . . . [But] *Declaration* believes that there has been some kind of cultural collapse. Doris Lessing: 'If there is one thing that distinguishes our literature it is a confusion of standards and the uncertainty of values'. Colin Wilson: 'I believe that our civilisation is in decline and that Outsiders are a symptom of that decline.'[14]

Harry Ritchie, whose recent work was noted above, devotes two chapters of *Success Stories* to Wilson. The first is an account of the 'rise and fall' that followed the publication of *The Outsider*. It is largely factual but Ritchie interposes in his account his own negative judgement on both Wilson and his work. In the second chapter, this judgement is itself exposed, for it is seen to rest on a failure to comprehend the argument even of the only five Wilson titles it discusses. It is true that Ritchie is writing an assessment of literature and the media in England in the Fifties, but if he presumes to pass judgement on Wilson's overall significance – as he does – then he has some obligation to treat a much broader range of Wilson's work. It is not enough simply to dismiss it thus:

Wilson has plodded on as a full-time writer in a prolific career (approximately sixty books to date) noteworthy for an unshakeable devotion to the spurious and the half-baked. His obsessive quest for something grander than normality has led him to investigations of 'psychology' and the paranormal, subjects he has tackled with all the thoroughness and insight promised by *The Outsider* – none.[15]

But Wilson was not published only in Britain. The American critic, Dwight Macdonald, was also unable to resist commenting, in 1956, on the public response to *The Outsider* and his judgement, too, must be quoted at some length, for apart from placing it in the American cultural context, it contains a fundamental confusion over Wilson's position.

The success of *The Outsider* is one more indication of the growth, since the First World War, of a public that habitually lives beyond its cultural means. These people are not the humble millions who read Will Durant's *The Story of Philosophy* or Wells' *Outline of History*. Nor are they exactly intellectuals. They might be called camp followers of the avant-garde. They want to keep up and they are attracted by large, new theories that seem to crystallise what is 'in the air'. There was James Burnham's *The Managerial Revolution*, in 1941, which resembled *The Outsider* in presenting a timely thesis in bold, poster-like outlines (yet conventionally fuzzy ones) and under a label that was sheer advertising genius. Mr Burnham's now almost-forgotten theory of Managerialism was discussed around innumerable academic campfires. In the same way, telling the Outsiders from the Insiders speedily became a London parlour game; a year earlier, the game was to discriminate, following Nancy Mitford's lead, between U and non-U word usage. . . .

As one trudges one's way through Mr Wilson's cultural wasteland, it slowly becomes clear that he is a Philistine, a Babbitt, a backwoods revivalist of blood-chilling consistency. The gospel he preaches is as hostile to art, letters, philosophy and other aspects of humanistic culture as was that of Savonarola, whom the Florentines burned, and John Knox, whom the Scotch didn't, thereby letting themselves in for cultural ravages they felt for centuries. . . .

'The Outsider's problems are the prophet's teething pains – Gradually, the message emerges'. The message attracts the camp followers for the same reason Marxism attracted them in the 'Thirties (I don't mean otherwise to acquaint Marxism and Outsiderism) – because it realistically recognises the depressing state of the here and now but points to a future in which all will be well. . . . The camp followers feel that culture is something to be possessed rather than something to be experienced. When an author explains difficult thinkers like Blake and Kierkegaard in down-to-earth terms, when he treats the great ones of art and thought with the slightly patronising

familiarity they would use themselves if they dared, and when
he does this with proper 'seriousness' and under the exciting
banner of the avant-garde, they naturally feel that he is their
man. I think they are right.[16]

The attempt to live 'beyond the cultural means' is as precise a
description of Wilson's philosophy as one is likely to find and it
is difficult to understand why Macdonald, who seems to concede
that the here and now is in a depressing state, finds such an
attempt unacceptable. Such an attempt has been the cornerstone
of human development and it *is* precisely the function of the avant
garde to engage in it. There is no preferred body of knowledge
lying in the hands of an elite body of artists and philosophers.
Furthermore, a philosophy that is obtuse to the point of incompre-
hension is useless to us. It is Wilson's contention that we are just
on the brink of learning how to apply consciousness in a manner
that will free us from our incapacity to understand what great
human beings have been wrestling with for centuries. By definition, camp followers are nomads but they *remain* with the camp.
Wilson represents the scout who advances ahead of the sleeping
camp, seeking out a safe site at which its members may spend
the next evening in safety. In the final analysis, culture is to be
neither possessed nor experienced: it is to be redesigned and re-
shaped until it accords with the vision that wells up again and
again in the human heart. Wilson understands Steinbeck's injunction that a man should not seek to gather around him a team of
disciples – for they shall surely lead their master to crucifixion.
The one certainty in the mind of the Outsider is that he must
separate himself from the camp followers and strike out alone in
search of his own identity. Wilson cannot be held responsible for
the public response to his work: nor can he fail to respond to the
sense that he is himself a leader. Whether others follow, and if
they do how they do so, must be left to them. In the cynicism
and sarcasm of his final sentence, Macdonald may be simply
wrong.

In 1965, Kingsley Widmer addressed the question of the 'rebel'
in literature and thus found himself face to face with Wilson. In an
essay which finds Wilson striking some authoritarian overtones,
lacking a sense of compassion or social justice, and engaged in an
attempt to impose his philosophy upon the whole of civilisation,
Widmer concludes thus:

Coming from 'outside' (in conventional social and psychological senses in a snobbish society), Wilson had the misfortune
to be published and praised for the process of his somewhat
uncertain, somewhat resentful, slightly rebellious, intellectual
education. But he was only a literary outsider, with a literary
message, and no other commitments or other intensity of
origin, experience or attitude (in contrast to a William Blake,
a John Clare or even his hedgingly idolised criminals). Litera-
ture-as-philosophy just isn't enough to make a real rebel. But
the rich traditions of British eccentricity tolerate much, and in
England, a Wilson may merit a decent minor place 'inside'.
That he should be taken for a rebel (or a writer or a thinker),
by himself and others, simply expresses the blurred role of the
rebel in modern culture.[17]

Writing in the *Chicago Review*, Richard Hack perceives that
Wilson is not interested in being a 'rebel' *per se;* that he has a
higher purpose.

What Wilson has searched for, in his wide-ranging study and
literary output is a path to the human energy centres, the
springs of evolution that drive all life, and especially humanity,
up to high levels of consciousness and achievement – i.e., an
energy, consciousness and power that know the conscious and
unconscious evils in modern thinking as irrelevant hindrances.
   The Mind Parasites is a novel that isolates and objectifies these
hindrances to productivity and happiness. Although it borrows
a little from the fantastic ideas of H. P. Lovecraft and is dedicated to August Derleth, 'who suggested it', *The Mind Parasites*
is really a piece of cultural history and parapsychology.
   Colin Wilson, with his commitment to clarity and at least
inward progress, is a powerful force in current philosophy. An
encyclopedic scholar, he unites the truth of religion with the
truth of science in a hopeful and progressive manner.[18]

While teaching at Hollins College in Virginia, Wilson met R. H.
W. Dillard, a member of the faculty who was editor of the college
Journal, *The Hollins Critic*. Dillard produced an issue of the journal
which featured Wilson's work, particularly his fiction. Perhaps it
was because they spent some time together discussing Wilson's
ideas, that Dillard was able to present a different approach in his

essay, 'Toward an Existential Realism'. Dillard sees a relationship between Wilson's ideas and those of Ralph Waldo Emerson.

> Colin Wilson thinks of himself primarily as a philosopher and the bulk of his writing has been critical and philosophical. Although the Outsider cycle is a sustained attempt to define a new synthesis of evolutionary humanism and phenomenological existentialism, he is no systematic philosopher. He is rather a man thinking through his ideas in print, a philosopher who feels, to use Emerson's description of the wise writer, 'that the ends of study and composition are best answered by announcing undiscovered regions of thought and so communicating, through hope, new activity to the torpid spirit'.
>   Like Emerson, Wilson sees man as a 'god in ruins' who must only be awakened in order to fulfil his godly potential, but because he is Anglo-Saxon and empirical by nature and heritage, his is a more specifically rational philosophy than Emerson's, depending more upon the analytical faculty than creative intuition. By phenomenological analysis, he argues, man can capture and extend moments of vision (like Nietzsche's on the hilltop in the storm or the mystic's vision of unity with God), can expand human consciousness, and can chart a 'geography' of the world of the inner mind. As he fulfils his own identity he will also find himself part of a larger identity, life itself: he will be able to attune himself fully 'to purpose and evolution' . . .
>   Wilson's novels, with their developing manner and matter, their movement towards a viable existential realism of inner as well as outer truth, show him to be a young man of real vision who has never ceased to grow and whose promise, for that reason, overshadows even his present achievement.[19]

In an afterword to his essay, written two years later, Dillard points out that 'Wilson has continued to grow in the ways in which I expected and in some new ways. His interest in psychology was certainly present in the Outsider cycle and in the novels, but it is taking a more tangible form than I could have predicted.'[20]

Dillard, writing eleven years after the publication of *The Outsider*, has the distinction of being the first to demonstrate a real grasp of the essential perspective from which Wilson approached his writing. He does not get it altogether correct – he failed to grasp what intuition meant for Wilson – but he does recognise the fundamentals. Few had done so before him.

The first book exclusively devoted to Wilson's philosophy was produced by John A. Weigel as a volume in the Twayne's English Author Series. Weigel wrote it with the aid of a number of research students, whose assistance he acknowledges, and the result is that it is an academic text rather than a popular introduction. In structure, it deals with the concept of the Outsider as expounded in Wilson's work and then utilises the concept as a term to epitomise Wilson himself. It devotes two chapters to the Outsider as philosopher, two to the Outsider as novelist and one to the Outsider as a critic-of-all-trades. It concludes with an evaluation of the New Existentialism and it may be that this conclusion is the most perceptive part of the full analysis.

Weigel notes that there has been a very significant development in Wilson as writer and philosopher over the two decades following publication of *The Outsider*.

> All in all, the time (1975) is a propitious one for Wilson's interests. Many young people have discovered the inadequacies of the facile enthusiasms of the preceding generations and are willing to study the subjects which concern them: supernatural phenomena, the role of sexuality, the rationale for crime and speculation about the future relevant to science fiction. More than one admirer of Colin Wilson has recently revived the legend that Wilson is the most important writer alive. Back in 1956, of course, there was no doubt about it – either in Wilson's opinion or in that of the careless critics who turned *The Outsider* into a sensational success without having read it carefully. This time, however, Wilson's success is not a flash, for he has finally earned the honour of being taken seriously by those readers he meant to take him seriously.[21]

Weigel's portrait of Wilson reveals an earnest philosopher grappling with the essential problems confronting a contemporary humanity that demands a clearer understanding of reality. There is an urgency in Wilson's approach to his task because he realises that it must be achieved against almost overwhelming odds. He has developed an analytic tool that reflects the urgency. He cuts through trivia and irrelevance in a direct assault on the problem.

But, in a real sense, Weigel notes, the method, no matter what final result it might produce, is less significant than the intensity of the investigation. Wilson is determined to survive the insistent waves of pessimism that threaten to drown humanity. He has won his optimism by dint of sheer effort and in this there is a critical lesson for his contemporaries.

Weigel intimates that Wilson's critics may have missed his message. It is pointless to assess him as either a 'good' or 'bad' philosopher – and never more so than when the assessment is based on an *argumentum ad hominem*. What Wilson does is to discard the wellworn maps of a familiar country and point in the direction of a promised land. It is this far distant horizon that must be assessed. Weak men, men fraught with fear and timidity, will not venture so far afield. Nor can they permit even the dreamers among them to be too persistent in their report of its attractions. Fearless, Wilson not only points in its direction; it may be that he beckons from it.

Weigel does not underestimate Wilson's complexity as a philosopher. He acknowledges him as representing a myriad syntheses: he is thinker and experimenter; realist and optimist; a mystic and a rationalist. The critic must be wary – and himself intelligent – for to pass a negative judgement on Wilson in one court is very often to exonerate him in another. Nor can this complexity be used as an excuse to evade the issues and hide in a self-satisfied ignorance. As Weigel concedes with Wilson, it *is* possible to formulate the shape of reality if the attempt is persistent and courageous.

Wilson's impatience with the exclusive application of the scientific method is well comprehended by Weigel. Because of the unchallenged premisses upon which it has rested for so long, modern science is not merely 'modestly inadequate' but 'arrogantly abusive' of the truth. Thus behaviourists reduced man to his experience of an interaction between a mindless body and an insensitive environment. For them, life is an experimental response to the prod of an external instrument. Wilson reasserts the potency of the mind – of consciousness – to impact with reality; to actually *extend* our perception of it, through the application of intentionality and relationality. The old Existentialism made the same mistake as behaviourism. The New Existentialism avoids it.

It is important to understand that Wilson's philosophy, which is avowedly now something other than traditional Existentialism or science, may eventually become scientific in the complete meaning of the noun-become-adjective. At present, he makes no claim to systematic completeness; but he is far from willing to renounce the possibility of knowing all about knowing, and so he has opted for extending the technique of finding out and for liberalising the modality for knowing *per se* by exalting intuition, vastations and peak experiences as valid modes of prehension leading to meaning-perception. Balanced then, at the edge of mysticism in a universe which is obviously not governed by any of the old Sunday School gods, Wilson asks as earnestly as Julian Huxley has, for religion without revelation. He would also develop a science without limitations on freedom. He urges man towards salvation by exhorting and stimulating him to see more, to hear more, to feel more, to touch more – that is, to apprehend what is *really* out there and what is *really* inside oneself. The Outsider is invited to embrace the whole universe and to cure his outsiderism.[22]

Weigel gives Wilson an assured place in the history of philosophy. The present sharp division of opinion between those who admire his work and those who renounce it, will finally disappear. The present academic insistent on an appropriate 'style' for philosophical debate will probably continue into at least a medium-term future but eventually, it too will be transformed by a deeper understanding of the mechanisms of human consciousness. When it is of such a nature as to admit Wilson's own exciting style, the debate will focus where it should always have focused – on the integrity of the ideas – and Wilson's value will be recognised. In a similar way, institutions, whether colleges and universities or learned academic journals, will lose their present stranglehold on our understanding of wisdom and dusty, secondhand copies of Wilson's books will become once again centrepieces of the coffee table, but for a vastly different reason than that which placed them in the sitting rooms of the Establishment in the Fifties.

If Weigel saw a real value in Wilson's work, there was also a measure of appreciation from Charles I. Glicksberg. Writing on the sexual revolution of the Fifties and Sixties, Glicksberg saw clearly that the sex in Wilson's novels was at a far remove from the salacious and the titillating. After a careful examination of the novels, during which he notes that Wilson shows that 'the life of sex is closely connected with the religious struggle for transcendence', Glicksberg draws the following conclusion:

> Colin Wilson's ideological message went unheeded. His warning that sex is not, and should not be made, an end in itself, that it is not to be reduced to a merely physiological function, was blithely ignored. The times were out of joint, and the English *avant garde* were not inclined to listen to Wilson's anachronistic blend of Shavianism and Existentialism, his pseudo-religious quest for salvation. Yet his discussion of the sexual problem, had much that was sound to offer the younger generation of intellectuals. A libertarian, a tireless searcher after the truth, he helped to puncture the myth that a fixed biogenetic difference divided the abnormal from the normal human being. His most notable contribution to the stormy debate that took place during the 'Sixties was his insistence that sexuality, if it were to be truly understood, had to be viewed in the context of life as a whole. The strivings of human beings to reach higher forms of consciousness, their need for an existential purpose that extends beyond the narrow confines of the self, their longing for transcendence – these were as essential parts of man as the cravings of the sexual instinct.[23]

Martha Eckman sought to understand Wilson's ideas from the perspective of his interest in the occult and it should be acknowledged that her address, 'Colin Wilson and the Occult', delivered to the Third National Meeting of the Popular Culture Association in 1973, is among the most intelligent and honest attempts to deal with them. To begin with, Eckman noted the change in climate between 1956 and 1973 in terms of the respectability of speaking or writing about the occult. What was revolutionary and suspicious in the Fifties was, twenty years later, far less so. To complicate matters further, there is the continually shifting definition of the term 'occult', with no two scientists, poets or even occultists seemingly able to agree. Eckman also refers to what she detects as a shift in Wilson's belief in 'the inquiries of science', although she does not provide any evidence to support her claim. After providing a brief but valuable account of Wilson's attitude towards his early critics, Eckman lays the foundation for the rest of her essay when she writes:

> My contention is that *The Outsider* contains the key ideas to
> understanding the twentieth century, and that it contains all the
> seminal ideas of Wilson's later works, though I would agree
> quickly that Wilson was probably unaware at that time of the
> direction his theories would take.[24]

Eckman correctly locates the sources of Wilson's basic ideas in
James' essay, *The Energies of Man*, Shaw's evolutionary concepts
as expressed in *Man and Superman* and Husserl's concept of intentionality. She points out that in *The Occult* he relates his central
theme to the major figures of the occult without surrendering a
sound 'objective distance' between himself and the eccentrics who
abound in the field. Once more, she is correct in identifying
Faculty X as the key to an understanding of *The Occult*. She
herself emphasises that the only two witches she has ever spoken
with have assured her that they deal with a normal 'facility' that
is available to the vast majority of people.

Wilson's novels, Eckman points out, are novels of ideas, in
which the main protagonist is frequently Wilson himself teasing
out his own theories and even quoting passages from his own
philosophical works.

Eckman clearly demonstrates her understanding of Wilson's
position by suggesting that its logical extension lies in the direction of a study of alpha and beta waves in the human brain: this
she does before Wilson has given any hint that he will concern
himself directly with the bicameral nature of the brain. For herself,
she then comments on the scientific state of research into brain
waves – by Jodi Lawrence, Herman Kahn and others – and concludes that Wilson's essential thesis contains nothing that contra-
dicts that investigation. She congratulates Wilson on his 'predilection for remaining within the framework of the verifiable
laboratory experiment while considering occult ideas'.

Eckman admits to a degree of concern and a measure of ambivalence as she contemplates Wilson. She expresses her concern
thus:

> I feel fairly strongly that Wilson has not developed any clear
> understanding of mysticism as distinguished from or related to
> the occult. All his novels and nonfiction seem to indicate that
> he is not particularly interested in spiritual developments nor
> in implications of consciousness expansion in a social context.

His chief interest seems to be simply in individual mind control *per se*. I find this 'tunnel vision', this indifference to the result of an evolved society of persons *all* possessed with Faculty X, difficult to reconcile with the impression of a man who has been described to me as a 'brave, gentle, stubborn man'. I suspect there is in Wilson, an ambivalence or at least an impatience towards the social implications of Faculty X.[25]

It is appropriate to interpolate here the fact that Wilson has, since these words were written, published *A Criminal History of Mankind* and *Marx Refuted*, both of which spell out a very clear concern for man's social nature. In a private conversation with the writer, Wilson insists that he *does* have an abiding interest in man's relationship with man.

Eckman's ambivalence is another thing. She expresses it by beginning with a statement of her sympathy with Wilson:

My ambivalence stems (1) from sheer admiration for Wilson's outsider concept, which I believe to be one of the crucial concepts for our era, (2) from an interest in the occult equally as sincere as Wilson's, (3) from a belief that 'Faculty X' or whatever we choose to call it is both possible and, sooner or later, inevitable, and (4) from a firm conviction that a pragmatic stance is inadequate for matters of expanded consciousness, that motivation (Wilson's own intentionality, if you will) does make a difference ultimately in the effects of individual and group mind control.[26]

In contrast to this acceptance however, Eckman quotes Dion Fortune as quoted by Wilson: 'Occult science, rightly understood, teaches us to regard all things as states of consciousness, and then shows us how to gain control of consciousness subjectively; which control, once acquired, is soon reflected objectively. By means of this conscious control we are able to manipulate the plane of the human mind. It is a power that is neither good nor evil in itself but only as it is used.'

Eckman's concern with this – and the root of her ambivalence – is that when men like Hitler or Stalin gain control of their consciousness, there seems to be no inner check on their behaviour and the social consequences can be devastating. She is concerned that the expansion of consciousness is not, of itself, enough to safeguard humanity against a paranoid egoism. In quest of an answer, she wrote to Wilson. Eckman found herself unsatisfied with his reply but it is quoted here as a statement of Wilson's perception of morality and of his confidence in his central contentions.

> In *The Outsider* and much more so in *Religion and the Rebel*, I suggested that if a man had the conviction of a saint or ascetic, and really made enormous efforts, he could finally overcome this problem, acquire a new sense of integration. However, I cannot agree with Dion Fortune that once this power is acquired by discipline, it may be used for good or evil. Like Ramakrishna, I would argue that in the process of acquiring it, a man becomes incapable of evil in the ordinary sense – which is basically immaturity, stupidity and lack of logic. In *Rasputin*, I argue that some men are born with an odd charisma in the way that some babies are born with two heads; and that these 'monsters' may well do evil things – as Hitler did – because they haven't acquired their power by the long, uphill route; they've won it on the football pool, so to speak. But bear in mind the basic thesis of *The Outsider*. The Outsider may begin as a tortoise, hiding in his shell. But ultimately, he must face the responsibility of becoming a leader; he must ultimately accept his responsibility fully. Most of the 'decadence' of our society is due to the failure of the artists to face their responsibility, to be courageous instead of whining and writing about defeat.[27]

Eckman has engaged herself in an attempt to grasp the central issues addressed by Wilson. She has verified what she could, accepted what made sense to her and challenged what she could not reconcile with her own perceptions. In this, she sets herself apart from a body of self-styled critics who have shown themselves to be content to dismiss contemptuously a body of knowledge they clearly did not begin to understand.

In Canada, the critical response has been as confused – and as variable – as any we have seen in England and the United States. When Robert Weaver lectured on the 'angry young men' at the 1957 Summer Couchiching Conference, he was misunderstood as pleading for the emergence of such a literary movement in Canada. While he was not advocating such an invasion he noted with surprise that there seemed to exist already, a vocal anti-angry-young-man movement, even before the majority of the primary works had become available to the Canadian reading public. (Weaver based the largest part of his lecture on the newly released *Declaration*.) Yet, it seems, there was enough material available for Weaver to draw his own conclusion:

The Angry Young Men are going to be with us for a while, and as a group they tell us a great deal about postwar England. Some of the things they tell us ought to disturb us: they are a discontented, more than a seriously angry generation, anti-intellectual, and possibly game for some smelly political nostrums. In some respects, they are the first American generation of English writers, but they lack the openness and the residual optimism that even the most embittered American writer still retains. They are the first generation of English writers who cannot begin to write as well as their American contemporaries. Some of the Angries, like Colin Wilson, seem already beyond redemption, and there are others like Kingsley Amis, pushed on by publicity and lazy about their craft, who are already flagging badly. The unfortunate paradox that threatens all the Angry Young Men is that their work has suffered because it appears to reflect all too faithfully the drabness and frustrations of postwar England against which they are determined to break their lances.[28]

1981 saw the publication of another Canadian essay – this one, bilingual – on Wilson; this time in the *Dalhousie Review*. Its author was Camille R. La Bossière and it bore the title 'Marcel Aymé and Colin Wilson on the Bourgeois, the Outlaw and Poetry.' La Bossière sees Wilson as a 'critic of the bourgeois world'. His annoyance at 'critics who ignore the ideas of my books, which seems to have become a critical tradition', is carefully noted. Le Bossière then proceeds to evaluate Wilson through the eyes of M. Pierre Lepage, a fictional character created by the French novelist, Marcel Aymé, to represent 'good sense'. Lepage, we are assured, would agree with Wilson that words are important for a healthy spiritual life. But it is this very importance that leads to a dispute between the two. Le Bossière quotes the passage from *Beyond the Outsider* in which Wilson writes: 'Man lives at the bottom of a fish tank whose glass is greasy, dusty and inclined to distort.

Certain experiences can endow him with a mental energy that momentarily rockets him clear of the top of the fish tank, and he sees *reality* as infinitely alien, infinitely strange.' We are then told:

> M. Lepage might object to Wilson's analogy here. The author of *Beyond the Outsider* seems temporarily to have lost his senses. . . . If a man is like a fish in a tank, and it is proposed that the fish, for its own spiritual well-being, spent its entire life outside that tank, then surely those who act on Wilson's counsel will rocket to death as well as to 'reality'. If man is prudent, on the other hand, and chooses like the bourgeois and normal fish, to remain in the tank, then surely he will not survive there either. Unlike Chaucer, Wilson seems not suf-ficiently to respect the literal sense of the terms of his analogy.[29]

Given that Wilson feels some measure of discomfort that living critics seem reluctant to deal with his ideas, we can do no more than wonder what he must feel when he is subjected to such analysis by a character from a novel.

From the time of his first publication, Wilson has had a large and attentive audience in the Soviet Union. The chief exponent of his ideas in that country has been Valentina Ivasheva, sometime Professor of Philology at the Moscow State University. Ivasheva has published two substantial essays in English on Wilson: 'The Struggle Continues: Some Comments on English Modernist Aes-thetics,' in 1960 and the later 'Colin Wilson', published in *Twenti-eth Century English Literature: A Soviet View.* Apart from having ready access to his work, she has visited England and held dis-cussions with him on at least two occasions.

While she does not directly associate its cause or even its first manifestation with Wilson, Ivasheva points to a 'crisis' in the sphere of English literature that began in 1956. She detected new developments during the period 1956 to 1960 that she traced back to various causes: difficulties being confronted by British imperialism, developing discontent across a wide range of British society, a defensive democratic stance against the prospects of a nuclear war and what she called 'the increasingly barefaced domination from across the Atlantic'. Ivasheva locates Wilson in this changing climate, as being essentially a disciple of Camus:

Colin Wilson proclaims himself the founder of a new philosophical stream; in reality what he does is merely to repeat certain relatively threadbare motives taken over from the works of Albert Camus. The basic presentation of man in *The Outsider*, as a creature torn from the life of society, is certainly no 'new discovery'. Wilson had an article published in the *London Magazine*, entitled *Existential Criticism and the Work of Aldous Huxley*. This production is not only full of references to Camus but is pervaded with reactionary, demoralising notions borrowed from the Frenchman such as the poetisation of the 'man–victim' and 'exploits' of the solitary free agent, capable, it would seem, the better to understand the world the more clearly he is aware of his isolation from it.[30]

By the time she came to write her second essay, Ivasheva had realised that Wilson was a great deal more than an imitator. By then, she was acknowledging that

no discussion of the philosophical trend in the English novel can ignore the work of Colin Wilson, no matter how wide-ranging his interests are in the fields of literature, philosophy and journalism. The author of a score of novels, not all of which, it is true, are of equal worth, he is still to this day, esteemed above all for such novels as *Necessary Doubt, The Glass Cage, The Mind Parasites* and *The Philosopher's Stone*. These novels of the 'Sixties, especially *The Mind Parasites*, put him among the major postwar English novelists.[31]

Ivasheva's pithy evaluation of Wilson reveals genuine insight:

It would be difficult to find a more ardent supporter than Colin Wilson of the view that the possibilities of the human intelligence are virtually unbounded. We may note that his belief does not only not contradict the findings of modern science but is determined by them, sometimes even anticipates them, regardless of Colin Wilson's philosophical premises. His own literary career is in itself a demonstration of the correctness of his basic views: his output, the number of his writings, is enormous. Only an author of iron will could have brought so many projects to fruition. And Colin Wilson has such will power.[32]

Wilson has attracted attention in Scandinavia and at least two students have submitted significant postgraduate theses on his work. K. Gunnar Bergstrom's doctoral thesis at the University of Uppsala was eventually published under the title, *An Odyssey to Freedom* by Almqvist and Wiksell in 1983. While it deals only with Wilson's fiction, and then only that published prior to its own publication date, this thesis clearly sets the fiction within the total field of Wilson's concern and in so doing provides a useful, although brief, introduction to it. The abstract of the thesis reads as follows:

This thesis contends that in order to understand Colin Wilson's novels properly, one has to consider their philosophical background. It is a study of these novels from a philosophical point of view. All of Wilson's novels are dealt with but the following are dealt with more thoroughly than the others: *Ritual in the Dark, Man Without a Shadow, The Glass Cage, The Mind Parasites, The Philosopher's Stone, The Killer, The God of the Labyrinth* and *The Black Room*. Chapter one gives a survey of Existentialism proper, the philosophical tradition to which Colin Wilson belongs, and outlines his own philosophy. In the following chapters, the novels are examined from the point of view of four themes with philosophical implications: the theme of the Outsider-hero, of the Outsider-criminal, sex and Faculty X – Wilson's term for man's latent power to intensify and expand consciousness, to achieve 'the visionary gleam'. The connections between Wilson's novels and his critical-philosophical works is thereby indicated. It is shown that the same questions are dealt with in both kinds of work; questions of freedom and of man's nature. In his first book, *The Outsider*, Wilson maintains that man is sick and self-divided but that there are certain people, whom he calls the outsiders, who are more aware of this than others and therefore anxious to cure man's disease. Two kinds of outsiders appear in his novels: the outsider-hero, who succeeds in overcoming his sick and split mind, and the outsider-criminal, who is defeated. The outsider-hero's inner strength and freedom develop from one novel to the next. This thesis tries to make evident this development, this odyssey to freedom.[33]

Ultimately, *An Odyssey to Freedom* never ceases being a university thesis. The examiner's shadow hovers over it at all times, yet it does have important insights and it does make clear significant relationships between many of Wilson's ideas. Its author must be regarded as significant in his own right for, as far as can be determined, he has been the first to take Wilson's philosophy as a theme for a doctoral thesis. It is impossible to doubt that many others will follow his lead. At the very least, Bergstrom has given us a clear example of a serious young man who has had greater insights into the work of a major writer than most of the literary critics who disseminate their ignorance in the pages of our journals and newspapers.

A review of the critical response to Wilson's work over thirty years leads one to wonder whether all of the critics were responding to the same writer. In part, this is because of the diversity of Wilson's interests, but that is not a sufficient explanation. It seems clear that the problem lies with the critics. By and large, too few of them have taken the trouble to see the network of ideas that constitute the body of his work. Thus their response is to a fragment of the work, and no matter how important the fragment might be, it cannot, of itself, provide a total comprehension.

There is evidence that many critics understand that *The Outsider* is the foundation that supports all of Wilson's work and this, in itself, is encouraging. But it is also clear that there is an inadequate understanding of the thesis presented in that first work. It may be this fact that has led to the tendency of the critics largely to ignore his subsequent works. Perhaps they find the task too difficult. Comprehension of Wilson's theories, like everything else of value, does not come cheaply. The reader must think them through carefully. What must be resisted, is the temptation, to which the schoolboy succumbs; to throw his pencil at the teacher because he does not understand the lesson. The personal abuse directed at Wilson, in the name of critical assessment, is one of the most dismal features of twentieth-century literary criticism and of the proud tradition to which it belongs.

The theological critic, Hilda Graef, provides us with a clear understanding of the problem. Consider the following passage:

Two facts have probably contributed to the extraordinary success of this really rather boring author. One is the title of his first book. No man likes to belong to the crowd; a great many people fancy themselves as something out of the ordinary.

Wilson himself tells us that he received loads of letters informing him that their writers too, were Outsiders. Further, this book enables readers who would never dream of consulting a history of literature, to absorb in an easy way, the names and contents, complete with commentary, of a large number of authors and books talked about at the moment so that, after perusing it, they have the pleasant feeling of knowing all about the trends of modern literature and thought. Unfortunately here too, Wilson is a most unreliable guide.[34]

That a vast populace finds in Wilson the promise of a satisfaction of their deepest needs – or at least a recognition of them – cannot seriously be disputed. The persistent attraction of his writing cannot be dismissed as an aberration produced by a lack of intelligence. In the face of this interest, the task of criticism is clear: it must address his ideas with the gravest seriousness and with the sharpest intelligence. If he is wrong, his readers want to know where and why. They read him precisely because they want to be free of self-delusion. They seek genuine insight into themselves and their world. A criticism which helps them achieve it will win their respect and their gratitude. What is certain is that they will not be impressed with the image of themselves that is represented in Graef's comment.

Perhaps the very nature of the critical response to Wilson is a powerful testimony to the validity of his thesis. Those who revile him do have something of a common mental set; as do those who respond positively to him. It might be that here we are witnessing a confrontation between left-brain dominance and right-brain dominance; between Outsiders and Insiders; between logic and intuition. Certainly there are two distinctive responses to his work that seem to have their origins in mutually exclusive modes of thinking, of looking at the world and of perceiving the function of philosophy and the nature of consciousness. To the extent that this is true, it behoves his critics to sustain their dialogue on his work until they themselves can forge something of the synthesis that he himself promotes. Hopefully, that dialogue can be carried forward in a more creative manner than that which prevails at present. It should certainly refrain from the personal abuse that has played so large a part in it in the past.

Wilson constitutes one of the most significant challenges to twentieth-century critics. It seems most likely that critics analysing his work in the middle of the twenty-first century, will be puzzled that his contemporaries paid such inadequate attention to him. But it is not merely for their sake that he should be examined. Critics who turn to him will find themselves involved in the central questions of our age and will be in touch with a mind that has disclosed an extraordinary resilience in addressing them.

Aphorisms

T HE following aphorisms have been col-
lected from Wilson's publications. They represent his skill in the
use of language and his capacity to formulate an idea succinctly.
They express ideas which are central to his philosophy and collectively they constitute a significant statement of that philosophy.
They have been arranged simply in alphabetical order according
to the first letter of the first word. The reference after each entry
refers to the bibliography that follows and in each case it is the
first edition of the work cited that is used. Thus, the reference
(7:22) indicates that the aphorism is to be found in book 7 of the
bibliography, that is the Gollancz edition of *The Strength to Dream*,
on p. 22.

1. A human being is more like a symphony than a painting:
    he is a process, not a thing. (85:37)

2. A novel should grow from its basic idea as an oak tree
    from an acorn. (45:185)

3. A novel that ends simply with the death of its hero is
    basically misconceived. (45:95)

4. All art is humanity's attempt to capture the affirmative
    experience. (45:44)

5. All forms of materialism are a slow and deliberate
    diminution of man's stature. (15:48)

6. All values are ultimately mystical. (45:219)

7. All works of art are connected to the artist by an umbilical cord of passion. (15:39)

8. Although the ultimate reality may be irrational, man's relationship to it is not. (2:286)

9. An accurately expressed question is already halfway towards the answer. (45:97)

10. Art is always a choice between compromise and integrity. (45:125)

11. Art is an attempt to focus a pair of binoculars on a distant meaning. (45:229)

12. At some point in his evolution, man will achieve complete control over the inner energy that creates the mystical experience. (27:18)

13. Boredom is as strange a mystery as cancer. (45:66)

14. Conscious man is a pygmy; a mere fragment of his true self. (50:86)

15. Consciousness means grasping relations. (50:593)

16. Criminality cannot exist in association with long-term purpose. (45:37)

17. Every human being contains the poles of Heaven and Hell – and the unimaginable tension between them. (15:47)

18. Everyday consciousness is a liar. (17:142)

19. Existentialism has more in common with science fiction than with academic philosophy. (17:161)

20. Existentialism is the philosophy of intuition. (15:56)

21. Freedom is a quality of consciousness. (89:502)

22. Freedom is the greatest burden of all. (1:185)

23. Go to the heart of a novel and you will find a question mark. (45:20)

24. Heroism, in its purest definition, is an appetite for freedom. (3:83)

25. Heroism is impossible for a man without beliefs. (15:50)

26. Human beings determine their own energy levels. (50:601)

27. Human beings experience a range of mental states which is as narrow as the middle three keys of a piano. (2:10)

28. Human beings will one day realise, beyond all possible doubt, that consciousness is freedom. (50:600)

29. I am like a mountain that suddenly discovers that it is an active volcano. (24:119)

30. If anything is an illusion, it is the present content of our consciousness. (17:143)

31. Imagination has increased man's autonomy more than any of the other senses. (8:241)

32. Imagination is man's act of increasing his freedom. (7:138)

33. Imagination is the herald of change. (7:115)

34. Imagination should be used, not to escape from reality, but to create it. (50:258)

35. In all intense sexual experience, there are never merely two people; there is always the invisible presence of a third. (24:114)

36. In his normal state, man lives in a mere corner of his being. (2:169)

37. In the very act of expressing the impersonal thought, man affirms the reality of his spiritual evolution. (15:19)

38. It remains to be seen whether our age will produce anyone strong enough to learn from their own failure. (15:127)

39. Laziness and timidity are no longer qualities that can be tolerated by the force behind evolution. (45:94)

40. Life is never exhausted because it is pure potentiality. (15:25)

41. Literary pessimism is usually a form of laziness. (7:17)

42. Literature, like nature, operates on the principle of the survival of the fittest. (45:55)

43. Love is an adventure in mutual freedom. (24:55)

44. Lovemaking is fundamentally a mystical experience in which the personalities of the participants are the least important part. (24:61)

45. Lovemaking is the nearest thing that most people have approached to magical possession. (24:133)

46. Magic is the art and science of using the will. (50:243)

47. Man has no alternative but eventually to become responsible for the whole universe. (15:109)

48. Man has not fallen: he has climbed a long way. (15:22)

49. Man is as much a slave to his immediate surroundings now as when he lived in tree huts. (1:45)

50. Man is free all the time, but he confronts his freedom only at long intervals. (3:115)

51. Man wants to know why he is not a god and how he can become one. (15:20)

52. Man's own inner being orders what he sees. (1:230)

53. Man's place is at the head of society; not at its bottom. (45:97)

54. Most men live from moment to moment, with no foresight or hindsight. (1:232)

55. Mystical experiences are not experiences of another order of reality but insights into this order. (2:69)

56. Neurosis is not the result of man's maladjustment to society, but to the whole of existence. (14:137)

57. No human situation is ever defined by the facts. (15:75)

58. No man has ever achieved total concentration. (2:269)

59. One cannot talk about the real issues of life: one can only show them. (2:298)

60. One half of the mind does not know what the other half is doing. (24:83)

61. Only the sexual impulse retains its autonomy and laughs at the calculations of the intellect. (24:147)

62. Our life is an attempt to discard false values. (17:155)

63. Our senses show us only a fraction of reality. (50:354)

64. Perception itself is a creative act. (50:593)

65. Pessimistic art is a contradiction in terms. (15:23)

66. Philosophy is nothing if it is not an attempt to take one's experience apart under a microscope. (2:13)

67. Reason also has its miracles. (7:99)

68. Religion is not the end: it is only a rest-house on the way. (2:242)

69. Sin is the drifting of higher forms of life towards an animal level. (2:103)

70. Terror is the beginning of beauty for all crises lead to beauty. (2:171)

71. The basic problem of philosophy is so simple that no philosopher has ever succeeded in stating it. (14:23)

72. The Christian–non-Christian conflict is less important than the life-negation–life-affirmation conflict. (45:35)

73. The concept of hell is only important insofar as it points to a concept of heaven. (2:55)

74. The concept of insanity only matters because it is a step towards supersanity. (2:55)

75. The Devil's idealism is sentimentality and spiritual laziness. (15:83)

76. The drive of male sexuality is the hunger of the will; the desire for the momentary sense of pure power. (24:35)

77. The first man to learn the secret of the control of consciousness will be the first true man. (14:135)

78. The foundation of the sexual impulse is a kind of astonishment. (24:19)

79. The idea of the superman is a response to the need for salvation. (1:135)

80. The mark of greatness is always intuition, not logic. (2:101)

81. The 'me' I have always taken for granted is not me at all – it is an imposter. (24:121)

82. The more one has to fight against, the more alive one can be. (2:12)

83. The most fundamental law of creativity is that you must worry a problem until you see all of its implications. (45:146)

84. The novel, like all great art, taught people to take themselves, and their lives, more seriously. (45:39)

85. The novel represents a new dimension of human freedom. (45:47)

86. The only trustworthy dogma is that there is no dogma. (2:283)

87. The peak experience is always associated with fulfilled purpose. (45:149)

88. The profession of adventure is not open to man in our time. (8:51)

89. The purpose of literature is not to record the world of immediacy but to get beyond it. (45:156)

90. The rare is reduced to the commonplace because we do not really believe in the rare. (24:51)

91. The reality behind human conflict is the will to power. (2:16)

92. The reason that few men of genius remain in their own town is that they know it too well. (45:84)

93. The spirit of science is a belief that our problems may be simpler than they appear to be. (7:98)

94. The unity of a great novel is created out of a tension of opposing forces. (45:201)

95. There is a greatness in the air. (15:20)

96. There is a mediator between flesh and spirit: it is called reason. (45:202)

97. There is a part of our being that knows far more than our conscious mind. (50:629)

98. To give a man only his personal ends to serve is to condemn him to triviality. (24:139)

99. Truth is the spiritual intensity of the man who apprehends it. (2:237)

100. Twentieth century pessimists are junior Romantics. (15:23)

101. We pant for breath when a single movement could open the window. (15:25)

102. We possess such immense resources of power that pessimism is a laughable absurdity. (45:9)

103. What we accept as everyday consciousness is thoroughly sub-normal. (50:75)

104. When a butterfly has emerged, it can never turn back into a caterpillar. (45:115)

105. When I open my eyes in the morning I am not confronted by a world but by a million possible worlds. (15:95)

106. When man thinks he has exhausted the world, he has really only exhausted his own mind. (45:66)

107. Wisdom is an increasing control of one's emotional experience. (2:193)

108. Wish-fulfilment is the true foundation of all creativity. (45:116)

109. You cannot get a clear note out of a slack guitar string. (24:63)

Bibliography

THIS bibliography is not intended to be exhaustive. It lists all the major publications by Wilson, including those he has jointly written with others. It includes all of his monographs. It also contains his introductions to books by other writers and those books containing significant evaluations of his work. Where they both exist, first English and first United States editions are listed. Readers interested in the complete bibliography are referred to: Colin Stanley, *The Work of Colin Wilson: An Annotated Bibliography and Guide* (Borgo Press, San Bernardino, 1989).

MAJOR WORKS

1. *The Outsider* (Victor Gollancz, London 1956; Houghton Mifflin, Boston, 1956).
2. *Religion and the Rebel* (Victor Gollancz, London, 1957; Houghton Mifflin, Boston, 1957).
3. *The Age of Defeat* (US: *The Stature of Man*) (Victor Gollancz, London, 1959; Houghton Mifflin, Boston, 1959).
4. *Ritual in the Dark* (Victor Gollancz, London, 1960; Houghton Mifflin, Boston, 1960).
5. *Encyclopedia of Murder* (with Patricia Pitman) (Arthur Barker, London, 1961; Putnam, New York, 1962).
6. *Adrift in Soho* (Victor Gollancz, London, 1961; Houghton Mifflin, Boston, 1961).
7. *The Strength to Dream* (Victor Gollancz, London, 1961; Houghton Mifflin, Boston, 1962).

8. *Origins of the Sexual Impulse* (Arthur Barker, London, 1963; Putnam, New York, 1963).

9. *The World of Violence* (US: *The Violent World of Hugh Greene*) (Victor Gollancz, London, 1963; Houghton Mifflin, Boston, 1963).

10. *Man Without a Shadow* (US: *The Sex Diary of Gerard Sorme*) (Arthur Barker, London, 1963; The Dial Press, New York, 1963).

11. *Rasputin and the Fall of the Romanovs* (Arthur Barker, London, 1964; Farrer Strauss, New York, 1964).

12. *Brandy of the Damned* (US: *Chords and Discords*) (John Baker, London, 1964; Crown, New York, 1964).

13. *Necessary Doubt* (Arthur Barker, London, 1964; Trident Press, New York, 1964).

14. *Beyond the Outsider* (Arthur Barker, London, 1965; Houghton Mifflin, Boston, 1965).

15. *Eagle and Earwig* (John Baker, London, 1965).

16. *Sex and the Intelligent Teenager* (Arrow Books, London, 1966; Pyramid, New York, 1968).

17. *Introduction to the New Existentialism* (Hutchinson, London, 1966; Houghton Mifflin, Boston, 1967).

18. *The Glass Cage* (Arthur Barker, London, 1966; Random House, New York, 1966).

19. *The Mind Parasites* (Arthur Barker, London, 1967; Arkham House, Sauk City, 1967).

20. *Voyage to a Beginning* (Cecil and Amelia Woolf, London, 1969; Crown, New York, 1969).

21. *A Casebook of Murder* (Leslie Frewin, London, 1969; Cowles, New York, 1969).

22. *Bernard Shaw: A Reassessment* (Hutchinson, London, 1969; Athenaeum, New York, 1969).

23. *The Philosopher's Stone* (Arthur Barker, London, 1969; Crown, New York, 1971).

24. *L'amour: The Ways of Love* (Crown, New York, 1970).

25. *The Return of the Lloigor* (Village Press, London, 1974).

26. *The Strange Genius of David Lindsay* (wtih E. H. Visiak and J. B. Pick) (US (abridged): *The Haunted Man: The Strange Genius of David Lindsay*) (John Baker, London, 1970; Borgo Press, San Bernardino, 1979).

27. *Poetry and Mysticism* (US (abridged): *Poetry and Mysticism*) (Hutchinson, London, 1970; City Lights, San Francisco, 1970).

28. *Strindberg* (Calder & Boyars, London, 1970; Random House, New York, 1972).

29. *The God of the Labyrinth* (US: *The Hedonists*) (Hart-Davis, London, 1970; Signet, New York, 1970).

30. *The Killer* (US: *Lingard*) (New English Library, London, 1970; Crown, New York, 1970).
31. *The Occult* (Hodder & Stoughton, London, 1971; Random House, New York, 1971).
32. *The Black Room* (Weidenfeld & Nicolson, London, 1971; Pyramid, New York, 1971).
33. *Order of Assassins* (Hart-Davis, London, 1972).
34. *New Pathways in Psychology* (Victor Gollancz, London, 1972; Taplinger, New York, 1972).
35. *Strange Powers* (Latimer New Directions, London, 1973; Random House, New York, 1973).
36. *'Tree' by Tolkien* (Covent Garden Press, London, 1973; Capra Press, Santa Barbara, 1973).
37. *Hermann Hesse* (US: *Hesse, Reich, Borges*) (Village Press, London, 1974; Leaves of Grass Press, Philadelphia, 1974).
38. *Wilhelm Reich* (Village Press, London, 1974).
39. *Jorge Luis Borges* (Village Press, London, 1974).
40. *Ken Russell: A Director in Search of a Soul* (Intergroup, London, 1974).
41. *A Book of Booze* (Victor Gollancz, London, 1974).
42. *The Schoolgirl Murder Case* (Hart-Davis MacGibbon, London, 1974; Crown, New York, 1974).
43. *The Unexplained* (Lost Pleiade Press, Lake Oswego, 1975).
44. *Mysterious Powers* (Aldus Books, London, 1975; Danbury Press, New York, 1975).
45. *The Craft of the Novel* (Victor Gollancz, London, 1975).
46. *Enigmas and Mysteries* (Aldus Books, London, 1975; Danbury Press, New York, 1975).
47. *The Geller Phenomenon* (Aldus Books, London, 1975; Danbury Press, New York, 1975).
48. *The Space Vampires* (Hart-Davis MacGibbon, London, 1976; Random House, New York, 1976).
49. *Men of Mystery* (US: *Dark Dimensions*) (W. H. Allen, London, 1977; Everest House, New York, 1977).
50. *Mysteries* (Hodder & Stoughton, London, 1978; Putnam, New York, 1978).
51. *Starseekers* (Hodder & Stoughton, London, 1980; Doubleday, New York, 1980).
52. *Science Fiction as Existentialism* (Brans Head, Middlesex, 1980).
53. *Frankenstein's Castle* (Ashgrove Press, Bath, 1980; Salem House, Salem, 1980).
54. *The Book of Time* (editor) (Westbridge Books, Newton Abbot, 1980).

55. *The War Against Sleep* (Aquarian Press, Wellingborough, 1980; Newcastle, New York, 1980).

56. *The Directory of Possibilities* (editor) (Webb & Bower, Exeter, 1981; The Rutledge Press, New York, 1981).

57. *Poltergeist!* (New English Library, London, 1981; Putnam, New York, 1981).

58. *Witches* (Paper Tiger, Surrey, 1981; A & W Publishers, New York, 1981).

59. *Anti-Sartre* (Borgo Press, San Bernardino, 1981).

60. *The Quest for Wilhelm Reich* (Granada, London, 1982; Anchor Press-Doubleday, New York, 1982).

61. *Access to Inner Worlds* (Rider, London, 1983).

62. *Encyclopedia of Modern Murder* (with Donald Seaman) (Arthur Barker, London, 1983; Putnam, New York, 1983).

63. *The Psychic Detectives* (Pan Books, London, 1984; Mercury House, San Francisco, 1985).

64. *A Criminal History of Mankind* (Granada, London, 1984; Putnam, New York, 1984).

65. *Lord of the Underworld* (Aquarian Press, Wellingborough, 1984).

66. *The Janus Murder Case* (Granada, London, 1984).

67. *'Rasputin'* in *Tales of the Uncanny* (Reader's Digest, New York, 1984).

68. *The Essential Colin Wilson* (Harrap, London, 1986; Celestial Arts, Berkeley, 1986).

69. *The Bicameral Critic* (Ashgrove Press, Bath, 1985; Salem House, Salem, 1985).

70. *Rudolph Steiner* (Aquarian Press, Wellingborough, 1985).

71. *Afterlife* (Granada, London, 1985; Doubleday Dolphin, New York, 1985).

72. *The Personality Surgeon* (New English Library, London, 1986; Mercury House, San Francisco, 1986).

73. *An Encyclopedia of Scandal* (with Donald Seaman) (Weidenfeld & Nicolson, London, 1986; Stein & Day, New York, 1986).

74. *The Book of Great Mysteries* (editor: with Christopher Evans) (Robinson, London, 1986).

75. *An Essay on the New Existentialism* (Paupers' Press, Nottingham, 1986).

76. *The Laurel and Hardy Theory of Consciousness* (Robert Briggs Associates, San Francisco, 1986).

77. *Spider World: The Tower* (Granada, London, 1987).

78. *Spider World: The Delta* (Granada, London, 1987).

79. *Marx Refuted* (editor) (Ashgrove Press, Bath, 1987).

80. *Aleister Crowley: The Nature of the Beast* (Aquarian Press, Wellingborough, 1987).

81. *The Musician as Outsider* (Pauper's Press, Nottingham, 1987).
82. *Jack-the-Ripper: Summing Up and Verdict* (Bantam Press, London, 1987).
83. *Autobiographical Reflections* (Paupers' Press, Nottingham, 1988).
84. *The Misfits* (Granada, London, 1988; Carroll and Graf, New York, 1988).
85. *Beyond the Occult* (Granada, London, 1988; Carroll and Graf, New York, 1988).
86. *The Mammoth Book of True Crime* (Robinson, London, 1988; Carroll and Graf, New York, 1988).
87. *The Magician from Siberia* (Robert Hale, London, 1988).
88. *The Decline and Fall of Leftism* (Paupers' Press, Nottingham, 1989).
89. *Written in Blood* (Equation, Wellingborough, 1989).
90. *Existentially Speaking* (Borgo Press, San Bernardino, 1989).

SHORT STORY

91. 'Time Slip' in John Grant (ed.), *Aries 1* (David & Charles, Newton Abbot, 1979).

MAJOR ESSAYS

92. 'Beyond the Outsider', in Tom Maschler (ed.), *Declaration* (MacGibbon & Kee, London, 1957; Dutton, New York, 1957).
93. The Existential Temper of the Modern Novel, in Findley Eversole (ed.), *Christian Faith and Contemporary Arts* (Abingdon, Nashville, 1957).
94. 'A Note Against Gardening', in James Turner (ed.) *A Book of Gardens* (Cassell, London, 1963)
95. 'The Dominant Five per Cent', in Nigel Morland (ed.), *The Criminologist* (Wolfe, London, 1971; Library Press, New York, 1972).
96. 'The Flawed Superman', in Michael Harrison (ed.), *Beyond Baker Street* (Bobbs Merrill, Indianapolis, 1976).
97. 'A Personal Response to Wuthering Heights', in Anne Smith (ed.), *The Art of Emily Brontë* (Vision, London, 1976).
98. 'Love as an Adventure in Mutual Freedom', in Herbert Otto (ed.), *Love Today* (Delta, New York, 1978).
99. 'Gorran', in Michael Williams (ed.), *My Cornwall* (Bossiney Books, St Teaths, 1973).
100. 'Spinoza – the Outsider', in Siegfried Hessing (ed.), *Speculum Spinozanum* (Routledge & Kegan Paul, London, 1977).

101. 'Royalty and the Ripper', in Marc Alexander (ed.), *Royal Murder* (Frederick Muller, London, 1978).
102. 'A New Look at the Paranormal', in Julian Shuckburgh (ed.), *The Bedside Book* (Windward, London, 1979).
103. 'George Bernard Shaw: A Personal View', in Michael Holroyd (ed.), *The Genius of Shaw* (Holt, Rinehart & Winston, New York, 1979).
104. 'The Realm of Experience', in D. B. Fry (ed.), *The Nature of Religious Man* (Octagon Press, London, 1982).
105. 'Literature and Pornography', in Alan Bold (ed.), *The Sexual Dimension in Literature* (Vision Press, London 1982; Barnes & Noble, New York, 1982).
106. 'King Arthur', in Anthony Roberts, (ed.), *Glastonbury: Ancient Avalon, New Jerusalem* (Rider, London, 1978).
107. 'Peak Experience', in Satish Kumar (ed.), *The Schumacher Lectures*, vol. 2 (Blond and Briggs, London, 1984).
108. 'Discovering Cornwall', in J. C. Trewin (ed.), *The West Country Book* (Webb & Bower, Exeter, 1981).
109. 'The Occult Detectives', in John Tate (ed.), *Genette is Missing* (David & Charles, Newton Abbot, 1979).
110. 'Why is Shiel Neglected?' in Reynolds A. Morse (ed.), *Shiel in Diverse Hands* (The Reynolds Morse Foundation, Cleveland, 1983).
111. 'Belief and Action', in Phillip L. Berman (ed.), *The Courage of Conviction* (Dodd Mead, New York, 1985).
112. 'Where Do We Go From Here?' in Themisticles Hoetis (ed.), *Zero Anthology*, no. 1 (Zero Press, New York, 1956).
113. 'The Search for the Real Arthur', in Brenda Duxbury (ed.), *King Arthur Country in Cornwall* (Bossiney Books, St Teaths, 1979).
114. 'Fantasy and Faculty X', in J. N. Williamson (ed.), *How to Write Tales of Horror, Fantasy and Science Fiction* (Writers Digest, Cincinnati, 1987).
115. 'Autobiographical Essay' in Adele Sarkissian (ed.), *Contemporary Authors Autobiography Series*, vol. 5 (Gale, Detroit, 1987).
116. 'My Search for Jack-the-Ripper', in R. G. Jones (ed.), *Unsolved* (Xanadu, London, 1987).
117. 'The Decline and Fall of Existentialism', in C. Crossley and I. Small, *Studies in Anglo-French Cultural Relations* (Macmillan, London, 1988).

INTRODUCTIONS

118. Campion, Sidney, *The World of Colin Wilson* (Muller, London, 1962).
119. De Foe, Daniel, *Moll Flanders* (Pan Books, London, 1965).
120. Sewell, Fr. Brocard, *My Dear Times Waste* (St Andrews Press, London, 1966).
121. Visiak, E. H., *Life's Morning Hour* (John Baker, London, 1968).
122. Drury, Neville, *The Search for Abraxis* (Neville Spearman, London, 1972).
123. Haining, Peter, *The Magicians* (Peter Owen, London, 1972).
124. Kelly, John, *Jack-the-Ripper: A Bibliography* (London Association of Assistant Librarians, London, 1972).
125. Harrison, Michael, *The Roots of Witchcraft* (Muller, London, 1973).
126. de Monfreid, Henri, *The Adventures of a Red Sea Smuggler* (Hillstone, New York, 1974).
127. Ollendorff, Robert, *Juvenile Homosexual Experience* (Tallis, London, 1974).
128. Arkle, William, *A Geography of Consciousness* (Neville Spearman, London, 1974).
129. Rosemblum, Arthur, *Unpopular Science* (Running Press, Philadelphia, 1974).
130. Pagram, Edward, *A View of London* (Hamish Hamilton, London, 1963).
131. Briussov, Valeri, *The Fiery Angel* (Neville Spearman, London, 1975).
132. Williams, Michael (ed.), *Murder in the Westcountry* (Bossiney Books, St Teaths, 1975).
133. Rumbelow, Donald, *The Complete Jack-the-Ripper* (W. A. Allen, London, 1975).
134. Foster, David, *The Intelligent Universe* (Abelard, London, 1975).
135. Reichel, Willy, *An Occultist's Travels* (Running Press, Philadelphia, 1975).
136. Harbinson, Alan, *Knock* (Intergroup, London, 1975).
137. Lindsay, David, *The Violet Apple and The Witch* (Chicago Review Press, Chicago, 1976).
138. Swedenborg, Emanuel, *Heaven and Hell* (Swedenborg Foundation, New York, 1976).
139. Lethbridge, Tom, *The Power of the Pendulum* (Routledge & Kegan Paul, London, 1976).
140. Holroyd, Stuart, *Briefing for the Landing on Planet Earth* (Corgi, London, 1977).
141. Dunning, John, *Truly Murderous* (Harwood Smart, London, 1977).

142. Alexander, Marc, *To Anger the Devil* (Neville Spearman, London, 1978).
143. Hay, George (ed.), *The Necronomicon* (Neville Spearman, London, 1978).
144. Conway, David, *Ritual Magic* (Dutton, New York, 1978).
145. Gaute, J. J. and Odell, Robin, *The Murderer's Who Who* (Harrap, London, 1979).
146. Roberts, A. and Gilbertson, G., *The Dark Gods* (Hamish Hamilton, London, 1980).
147. McIntosh, Christopher, *The Rosy Cross Unveiled* (Aquarian Press, Wellingborough, 1980).
148. Graves, T. and Boult, J., *The Essential T. C. Lethbridge* (Routledge and Kegan Paul, London, 1980).
149. Smyth, Frank, *Cause of Death* (Orbis, London, 1980).
150. Campbell, J. and Roberts, Richard, *Tarot Revelations* (Phoenix, New York, 1979).
151. Sellin, Bernard, *The Life and Work of David Lindsay* (Cambridge University Press, Cambridge, 1961).
152. Cracknell, Robert, *Clues to the Unknown* (Hamlyn, London, 1981).
153. Weinstein, Marion, *Positive Magic* (Phoenix, Surrey, 1978).
154. Reynolds, Alfred, *The Hidden Years* (Cambridge, London, 1981).
155. Sewell, Fr. Brocard, *Like Black Swans* (Tabb House, Padstow, 1982).
156. Farson, Negley, *Behind God's Back* (Zenith, London, 1983).
157. Locker, Leonard, *Holistic Healing for Dowsers* (Privately printed, 1983).
158. Scott, Ernest, *The People of the Secret* (Octagon, London, 1983).
159. Hopkins, Bill, *The Leap* (Deverell and Birdsey, London, 1984).
160. Salwak, Dale, *Britain's Angry Young Men* (Borgo, San Bernardino, 1984).
161. Lander, June, *Eccentrics in Cornwall* (Bossiney Books, St Teaths, 1983).
162. Peat, David, *The Armchair Guide to Murder and Detection* (Deneau, Ottowa, 1984).
163. Williams, Michael, *Westcountry Mysteries* (Bossiney Books, St Teaths, 1985).
164. Bourne, Lois, *Witch Amongst Us* (Hale, London, 1985).
165. Crabtree, Adam, *Multiple Man* (Collins, Toronto, 1985).
166. Holiday, Ted, *The Goblin Universe* (Llewellyn, St Paul, 1986).
167. Crowe, Catherine, *The Night Side of Nature* (Aquarian Press, Wellingborough, 1986).
168. Barrett, Sir William, *Death-Bed Visions* (Aquarian Press, Wellingborough, 1986).

169. Marsden, Simon, *The Haunted Realm* (Webb & Bower, Exeter, 1986).
170. Taylor, Bernard and Knight, Stephen, *Perfect Murder* (Grafton, London, 1987).
171. Reynolds, Bernard, *Heart of Herts* (privately published, 1987).
172. Denton, William, *The Soul of Things* (Aquarian Press, Wellingborough, 1988).
173. Lombroso, Cesare, *After Death – What?* (Aquarian Press, Wellingborough, 1988).
174. Collins-Smith, Joyce, *Call No Man Master* (Gateway Books, Bath, 1988).
175. Lindsay, David, *Sphynx* (Xanadu, London, 1988).
176. Robertson, Sandy, *The Aleister Crowley Scrapbook* (Foulsham, London, 1988).
177. Lampo, Hubert, *Arthur and the Grail* (Sidgwick & Jackson, London, 1988).
178. Moody, Raymond, *The Light Beyond* (Macmillan, London, 1988).
179. Conan-Doyle, Sir Arthur, *The Wanderings of a Spiritualist* (Ronin, Berkeley, 1988).
180. Neville, Bernie, *Educating Psyche* (Collins Dove, Melbourne, 1989).
181. Burrell, Philippa, *The Dance of the Opposites* (Charles Skilton, Haddington, 1989).
182. Robins, Joyce, *The World's Greatest Mysteries* (Hamlyn, London, 1989).
183. Turner, Robert, *Elizabethan Magic* (Element Books, Shaftesbury, 1989).

EVALUATIONS

184. Booker, Christopher, *The Neophiliacs* (Collins, London, 1969).
185. Allsop, Kenneth, *The Angry Decade* (Goodchild, Wendover, 2nd edn, 1985).
186. Hewison, Robert, *In Anger* (Weidenfeld & Nicolson, London, 1981).
187. Dillard, R. H. W. *et al.* (eds), *The Sounder Few* (University of Georgia, Athens, 1971).
188. Weigel, John A., *Colin Wilson* (Twayne, Boston, 1975).
189. *20th Century English Literature: A Soviet View* (Progress Publishers, Moscow, 1982).
190. Tredell, Nicolas, *The Novels of Colin Wilson* (Vision, Barnes & Noble, London, Ottawa, 1982).

191. Bendau, Clifford P., *Colin Wilson* (Borgo Press, San Bernardino, 1979).

192. Bergstrom, K. Gunnar, *An Odyssey to Freedom: Four Themes in Colin Wilson's Novels* (Almquist & Wiksell, Stockholm, 1983).

193. Ritchie, Harry, *Success Stories* (Faber & Faber, London, 1988).

194. Stanley, Colin (ed.), *Colin Wilson: A Celebration* (Cecil Woolf, London, 1988).

Notes

INTRODUCTION

1. Colin Wilson, *Religion and the Rebel* (Victor Gollancz, London, 1959), p. 310.
2. This translation from Fyodor Dostoevsky's, *Notes from Underground* was used in the BBC programme on Dostoevsky in the series 'Ten Modern Novelists'. The Translator was unacknowledged.
3. Colin Wilson, *Spider World: The Delta* (Grafton, London, 1987), pp. 212–13.

CHAPTER 1. THE MAN

1. Sidney Campion, *The World of Colin Wilson* (Frederick Muller, London, 1962), pp. 9–10.
2. Ibid., p. 11.
3. Colin Wilson, *Autobiographical Reflections* (Paupers' Press, Nottingham, 1988), pp. 8–9.
4. Campion, op. cit., p. 197.
5. Ibid., p. 41.
6. Quoted in ibid., p. 56.
7. Colin Wilson, 'On the Bridge', *Encounter*, April 1960, p. 23.
8. Stuart Holroyd, *Contraries* (Bodley Head, London, 1975), p. 16.
9. Quoted in Campion, op. cit., pp. 112–13.
10. Holroyd, op. cit., p. 66.
11. *Sydney Morning Herald*, 2 March 1957, p. 2.
12. Colin Wilson, 'Gorran' in Williams, Michael (ed.), *My Cornwall* (Bossiney Books, St Teaths, 1973), pp. 73–4.
13. Extract from a letter by Victor Gollancz generously provided by Daniel Farson. © Livia Gollancz c/o Victor Gollnacz Ltd.

14. Ibid.
15. Colin Wilson, 'Publisher be Damned', review in *Yorkshire Post*, 19 February 1987.
16. Quoted in Daniel Farson, *Henry* (Michael Joseph, London, 1982), pp. 149–50.
17. Colin Wilson, 'Writer in Residence', *Encounter*, June 1969, pp. 78–9.
18. Ibid., p. 80.
19. Interview with Colin Wilson by Daniel Grotta-Kurska, *Oui*, December 1973, p. 130.
20. Colin Wilson, *Access to Inner Worlds* (Rider, London, 1983), p. 139.
21. In a letter to the author, 23 March 1988.
22. Daniel Farson, *Out of Step* (Michael Joseph, London, 1974), pp. 132–3.
23. Nicolas Tredell, *The Novels of Colin Wilson* (Vision, Barnes & Noble, London, New York, 1982), pp. 20–1.
24. Cecil Beaton, *The Face of the World* (Weidenfeld & Nicolson, London, undated), p. 225.
25. Fr. Brocard Sewell, Introduction to Colin Wilson, *Voyage to a Beginning* (Cecil & Amelia Woolf, London, 1968), pp. xi and xiv.

CHAPTER 2. THE PHILOSOPHY

1. Jacques Barzun, 'Romanticism', in *Collier's Encyclopedia* (Crowell-Collier Publishing Co., New York, 1965), vol. 20, p. 163.
2. Colin Wilson, *Beyond the Outsider* (Arthur Barker, London, 1965), pp. 38–9.
3. Barzun, op. cit., p. 164.
4. Ibid.
5. Ibid.
6. Søren Kierkegaard, quoted in Wilson, *Beyond the Outsider*, p. 22.
7. Quoted in Colin Wilson, *Anti-Sartre* (Borgo Press, San Bernardino, 1981), p. 5.
8. Ibid., pp. 4–5.
9. Colin Wilson, *Introduction to the New Existentialism* (Hutchinson, London, 1966), pp. 96–7.
10. Colin Wilson, *Religion and the Rebel* (Gollancz, London, 1957), pp. 243–4.
11. Ibid., pp. 47–8.

12. Colin Wilson, *The Outsider* (Victor Gollancz, London, 1956), p. 14.
13. Colin Wilson, *Poetry and Mysticism* (Hutchinson, London, 1970), pp. 39–40.
14. Wilson, *Beyond the Outsider*, p. 108.
15. Wilson, *Religion and the Rebel*, p. 160–1.
16. Wilson, *The Outsider*, p. 197.
17. Wilson, *Religion and the Rebel*, p. 315.
18. Colin Wilson, *Introduction to the New Existentialism* (Hutchinson, London, 1966), pp. 44–5.
19. Colin Wilson, *The Craft of the Novel* (Victor Gollancz, London, 1975), p. 226.
20. Wilson, *Introduction to the New Existentialism*, pp. 53–4.
21. Wilson, *Poetry and Mysticism*, pp. 59–60.
22. Ibid., pp. 60–1.
23. Wilson, *Introduction to the New Existentialism*, p. 180.
24. Wilson, *Beyond the Outsider*, p. 143.
25. Wilson, *The Craft of the Novel*, p. 68.
26. Colin Wilson, *The Strength to Dream* (Victor Gollancz, London, 1962), p. 106.
27. Wilson, *Religion and the Rebel*, p. 268.
28. Wilson, *Poetry and Mysticism*, p. 124.
29. Wilson, *Beyond the Outsider*, p. 164.
30. George Bernard Shaw, quoted in Wilson, *Religion and the Rebel*, op. cit., pp. 251–2.
31. Wilson, *Religion and the Rebel*, p. 257.
32. Quoted in Wilson, *Religion and the Rebel*, p. 261.
33. Wilson, *Religion and the Rebel*, p. 262.
34. Sir Oswald Mosley, *The European* (London, part 48, 1957), p. 124.

CHAPTER 3. THE PSYCHOLOGY

1. See 'The Analysis of an "Outsider"' in John A. Linden, *The Psychoanalytic Forum*, vol. 3 (International Universities Press, 1972), pp. 275–303.
2. Quoted in Colin Wilson, *The Outsider* (Victor Gollancz, London, 1956), p. 149.
3. Colin Wilson, *New Pathways in Psychology* (Victor Gollancz, London, 1972), pp. 68–9.
4. Ibid., p. 87.
5. Ibid., p. 96.
6. Ibid., pp. 96–7.

7.   Colin Wilson, *Lord of the Underworld* (Aquarian, Wellingborough, 1984), p. 139.
8.   Wilson, *New Pathways in Psychology*, p. 111.
9.   Ibid., pp. 19–20.
10. J. F. T. Bugental, (ed.) *Challenges of Humanistic Psychology*, (McGraw-Hill, New York, 1967).
11. Colin Wilson, in his essay 'Peak Experience' in Satish Kumar, *The Schumacher Lectures*, vol. 2 (Blond & Briggs, London, 1984) pp. 67–8.
12. Colin Wilson, *A Criminal History of Mankind* (Granada, London, 1984), p. 669.
13. Wilson, *New Pathways in Psychology*, pp. 197–8.
14. Quoted in ibid., p. 200.
15. Wilson, *A Criminal History of Mankind*, p. 134.
16. Colin Wilson, *The Laurel and Hardy Theory of Consciousness* (Briggs and Associates, Mill Valley, 1979), p. 5.
17. Wilson, *New Pathways in Psychology*, p. 207.
18. Ibid., pp. 250–1.
19. Ibid., pp. 258–9.
20. Ibid., pp. 219–20.
21. Ibid., pp. 268–9.
22. Wilson, Colin, *Access to Inner Worlds* (Rider, London, 1983), pp. 133–4.

CHAPTER 4. THE SEXOLOGY

1.   Colin Wilson, *The Strength to Dream* (Victor Gollancz, London, 1962), p. 148.
2.   Colin Wilson, *Origins of the Sexual Impulse* (Arthur Barker, London, 1963), p. 26.
3.   Quoted in ibid., pp. 28–9.
4.   Quoted in ibid., p. 73.
5.   Colin Wilson, *Origins of the Sexual Impulse*, p. 42.
6.   Ibid., p. 47.
7.   Ibid., p. 21.
8.   Ibid., p. 28.
9.   Ibid., p. 79.
10. Ibid., pp. 230–1.
11. Ibid., p. 242.
12. Ibid., p. 154.
13. Colin Wilson, *Sex and the Intelligent Teenager* (Arrow Books, London, 1966), pp. 54–5.
14. Ibid., p. 187.

15. Colin Wilson, *The Misfits* (Granada, London, 1988), p. 36.
16. Ibid., p. 39.
17. Ibid., pp. 112–13.
18. Ibid., pp. 45–6.
19. Ibid., p. 215.
20. Colin Wilson, in Alan Bold (ed.), *The Sexual Dimension in Literature* (Vision Press, London 1982; Barnes & Noble, New York, 1982), p. 216.
21. Colin Wilson, in Robert Ollendorff, *Juvenile Homosexual Experience* (Tallis Press, London, 1974), pp. xviii–xix.
22. Percy Grainger, quoted in Wilson, *The Misfits*, p. 206.
23. Ibid.
24. Wilson, *The Misfits*, p. 253.

CHAPTER 5. THE CRIMINOLOGY

1. Colin Wilson, *Encyclopedia of Murder* (Arthur Barker, London, 1961), pp. 21–2.
2. Ibid., pp. 42–3.
3. Quoted in Colin Wilson, *A Casebook of Murder* (Leslie Frewin, London, 1969), p. 13.
4. Ibid., p. 273.
5. Ibid., p. 14.
6. Quoted in ibid., pp. 20–1.
7. Ibid., p. 21.
8. Ibid., p. 28.
9. Colin Wilson, *Order of Assassins* (Hart-Davis, London, 1972), p. 189.
10. Colin Wilson, *A Criminal History of Mankind* (Granada, London, 1984), p. 70.
11. Ibid., p. 73.
12. Colin Wilson, and Robin Odell, *Jack-the-Ripper: Summing Up and Verdict* (Bantam Press, London, 1987), p. 12.
13. Colin Wilson, *A Criminal History of Mankind*, p. 514.
14. Ibid., p. 503.
15. Ibid., pp. 13–14.
16. Colin Wilson and Donald Seaman, *Encyclopedia of Modern Murder* (Arthur Barker, London, 1983), p. xv.
17. Colin Wilson, *Crimes of Freedom and Their Cure* (Twentieth Century, London, Winter 1964–5), p. 29.
18. Quoted in Wilson, *A Criminal History of Mankind*, p. 3.
19. Quoted in review of Colin Wilson, *A Criminal History of Mankind*, *Time Out*, 29 March 1984, p. 18.

20. Wilson, *A Criminal History of Mankind*, pp. 213–14.
21. Laurie Taylor, 'The Dark Side', Review of Colin Wilson, *A Criminal History of Mankind, New Society*, London, 29 March 1984, pp. 488–9.
22. John Moses, 'Darker Side of Humanity', Review of Colin Wilson, *A Criminal History of Mankind, The Weekend Australian*, 7–8 July 1984, p. 14.
23. Gordon Hawkins, 'A Criminal History of the History of the Criminal', Review of Colin Wilson, *A Criminal History of Mankind, Melbourne Age Extra*, 29 September 1984, p. 12.
24. Laurie Taylor, op. cit.
25. Colin Wilson, *Written in Blood* (Equation, 1989), p. 499.
26. Wilson, *A Casebook of Murder*, pp. 22–3.

CHAPTER 6. THE OCCULTISM

1. 'What We Need is Faculty X', *Times Literary Review*, 26 November 1971, p. 1411.
2. Alan Hull Walton, 'Wilson's Occult', *Books and Bookmen*, December 1971, p. 50–1.
3. Colin Wilson, *The Occult* (Hodder & Stoughton, London, 1971), p. 89.
4. Ibid., pp. 559–60.
5. Ibid., p. 33.
6. Colin Wilson, *Poetry and Mysticism* (Hutchinson, London, 1970).
7. Ibid., pp. 110–11.
8. Wilson, *The Occult*, p. 91.
9. Colin Wilson, *Strange Powers* (Latimer New Directions, London, 1973).
10. Ibid., p. 63.
11. Colin Wilson, *The Unexplained* (Lost Pleiade Press, Lake Oswego, 1975), p. 37.
12. Wilson, *The Occult*, p. 47.
13. Ibid., p. 58.
14. Quoted in ibid., p. 58.
15. Ibid., p. 276.
16. Ibid., p. 279–80.
17. The *American Poetry Review*, Jan.–Feb. 1973, pp. 8–9.
18. Wilson, *The Occult*, pp. 501–2.
19. Colin Wilson, *Mysteries* (Hodder & Stoughton, London, 1978).
20. Ibid., p. 40.
21. Colin Wilson, *The Janus Murder Case* (Granada, London, 1984), See the Appendix on Multiple Personality, p. 229.

22. Quoted in Wilson, *Mysteries*, p. 67.
23. Ibid., p. 70.
24. Ibid., p. 56.
25. Ibid., p. 59.
26. Ibid., p. 76.
27. In the Introduction to Tom Graves and Janet Hoult (eds), *The Essential T. C. Lethbridge* (Routledge & Kegan Paul, London, 1980), p. xiv.
28. Neil Powell, *Alchemy: The Ancient Science* (Aldus, London, 1976), p. 8. Colin Wilson served as an editorial consultant to the twenty-volume series, *Library of the Supernatural*, in which this work appeared.
29. Wilson, *Mysteries*, p. 435.
30. Ibid., p. 204.
31. Colin Wilson, *Poltergeist!* (New English Library, London, 1981).
32. John Grant, 'Things That Go Crank in the Night', *Common Ground*, no. 4. February 1982, pp. 16–18.
33. Colin Wilson, *Afterlife* (Harrap, London, 1985).
34. Quoted in ibid., p. 130.
35. Quoted in ibid., p. 152.
36. Ibid., pp. 35–6.
37. Ibid., p. 237.
38. Colin Wilson, *Beyond the Occult* (Bantam, 1988), p. 347.
39. Ibid., p. 332.
40. Martin Gardner, *Order and Surprise* (Oxford University Press, Oxford, 1983), pp. 361–2.
41. Ibid., pp. 363–4.
42. Colin Wilson, *Afterlife*, p. 256.

CHAPTER 7. THE CRITICAL THEORY

1. Colin Wilson, *The Strength to Dream* (Victor Gollancz, London, 1962), p. 14.
2. Colin Wilson, *The Age of Defeat* (Victor Gollancz, London, 1959), p. 17.
3. Colin Wilson, *Eagle and Earwig* (Arthur Barker, London, 1965), p. 88.
4. Ibid., p. 91.
5. Quoted in Colin Wilson, *The Strength to Dream* (Victor Gollancz, London, 1962), p. 95.
6. Wilson, *The Strength to Dream*, p. 97.
7. Colin Wilson, *The Craft of the Novel* (Victor Gollancz, London, 1975), p. 114.

8.   In a tape in the possession of the writer.
9.   Colin Wilson, *The Craft of the Novel*, op. cit., p. 219.
10. Colin Wilson, Introduction to David Lindsay, *The Violet Apple and The Witch* (Chicago Review Press, Chicago, 1976), pp. 8–9.
11. Ibid., pp. 10–11.
12. Wilson, *The Craft of the Novel*, pp. 129–30.
13. Quoted in Wilson, *The Strength to Dream*, p. 216.
14. Ibid., p. 217.
15. Colin Wilson, *The Outsider* (Victor Gollancz, London, 1956), p. 55.
16. Ibid., pp. 51–2.
17. Wilson, *The Craft of the Novel*, p. 106.
18. Ibid., pp. 150–1.
19. Quoted in Wilson, *The Strength to Dream*, p. 190.
20. Ibid., pp. 200–1.
21. Quoted in Colin Wilson, *Poetry and Mysticism* (Hutchinson, London, 1970), p. 106.
22. Ibid., pp. 110–11.
23. Quoted in ibid., pp. 120–1.
24. Colin Wilson, *Brandy of the Damned* (John Baker, London, 1964), pp. 57–8.
25. Wilson, *The Age of Defeat*, p. 146.

CHAPTER 8. THE FICTION

1.   Colin Wilson, *Voyage to a Beginning* (C. & A. Woolf, London, 1968), pp. 160–1.
2.   Nicolas Tredell, *The Novels of Colin Wilson* (Vision Press, London 1982; Barnes & Noble, New York, 1982), p. 147.
3.   Ibid., p. 79.
4.   John Lehmann, *Chicago Review*, Summer 1960, p. 126.
5.   Colin Wilson, *Ritual in the Dark* (Victor Gollancz, London, 1960), p. 135.
6.   Colin Wilson, *Man Without a Shadow* (Arthur Barker, London, 1963), p. 35.
7.   Ibid., p. 16.
8.   *Time*, 31 May 1963, p. 52.
9.   *Spectator*, 27 June 1970, p. 5.
10. Colin Wilson, *The God of the Labyrinth* (Hart-Davis, London, 1970), pp. 304–5.
11. Colin Wilson, *The Craft of the Novel* (Victor Gollancz, London, 1975), p. 236.

12. Daniel Farson, *Soho in the 'Fifties* (Michael Joseph, London, 1987).
13. Colin Wilson, *Adrift in Soho* (Victor Gollancz, London 1961), p. 215.
14. Bernadine Bishop, review of *Adrift in Soho*, *The Aylesford Review*, Winter 1961–2, p. 204.
15. Colin Wilson, *The World of Violence* (Victor Gollancz, London, 1963), pp. 37–8.
16. Ibid., p. 40.
17. Colin Wilson, *The Essential Colin Wilson* (Harrap, London, 1985), p. 213.
18. Tredell, op. cit., p. 82.
19. Colin Wilson, *Necessary Doubt* (Arthur Barker, London, 1964), pp. 253–4.
20. Stuart Curran, '"Detecting" the Existential Blake', *Blake Studies*, vol. 2, 1970, pp. 75–6.
21. Ibid., p. 72.
22. Colin Wilson, *The Glass Cage* (Arthur Barker, London, 1966), p. 203.
23. Colin Wilson, 'Rasputin', in *Tales of the Uncanny* (Reader's Digest, New York, 1983), p. 589.
24. Colin Wilson, *Rasputin and the Fall of the Romanovs* (Arthur Barker, London, 1964), p. 19.
25. Tredell, op. cit., p. 118.
26. Graham Zellick, 'Shock Treatment', *New Law Journal*, 3 December 1970.
27. Colin Wilson, *The Killer* (New English Library, London, 1970), p. 221.
28. Tredell, op. cit., p. 131.
29. Colin Wilson, *The Black Room* (Weidenfeld & Nicolson, London, 1971), pp. 316–17.
30. Colin Wilson, *The Personality Surgeon* (New English Library, London, 1985), pp. 244–5.
31. Ibid., p. 327.
32. George Hay, (ed.), *The Necronomicon* (Neville Spearman, London, 1978).
33. Colin Wilson, *The Mind Parasites* (Arthur Barker, London, 1967), pp. 130–31.
34. R. H. W. Dillard, 'Toward an Existential Realism', in *The Sounder Few*, University of Georgia, Athens, 1964), p. 294.
35. Colin Wilson, *The Philosopher's Stone* (Arthur Barker, London, 1969), p. 313.
36. Glen St John Barclay, *Anatomy of Horror* (Weidenfeld & Nicolson, London, 1978), see Chapter 5.

37. Joyce Carol Oates, introduction to *The Philosopher's Stone* (Warner Books, New York, 1974), p. 9.
38. John Grant, *Aries 1* (David & Charles, Newton Abbot, 1979).
39. Colin Wilson, *The Space Vampires* (Hart-Davis MacGibbon, London, 1976), p. 112.
40. Wilfred De'ath, review of *The Schoolgirl Murder Case*, *Punch*, 29 May 1974, p. 922.
41. Colin Wilson, *Spider World: The Tower* (Granada, London, 1987), pp. 280–1.
42. Colin Wilson, *Science Fiction as Existentialism* (Brans Head, Hayes, 1978), p. 10.
43. Hilary Corke, review of *The Mind Parasites*, *The Listener*, London, 16 February 1967, p. 237.
44. Ibid.
45. Daniel Farson, review of *Spider World: The Tower*, *The Literary Review*, London, April 1987, pp. 8–9.
46. Colin Wilson, *The Craft of the Novel*, p. 241.

CHAPTER 9. THE CRITICAL RESPONSE

1. Anthony Burgess, 'Whips and Petticoats', *The Observer*, 21 February 1988, p. 27.
2. Colin Wilson, 'Love as an Adventure in Mutual Freedom', in *The Bicameral Critic*, (Ashgrove Press, Bath, 1985), pp. 55–72.
3. Cyril Connolly, 'Loser Take All', *Sunday Times*, 27 May 1956, p. 5.
4. A. J. Ayer, 'Mr Wilson's Outsider', *Encounter*, September 1956, p. 76.
5. Joseph C. Mihalich, *Existentialism and Thomism* (Philosophical Library, New York, 1960), pp. 86–7.
6. Marilyn Ferguson, Introduction to *The Outsider* (Tarcher, Boston, 1982), p. xii.
7. Quoted in Kenneth Allsop, *The Angry Decade* (John Goodchild Publishers, Wendover, 1986), 2nd edn, p. 25.
8. Allsop, op. cit., pp. 182–3.
9. Leslie Paul, 'The Angry Young Men Revisited', *Kenyon Review*, Spring 1965, p. 350.
10. Derek Stanford, *Beatniks and Angry Young Men* (Meanjin, Melbourne, December 1958), p. 416.
11. John Lewis, *The Fifties* (Book Club Associates, London, 1978), p. 169.
12. John W. Aldridge, *Time to Murder and Create: The Contemporary Novel in Crisis* (McKay, New York, 1966), p. 234.

13. Robert Hewison, *In Anger* (Weidenfeld & Nicolson, London, 1981), p. 132.
14. Op. cit.
15. Harry Ritchie, *Success Stories* (Faber & Faber, London, 1988), p. 172.
16. Dwight Macdonald, *Against the American Grain* (Da Capo, New York, 1983), pp. 216–17.
17. Kingsley Widmer, *The Literary Rebel* (Southern Illinois University Press, 1965), p. 167.
18. Robert Hack, *Chicago Review* (Winter 1972), pp. 158–9.
19. R. H. W. Dillard, *The Sounder Few* (University of Georgia Press, Athens, 1971), pp. 284 and 294.
20. Ibid., p. 296.
21. John A. Weigel, *Colin Wilson* (Twayne, Boston, 1975), p. 31.
22. Ibid., p. 131.
23. Charles I. Glicksberg, *The Sexual Revolution in Modern English Literature* (Nijhof, The Hague, 1973), p. 231.
24. Martha Eckman, 'Colin Wilson and the Occult', in F. N. Magill, (ed.), *The Contemporary Literary Scene* (Salem House, Englewood, 1973), p. 63.
25. Ibid., p. 68.
26. Ibid., p. 71.
27. Colin Wilson, quoted in ibid., p. 72.
28. Robert Weaver, 'England's Angry Young Men', *Queens Quarterly* (Summer 1958), p. 193.
29. Camille R. La Bossière, 'Marcel Aymé and Colin Wilson on the Bourgeois, the Outlaw and Poetry', *Dalhousie Review*, Spring 1981, p. 109.
30. Valentina Ivasheva, 'The Struggle Continues', *Zeitschrift für Anglistik and Amerikanistik*, vol. 8, 1960, p. 419.
31. Valentina Ivasheva, *Twentieth Century English Literature: A Soviet View* (Progress Press, Moscow, 1982), p. 288.
32. Ibid., p. 291.
33. K. Gunnar Bergstrom, *An Odyssey to Freedom* (Almqvist & Wiksell, Uppsala, 1983), frontispiece.
34. Hilda Graef, *Modern Gloom and Christian Hope* (Regnery, Chicago, 1959), p. 60.

Index